Architecting Enterprise Solutions

Architecting Enterprise Solutions

Patterns for High-Capability Internet Based Systems

Paul Dyson
Andy Longshaw

John Wiley & Sons, Ltd

Other Wiley Editorial Offices

John Wiley & Sons Inc., 111 River Street, Hoboken, NJ 07030, USA

Jossey-Bass, 989 Market Street, San Francisco, CA 94103-1741, USA

Wiley-VCH Verlag GmbH, Boschstr. 12, D-69469 Weinheim, Germany

John Wiley & Sons Australia Ltd, 33 Park Road, Milton, Queensland 4064, Australia

John Wiley & Sons (Asia) Pte Ltd, 2 Clementi Loop #02-01, Jin Xing Distripark, Singapore 129809

John Wiley & Sons Canada Ltd, 22 Worcester Road, Etobicoke, Ontario, Canada M9W 1L1

Wiley also publishes its books in a variety of electronic formats. Some content that appears
in print may not be available in electronic books.

Library of Congress Cataloging-in-Publication Data

Dyson, Paul.
   Architecting enterprise solutions : patterns for high-capability
Internet-based systems / Paul Dyson, Andy Longshaw.
      p. cm.
  Includes bibliographical references and index.
  ISBN 0-470-85612-2 (cloth : alk. paper)
 1. Internet programming. 2. Computer architecture. 3. Computer
systems.
I. Longshaw, Andy. II. Title.
  QA76.625.D97 2004
  005.2′76--dc22
                            2004001727

British Library Cataloguing in Publication Data

A catalogue record for this book is available from the British Library

ISBN 0-470-85612-2

Typeset in 10/12pt Sabon by Laserwords Private Limited, Chennai, India
Printed and bound in Great Britain by Biddles Ltd, King's Lynn
This book is printed on acid-free paper responsibly manufactured from sustainable forestry
in which at least two trees are planted for each one used for paper production.

Contents

Acknowledgements

No book is ever purely the work of the authors alone. There are those that help shape the ideas that form the core of the book, those that help the authors to actually write the book, and those that support the authors through the writing process. We'd like to take the time to thank those people here.

The first public outing for some of the core ideas in the book came at a workshop at the OT2002 conference in Oxford, England. We'd like to thank Anthony Barnes, Andrew Broughton, Mark Campbell, Stephen Hutchinson, Clive Menhinick, Vera Peeters, Rajiv Tyagi, Louise Whelan, and Eoin Woods for their contributions at the conference. Following this we submitted two pattern language papers to consecutive EuroPLoP conferences (in 2002 and 2003, both at Kloster Irsee) for peer review. There are too many reviewers to list individually here, but we would like to say a big thank you to all the members of our writers' workshops: you know who you are. We would particularly like to thank Peter Sommerlad and Klaus Marquardt who each shepherded one of the papers.

We would also like to thank the people who have taken the time to review and comment on this book through its various stages of development: Aaldert Hoffman, Arno Haase, Bobby Woolf, Kevlin Henney, Markus Völter, Michael Jackson, Steve Berczuk, and Wolfgang Keller. Klaus Marquardt deserves a special mention. Klaus, the time and effort you must have spent in all your reviews and the attention to detail of your comments, amazed us both. This book is certainly improved through your many contributions – cheers!

Finally, we'd both like to thank Michael Stal for shepherding this book and our editor Gaynor Redvers-Mutton. You've both stuck with us from beginning to end and your help and support have been invaluable.

Paul Dyson would particularly like to thank James Spalding and Rod Williams of e2x limited for their backing whilst writing this book. I would also like to thank Bruce Anderson who got me started on all this 'architecture stuff' and still challenges and guides a lot of my thinking, as well as being a good friend. Lastly, I can't really say how much the love and support of my wife Angela and my son Josh mean to me, despite the hours locked up in my study or sitting on the sofa with my laptop – thank you both.

Oh, and Andy: it's been a pleasure working with you over the past year or so – I've learned a lot and really enjoyed the experience. But I have to sing: 'Since City were the champions, my true love gave to me: Eight Premiership titles, Seven FA Cup victories, Six past the Arsenal, . . ., and a treble winning season'.

Andy Longshaw's main thanks go to Sarah, Adam and Josh for putting up with the extra work and late nights required to write this book, for their indulgence of the consequent grumpiness, and for the drawings and cups of tea delivered while writing. They are far too familiar with my working pattern and some day I may actually stop doing it, balance my life and learn to appreciate them properly. I would also like to thank Dave de Naeyer for allowing me to architect his system and write this book in parallel and for his perceptive questioning. A vote of thanks is also in order for the many people with whom I've had great discussions about architecture over the past two years including Eoin Woods, Kevlin Henney, Arno Schmidmeier and many more.

And finally to Paul, who has been a joy to work with – I have learned a lot from this and I thank you for that. Also, I admire your fortitude in continuing with this book in the face of '1 easy point' last season and I hope you appreciate the level of stick I *could* have given you for being a United fan who lives nowhere near Manchester.

An All-Too-Common Story

In the beginning . . .

The leadership team of the project sits down to discuss the new system they are about to build: the corporate Internet platform for delivering services to business and consumer customers around the globe. The use cases have been defined, in a more-or-less coherent fashion, and the project methodology has been chosen. The toolset has been mandated as part of a company-wide strategic technology initiative and the development and test environment has been specified.

The meeting starts with a round-the-table review of everyone's position. The customer is happy: at last work is about to start on the system they really needed several months ago. The project manager is happy: the plan can be developed from the requirements once the developers have had a chance to produce estimates, and the roles and responsibilities are clear. Okay the deadline is a little tight (three months to go live) but the team is dedicated and this is an important project.

The development coach is happy: she has chosen the development process and environment and everything is more or less as she wishes. Even the QA manager is happy: the use cases are a good starting point for defining test cases and the development process places a lot of emphasis on developer-driven testing – he's hoping this is going to be a relatively easy project. Only the system architect is looking a little unsure (and is starting to feel a bit out of place in this highly-positive meeting).

'The use cases are the only requirements we have, right?' he says.

'Well, we have the UI templates from the design agency which put the use cases into context, and of course we've all read Charlie's strategic vision document', says the project manager, grinning at his customer.

'What about non-functional requirements? How many people are likely to access the system at the same time?'

'Well, obviously, we have no way of knowing how popular this service is going to be', says Charlie, the customer. 'We think that the consumer side will have somewhere between 500 and 10 000 users accessing the system at once. The business side is a bit harder to call – we're currently canvassing our customers to see how many of them are set up to place orders electronically. Potentially there are as many as 40 000 users out there but we've no real idea how many of them will use the service.'

'500 to 10 000? That's quite a range.'

'Well clearly we'll only get as many as 10 000 when we do a large promotion for a new product or something. I guess the average will be about 2000, I don't know.'

'Okay, and what about security?'

'Security is really important. We don't want any embarrassing stories about hackers stealing our details or placing false orders.'

'Mmm, and I suppose it has to be fast too?'

'Well of course. Look, you're the techie, you know how to do this. Make it fast, secure and flexible; it needs to be able to cope with whatever the users throw at it.'

In the middle . . .

Work has started. The deadline is proving to be a bit overly ambitious and the harassed project manager is trying to convince Charlie, the customer, either to extend the deadline ('Can't do that, we have a marketing campaign in place for the launch.') or to prioritize the requirements so some can be delayed until the second phase ('But they're all high priority.'). Then an email arrives from Charlie and the project manager calls the system architect into his office.

'Charlie's worried about uptime.'

'Uptime? He's never worried about that before, what's happened?'

'Well, he's read an article that claims a web site that is down for just 20 minutes a day can lose something like 20% of its potential users every month.'

'But we were going to take the system down for 30 minutes every day for maintenance and updates, at least for the first two months of operation. He's agreed to that.'

'Well, now he's saying that the first two months are critical for getting users on board, particularly the business users. You'll have to think again.'

In the end . . .

The system has gone into production. The customer finally agreed to a phased approach with a subset of functionality going live in the first phase and a further two phases agreed to implement the rest of the functionality. Because of delays in development, the system went live before the full QA cycle could be completed and the system currently has to be taken down for between 30 and 60 minutes every day for bug-fixes and minor updates. The customer really isn't happy about this but there wasn't much alternative other than to delay the live date. To slightly pacify the customer, these updates take place at midnight – after the consumer peak between 6 pm and 10 pm. The overtime payments for the deployment team are adding significantly to the initial support costs of the system.

And things are about to get a bit trickier. A new agreement has been signed with a major service provider in the US to jointly promote a number of new services. This is a major coup for the company but they are concerned that the system in production isn't up to the job. In particular, the current time for taking the system down for maintenance is 7 pm in New York which is right in the middle of the consumer peak in the US. The ideal time for maintenance from the American point of view is 1 am California time, which is right at the start of the working day for the company's local business customers.

Another worry is that promotion of the site by such a major US Internet presence will massively increase the average number of simultaneous users. The best guess is that the figure will be closer to 8000 than 2000, with an expected peak of 15 000–20 000 when major promotions are run. Although money has been made available for additional hardware, the big question is whether the software can scale to cope with this level of demand.

The final area of concern is the ability of the system to cope with major changes in functionality. The deal with the service provider has led to a number of new functional requirements, but with a further two phases required to implement the original requirements and massive restrictions on how often and for how long the system can be taken down for maintenance, the idea that large functional changes can be made quickly and easily seems fantasy. Sadly, despite the claims of all the individual vendors from whose components the system is built, the system simply isn't 'flexible' enough.

CHAPTER 1

Introduction

What this Book is About

Many of today's 'enterprise solutions' – systems that execute the fundamental business functions of an organization – are being implemented using Internet technology. Whilst there are many reasons for choosing this type of technology, one of the strongest is the ability to open up these systems to new users, from the end consumer to business partners and internal parts of the organization that didn't previously have access.

This book is about defining and evolving architectures for high-capability Internet technology systems. 'Internet technology systems' encompass all systems that use Internet technology to deliver information and services, including:

- Systems that are available to the public or a select range of partners and customers, or that are completely internal to an organization.

- Systems that provide information and services to other business and organizations as well as systems intended for individual users.

- Specialist systems that offer a very tightly-integrated set of services and general systems offering a broad range of loosely-coupled services.

Whilst our definition of the types of system encompassed by the term 'Internet-technology system' is pretty broad, the scale of the systems we are considering is more restrictive. This book is aimed at non-trivial, large-scale, mission-critical, enterprise systems.

Given that definition of Internet technology systems, what do we mean by 'defining and evolving architectures'? A system's architecture specifies the structure of the system, in terms of both the software that implements the system functions and the hardware that provides the operating environment for the software. For any given system there will be many viable ways to structure the system – and each different structure will exhibit different non-functional characteristics.

This book describes a set of patterns that can be used to define or evolve the architecture of Internet technology systems. The patterns are described both in terms of their effect on the structure of the system and also in terms of their relationships with each other. The pattern relationships define how each pattern reinforces or balances other patterns to form an inter-related pattern language. Application of the patterns will help you to tailor the important non-functional characteristics in your system.

What this Book is Not About

This book is not intended to be an all-encompassing manual for building Internet technology systems. Each of the topics we consider in the book could be expanded to a full book in its own right and such books do exist, written by, for example, specialists in security or performance. The role of the system architect is to understand enough about each aspect of the system to be able to balance the various system characteristics and requirements. We believe that we have presented the information in this book to the appropriate depth required by practising architects. It should allow architects to understand the issues sufficiently to achieve a balance without requiring that they become expert in every area.

This book is also not about processes for developing the architecture of the system. Although we do talk about an evolutionary approach to architecture definition, we don't restrict ourselves to a particular view about how and when that evolution should take place, how the definition should be represented, or who should be involved. These sorts of questions are going to be influenced much more by your choice of project and development process or processes.

Finally, this book is not about a particular technology specification such as Microsoft's .NET or Sun's J2EE, or a particular product set such as the Oracle Application Server. We have taken a general view of Internet systems – we're interested in the architectural components of the system and how they are arranged. Where appropriate we have described how a particular technology, platform, or product supports the general concepts or how the concepts must be refined to work with a particular technology. We also use specific technologies when giving examples of how the patterns would work out in practice. This includes some idea of the relative cost of different solutions since, as a system architect, you will almost certainly get involved in some financial horse-trading at the start of the project cycle when the initial architecture is defined. Cost is a non-functional requirement that is seldom discussed in technical circles.

Why Write this Book?

The previous chapter described the sort of scenario that many system architects have encountered at one time or another. In all but a few business domains the days of the three-year project are numbered, instead software projects are expected to deliver business value within a few months and then be built on in a number of phases. This is certainly no bad thing – we build these systems to deliver business value and the quicker that value is delivered the better. However, developing complex systems in short timeframes and dealing with changing requirements present problems to the architects of the system.

With almost all Internet systems being needed 'yesterday', project managers are always looking to squeeze development of the most functionality into the shortest space of time. This usually means that non-functional requirements are ignored or are paid lip service. In a project delivered over a number of three- to six-month phases, the initial phases of the project are almost totally concerned with getting functionality out the door. Because this is what adds business value, right?

Well, sort of. Certainly a system that provides all the required functionality is an asset to the business. But if this functionality has been developed with little or no consideration of the non-functional characteristics of the system, the pleasure that the business draws from its new system will be short-lived. If the system keeps falling over, the users will experience a patchy service and will (rightly) consider the system to be unstable. If performance is poor, they will decide it is unusable. If security is poor, the system may come under attack with consequences ranging from lack of availability due to denial of service attacks through to a damaged reputation due to the theft of sensitive data.

The problems listed so far just address the customer-visible side of the system. If the system is hard to manage and maintain, the business can suddenly find it is restricted by the live system. It wants to update and evolve the system but can't do so without serious interruption in service. This places the business squarely between a rock and a hard place. From the point of view of the user, frequent interruption in service is just as bad as a system that keeps falling over. However, a system that doesn't evolve in line with the customer's needs becomes less and less useful over time. Hence, a system that was quickly hacked together and now can't easily be changed will stagnate. So what started out as a 'quick win' has rapidly become a liability and this is the point where a project for 'version two' (or 'three', or 'four') is usually commissioned.

But surely the solution is obvious – problems like poor performance, poor reliability, lack of security and inability to evolve are down to an inadequate system architecture. If the architecture had been developed with these in mind, the chances of such problems occurring would be much lower. While this is absolutely right, how much time is there for evolving the architecture in a three-month project? How much investigation and prototyping can be done to ensure the system is highly available, performs well, is secure, but can also scale to deal with massively increased user loads? Oh, and it must be easy to update as well.

This is the kind of problem facing the system architect of an Internet technology system. The demands placed on the system by the user population are unpredictable, whilst the availability, performance and scalability always have to be excellent at the very least. The system needs to be flexible in the face of change and it must be delivered in a super-short timeframe. So the system architect must produce the initial architecture in a similarly super-short timeframe: if the project is to be delivered within three months, the system architect probably has three days to produce the architecture; if the timeframe is six months, they may get a week.

What so often happens in these cases is that an initial architecture is rapidly drawn up and then it is constantly updated, amended and tweaked throughout the project. This isn't necessarily a bad approach but it runs the risk that the architecture will become brittle. Fixes are bolted onto the initial architecture and far-reaching changes are avoided as these will place the delivery timescale under threat. The architectural direction becomes governed more by the latest problem to be solved than by the high-level objectives for the system.

Our intention is to provide support to system architects put in the awkward position of having to produce an architecture that will last the lifetime of the system, but where that architecture must be created initially in a very short space of time and then evolved throughout the system's development. We see patterns as being very useful in this situation as they act as templates that can be adapted to the specific technologies and systems in use and, as is the nature of patterns, the strategies described have been shown to work in real-world systems.

Who Should Read this Book?

Architects

Practicing system architects are the people we believe will get the most from this book. The patterns in the language deal with the problems that system architects face every time they consider the non-functional characteristics of the systems they work on. The patterns are taken from our experience as system architects and the experience of other system architects – this is not a theoretical text.

We are well aware that 'system architect' is a role and not necessarily a job description to be filled by one person. In some projects the role of 'system architect' is split between two or more people, possibly divided between software and hardware architecture. In other projects, there may be no identified architect, with the role being split among the development team. However, every system has an architecture and, on any project, there should be at least one person thinking about how the system should be structured across both hardware and software. If you are that person (or one of those people), this book is for you.

Developers

Even when there is a person on the project with 'system architect' as a job title, all the developers on a project have a part to play in developing the system architecture. The developers are usually the principal 'consumers' of the architecture and so will usually be amongst its first reviewers and critics. Then, throughout the development of the system, one of the roles of the developers is ensuring that the code they develop is consistent with the architecture that has been defined. This pattern language will help developers gain a greater understanding and appreciation of the system architecture they have to live with.

Project Managers

Some project managers like to understand a lot of the technical detail of the system their team is building, others delegate that to the system architect. Those that like to understand the detail will benefit from this pattern language in a similar manner to developers – they will gain a better understanding and appreciation of the architecture their team is working with. Those that prefer not to be too close to the technical detail may gain some benefit simply from understanding better the terminology and broad techniques used by their team.

Students and Trainees

Whilst this book is certainly not intended to be a training manual, the approach we have taken, of evolving a system architecture from first principles, may provide useful insight to those that are learning about Internet technology systems or are about to embark on their first project to develop one.

The Structure of the Book

The book is presented in three parts. The first part sets the context for the pattern language – we look at both system architecture and Internet technology as subjects, and define the example that will be used throughout the discussion of the patterns. The second part of the book presents the patterns themselves.

The final part of the book discusses the application of the patterns. We revisit the example system to examine its architecture as a whole, and then examine other systems to see how the application of the patterns can produce quite different architectures.

The appendix contains a complete set of pattern summaries. These are intended to complement the patterns in the second part of the book, helping the reader that wishes to use the book as a reference to get at the information more quickly.

Part 1 Architecture, Patterns and Internet Technology

- System Architecture – we look at how the functional requirements and non-functional characteristics drive system architecture.
- Internet Technology Systems – we look at Internet technology systems and examine why they are difficult to architect successfully.
- Architectural Patterns for Internet Technology Systems – we describe why we have used patterns in this book and provide a roadmap for navigating through the pattern catalogue.
- The GlobalTech System – we introduce the example that will be used throughout the exploration of the pattern language.

Part 2 The Patterns

- Fundamental Patterns – we examine two core patterns that impact almost every non-functional characteristic of the system and determine the 'shape' of the system.
- System Performance Patterns – we describe the patterns that enhance the overall performance of the operational system. These patterns are chiefly concerned with the availability, short-term scalability and end-to-end performance of the system.
- System Control Patterns – we describe the patterns that enhance the organization's ability to control the operational system. These patterns are chiefly concerned with the manageability, security and maintainability of the system.
- System Evolution Patterns – we describe the patterns that enhance the ability to evolve the system over a period of time. These patterns are chiefly concerned with the long-term scalability, flexibility, maintainability and portability of the system.

Part 3 Application of the Patterns

- GlobalTech Revisited – we examine the end-to-end evolution of the architecture for the example system.

- Applying the Patterns – we discuss how applying the patterns can lead to different architectures from the example one.
- Moving on from Here – we present some of the current trends in Internet system architecture and how to build on the work presented in the patterns.

Reading the Book

Although we have tried to provide a good story in this book if you read it from front to back, we realize that it is also useful as a reference or for solving specific problems. We therefore anticipate that the book could be used in different ways depending on the objectives and background of the reader. However, we would encourage all readers to read the first three chapters of Part 1. These chapters describe our view of what architecture, Internet technology and patterns are about. Understanding this view is important if the reader is to get the most from this book.

The ways in which we anticipate readers approaching the book are:

- *'I want to learn about Internet technology system architecture from scratch'*. Treat this book as a tutorial – read it from front to back.

- *'I know about Internet technology system architecture but I want to fill in gaps'*. Go to 'Navigating the language' in Chapter 4 to identify unfamiliar patterns. From there you can proceed into the detailed patterns in the subsequent chapters or refer to the outlines in the Appendix for a more concise description.

- *'I have built one or more Internet technology systems and I want to compare my thinking with yours'*. Go to Chapter 10 and examine the shape of the refactored example system. Refer to the detailed patterns in the main pattern chapters or the outlines in the Appendix to determine any unfamiliar concepts and patterns.

- *'I am building an Internet technology system that does not look like your example system'*. Go to Chapter 11 and examine the pattern combinations described there for different types of Internet technology system. Identify a system that is similar to the problem space you are addressing and refer to the details in the main pattern chapters or the outlines in the Appendix for any patterns that are unfamiliar to you.

So, take your pick and read on.

PART 1

Architecture, Patterns and Internet Technology

CHAPTER

2

System Architecture

Architecture, Design and 'Goodness of Fit'

Christopher Alexander is an architect from the world of bricks, steel and concrete who has inspired much of the patterns work in the computer industry. One of the cornerstones of his work on architectural patterns is the consideration given to the forces that are at work in the system being considered. A force is a consideration or concern that 'pulls' the design in a particular direction, perhaps towards better performance or greater simplicity. Often these forces are in tension with each other, or add an extra level of complexity to the problem being addressed, and so they need to be resolved – we need to find a design or architecture that somehow gives good performance and yet is also simple, at least as far as is possible. Resolving these forces is the role of the architect.

In talking about the role of the architect in resolving forces, Alexander gives an example of how forces interact in the 'simple design problem' of choosing the materials to be used in the mass production of 'any simple household object like a vacuum cleaner' [Alexander 1964].[1]

[1] No, 'Mr Dyson the vacuum cleaner man' isn't any relation of Paul Dyson, just in case you were thinking of asking.

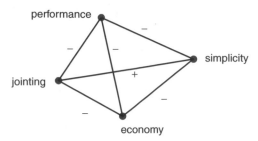

Figure 2.1 Interaction of forces in choosing materials for a vacuum cleaner.

Alexander draws something similar to Figure 2.1, which illustrates the tensions between the desirable characteristics for a vacuum cleaner. These characteristics are self-explanatory except for 'jointing' which refers to the ability to fit the parts together and fix them in place. Assuming that the chosen design for the vacuum cleaner implements its basic function (vacuuming), there are still a number of choices and trade-offs, such as:

- Do we choose a simple set of materials (because they are easy to source and work with) or do we choose the best materials for the job, trading off simplicity against performance?
- Do we choose the best materials for the job or do we pick a set that are easy to fit together, trading off performance against jointing?
- Do we choose the cheapest set of materials, which may result in a vacuum cleaner that is not simple, not performant, and is hard to fit together?

As the diagram shows, however, not every force represents a trade-off. There is a positive force between jointing and simplicity:

- If a simpler set of materials is chosen, the job of fitting them together becomes easier.
- If more emphasis is placed on the ease of jointing, a simpler set of materials is likely to be chosen.

Whilst this is generally true, jointing and simplicity are still different characteristics and have to be balanced separately. For example, the wide use of a single material that is very hard to join, even to itself, improves simplicity and improves jointing in the sense that there is only one jointing problem to solve, but we are left with one very hard jointing problem. Given each of these general forces, there are still detailed trade-offs to be made.

Having discussed these kinds of trade-off, Alexander goes on to talk about 'goodness of fit'. Given all the possible trade-offs that can be made between the four variables considered here, there must be one that optimally balances the forces. However, what is optimal depends on the unique type of vacuum cleaner being built. For a high-end product, we may choose to sacrifice economy over performance but still strive for simplicity and ease of jointing (because the cleaner has to be mass-produced). For a 'cheap and cheerful' cleaner, economy is the primary force. For every object being designed there is a context that defines what is meant by optimal in this unique case.

How does this Relate to System Architecture?

Alexander's diagram deals exclusively with the non-functional characteristics of the vacuum cleaner; it says nothing about how 'vacuuming' is achieved and simply focuses on the way the cleaner is built and how well it fulfils its function once it is built. When designing and developing computer systems we often talk about functional and non-functional requirements:

- Functional requirements describe what the system is to do, broken down into some structured form such as use cases [Cockburn 2001] or user stories [Beck 2000].
- Non-functional requirements describe the tolerances, boundaries and standards that must be adhered to by the system in delivering its functionality to its users. For example, 'the system must handle at least 3000 transactions per hour' or 'the system must be up for more than 99.5% of its operating time'.

Non-functional characteristics have the same relationship to non-functional requirements as functionality has to functional requirements: they are the realization of those requirements in the system. So, system architecture is really all about balancing the non-functional characteristics of the system we are building in order to fulfil the non-functional requirements.

A System View: Hardware and Software

We should be clear that when we talk about meeting non-functional requirements and balancing non-functional characteristics, we are concerned with the 'whole system' architecture. In defining a system architecture we have to define both the software elements that implement the functionality and the hardware elements that provide the execution environment for the software. Although hardware and software are usually dealt with separately (see 'Defining system architectures' later in this chapter), and the definition of hardware and software architectures are often considered very different disciplines, the non-functional characteristics of the system will be determined by the combined capabilities of all of its constituent software and hardware parts. So balancing the non-functional characteristics requires working with both hardware and software elements.

System architects are often faced with a problem that requires the alteration of one or more non-functional characteristics (such as improved performance and scalability). This will need a decision on whether such an improvement can be delivered through hardware, software or a combination of both:

- Sometimes we can only achieve an improvement in a particular non-functional characteristic by changing the hardware (or software) structure of the system: we have no choice. For example, if our system is running on a single hardware server then the availability of the system cannot be improved beyond that of the hardware server itself no matter how much software we add. To improve the availability of the system beyond that of the hardware server we must add more hardware.

- Sometimes we may be able to achieve the improvements we require by altering either the hardware or software structure.

   In some cases, the improvement may be the same but the solution is very different depending on whether we choose a hardware or software solution. For example, we may gain a major performance improvement by improving the speed of the network connections between the various system elements, but we may get similar gains by introducing a LOCAL CACHE.

   In other cases, the solution may be fundamentally the same whether it is implemented in hardware or software, For example, we may want to direct customers to different parts of the system based on certain parameters. This could be done by software, using a Front Controller [Alur *et al*. 2000], or by a hardware content switch.

- Sometimes a particular improvement in the non-functional characteristics of the system can only be achieved if we alter the hardware and software structures in tandem. For example, we may decide we need to introduce a redundant web server in order to improve the availability of the system. We could simply add a redundant instance of the web server software on the same hardware as the non-redundant web server but this doesn't help if the hardware fails. We only get the full improvement in availability if the redundant web server runs on a different, equally redundant, piece of hardware.

Without a working (but not necessarily in-depth) knowledge of both hardware and software, the system architect would not be able to make such judgement calls.

A System View: The Big Picture

Another aspect of being concerned with the system architecture is that we tend to be particularly interested in the 'big picture' of the system. We strongly believe that 'architectural thinking' (being concerned with the structure and the non-functional characteristics of the system) should be applied at all levels of software and hardware design. However, we can most affect the non-functional characteristics of the system by evolving the high-level structure and this is where the hardware and software really combine to form a system. So, throughout this book, we shall focus on how the major hardware and software elements of the system combine, rather than the detail of building each of those elements.

What are the Non-functional Characteristics we Care About?

In this book we consider the following non-functional characteristics:

- Availability
- Performance
- Scalability
- Security
- Manageability
- Maintainability
- Flexibility
- Portability

As you can see, most of these characteristics end with 'ility' which has led them to be referred to by some people as the 'ilities'. Regardless of the generic term used for them ('system qualities' and 'systemic qualities' are also popular), the list of core characteristics is reasonably constant. Given that these core characteristics are our focus, we need to be clear about what we mean by them.

Availability

No system can start running and then run forever completely uninterrupted. Things will go wrong (the failure of one or more system elements, for example) and there will be a need for system maintenance that requires the system to be 'taken down'.

Availability is an indication of the 'up-time' of the system: how much of the time is the system available to users? The availability of a system is based on the reliability of individual system elements and the robustness built into the architecture.

Reliability is a measure of how long a particular system element will perform its job without failing. The reliability of all types of hardware is defined as the 'mean time between failure' (MTBF). Increasing the MTBF by buying a better quality network card can improve the reliability of the system. Software reliability can be more difficult to quantify, as many software elements will tend to fail partially. For example, a memory leak in a messaging system may start to restrict the size of message that can be dealt with. Again, as this will stop part of the system running, it will affect the availability of the system.

Robustness characterizes how well the system copes with failure. Even a network card with a long MTBF can fail but does this failure cause the entire system to stop functioning? If it does then the system isn't very robust. If the system can continue to function, either fully or in some reduced capacity, then it is reasonably robust.

Good availability can be achieved by increasing reliability, robustness or both together. Given a system made up of extremely reliable components we don't need to worry too much about robustness in normal operation. However, even if an element of the system doesn't fail, we may want to perform maintenance on it to upgrade it, replace it or change its operation. Hence, most contemporary systems tend to increase availability by increasing robustness – we don't necessarily aim to use elements with poor reliability but it is more important that the system continues to function if they fail or need maintenance than that the elements never fail.

Performance

When users make a request of a system, they expect a response, preferably sometime soon after they made the request. Performance is an indication of the system's ability to provide that response in a timely manner. Performance should also be viewed at a system level: we not only want to ensure that individuals enjoy good performance, but that all users of the system enjoy good performance consistently. It is no good for 5% of the users to experience a very fast system if the remaining 95% get poor response times. We also don't want everyone to experience equally poor performance.

There are various other measures of system performance that may be of importance to a system architect. The overall throughput of a system is important to keep in balance with the perceived performance of the user. It would be quite possible to produce a system where each server only services a few users. This would give good perceived performance but poor overall throughput. There are also individual aspects of internal system performance that will appear as bottlenecks during scalability testing, such as the speed with which database connections are allocated and recycled.

Scalability

No non-trivial system of the type we have been discussing has a single user – user communities are usually measured in the thousands or millions with hundreds or thousands of users accessing the system at any one point in time (tens of thousands in the case of some large-scale systems).

Whereas performance is concerned with ensuring a predicted group of users all get good response times, scalability is concerned with ensuring performance doesn't catastrophically degrade as the number of users grows significantly. This view of scalability is concerned with both short-term growth (the user numbers ebbing and flowing over the course of the day, week, month or year) and long-term growth (the average number of users increasing as the take-up of the services grows).

Security

No system is 100% secure, totally impenetrable to any form of malicious attack. Equally, there are very few systems in the world that can get away with being 100% open with no defences whatsoever against those who would seek to disrupt the service or steal information. Security is concerned with putting in place sufficient defences to ensure that the system can operate normally while ensuring a reasonable degree of privacy towards its information and controlled access to its functionality.

Manageability

Manageability deals with the ability to monitor and alter the system's runtime behaviour. Any non-trivial system requires a certain degree of monitoring to ensure that it is functioning correctly and monitoring information can often reveal ways in which certain system parameters, whether functional or non-functional, could be altered to enhance the system's operation or cure recurrent problems.

Manageability is a notoriously difficult requirement to define. In theory we want to capture information about every aspect of the system and its performance. We also want to vary the runtime characteristics of the system in a multitude of ways, possibly many times each day, to ensure the system is always optimized for its current user population and workload.

In practice, a huge amount of information about the system and a large degree of variation in its runtime characteristics make the system less manageable rather than more manageable. A mass of information makes it difficult to pick out salient details and to make sense of the patterns and trends in the data. Equally, lots of opportunity to vary the system characteristics presents lots of opportunity to set up the system in error or to tinker unnecessarily – which may render management information invalid.

Maintainability

Systems will always need upgrading and maintenance fixes. This is often required to support other non-functional requirements. For example, part of the security strategy will require that the latest security patches are applied to system elements. On the other hand, an increase in the required level of scalability may lead to the introduction of more or better hardware.

At first glance, maintainability may look to be part of flexibility. While the two are somewhat related, flexibility implies that you are changing something – almost a measure of 'upgradeability' or 'developability', or of how well you can re-configure the system in the face of change (e.g. different inputs or outputs). Maintainability is more a measure of how easy or hard it is to fix problems in the existing system or to upgrade parts of the system independently (such as applying a new service pack to the operating system).

Flexibility

Very few, if any, systems are developed, deployed and then left unchanged for their entire operational lifetime. Whilst manageability is concerned with the ability to alter system parameters at runtime, flexibility is concerned with the ability to produce new versions of the system within the development environment. Such new versions may take the current system elements and restructure them to provide new functionality or to alter the non-functional characteristics of the system. Alternatively, there may be new requirements that cause entirely new elements to be added to the system.

Portability

Any system operates within an environment. Just as the system itself is unlikely to remain unchanged throughout its operational lifetime, so the environment will be subject to change. Portability is concerned with the ease with which the system can be migrated to new environments. These environments may be hardware platforms, operating systems or virtual platforms (such as Java 2 Enterprise Edition – J2EE – or Microsoft's .NET framework).

And the Rest

You will find many other non-functional characteristics listed in various discussions. Examples of these include usability, reusability, integratability, internationalizability, buildability, testability, and so forth. Although they all reflect good practices and are of key interest to certain stakeholders in the project, we do not perceive them as key characteristics at the level of system architecture.

Balancing the Non-functional Characteristics

We began the chapter with Christopher Alexander's discussion of the need to balance a set of inter-related forces in the design of buildings and other structural or mechanical constructions. As architects of Internet technology systems, the forces with which we must contend are the non-functional requirements imposed upon the system.

The example drawn from the work of Alexander used a diagram to explore the relationships between the forces in the construction of a vacuum cleaner. In a similar vein to Alexander's diagram, Figure 2.2 shows the forces between the non-functional characteristics that we, as architects of Internet technology systems, are interested in.

It can be difficult at first glance to see how each of these characteristics affects the others. To try to simplify things, we have grouped the characteristics:

- **System performance.** This group contains performance, availability and short-term scalability. The driving force behind these characteristics is that the system is always there and always responds quickly.

- **System control.** This group contains security, manageability and maintainability. The driving force behind this group is that the system is always under control.

- **System evolution.** This group contains flexibility, portability and long-term scalability. The driving force here is to make it easier to change or add to the functionality of the system or to migrate it between technologies and platforms as time goes on.

Let us consider each group in turn and how the characteristics within each group interact with characteristics from other groups and also with other characteristics within their own groups. Bear in mind that since we currently have no context

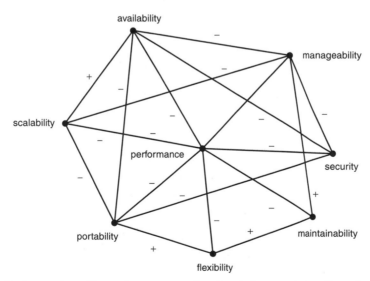

Figure 2.2   Interaction of forces between non-functional characteristics of a software system.

(no fixed set of requirements or initial architecture), the discussion is in general terms and there will always be specific situations in which tensions are lessened or even inverted.

System Performance

Performance is at the centre because it is in tension with every other non-functional characteristic. This is not surprising. If we were building a system where speed of response was of absolutely paramount importance, to the point where the other non-functional characteristics were unimportant, we'd ruthlessly omit every 'extraneous' element we could. Anything that added, say, some reporting or robustness to the system would be sacrificed for maximum execution speed.

This can present something of a dilemma for the system architect. More than any other characteristic, performance is traded to achieve improvements in the other non-functional characteristics. Equally, zealous pursuit of performance (and there is *always* a requirement for good performance whether it is explicitly stated or not) can have a severely detrimental effect on the other characteristics of the system. The role of the system architect will always involve balancing the forces between performance and the other non-functional characteristics.

Availability is generally in tension with the system control characteristics because, in general, availability is improved through the introduction of more system elements (hardware or software) following the principles of redundancy and replication described in Chapter 7. Adding more elements to a system makes it more difficult to manage and to secure due to the added complexity and the amount of management data that must be processed or the number of security checks that must be performed.

Availability has a more balanced relationship with maintainability. On the one hand, extra steps will usually be required when performing maintenance on a system that is highly available, such as introducing backup servers in order to take primary servers offline for maintenance. However, the steps taken to make a system more available will tend to enhance the maintainability of a system – having more than one machine at least makes it possible to maintain one while the other takes the strain.

Availability is also in tension with system evolution characteristics because availability techniques often require or build on bespoke features of the system software and hardware. Availability functions of elements with bespoke features are not easily abstracted. Performance suffers with improved availability typically because additional processing will be added to ensure the system can survive the failure or removal for maintenance of one or more of its elements.

Scalability and availability generally have a reinforcing relationship with one another. This is simply because a number of the techniques for improving availability can be applied to scalability and vice versa. Even when the technique isn't common between the two, it is rare that something done to improve the number of users that can comfortably access the system will actively worsen the chances that the system is available for them to use.

Scalability is usually in tension with manageability – as with availability, the addition of new hardware and software elements to cope with the additional load makes the job of monitoring and controlling the system harder. There is a similar, if less drastic, tension with security as the addition of more elements creates the possibility of more security holes. Scalability does not tend to impact the maintainability of a system.

Scalability generally affects performance, because the provisions made for dealing with extra load will often require additional processing that affects the end-to-end responsiveness experienced by the individual user. Finally, scalability can worsen the portability of the system when it uses techniques that depend on bespoke features of the system's hardware and software.

System Control

Improved manageability often results in worsened security. Manageability can be improved by increasing the amount of management information provided by the system. This information must be carefully guarded, as it can be very useful to hackers. Manageability can also be improved by increasing the number of system parameters and settings that can be altered at runtime. This degree of control has to be weighed against the possibility that breaches in security could arise due to changing these settings. If the security implications of a combination of system settings are not analysed in advance it makes it difficult to determine how secure the system is with those settings in place.

Manageability is also generally in tension with performance. Runtime checking of parameters, or production of management information, requires processing that doesn't directly contribute to the execution of an individual user request, hence end-to-end response time suffers.

Improvements in maintainability usually occur alongside improvements in both manageability and flexibility. The manageability of the system is improved by increasing the amount of information on what the system is doing when it fails. This information is a key part of delivering maintainability since, in order to fix a problem in the system, we need as accurate a picture as possible of what it was doing when the failure occurred. Once the source of the failure is identified, we need to apply a fix with as little disruption to the system as possible. This can be achieved by isolating elements so that each element can be fixed independently of the others. Such isolation can be achieved by judicious partitioning or by the introduction of isolating layers and adapters (see Chapter 9). This type of partitioning can also allow the elements to evolve independently of each other, improving flexibility. In common with the other characteristics, maintainability is in tension with performance: adding debug information and isolating elements from each other both have a negative impact on the end-to-end performance of the system.

Security techniques typically lead to worse performance simply because of the additional checks and processing required in order to make the system or function secure. Security is also in tension with portability as security measures may well require or build on bespoke features of the hardware and software elements.

System Evolution

Flexibility is generally in tension with performance as the principles employed to produce a flexible system, such as abstraction and layering, typically lead to additional processing that wouldn't be required if our only concern was optimal fulfillment of the request. However, flexibility and portability are generally not in tension. In some respects, portability can be considered to be a specialist form of flexibility, the objective being to run the same system within a different environment rather than to add new functionality. So making a system more flexible is generally likely to make it more portable and vice versa.

Portability is in tension with performance for much the same reasons that flexibility is – abstraction and layering are key principles in achieving portability. In reverse, a key technique in optimization is to remove abstractions and generalizations and work directly with the bespoke features and interfaces of the hardware and software elements of the system. This reduces portability.

Cost as a Non-functional Characteristic

Alexander's diagram explicitly considers economy or cost. We have not included this in our diagram because it is not *directly* a non-functional characteristic of an Internet technology system. However, controlling cost is a feature of every project and, as system architects, we always have to work within cost constraints. You will have to balance cost in terms of both finance and time. In some cases, the project may be able to bear the financial cost of additional capabilities, but those capabilities cannot be delivered in the required timescale. It is not always as easy as just adding more people (see [Brooks 1995] for a discussion of why this is the case).

Cost is, in some respects, in tension with all of the non-functional characteristics considered above. Occasionally we can make an improvement and save money at the same time but, generally speaking, in order to improve any of the characteristics we must spend time – and hence money. Sometimes the improvement will also require purchasing additional hardware or software. Such costs cannot be avoided but they can be minimized. Throughout our consideration of how to improve the various non-functional characteristics of an Internet technology system we will also consider relative cost.

Defining System Architectures

Having talked about what system architecture is, we have to say a little about how we define a system architecture. After all, this book is about patterns that can be combined to define architectures for Internet technology systems.

Architectural Views

In a typical project you will probably find at least the following architectural views [IEEE 2000] that describe the system being built:

- The logical view describes the components and software elements of the system. It bundles the software elements of the system into logical units and describes the relationships between these units.
- The infrastructure view shows the hardware devices (servers, routers, etc.) used by the system and how they are connected.
- The deployment view shows how the logical components are assigned to the various hardware elements in the system.

For each of these different views there are a number of diagrams that can be drawn and many levels of detail that can be considered. For example, if we are interested in showing the detail of how objects collaborate to implement a particular function, we may draw something like a UML sequence diagram. On the other hand, if we wish to get an overview of the hardware environment for the system, we may draw a network diagram of the whole of the infrastructure.

There is no accepted single representation of the overall system architecture. Instead the system architecture is described using a number of representations of all of these views, at different levels of detail.

We are not particular fans of any single notation or model for representing these different views (and we use a home-grown notation throughout the book). Our position is that an architectural definition is something that answers three questions:

- What are the structural elements of the system?
- How are they related to each other?
- What are the underlying principles and rationale that guide the answers to the previous two questions?

This 'something' could be a sketch on the back of a napkin, drawn as part of a lunchtime conversation; reams of technical diagrams and related descriptions; or a short description of the patterns along with a couple of block diagrams as used in this book. Whatever the technique, the views or representations used to answer the first two questions and the level of detail they contain will depend on the stakeholders in the project and their particular concerns. The combination and type of views required will be unique to each project. However, the understanding of system architecture that lies behind the third question forms a common link between successful Internet technology systems. It is in this area that the patterns described in this book come into play.

Servers, Components and Elements

When defining the architecture of systems that are made up of different combinations of software and hardware, inconsistent terminology can be a hindrance. In this book, we use the term 'server' a lot for both hardware and software. Sometimes it isn't really necessary to distinguish between the two and, where it is, we will talk about 'hardware server' or 'software server'. Hardware servers are usually machines that host some part of the system software and software servers are applications that implement some part of the system functionality.

We try to avoid using the term 'component'. Component tends to have a very specific meaning in software (although there do seem to be many interpretations of that specific meaning) and in hardware it usually implies a part of a larger assembly. Instead of component we use the term 'element' (sometimes 'system element') when we want to be more abstract than 'server', particularly when we discuss a piece of hardware such as a switch (which is not really a hardware server) or a logical part of an application (which is not a software server and could be implemented using a number of software components).

Why do we Care About System Architecture?

Having just spent an entire chapter discussing what system architecture is and how it affects the system, this may sound like a pretty stupid question. However, it is surprising (and worrying) just how many projects don't really care about system architecture. A number of projects we have seen have architecture documents (and architects) that seem to belong only in an ivory tower. This type of architecture is particularly concerned with being abstract (although they are more often vague – definitely not the same thing) and general. These architectures are produced in isolation and presented as a blueprint for development to the people who have to implement the system. Often these types of document rarely change as the system is developed, not because they are being closely adhered to but because they are so disconnected from what is actually going on as to not be affected.

In other projects, we have seen concerted efforts to define either the software or hardware architectures (or both) with little co-ordination or balance between the two. Whilst this is better than the ivory tower situation, it is still ignoring the overall system. And, let's face it, building a system rather than an application or some infrastructure is what we're interested in here.

We think there are two reasons why we really need to focus on system architecture. Firstly, the creation of an architecture for a large-scale system is not a trivial task – it is definitely a hard problem. Secondly, the system architect is concerned with the delivery of a 'complete' system, however far that may reach. This combination of difficulty and responsibility arises from the scale and scope of the systems we are creating.

As the size of the system increases, it becomes more difficult to create an architecture for it that balances all of the requirements placed on the system. The number of elements in the system increase and hence the number of possible interactions in the system increase, potentially in a exponential way. A large system can consist of hundreds of 'moving parts', each of which has its own configuration and comes from one of a variety of different vendors. It is easy for the system to become mired in complexity without an overall vision of (relative) simplicity and form. Additionally, as the system increases in size, so too do the size of the individual problems within the system. For example, the data flowing back and forth in a system that must support hundreds of thousands of users is like a primeval force compared to the smaller flows in a departmental system. Any system element not prepared for the scale of such flows will bend or break under the onslaught, which will inevitably lead to problems achieving the required non-functional characteristics. The system architect must predict such intense forces and put in place strategies to cope with them.

The level of difficulty for the system architect also increases as the scope of the system increases. A public Internet system, or a large-scale intranet system, will stretch out across the world, relying on intermediate network connections and browsers on client systems for its delivery. Whether inside or outside of an organization, these links and the client systems are largely outside the system architect's control. However, and this is the difficult part, the system architect must still worry about them. This additional responsibility comes as the scope of the system increases. The creators of individual software elements will be concerned that the elements perform to their specifications, but they bear little or no responsibility beyond that for the overall performance of the system in which they are used. Similarly, a team that writes a packaged product for installation on a PC specifies some basic hardware requirements on the side of the box and their duty is largely discharged. A project team that must develop a traditional client–server application with a thick client, for consumption within an organization, will be responsible for the end-to-end performance of the system but potentially nothing is outside of their control as they may be able to change client processing power, network bandwidth, client software and so on. Once you move into a large-scale system, the amount of control over anything outside of your immediate, server-focused data centre diminishes rapidly. Despite this lessening of control, the team building the system (and hence the system architect) still remains responsible for the overall performance of the system, regardless of who controls which parts. The system architect must identify bottlenecks, or limitations on performance, and issues with the delivery of functionality to potentially differing client platforms.

These concerns should come as no surprise as it is the size and scope of a system that generally governs its need for stringent non-functional requirements. As a system widens its reach, the functional model will probably stay pretty much the same. However, with reach comes concerns about privacy of data, responsiveness across a widely-distributed network and the number of customers who may come to use the system. Someone needs to be concerned that the system as a whole

War Story

One of the authors was involved with the delivery of an internal Internet-technology development deployed through a web browser. As the system scaled, there were reports of the application 'crashing'. Most of the application functionality resided on a server farm and this part of the system was well monitored for potential failure. However, the problem in this case was occurring in the browser inside a mixture of DHTML, JavaScript, active content and data download. The users did not perceive that 99% of the system was working fine – their perception was that the system was crashing. It did not matter to them whether it was due to a bug in the browser (as turned out to be the case) or in the client-side code downloaded to it. Basically, the whole system was tarred with the same brush, much to the displeasure of the business sponsors.

meets the non-functional requirements necessary for it to succeed. It is the job of the system architect to close the gap between characteristics and requirements. Ultimately, as system architect, you 'own' the overall system and the way in which it meets customer needs. When it comes to meeting non-functional requirements, user perception is everything (whether those users are customers, developers or the operations team). High-capability, high usage Internet technology systems carry with them a high profile and a high price of failure. These systems rely on having a system architecture that delivers their key non-functional characteristics consistently and the responsibility for this lies squarely with the system architect.

We need to get this right.

Summary

In this chapter, we defined system architecture and contrasted it with software architecture. We gave reasons why system architecture is important to the types of system this book focuses on (Internet technology systems) and how the architectural considerations of such systems differ from other systems. We looked at the main aspects of system architecture – the non-functional characteristic – and how system architecture may evolve over time as the system and its requirements evolve. We listed and defined the main non-functional characteristics in which we are interested during the rest of the book and why these characteristics are important. Finally, we put forward arguments for why the creation of system architecture is fundamentally difficult and cannot be subjected to simplistic analysis.

In the next chapter, we will continue laying the groundwork for our pattern language by examining Internet technologies and the types of system that are built with them.

Internet Technology Systems

For the purposes of this book, an Internet technology system is any system that uses the Internet to deliver content and services to end users and/or other systems. At its heart, 'Internet technology' means the TCP/IP protocol family, which includes FTP for transferring files, SMTP and POP3 for sending and receiving email, and HTTP for accessing the World Wide Web. These protocols provide Internet technology systems with the basic mechanisms through which users or systems can request data and services.

If you have been a user of the Internet for a few years now, you may have come across all of the protocols listed during everyday interactions with web sites. So aren't we using 'Internet technology system' as a fancy term for 'web site'? Well no, we're not. Certainly, a web site is one of the more common ways of providing a human interface to the content and services provided by an Internet technology system but it is by no means the only way. And, even if a system has a web site as its primary interface, the term can be disarmingly simplistic. Consider Amazon.com, eBay.com, Google.com, late-availability travel sites, online grocery shopping sites, Internet banks, and news sites – the list is almost endless. All of these web sites provide a relatively simple front end for what can be a highly-complex, highly-transactional system.

Some Internet technology systems don't provide a recognizable web site as a front-end. Some provide information and services to specialist clients such as PDAs, mobile phones, set-top boxes (even, increasingly, consumer appliances such as Internet radios, TV sets and video- or DVD-recorders). Others only interface to other systems, using the TCP/IP protocols and more specialized web service protocols such as SOAP and WSDL.

In this chapter we will examine the different forms that Internet technology systems take and the technologies, platforms and products that they use to deliver their content and services.

Types of Internet Technology System

Probably the most common type of Internet system that people are familiar with is the business-to-consumer (B2C) e-commerce site that sells books, electrical items and even groceries to the public across the Internet. We can classify Internet technology systems based on the type of business or exchange they perform (the style of the system) and the intended audience (the focus of the system). Based on these classifications we can then start to examine the levels of particular non-functional characteristics typically required by each type of system.

Style of an Internet Technology System

Business-to-Consumer (B2C)

An organization uses a B2C site either to deliver information to customers or to sell goods and services to them (or both). The customer accesses the site through a web browser and the system interface is defined as a set of web pages (frequently, dynamically generated pages) that are accessed using Internet protocols.

AKA:[1] e-commerce site, company web site, online support

Examples: Amazon.com, Dell.com, Tesco.com

Business-to-Business (B2B)

A B2B system is intended to interact with systems from other organizations to exchange information, place orders, make payments and so forth. As the client for the functionality is another system, there is no user interface in the form of web pages. Instead, there is a set of defined business messages that can be sent and received over Internet protocols. In this area, XML has made large inroads as the

---

[1] In each style, the AKA section gives other names by which this type of system is known.

way of encoding business data to be exchanged. Most B2B systems now being built use some form of web service interaction.

AKA: Extranet, supply chain management, e-business site, Internet-based EDI

Example: Boeing Supplier Portal

Business-to-Employee (B2E)

A B2E system is part way between a B2C system and a B2B system. It has many of the facets of a B2C system (web user interface, mix of information and functionality) but differs in audience and mechanisms. The audience for a B2E system is fixed as a set of employees in another company. Two major variants are systems that enable collaboration between employees of different companies and systems that provide procurement facilities for employees of an organization (buying things with the company's money!). Again, the front-end uses web pages, but the back-end will use B2B mechanisms to fulfil the exchange of services.

AKA: e-procurement system, B2B collaboration, extranet

Example: Microsoft's MS Market e-procurement system

Consumer-to-Consumer (C2C)

A C2C site is primarily intended to facilitate interaction between customers or users who wish to exchange information, data, or goods and services (auction sites). These sites will tend to use web front ends, or small applications with extended functionality that enable specific types of exchange over Internet protocols.

AKA: auction site, peer-to-peer (in some guises)

Examples: friendsreunited.com, Napster, eBay

Consumer-to-Business (C2B)

A C2B site lets customers club together and create a demand for a particular product or service at a particular price. This need can then be filled by a supplier willing to meet that price. Again, a web front end is the usual way of accessing such sites.

AKA: reverse auction site

Example: letsbuyit.com

Focus of an Internet Technology System

Categorizing Internet technology systems based on their intended audience will usually give us an indication of the importance that the system will place on non-functional characteristics such as scalability and availability.

Public Internet Systems

Public Internet systems are just that – Internet technology systems usable by anyone. Typically they are used to promote a company and its business and/or to provide content and services to the public at large. The defining characteristic of a public Internet system is that it can be accessed by anyone, either anonymously or through a process of non-vetted registration, regardless of whether they represent an individual or another company. There are many examples of this type of system: Amazon.com and eBay.com are two of the most well-known.

Consider an Internet auction site. This web site is highly dynamic in nature with the bulk of its content being derived from auctions that are set up over time by its users. There is a set of 'core' services such as user registration, auction set-up, bid placement, auction finalization and searching. In addition there may be a number of peripheral services such as automated bidding, auction notification, anonymous email, message boards and payment. So behind the web site lies a highly complex system.

As you saw in the previous section, many people distinguish between sites based on their style. When considering system architecture, we make no such distinction as the precise nature of the functionality takes second place to the delivery of the appropriate non-functional characteristics to meet the system's non-functional requirements. Public Internet systems will tend to have high requirements for characteristics such as availability and scalability regardless of the services that they deliver. As the user base of a public Internet system is far more unpredictable – both in terms of size and usage – than more controlled systems, public Internet systems pose a unique challenge.

Intranet Systems

An intranet system is a system delivered using Internet technology for use exclusively within a company or organization. A simple intranet system might provide basic content about the business and offer a number of services to employees. For example there might be a company news section, a section providing electronic versions of important company documents, plus a number of calendar-based services such as event-, meeting- and holiday-booking.

This is a simple system targeted at the general routine of keeping a company running. For example, companies are delivering corporate purchasing systems in the form of intranet functionality that replaces paper-based forms. Microsoft's MS

Market internal ordering system for office supplies has knocked $30 million off its annual procurement costs. Other organizations are building intranet systems to implement the functions that form part of the company's core business. This can range from fairly generic customer service applications (complaints, enquiries, etc.) through to market-specific insurance and banking functionality. These systems are then used by employees in stores, branches or call centres to deliver services to customers.

Extranet Systems

Extranet systems generally come in one of two forms: user-facing or B2B. A user-facing extranet is very much like an intranet system but the users may include (or exclusively be) external customers of the business. The customers are either pre-approved (the business decides who should use the system) or must go through some form of application process. The user community is essentially closed and there is a decision process to go through in order to add users to the community. Many banks offer extranet systems to their customers – the users can check their account details and perform simple transactions online but must be account holders in order to access the system.

Similarly, businesses are starting to use extranet systems to interface with other businesses that are their major customers and suppliers. These system-to-system extranets will allow authorized customers or suppliers to deliver purchase orders and invoices and perform other business processes across the Internet or a dedicated link.

How Big is your System?

As an extranet system becomes larger in scope, the users can number many tens of thousands. This means that, in terms of concurrent users, such systems will start to match public Internet systems. Although there is not the same level of unpredictability in the absolute number of users, the usage pattern of a large extranet system remains as uncertain as a public Internet system. Indeed, some of the largest intranet systems in the largest companies (e.g. IBM and General Motors) may reach high levels of unpredictable usage that would push them into the same category.

The bottom line is that you can find examples of each of these types of system that require high levels of certain system qualities. As Internet technology becomes more widely used inside organizations and between business partners, the boundaries between the types of system are blurring. A general-purpose intranet system used within a large global corporation may be more like a large public Internet system than is a public system catering for a small, well-defined set of users. Our concern in this book is Internet technology systems that must support high levels of certain non-functional characteristics. If we considered all of the systems in the world that have these requirements, we would probably find that 70% of them are public Internet systems, 20% are extranet systems and 10% are intranet systems. Because of the bias in this split towards public Internet systems, this remains our primary focus. However, the techniques and principles are just as applicable to top-end intranet systems and high-volume extranet systems.

Characteristics of Internet Technology Systems

Different types of Internet technology systems have different characteristics. We can couch these differences (and similarities) in terms of the level of non-functional characteristics they require. We will generally focus on the requirements of public Internet systems.

Table 3.1 Comparison of Non-functional Characteristics

REQUIRED CHARACTERISTIC	INTRANET	EXTRANET	PUBLIC INTERNET
Availability	Based on the criticality of business function within the company. A mission-critical system for a global business will need to be available 24×7 all year round; a less critical system or one for a much smaller business may have large windows for downtime.	Based on the needs and expectations of the company's customers. If they are distributed globally, the system may need to be available 24×7 all year round, even if the company itself only uses the system for a relatively short proportion of that time.	Based on the needs and expectations of anyone who may be interested in using the system. More often than not, the system needs to be available 24×7 all year round.
Performance	Based on the expectation of the users for the speed of the business function being performed. Users are likely to be more forgiving of a slow response time if the function is complex but less forgiving if the function is perceived to be simple. Users can be educated as to 'reasonable' expectations.	Based on the expectation of the customers for the speed of the business function being performed. Users can be educated as to 'reasonable' expectations.	Based on the users' expectations of what the performance of a 'fast' Internet system should be, often regardless of the complexity of the function being performed. Users definitely cannot be 'educated' about response times.
Scalability	Based on the number of employees who are likely to need to access the system. It is often possible to predict how many users are likely to access the system over time reasonably accurately and so the scalability requirement should be reasonably low.	Based on the number of users. If they are a defined and quantifiable set (such as the company's suppliers), the scalability requirement should be relatively low. If the user population is less predictable (such as for an online banking system), scalability is more in line with that for a public Internet system.	Based on the number of users. It is often near impossible to predict how many users are likely to access the system over time. In fact, a common measure of the system's success is the number of users it manages to attract. So the scalability requirement is likely to be very high.

Table 3.1   (*continued*)

Security	Based on the environment into which the system is deployed. If it is secure from outside attack, the security requirement for the system is reasonably low – restricted to taking reasonable precautions against rogue employees.	The security requirement is very high: only approved extranet users may connect to the system, particularly as accessing the system often gives access to sensitive information provided by the company and the extranet customers themselves.	Users must be able to connect easily to the system and access its content and services. In fact, such access needs to be actively encouraged. However, information stored within the system, usually supplied by the users themselves, must be protected.
Manageability	Because the users, and their objectives for the system, are reasonably predictable, the emphasis is likely to be on monitoring rather than the ability to change system parameters at runtime.	Whilst there will be a requirement for monitoring, similar to intranet systems, the need to adjust system parameters at runtime is likely to be greater due to the less predictable nature of the customers.	Monitoring is extremely important because it will reveal information about how the users actually use the system – something that cannot easily be predicted for a system usable by anyone. Similarly, there is likely to be a high need to adjust the system's parameters in response to the information gathered.
Maintainability	All Internet technology systems need to be able to be maintained.	All Internet technology need to be able to be maintained.	All Internet technology need to be able to be maintained.
Flexibility	Based on the business objectives for the system.	Based on the business objectives for the system.	Based on the business objectives for the system.
Portability	Based on the likelihood of the environment to be changed.	Based on the likelihood of the environment to be changed. The presence of external customers who will have their own policies for environments they work with may influence the company's decisions on how and when to port the system to a different environment.	Based on the likelihood of the environment to be changed. A common exception is when the project's funds are 'staged' depending on how successful the system is at attracting new users. Initial system versions are often deployed on 'cheap and cheerful' environments and then ported to more 'robust' (performant, scalable, secure) environments if they are successful.

Why do we Build Systems Using Internet Technology?

Given that Internet technology systems can be internal or external, can have a controlled and predictable set of users or be used by anyone, and deliver 'content and services' to their users, it is clear that almost any system could be implemented using Internet technology. So why would you choose to do so (or, perhaps more importantly, why would you choose not to)? There are a number of advantages in using Internet technology as the foundation for a system:

- Ubiquity – the principal reason for the adoption of Internet technology is the widespread availability of the technology. Implementations of Internet protocols exist for all popular operating systems, as do applications built on these protocols. Although the Internet is often considered as a single entity, it comprises an extremely heterogeneous and volatile set of networks running on a massive range of hardware and operating systems. Internet technology binds this huge mixture of different technologies into something we can treat as a single entity.

- Simplicity – one of the main reasons for the ubiquitous nature of Internet technology is its simplicity. Although a number of much more complex application protocols have been developed to deliver richer services over TCP/IP, the 'core' Internet protocols are extremely simple. This simplicity means that it is relatively easy to deliver content and services across the ubiquitous Internet. Note that it is the technology that is simple and not necessarily the applications built using it, as evidenced by the rest of the book.

- Reach – a consequence of the ubiquity of support for Internet technologies is that almost all potential customers or users have access to it. If your application is fronted by web pages written using HTML version 3.2 and JavaScript, all but the oldest web browsers will be able to access your application. You do not have to limit your client base or issue your clients with a specific piece of software just to use your system. Since an application fronted by web pages is accessed over HTTP, there should be no issues with customers being able to get to it as their Internet connection will use TCP/IP and the various firewalls will be configured to permit HTTP traffic.

- Cost – a direct consequence of the ubiquity and simplicity of Internet technology is that it is relatively cheap to adopt. Many of the products (both software and hardware) that implement Internet protocols cost so little as to have only a minor impact on a project's budget. Certainly they are rarely more expensive than their 'proprietary', non-Internet technology equivalents.

- Skills – a proprietary vendor solution may give you difficulty recruiting, training and retaining people with the appropriate skills, no matter how much money you are willing to throw at the issue. There is far more widespread availability of people who can create JSPs, servlets or ASP.NET pages than those who can customize Notes pages with LotusScript.

- Vendor lock-in – over the years, almost all software and hardware vendors have endeavoured to create proprietary solutions to problems, using proprietary protocols. Once you opt for such a solution there is a large cost associated with changing to another vendor. The use of Internet protocols generally provides the ability to 'plug and play' at the protocol boundaries (i.e. between web browser and web server). Ironically, most vendors now have Internet protocols at the heart of their development efforts, meaning that it can sometimes be difficult to avoid the use of Internet protocols even if you want to.

- Widespread acceptance – as all vendors have accepted the use of Internet protocols, continued support for these protocols in all relevant products is assured.

These advantages have to be weighed against the disadvantages:

- Unpredictable response times – because TCP/IP is a packet-switching technology it is impossible to guarantee the route a request will take through the network and, hence, how long it will be until the system receives the request. This makes Internet technology unsuitable for any system that needs predictable or guaranteed response times, or strict time-based processing.

- Limited user interfaces – although HTML is ubiquitous, it is also limited in many ways. The simplistic nature of HTML means that you cannot build a sophisticated user interface from it without starting to restrict the number of browsers that can successfully use the interface. More sophisticated interfaces can be created with Flash and DHTML but these can be harder to integrate with dynamic server page languages.

- Performance – the general nature of Internet protocols means that they are predominantly text-based. This is not as efficient as it would be using a binary protocol. The worst offender here is XML as it encodes most of its data in text format (you can attach binary chunks such as images if you like). This is far more inefficient than an equivalent binary data protocol, but it provides far more interoperability and is less brittle in the face of change.

- Slow standards evolution – although Internet protocols have emerged very quickly compared to other protocols, the very fact that they are widespread and interoperable does tend to restrict their evolution. As an example, the version of IP on which the Internet generally runs is version 4. The address space for version 4 is very limited compared to the number of IP-enabled devices in the world. However, the progress of its successor, IP version 6, has been comparatively slow as its introduction will cause a major disturbance in the implementation. It has been held back by a combination of interoperability requirements, availability of hardware and software that supports version 6, and the desire to get as much functionality as possible into it since people do not want another major upgrade again in a few years time. If IP were controlled by one vendor, the pressures from their customers would probably have led them to introduce the features gradually over time in a more piecemeal way.

■ Expectations and bleeding edge development – the Internet is very subject to hype surrounding technologies and possibilities. You may find that you have to do some of your development on the leading (or bleeding) edge of standards development to satisfy some elements of your customer base. The use of web service protocols is a good recent example of this. In such an environment you may need to limit the type of clients that can access the service or undertake your own thorough testing against likely types of client.

This set of advantages and disadvantages has a strong influence over how Internet systems are built and how they offer their functionality. The disadvantages in particular can make it far more difficult to achieve some of the desired non-functional requirements of a system, such as high performance.

Building Blocks of Internet Technology Systems

The systems we are talking about are large-scale and complex. This is why good architecture is critical to the success of the system. With such a degree of complexity, the system is never developed directly on top of the Internet protocols. Instead, it is built on a number of higher-level elements. When we look at specifying elements in the architecture of an Internet technology system, these building blocks will be used to provide much of the functionality we identify.

Web Server

A web server handles multiple simultaneous HTTP requests and returns the appropriate responses. Web servers can be used to serve a wide variety of responses: pages in a particular mark-up language (HTML, WML, etc.); binary resources (images, audio and video files, binary documents, etc.); and general documents (style sheets, etc.).

A web server also acts as a gateway to other functionality. For browser-based clients, this involves receiving data from the browser as a set of name/value pairs and passing it on to some plug-in such as a Java servlet or an ASP page, which will generate a page of mark-up as a response. For B2B exchanges, the data sent is usually an XML document (often as part of a SOAP message) and the response will be an XML or SOAP response.

Commonly used web servers include Apache, Microsoft IIS and iPlanet Web Server.

Application Server/Framework

Internet technology systems are rarely built from the ground up. Instead an application server or framework is used to 'host' the application logic, wrapping it with infrastructure-level capabilities such as multi-threading, database access, etc. These servers or frameworks often provide 'server page' capabilities, allowing pages in HTML, WML or other mark-up languages to be constructed dynamically. There is a broad range of application servers and frameworks, some completely proprietary and some adhering to a standard such as J2EE.

The J2EE model refers to a 'Web container' which hosts the servlets and JSPs that dynamically generate pages. This is not to be confused with the Web server which handles requests for pages and other resources. In both J2EE and .NET it is possible to host the software that dynamically generates pages in the Web server, but we shall see that it is important to distinguish between the two.

Commonly deployed application servers/frameworks include IBM WebSphere (J2EE-compliant), BEA WebLogic (J2EE-compliant), the Microsoft .NET framework (Microsoft-specific but standardized through ECMA), ATG Dynamo (J2EE-compliant but also supports a proprietary software component model), ColdFusion (proprietary) and Broadvision (proprietary).

Database

Every large system needs to store data and databases are as ubiquitous in Internet technology systems as web servers. Most databases are relational so that the data is stored in tables, although other variants include object databases and XML databases. Databases allow data to be queried in standard SQL and also with their own variants of SQL. You can run some of your business logic and rules using stored procedures to embed SQL scripts in the database. Some databases will also allow you to run software components, such as Java objects, inside them. Commonly used databases include Oracle, Microsoft SQL Server and IBM DB2.

Router

A router provides a link between different parts of the network on which Internet systems are built. Some routers connect the system to the outside world, others connect different parts of the system, and others connect the system to internal servers and services. Routers are usually dedicated hardware devices that not only route but can also filter network traffic to block certain types of traffic on certain routes. Common router vendors include Cisco, Bay Networks and 3Com.

Firewall

A firewall is a combination of hardware and software in a particular configuration that is intended to protect parts of the system from unauthorized access or attack. A firewall will commonly consist of filtering routers and a firewall host (sometimes now embedded as an extra 'blade' in a hardware router). Common firewall products include Firewall-1, Gauntlet, and SonicWall.

Load Balancer

A load balancer is a type of router that balances network requests between a set of servers. All traffic for the set of servers goes to the load balancer and the load balancer determines which particular server should service any new connection. The objective is to ensure that, as far as possible, client sessions are distributed evenly over the set of servers. The load balancer will typically engage in conversation with the servers and use some of their performance information (such as CPU load and memory usage) as part of its calculation of which server currently has the lightest load and hence should have the next request routed to it.

A load balancer usually takes the form of a separate hardware router or an optional 'blade' that can be installed in the router. Some clustering mechanisms, such as that provided with Windows 2000 Server, provide software load-balancing between the members of the cluster so that no additional hardware is required (although this will be slower than hardware load-balancing). Load balancers are also known as content switches. As they are generally optional parts of hardware routers, load balancers usually come from the same vendors as routers.

Email Server

An email server allows your application to send or receive email. It has two parts – SMTP for sending email and POP or IMAP for accessing email in a message store. SMTP mail servers handle multiple simultaneous SMTP connections from clients or other servers. SMTP messages are passed from server to server until they arrive at their destination. POP and IMAP servers are less common than SMTP servers in Internet technology systems simply because we usually want the system to send mail rather than receive it. However, email may well be used to interface with the system; in which case, access to a message store will be required. More commonly, even if the system itself doesn't process the email, a message store will be required to deal with any 'return path' mail. Commonly used email servers include sendmail, qmail, Microsoft Exchange and Lotus Notes.

Management Console

When operating complex Internet systems, you can use a management console to monitor the health of the hardware and software elements that make up the system. There are standard protocols, such as SNMP, that are used to gather management information from different system elements. Examples of management consoles include Tivoli and OpenView.

Isn't this Enough?

Given this list of building blocks, do we really need to worry about the non-functional characteristics of the system we are building? Surely if we choose established products that have all been proven in real systems, we will get good performance, availability, security, etc., if we simply put them together correctly.

Whilst it might be wonderful if this were the case, it simply isn't. Certainly it is true that some products will exhibit excellent scalability or provide fantastic management functions, but we are concerned with a system here, not a set of individual elements. There is no point in having a web server that can handle millions of requests per second if your application can only service a fraction of those requests. The non-functional characteristics of the system are determined by the combination of all its elements (sometimes combining unexpectedly) and it is often the case that one 'weak link' seriously affects the characteristics of the system as a whole.

Even if the building blocks being considered are all well matched, there is still the consideration of 'goodness of fit'. Just because a vendor claims their application has 'excellent scalability' doesn't mean it is good enough for what we need. Or, perhaps, it provides far more scalability than we need but provides much less in the way of manageability – an area that, for this unique system, we are particularly concerned about. Choosing building blocks that provide good non-functional characteristics is not the same as picking those with the right ones.

This is not to say we ignore the capabilities of these building blocks. What we are concerned about is that we ask the right questions in choosing them and that we have enough techniques at hand to cope with any gaps or deficiencies in the set we choose. The patterns in this book examine these questions and provide answers that can be used to help choose the right product or fill the gaps.

Why is it Difficult?

The intention of this book is to consider the architecture required to implement systems that can cope with exposure and use across the public Internet. The public

Internet environment is unpredictable in many ways and potentially hostile. In order to fully appreciate the tradeoffs that must be made later when considering the architecture of systems for this environment, we will quickly explore the specific areas of concern for Internet systems and also some examples of the serious failures that may occur and their consequences.

A Sea of Troubles

One of the important pieces of information required by the system architect is the user profile. You need to answer questions such as:

1. Who will be the users or customers for the system?
2. How many of them will there be when the system is deployed? How many will there be in 12 months, two years and five years?
3. How will these users use the system? Can we obtain any typical usage patterns based on common business processes or interactions?
4. When will the users use the system? Are there any times that are particularly busy or quiet?
5. What sort of additional functionality might these users want as time goes on?

For a system that serves internal customers you may get quite precise answers to these questions. However, for a public Internet system, the answers will probably be as follows:

1. We have an idea of our target market and this is likely to form the bulk of the initial users. However we cannot limit users to this target market and we cannot predict how the user profile will evolve over timeframes even as short as six months.
2. We predict an initial market of N thousand users, 10% of whom will typically be online at any one time. We anticipate that we will have $3 \times N$ users in 12 months, but successful promotion and uptake of the service could lead to as many as $10 \times N$ users at that point. We have no firm idea of how many users the system will have in 2 to 5 years.
3. There are multiple distinct use cases for the main system functionality. However, there is no indication of the balance of use cases and which particular functions will prove most popular. As this is a new service, there is no historical data on which we can base predicted patterns of use.
4. As the system has global reach and we anticipate users in most parts of the industrialized world, user activity could take place at any time. There are no particular quiet times. Peak times are anticipated as early to mid

evening in our main markets at which time up to 50% of the users could be online. In response to major promotions, we may need to handle loads of up to 80%.

5. We have no idea.

The main problem here is unpredictability. There is no guarantee that even one customer will turn up to use the system, but you have to figure out what will happen in the worst case scenario (or the likely worst case). You will not have every Internet user in the world accessing your system at the same time (or even over several years), but if you are a global company, a major sales promotion may cause huge peaks of demand and associated large spikes in usage. This may also happen even if you are not selling products since a major news story involving your company may trigger large amounts of interest. Peak usage may be a factor of 10 or 20 times higher than your average usage. This obviously poses a problem as you cannot have all the resource needed to handle this peak demand sitting idly by for the rest of the time. Equally, it is unacceptable for the system to fall over or grind to a halt as it reaches peak load. If your load is seasonal (for example, toy sales at Christmas) then you may need more capacity for a time after which the demand drops away again for a long period.

The other way in which 'users' of public Internet systems are unpredictable is in their intent. Almost all of your users will want to use the system for the purpose it was intended. However, there are always a few individuals in your public user base (particularly an anonymous user base) who will want to challenge your security expertise. Such crackers (also known as 'hackers') can bring your system to a halt, damage your reputation or steal your customers' money.

Oh, to be back creating two-tier internal systems with Visual Basic...

Internet System Horror Stories

As you have seen, the very nature of public Internet systems makes them a very visible part of an organization. This is made trickier by the fact that such systems are difficult to architect. It is impossible to mitigate every risk associated with the creation and maintenance of such a system, and things can often go wrong.

It's not there...

At 7.50 pm on Thursday 10 June 1999, the eBay online auction house effectively went offline for around 22 hours due to a software failure. According to Wired News (www.wired.com/news/business/0,1367,20190,00.html): 'A spokesman said Friday a failure in the software used to list items for sale and update bids caused the service to crash.'

eBay had worked very closely with their primary vendor – Sun Microsystems – to create and run the auction site. eBay was one of the prime reference sites for Sun's

Professional Services division, which delivers consultancy to assist with the creation of public Internet systems.

The consequences of this outage included:

- A financial loss for eBay in the region of $3 million to $5 million, including lost revenues and refunds.
- A loss of confidence in eBay by its user community that would take months to rebuild.
- A loss of credibility for Sun, their software and their Professional Services division.
- A further two-hour maintenance outage two days later while patches were applied.
- A major loss of 'face' all round.

From a system architect's viewpoint, this is when it hits home that the responsibility sits at the system architect's door. Senior Sun Professional Services people still refer to 'the eBay moment', meaning a time when the bottom drops out of your world.

It's not Secure...

In early January 2000, an 18 year old Russian cracker doled out 25,000 stolen credit card numbers, complete with expiry dates and address information, before his site was taken offline. He had stolen the information from the online store CDUniverse and released the information publicly when his efforts to blackmail the company came to nothing.

According to internetnews.com (www.internetnews.com/ec-news/article.php/4_278091):

> *The cracker, who goes by the nickname Maxus, claimed in an e-mail to Internet-News.com to have breached the security of CDuniverse.com, an online music store operated by eUniverse, Inc. of Wallingford, Conn. Maxus said he had defeated a popular credit card processing application called ICVerify, from CyberCash (CYCH) and obtained a database containing more than 300,000 customer records from CDUniverse.*

The consequences of this security breach included:

- Reduced trust, and hence trade, for CDUniverse.
- A potential financial loss for those customers whose card information was stolen.
- Legal exposure for CDUniverse resulting from the theft.

■ An overall reduction of consumer confidence in the security of the Internet. As a consequence, anticipated savings from transfer of 'bricks and mortar' sales to online sales failed to appear.

Having bought a specialist product for processing credit cards, the system architect might hope that this would solve any concerns about this part of the application. However, there is a common security tradeoff: widespread software is more widely tested but the downside is that its popularity may encourage crackers to seek an exploit.[2]

It's Running Really Slow Today...

In September 1998, special prosecutor Kenneth Starr published the report of his investigation into the Clintons on several US government web sites. Although these sites (including the White House's official web site) were used to providing a large number of users with information about every aspect of government, they were simply incapable of meeting demand. According to the Houston Chronicle:

Starr's report was first posted to several government web sites in the early afternoon. But the sites were swamped even before the document made it online. "Your chances of getting to these sites are down to less than 10 percent," said Umang Gupta, chief executive of Keystone Systems, a company that monitors web traffic from its offices in San Mateo, Calif. "In other words, you've got a 90–95 percent failure rate."

The consequences of this lack of scalability included:

■ A lack of availability of the report to the people that it was intended for. Posting it to servers incapable of meeting demand defeated the purpose of making it available over the Internet.

■ The complete inability by these sites to carry out their normal function: providing official documents published by the US government

■ A knock-on effect as people who couldn't reach the report tried other government sites (some of which didn't actually carry the report) and also overloaded them.

Whether the people that placed the report on the servers didn't know just how many users would try to download it, or whether they over-estimated the capability of their servers is irrelevant. They simply weren't prepared for the load placed on the system and it failed to cope.

---

[2] In Internet security terminology, an exploit is a security hole of which a potential attacker can take advantage.

Summary

In this chapter we have discussed Internet technology and the types of system built from it. We have explored the types of non-functional characteristics typically required from such systems and we have defined the target application type for this book: large-scale public Internet systems. You have seen why building such systems is difficult and fraught with danger should parts of the system fail.

In the next chapter, we will examine how a pattern language for the creation of Internet technology systems can help to deliver systems that exhibit the required non-functional characteristics.

CHAPTER 4

Architectural Patterns for Internet Technology Systems

This book captures a set of patterns that will help to guide system architects in the creation of Internet technology systems. In order to get the most from the patterns here, we need to understand what a pattern is, how it is used, and how the patterns in this book are organized.

Patterns, Languages and Internet Technology

The patterns movement within software and computer systems originated from the work of the architect Christopher Alexander. 'Each pattern is a three-part rule, which expresses a relation between a certain context, a problem, and a solution.' [Alexander 1979]

This 'definition' has been condensed, expanded and metamorphosed in the various patterns books that have been published dealing with software and computer technology. Many different types of patterns have been published for software and hardware; the most common are design patterns, but there are also idioms (programming language patterns), architecture patterns, network and communication patterns, and so on.

Patterns are an area of much discussion in software and computing in general. They are subject to intense and sometimes heated debate about what is and is not a pattern and how 'true' particular patterns and definitions are to the original intent. We're not interested in such discussions here; we use patterns to capture common decisions in evolving a system architecture as they are a useful way of framing problems and their solutions.

In this book we are not going to provide further definitions of what a pattern is, but instead return to Alexander's original concept [Alexander 1979]:

As an element in the world, each pattern is a relationship between a certain context, a certain system of forces which occurs repeatedly in that context, and a certain spatial configuration which allows these forces to resolve themselves.

As an element of language, a pattern is an instruction, which shows how this spatial configuration can be used, over and over again, to resolve the given system of forces, wherever the context makes it relevant.

Alexander uses the term 'spatial configuration' to describe the combination of elements found in the proposed solution. This is basically the 'shape' of the solution which, in computer system architecture terms, will be the combination of hardware and software elements that solves a particular problem.

We have already discussed how the role of the architect is to resolve the forces of non-functional characteristics in order to produce the greatest 'goodness of fit' for their unique situation. The patterns in this book describe elements in the world of Internet technology systems. They may occur many times in the architecture of a single system, and are usually found in every successful system of a particular type, because the relationship between the context, the forces in that context and the spatial configurations occurs in all these systems, often many times over.

Alexander suggested that patterns frequently form a language or vocabulary that relates to a particular area, such as town planning. The patterns in this language would complement each other and work together to create the overall shape of the town.

In defining his language, Alexander described not just the patterns that he saw, but also the relationships between the patterns in terms of how they complement or contradict each other, or how they can be combined. Similarly, we have defined relationships between our patterns to form what we see as a pattern language, where the best solutions are obtained by the combination and repetitive application of a number of patterns rather than just one or two in isolation.

Why do we use Patterns?

The purpose of this book is to communicate practical experience of architecting Internet technology systems. We can't describe a simple example architecture to achieve this; given that there are many ways to balance the non-functional characteristics described in the previous chapter, there are many possible architectures that could be developed for a given system. By stating a set of required characteristics, we can narrow down the options within this space to create a more restricted set of architecture options. The more precise the stated characteristics, the more specific a matching architecture becomes. So an example architecture, or even a number of example architectures, can only cover a tiny portion of the space of possible architectures that can be defined. However, the architectures within this restricted space are only relevant if your combination of characteristics match the set we have stated. Hence, even if they work well as exemplars, the task of bridging the gap between the examples provided and the architecture required to match your own set of characteristics is left to the reader.

We also can't achieve our aim by providing a design decision tree or single 'recipe' for defining Internet technology system architectures. As before, the range of possible choices is simply too large for a flowchart or decision tree to accommodate. And even if this were possible, it assumes we understand the complete space of architectural decisions. This simply isn't the case – although there is a large amount of similarity between the many system architectures that have been implemented, it is rare that a system architecture doesn't contain some unique elements. Some vendors attempt to define 'prescriptive' architectures that you can follow when defining your own systems. However, these usually only cover a small set of system types, albeit common ones.

Instead of either of these approaches, we have concentrated on capturing the similarities between architectures we have seen (or been involved in defining) in a way that allows the architect to draw on the experience of others and apply that experience to their unique situation. Patterns are a suitable tool for achieving that goal but we didn't want to restrict ourselves to a loose catalogue of architectural patterns – this still leaves the architect with the task of figuring out how the patterns should be combined to achieve their goal. Instead we have developed a language, with pattern relationships explicitly defined, and guidance on when and how to use techniques that others have employed before.

As a system architect or designer, you should be able to read, understand and apply these patterns in the context of your own requirements. If your requirements differ from the example system (GlobalTech) or those of the sequences, you should still be able to determine whether a particular pattern applies to the context in which you are architecting and whether the stated problem exists in your proposed system. You can then follow the pattern and apply it in your particular context.

Patterns vs Principles

Often when we were developing the patterns in this book we would use certain terms again and again to describe what we were seeing in recurring spatial configurations.

For instance, we'd look at an example of using the LOAD-BALANCED ELEMENTS pattern and we'd talk about the use of 'replication' for each of those elements. After a while we began to wonder if these terms (replication, redundancy, one-way dependency, etc.) were actually patterns themselves. So we set about trying to write them up as patterns and failed miserably. We simply couldn't see what specific problem replication was trying to solve or how to implement replication as a solution. Of course, we knew replication was a useful technique to apply in improving availability and scalability, and we knew that any element in the system could, potentially, be replicated. But what we were really trying to do in the patterns was to describe which elements should be replicated, how they should be replicated, and why they should be replicated.

So we ditched the replication pattern but we kept coming back to it as an important concept to understand in both appreciating and applying some of the patterns. Eventually we asked ourselves 'why is this important; why does it keep recurring?' And then it struck us: replication is simply an underlying principle common to many of the patterns concerned with availability and scalability. If you understand the abstract concept of replication, you can more easily understand and apply a pattern that it underpins. In addition to the patterns presented, we also present the principles that appear in a number of the patterns.

Organization of the Patterns

The primary driver in defining these Internet technology patterns is the desire for the system to meet certain non-functional requirements. In Chapter 2 we defined the non-functional characteristics in which we are interested and split them into three groups:

- System performance
- System control
- System evolution

In defining this language, we have used these groupings as the basis of the chapters in which we discuss the patterns. These chapters are preceded by an initial chapter discussing some fundamental patterns that provide the foundation for the others.

Fundamental Patterns

The fundamental patterns are:

- APPLICATION SERVER ARCHITECTURE. Group all the application functionality into a single application rather than multiple collaborating applications.

■ PERIPHERAL SPECIALIST ELEMENTS. Separate out 'extraordinary' functionality into specialist or dedicated elements. Place these elements at the periphery of the core application and manage them separately.

System Performance Patterns

■ ACTIVE–REDUNDANT ELEMENTS. For each critical system element that may be subject to failure or maintenance (usually all of them), introduce an additional, functionally-identical, redundant element that can be brought into service if the active element fails or needs to be taken out of service for maintenance. The redundant element is usually significantly cheaper and of lower capacity than the original, active element.

■ LOAD-BALANCED ELEMENTS. For each critical system element that may be subject to failure or maintenance, introduce one or more additional, functionally-identical elements of a similar capacity. Add a load balancer that spreads the load evenly amongst these elements. Make the load balancer dynamically configurable so that additional elements can be added to the load-balanced set on demand.

■ SESSION FAILOVER. Save the state of the user session whenever it changes so that it can be retrieved by any element that might need to get at it. Implement a failover mechanism that causes the element that takes over interacting with the user to retrieve the session state as necessary.

■ DEDICATED WEB AND APPLICATION SERVERS. Split the application into software optimized for handling user requests and software optimized for processing those requests. Deploy these on different servers.

■ COMMON PERSISTENT STORE. Implement a single persistent store that is shared between all the application servers. It holds a single consistent set of the system data, with all the servers accessing and updating that single set.

■ DATA REPLICATION. Replicate dynamic data between one or more data sources. Ensure that each update of data is only complete when the update has been successfully performed on each replica of the data – failure to update one should mean that none are updated. Provide load-balanced or active–redundant servers for all data access.

■ CONNECTION LIMITATION. Limit the number of connections to a potentially constrained resource. Use this limit to balance the need to maximize the number of connections with per connection throughput.

■ RESOURCE POOLING. Implement a pool of resources such that a resource can be 'checked out' when required and 'checked back in' when finished with, for use by other processes or threads.

■ LOCAL CACHE. Implement a mechanism that caches frequently used information 'locally' to the system element that uses the information.

■ OFFLINE REPORTING. Take a snapshot of the live data into an offline database. Run the report generation routines against this offline database.

System Control Patterns

■ CONTINUAL STATUS REPORTING. Define a reporting interface or protocol for every type of system element that can seriously affect the operational health of the overall system (usually all or nearly all of them). Have each individual system element continuously report its status according to its type. Log some or all of the data generated so that it is available for subsequent offline analysis.

■ OPERATIONAL MONITORING AND ALERTING. Have all system elements report their status at an appropriate frequency. Implement an automated process that watches for indicators of a failing system and warns the system operations team – allowing them to take preventative action if possible.

■ 3-CATEGORY LOGGING. Implement a mechanism to log system events and system execution information. This mechanism should be able to log three different types of data: debug, information and error.

■ SYSTEM OVERVIEW. Provide agents that monitor all the interfaces to each of the system elements individually. Implement a further layer of monitoring agents that extract relevant data from each of the individual monitoring agents, merge it together and abstract from it to give a single picture of the system. This SYSTEM OVERVIEW is presented as a number of aggregated elements.

■ DYNAMICALLY-ADJUSTABLE CONFIGURATION. Identify key parameters that fundamentally affect the non-functional characteristics of the system and allow them to be altered at runtime.

■ DEMILITARIZED ZONE. Create a secure 'de-militarized zone' (DMZ) between the organization and the outside world.

■ INFORMATION OBSCURITY. An essential set of sensitive information should be obscured at all times unless it is being directly used in a relatively safe environment.

■ SECURE CHANNELS. Use encrypted communication channels to protect sensitive information in transit.

■ KNOWN PARTNERS. Use digital certificates to prove client and server identity before engaging in the exchange of data and requests.

System Evolution Patterns

■ DYNAMICALLY-DISCOVERABLE ELEMENTS. Identify the points in the architecture where you are likely to want to introduce new system elements. Determine whether that introduction would necessarily involve taking the system down. If not (e.g. introduction of identical elements to improve scalability and availability), introduce a mechanism that allows new elements to be discovered at runtime.

- VIRTUAL PLATFORM. Choose a technology stack and infrastructure for the system that, for every type of element, offers one or more alternatives that can be relatively easily migrated to. This does not mean that the elements have to be 'plug and play compatible', more that their introduction should not require a major new project in order to port to them.

- EXPANDABLE HARDWARE. Ensure that hardware (both servers and network) has internal capacity for expansion when the system is first installed and for each addition of new hardware.

- SWAPPABLE STAGING ENVIRONMENT. Create a parallel 'live' environment in which a new version of the system can be deployed and tested. Potentially, users can be migrated to the parallel environment as a way of upgrading the application.

- SEPARATE SYSTEM-MANAGED DATA. Identify data that is updated by users as part of their interaction with the system and data that is used and controlled entirely by the system itself. Use this as the basis for partitioning the data in your system to ease data migration issues during upgrades.

Presentation of the Patterns

The patterns are presented in two forms: in the main chapters of the book the patterns are presented in detail using a narrative form. In the Appendix, a summary form is used that highlights the most important points of the detailed pattern in a template.

Patterns in the Main Chapters

Although the patterns are presented in a narrative form, the narrative has the same flow in all cases. Each pattern description roughly follows this sequence:

- A preamble, including a description of the problem in a more general context and then relating the problem to the specific context.

- The problem statement (in bold). This statement is the same in the main pattern and in the reference pattern.

- A detailed description of the problem in the context of computing and Internet systems and the forces at work.

- A detailed description of the problem in the context of the GlobalTech system example (see Chapter 5 for details of the requirements of this system) and the forces at work.
- The solution statement (in bold). This statement is the same in the main pattern and in the reference pattern.
- A detailed description of the solution in the context of the GlobalTech system.
- A discussion of the implementation options for this particular pattern.
- A discussion of how the application of this pattern impacts the non-functional characteristics of the system.

Patterns in the Appendix

The patterns are described in a shortened, or reference, form in the Appendix. Each reference pattern consists of a set of headed sections in the following order:

- Pattern name
- Problem
- Context
- Example (of the problem)
- Forces
- Solution
- Example resolution
- Resulting context (what the application of the pattern does for the non-functional characteristics of the system – this is the same as the table at the end of the main pattern)
- Implementation (whether the solution is usually implemented in hardware or software)
- Related patterns and principles

The reference patterns are intended for quick reference if you want to understand the essence of a pattern without reading the full discussion.

Navigating the Language

The easiest way to navigate the language (other than just to read it from start to finish) is to use the pattern relationships (summarized in the diagram on the inside of the back cover of the book). Each pattern identifies the direct relationships it has with other patterns that build on it, complement it, or offer an alternative to it. These tend to be 'localized' in the sense that patterns that address one or two non-functional characteristics, such as the management patterns in Chapter 8, tend to be related to each other.

Patterns are also indirectly related to each other through the tensions identified between the non-functional characteristics. A pattern that improves security, for example, is likely to have a negative impact on performance to some degree. If we can't really afford a loss of performance (either because we are just meeting the non-functional requirements for performance or are yet to meet them) we need to counteract the effect of the security pattern by applying one or more performance patterns. So, after navigating a 'local' group of patterns related by a non-functional characteristic they address, we may wish to navigate to patterns that can be used to balance the negative effects they have on other characteristics.

Table 4.1 summarizes the effects each of the patterns has on the non-functional characteristics identified in Chapter 2. A plus (+) indicates that the characteristic is improved by the pattern, a minus (−) that the characteristic is negatively impacted and a 'u' that the characteristic is unaffected by the pattern. Sometimes the relationship between the characteristic and the pattern is more complex in that the pattern may improve or degrade the characteristic depending on the implementation. Such cases are indicated by a question mark (?) – for further discussion on these points, see the 'Impact of the pattern on non-functional characteristics' section of the relevant pattern. Cost ratings are given in terms of currency symbols, with '£' indicating some initial cost increase and '££' indicating a significant initial cost increase.

Summary

In this chapter we have looked at the ideas of patterns, pattern languages and principles as well as giving a brief introduction to the pattern language presented in this book and how to navigate it. In the next chapter we will introduce the GlobalTech system – a fictional system that we use as an example throughout the rest of the book. This is followed by the four chapters that contain the patterns themselves.

Table 4.1 Effect of the Patterns on the Non-functional Characteristics

	AVAILABILITY	PERFORMANCE	SCALABILITY	SECURITY	MANAGEABILITY	MAINTAINABILITY	FLEXIBILITY	PORTABILITY	COST
Application Server Architecture	U	+	U	+	+	+	−	U	?
Peripheral Specialist Elements	+	+	U	−	+	+	+	?	££a
Active–Redundant Elements	+	Ub	U	−	−	U	U	U	££
Load-Balanced Elements	+	−	+	−	−	U	U	U	£
Session Failover	+	−	U	−	−	+	U	U	£
Dedicated Web and Application Servers	+	?	+	−	−	+	U	U	££
Common Persistent Store	−	−	−	+	−	+	U	U	££
Data Replication	+	−	U	U	−	U	U	−	££c
Connection Limitation	−	+	+	U	−	U	U	U	£
Resource Pooling	U	+	+	U	−	U	U	U	£
Local Cache	?	+	U	?	−	U	U	U	?
Offline Reporting	U	+	U	−	−	U	U	U	?
Continual Status Reporting	+	−	U	−	+	+	U	U	£
Operational Monitoring and Alerting	+	−	U	U	+	U	U	U	£
3-Category Logging	U	−	U	U	+	+	U	U	£
System Overview	U	U	+	U	+	U	+	U	£
Dynamically-Adjustable Configuration	U	−	U	U	+	U	U	U	£
Demilitarized Zone	−	−	Ud	+	−	U	U	U	££
Information Obscurity	U	−	U	+	−	−	−	−	£
Secure Channels	−	−	−	+	−	U	U	−	£
Known Partners	−	−	U	+	−	U	U	U	£
Dynamically-Discoverable Elements	+	−	+	−	−	+	+	U	£
Expandable Hardware	−	U	+	+	+	U	+	U	£
Virtual Platform	U	?	U	U	+	+	U	+	?
Swappable Staging Environment	+	−	U	U	−	+	U	U	£
Separate System-Managed Data	+	U	U	U	−	+	+	U	£

a. Only if the specialist elements are given their own dedicated hardware.

b. There may be a very small negative impact but not enough to warrant a '−' rating.

c. If Data Replication is built into the component that implements the Common Persistent Store, it will generally increase the cost of that component.

d. This is unaffected as long as the new elements introduced are themselves scalable.

The GlobalTech System

Before we get into the detail of patterns we will take a look at the GlobalTech system which is the example we use throughout the book. GlobalTech is a fictional system but is an amalgam of a number of systems that we have worked on and reviewed.

GlobalTech is a major manufacturer of consumer goods which range from low-value, high-volume products right through to specialist-market, big-ticket items. The outlets for GlobalTech's products range from small, independent outlets (particularly for the high-end products) to multi-national retailers.

The GlobalTech system discussed in this chapter is used throughout the rest of the book in three distinct ways:

- Each pattern will have an explanation of how it would be embodied in a real solution, and hence what it would imply in the type of system being created for GlobalTech.
- A fully evolved form of the GlobalTech system, in terms of the patterns applied to meet the requirements stated in this chapter, is described in Chapter 10.

■   Some variations on the GlobalTech system are discussed in Chapter 11. These variations come about as certain requirements are emphasized to the detriment of other requirements. Hopefully, this should help you to see how the patterns relate to other types of system, such as those where security is paramount. You will see that the applicability and relevance of certain patterns, and the interaction between the patterns, alters as the requirements change.

The Business Case

Before any system is created, its creation must be justified. At present, Global-Tech has a fairly typical 'corporate presence' web site that holds information about the company and its subsidiaries together with an online version of their product catalogue.

After a recent strategy review, GlobalTech has decided to extend its Internet presence beyond the current web site. GlobalTech currently spends a huge amount of money on customer support, provided by specialist call centres throughout the world. The call centres deal with customers who need help with anything from replacing a lost product manual, to step-by-step analysis of set-up problems, to locating a local retailer that stocks a particular product. Analysts have predicted that GlobalTech could save around $80 million over three years if it diverts 20% of the customers who currently call the support centres to the web site and deals with their requests there. So the customer support department wants to work with the marketing department to create a new site that carries not only the promotional catalogue of products, but also all the customer support materials related to each of those products, as well as a searchable database of retailers and the products they stock.

In addition, GlobalTech's sales department has been looking at ways to update their operation – again with a view to cutting costs. GlobalTech does not currently sell direct to the consumer and has a highly-developed dealer network. However, the relative cost of sale through smaller dealers has been rising over recent years as the smaller dealers have faced shrinking margins due to increased competition with the larger retailers. GlobalTech won't drop the high-end products that these smaller dealers tend to sell from its ranges as they give the company consumer credibility that helps to shift the higher-volume items. However, if the trend cannot be halted, the smaller dealer network will have to be sacrificed, leaving only the larger retailers to sell the high-end items.

Each of the retailers is assigned a sales manager based in a regional office. The retailers place orders on an *ad hoc* basis (whenever they need stock or whenever a particular product is 'hot' in the marketplace). This leads to massive fluctuations in the workload of the manager, which has led to growing dealer dissatisfaction as the number of managers has been reduced in an attempt to cut costs – on average each manager is now dealing with nearly twice as many retailers as they did two years ago.

In a recent survey, a significant proportion of what GlobalTech classifies as 'specialist retailers' responded that they would rather place orders through a dedicated ordering system than work through the account manager. However, their major caveat was cost – they wouldn't pay to have dedicated machines that could only be used for ordering from GlobalTech in their offices. There was also a very strong indication that any such system would have to be easy to use otherwise the retailers just would not use it.

So the sales department is interested in creating an extranet for the retailers, both big and small. The extranet would allow each retailer to place orders for stock and review the status of an order. In addition, many of the 'housekeeping' functions currently performed by the account managers (such as keeping the contact details for each of the retailers up to date) could be performed by the retailers themselves via the extranet system.

The System Overview

Although these two departments have very different functional requirements, there is a lot of overlap in what they are trying to achieve. Both want a system that is available over the public Internet (although the sales department wants it to be restricted to retail partners). Both want a system that can be made available in many different countries and in many different languages – this is a global corporation, after all. And both want a non-trivial set of functionality to be accessible by a large number of users, which necessitates a significant investment in the hardware and software infrastructure, and in the development of the application.

A meeting of the GlobalTech board decides that the two projects should have their budgets and objectives combined. A single project will build a single system that meets the requirements of both the customer support and sales departments, as well as integrating (or replacing) the current online catalogue run by the marketing department.

Functional Requirements Overview

The functional requirements for the system come from three main sponsors: the customer support, retailer sales, and marketing departments. We will describe these functional requirements at a very high level.

Customer Database

When a customer calls customer support, this is one of the few opportunities GlobalTech has of gathering personal information about its customers. Whilst this information is passed to the marketing department, its primary usefulness is in reducing the length of a customer call – the more details customer support has on a customer, the quicker they can deal with them.

Moving customers to the web site will not necessarily stop them from ever calling customer support, but not gathering any information on them at an early stage in their interaction with the support process could negate the savings made by pushing them to the web site. So customer support wants to force customers to register their personal details with the site as part of the support process. This customer database should be available to the support centres, possibly via an extranet.

Marketing wants to extend customer support's idea of a customer database to include data about a customer beyond their contact information and what products they own. They are interested in basic 'segmentation' data, such as sex, age and income, and also in information such as the customer's interests and hobbies and the non-GlobalTech products they own.

Customer Support Materials

A significant proportion of calls to customer support are requests for information that either was supplied with the product and has been lost, or was not included with the product in the first place. Such information includes user manuals, warranty information, software and after-sales care guides.

When a user calls to request such materials, they are shipped from the warehouse to the user's home. This process is lengthy (often taking in excess of 10 days from the call being received) and expensive (the average cost of taking the call, placing the order for the materials and shipping them is estimated at $30) leading to a perception of poor (i.e. slow) service for the customer and a massive budget for customer support.

Customer support wants to make all the materials that can be stored in electronic form available on the web site so that they can be downloaded by anyone that has registered. They also want the ability to 'push' new versions of support materials (such as corrected versions of user manuals that originally contained erroneous or misleading information) to registered customers where appropriate.

Troubleshooting Software

The customer support centres have an expert system that guides operators through various troubleshooting procedures when a customer calls with problems operating the product. Although the operator needs training for the system itself, the knowledge bases and the troubleshooting procedures have been written assuming the operator has no familiarity with the product whatsoever.

The success of the expert system within the call centres (replacing an organization where there used to be 'product experts' within the support centres, each dealing with a small range of products) suggests that anyone who is familiar with standard web searching techniques (such as those employed on Google) could use the system. Customer support wants to trial a user interface to the expert system for a small range of products that are targeted at 'innovators and technophiles'. This will be available as part of the web site for any registered customer.

Retail Outlet Finder

The customer support centres maintain a database of local retail outlets that GlobalTech supplies and a list of the products supplied to each outlet. In the case of specialist retailers this list is derived from the actual orders placed by the retailer. In the case of the larger retailers – who usually place many orders centrally and then do their own distribution – this is an indicative list of the products usually stocked.

Each of the customer support centres has a phone number that a customer can call. Given the customer's address or postal code and the product they want to buy (or the range of products they are interested in), the support centre can supply the customer with the details of retail outlets in their area that are likely to stock the product.

The customer support department would like to totally remove this facility from the support centres. In addition to the cost of answering calls, the maintenance of the database is a significant operation as it has to be regularly updated and then localized for each of the support centres as operators are not required to speak English. They would like to have the function available through the web site only with the cost of update and localization transferred to the marketing department.

Retailer Database

A significant proportion of the account managers' work is maintaining information about each of the retailers they deal with. This includes details of contacts at both a local and (if applicable) national or international level and details of the retailer's outlets.

The process of keeping these details accurate and up-to-date is a frustratingly time-consuming and expensive one, for both GlobalTech and the retailer. The sales department wants to give the retailers the opportunity to update their own details directly. This means the retailer can maintain their details whenever they want to and can ensure that the information is accurate.

Marketing doesn't want to take over the maintenance of the retail outlet database from customer support but the board agrees that customer support should phase out the retailer outlet locator phone numbers. In order to lessen the cost of maintaining the database, marketing wants to extend the sales department's concept of a retailer database to include information about what each retail outlet stocks so that the retailer themselves can maintain the information used by the retailer outlet location functionality.

Retailer Orders

An even greater proportion of the account manager's time is spent taking orders from retailers. These are usually delivered by fax (specialist retailers) or EDI. For faxed orders, the order has to be entered into GlobalTech's supply-chain management system and the order confirmation from this faxed back to the retailer for checking. EDI orders go straight through to the supply-chain management system.

The sales department wants to allow retailers to enter orders directly, again enabling the retailers to place orders whenever they want and to ensure the order is accurate. In addition to the basic ordering facility, the system should maintain an order history (allowing orders to be reviewed and copied to new orders).

Order Status Reports

Currently, order status reports are generated as part of the supply-chain management system and sent to the retailer directly. In the case of the larger retailers, this consists of a large list of goods to be supplied, estimated supply times and other information that is distributed variously by EDI, data tape, CD-ROM or paper. For the specialist retailers, fax is the only option offered.

The system works and the proportional costs are relatively low. However, the sales department wants to present a uniform interface to its retailers and encourage as many of them as possible to move to the web-based system. So they want the system to provide two forms of order status reporting. Firstly the retailer should be able to review the status of orders via the web site, as part of the order history functionality. Secondly, retailers should be able to opt to have order status reports delivered electronically, via encrypted email, on a daily, weekly or monthly basis depending on their size and the frequency of their orders.

Retail Materials

Retailers can order materials such as promotional bins or displays, or training information via their account manager. Unlike product orders, these materials are not supplied through the supply-chain management system as GlobalTech usually outsources their production.

The sales department wants to allow retailers to order physical materials through the web site. This means the site needs to take the order and then relay it to the supplier either via automated fax or email. If the materials can be delivered electronically (such as a training manual for a particular new product or interactive demo software), the retailer should be able to download them.

Product Catalogue

The marketing department wants the full product catalogue to be available online, as a significant proportion of GlobalTech's potential customers use the Internet to research their product purchases. And they want something more than just a direct translation of the paper-based catalogues to the web site. In addition to a category-based hierarchical catalogue, they want a number of 'dynamic views' where the user can decide to find and group products by features/benefits, form (portable products, 'lifestyle' products, high-fidelity products, etc.), price, and so on.

Promotions

Marketing sees the new web site as an excellent tool for promoting GlobalTech products to consumers. They want to use two different promotional techniques: online promotions and email promotions.

Online promotions will use personalization techniques to alter site content based on a user's segment. Several promotions will be run at any one time, but only one will ever be displayed to a particular user for a particular interaction with the site. If the user has registered with the web site and logs in, the promotion will be chosen based on the information stored against them in the customer database. If they have not identified themselves to the system, the promotion will be chosen based on the pages viewed during the interaction with the web site.

Email promotions will start with the sending of a personalized email to every user within a segment derived from the customer database. These emails will induce the receiver to visit a specialist web site (usually developed and hosted outside of the system being discussed here) where they will be given incentives to provide information about themselves or their experiences of using GlobalTech products.

Non-functional Requirements Overview

As system architects we have a significant interest in the functional requirements, partly because we are involved in delivering a system that must implement them and partly because they can directly influence the non-functional requirements and the architecture. For example, we have a functional requirement to make the customer profile information available to the customer support department. This implies a level of performance (it needs to be fast enough for the telephone support operator to access while on the phone) and security (operators have to be able to access, and probably update, customer profiles online).

Some of the non-functional requirements will be implied by the functional ones in this way and others will be more explicit (e.g. a requirement for a certain amount of uptime in a given period). This section reflects a typical statement of non-functional requirements for a corporate system.

Availability

The system is going to provide both public Internet and extranet facilities for a global corporation. Consumer and business customers will want to access the system via its web site interface from over 100 countries all around the world. This web site will expose functionality that forms a core part of GlobalTech's business. If the system is not available to take an order from a retailer, or to provide customer support, it will not meet the objectives set for it – to reduce the cost of both the customer support and retail sales departments.

The average consumer interaction time (the amount of time from the point where the user browses to the site until the point where they navigate away) is expected to be no more than 5 minutes, with a predicted maximum of around 20 minutes. However the average extranet user interaction time is estimated to be around 60 minutes with a maximum of 4–6 hours. These longer interaction times, combined with the global distribution of users, mean the system must be 100% available – there is no 'dead time' when the system can be taken down for maintenance.

It is extremely difficult (i.e. expensive) to make a system 100% available, so the following availability criteria are defined:

- The system should be able to withstand major hardware or software failure without loss of availability.
- The system should remain available whilst routine maintenance is carried out.
- The system can be taken down for a period of up to one hour for a planned minor upgrade. These upgrades should happen no more than once per month.
- The system can be taken down for a period of up to four hours for a planned major upgrade. These upgrades should happen no more than once per quarter.
- Outside of planned maintenance, the system must be available at least 99.9% of the time (this equates to downtime of up to 90 seconds per day) when averaged out over the course of a month.

Performance

Performance criteria are usually presented in terms of maximum response times. These are usually derived from estimated figures for different types of interaction based on user expectation and tolerance:

- Less than three seconds for the home page and other common 'landing pages'
- Less than six seconds for any other content pages (static or generated)
- Less than 10 seconds for a 'simple' search operation
- Less than 20 seconds for an 'advanced' search operation

These times are for the public Internet and represent the expectations of an 'average' user.

Extranet users may well be more tolerant of longer response times when they are aware that what they are doing is 'significant' but they still need enough performance from the system for it to be usable:

- Less than 20 seconds for an order status request
- Less than 60 seconds for an order placement request

All times are end-to-end, from the point the request is submitted to the browser to the point where the page is substantially loaded such that all the relevant information is in the browser, even if some images or extra information are still downloading. (The 'time to last byte' may also be used as a performance measure, counting from when the request was made to the point at which all parts of the page have been loaded and the browser is quiescent again.) All such measurements obviously include time introduced by network latency – one of the major disadvantages with requiring system access over the public Internet being that this latency is uncontrollable and largely unpredictable. For the GlobalTech system these figures are required for interactions in Europe, North America, Australia and New Zealand. For other areas, such as Asia, where Internet infrastructure is predictably poorer, the figures can be relaxed by 100%. This clearly isn't desirable, however.

Performance measurements must also take into account the anticipated access mechanism used by customers and retailers. Retailers can be expected to use some form of high-speed access, preferably xDSL but at least ISDN. However, consumers may be accessing the system over a modem running at as little as 9600 baud. In either case, the performance targets for the different aspects of functionality must be hit when simulating the target access mechanism.

Scalability

The scalability requirement is derived from the budgeting scenarios identified by the analysts. For the system to return its budget over three years, 20% of the customer support requests and 100% of the specialist retailer interactions must go through the system (100% is unlikely; 80% more realistic but the shortfall would be offset by 8–10% of major retailer interactions being moved to the system) within two years of the system going live. Given the best analysis of global data from the customer support and retail sales departments, this level of usage would translate to roughly 6000 public Internet users and 1200 specialist retailer users accessing the system at any one time, with peaks of up to 8000 and 2000 respectively.

This is the best case scenario; the project would still be viable with averages of 1200 public Internet and 300 specialist retailer simultaneous users (peaks of 2000 and 500). However, this does not include the users of the current online catalogue. The average number of simultaneous users is just 500, however peaks of 10 000 users are not unknown when GlobalTech launches a major new product.

Considering all of these figures, the following has been agreed:

- The system must support an average of 2000 simultaneous public Internet users and 500 retailer users at the outset.

- Peaks of 3000 and 700 must be catered for at the outset – the system performance can degrade by up to 20% at peak load

- The system must be expandable so that it can grow to support averages of 7000 and 1200 (peaks of 8000 and 2000), respectively, through the purchase of new hardware and/or software should demand require it.

- The system must be temporarily expandable to support up to 20 000 public Internet users (when there is a major new product launched), whilst still supporting the average and peak number of extranet users.

Security

In terms of access to the system, there is no security requirement for browsing the online catalogue – it is available to anyone anonymously. This is also true of the retail outlet locator and peripheral pages such as legal notices and contact information. Online promotions will usually be displayed on these public pages.

Customer support materials and the troubleshooting software can only be accessed by users who have signed up to the customer database. The user must supply a login name and password that they have specified as part of registration. The registration process and login must be secure from external 'snooping' to capture user details, as must any interaction with the customer database to update the customer's details.

Access to any of the retailer functions must be restricted to retailers who have explicitly signed up with the extranet. There can be no opportunity to snoop information passed between the user and the system for any function. In addition, it must be possible to prove that a particular order came from the user who submitted it and not anyone else.

The system itself must be well-protected against hackers. Hackers should not be able to gain access to the system in order to obtain or alter the executable code. The data held by the system should also be protected and, even if the customer data is somehow obtained, sensitive information such as passwords should not be usable by the hackers. Additionally, even if hackers are able to compromise the system and data related to the public Internet functions, they should not be able to access the order-placement functions or any of the extranet data.

Manageability

The management information requirements for the GlobalTech system can be defined in terms of the questions the system administrators and the business are interested in answering:

- How many users are on the system at any one time? What types of user are they (anonymous, registered, retailer)? Roughly, what they are doing?
- How many users have registered with the system? How many of the registered users return to use the system more than once?
- What are the current average and maximum response times the users get depending on which parts of the system they are accessing?
- What is the average uptime of the system as a whole? What are the average uptimes of its individual elements?
- Which elements of the system are regularly failing? What is causing their failure?
- How efficient is the usage of the system as a whole (how does average throughput relate to maximum throughput)? How efficient is the usage of the individual elements of the system?

The requirements for variation in the runtime characteristics of the system can be defined in terms of those characteristics:

- Availability. It should be possible to alter the level of availability by dynamically adding (or removing) resources.
- Performance. It should be possible to vary performance characteristics by altering system values (buffer sizes, queue sizes, etc.).
- Security. It should be possible to revoke security privileges and to change security settings.
- Manageability. It should be possible to change the amount or level of detail of the information captured.

Maintainability

The GlobalTech system should be easy to maintain. This is a fatuous statement but it is often the level of requirement given for the maintainability of a system. Maintainability is extremely hard to specify: we could give maximum times it should take to identify and fix a bug or fault in the hardware, but this is not something you can architect (or even plan) for. By their very nature, these defects are unknown until they happen, so how can we mandate how easy they should be to fix.

One of the best approaches to specifying maintainability that we have seen is the 'measure and continuously improve' approach. Any defects fixed are logged with the time taken to find and fix. After a number of these are done, a review is made to see if there is anything (technically or in the process) that can be changed to reduce the find and fix cycle. The changes are made and the process starts again.

This is not to say that we ignore maintainability for the first iteration, however. There are some sensible precautions we can take to start with and then improve from there. So we will make the initial system as easy to maintain as we can, given our other constraints.

Flexibility

To give some indication of the required flexibility we can look at the future enhancements that the system is likely to need to support. Most of these are new areas of functionality such as warranty registration, a shopping basket for limited direct selling, a newsroom, etc. So the addition of new services is emphasized more than expanding existing services to take account of new types of information (e.g. the notion of what the catalogue holds is unlikely to change significantly in the foreseeable future).

Additionally, the nature of the system as a 'platform' on which multiple public Internet and extranet services are offered indicates that future services may well require further integration with 'back office' and third party systems. So integration mechanisms are another area where we need to focus efforts to build in flexibility.

Portability

A common practice for dotcom start-ups is to produce a 'cheap and cheerful' version of their system in order to prove their business model and secure further funding. This is then ported to a more robust and scalable environment, often resulting in some elements of the system being directly ported and some being thrown away and replaced.

GlobalTech, however, has no such need. Although they want to start small and expand once the concept is proven, they wish to do that through scalability – starting with a production-ready environment and expanding it rather than starting with something particularly cheap and porting across. Despite this, GlobalTech does have a major requirement for portability. Like many large corporations, it likes to maintain a degree of independence from its suppliers. So, where it chooses a supplier (particularly for software rather than hardware) for a particular system element, it wants the option of porting to an alternative supplier if the first choice proves to be unreliable (technically or financially) or if 'political' issues arise around the continuing use of that supplier.

Summary

In this chapter we have described the GlobalTech system that is used as the example throughout this book. We have looked at its intentions and origins and the resulting functional and non-functional requirements.

Over the next few chapters, we look in detail at the patterns for Internet technology systems. As we apply these patterns, you will see how the non-functional requirements defined earlier lead us to adapt and refactor the GlobalTech system architecture until it is of sufficient capability.

PART 2

The Patterns

CHAPTER 6

Fundamental Patterns

Getting the Shape Right

Now we have the functional and non-functional requirements for the GlobalTech system, we need to start developing the architecture. Unfortunately, as with so many jobs, getting started can be the hardest part. What is the right starting point for the GlobalTech architecture?

This chapter introduces two 'fundamental' patterns: APPLICATION SERVER ARCHITECTURE and PERIPHERAL SPECIALIST ELEMENTS. We've identified these patterns as being fundamental because they describe the basic shape that most Internet technology systems adopt, and so underpin most of the architectural decisions that we will examine in the other patterns in the language.

APPLICATION SERVER ARCHITECTURE

A number of the early Internet technology systems started out with a logical architecture similar to Figure 6.1.

These architectures followed the principle of software modularity: a registration and personalization application was constructed along with a 'profile' database

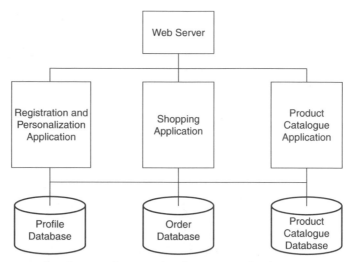

Figure 6.1   Logical architecture for typical early Internet technology system.

where it could store information about registered users. The other applications would follow the same principle of supporting an identified subset of overall application functionality, with registration/personalization, shopping and product catalogue being some of the most common. These applications were designed to run 'semi-autonomously', the idea being that they would be deployed onto separate hardware servers or separate processes on a single hardware server.

Unfortunately, despite the fact that this type of architecture supports partitioning of the system software, we shall see that there are a number of problems with it in terms of its non-functional characteristics – particularly when we consider deployment. So the question remains:

What is a good starting point for the architecture of an Internet technology system?

Let's look in detail at some of the problems of the architecture described above in terms of the non-functional characteristics we care about.

■ **Availability.** Partitioning the system in this way does not really improve its overall availability. If the shopping application fails (or needs to be taken down), users can still browse the product catalogue but can't purchase anything. If the product catalogue goes down, there is no point in being able to purchase as they won't be able to navigate to the product they want to buy. The different applications collaborate to implement the total functionality of the system and being able to access only some of that functionality is sometimes useful, but often not.

- **Performance.** A single web page is likely to contain elements that touch on a number of the applications, possibly all. A 'personalized home page' will contain personal details from the registration/personalization application and may also contain a summary of the shopping basket and direct navigation into the product catalogue. Rendering that page requires separate interaction with all three applications – very costly in terms of response time.

- **Scalability.** There is no obvious way of scaling this system without simply increasing the capacity of each of the different applications. And we will always be at the mercy of the most loaded or least scalable application as most pages will require interaction from more than one of the applications. If the catalogue application is overloaded, the personal home page will be very slow to construct even if the registration/personalization and shopping applications are fine.

- **Security.** Security is not particularly negatively impacted. Different applications may need to be accessed by different people, and the data they store may have different levels of sensitivity. But it is unlikely that completely different security policies will be specified and implemented for each of the different applications – doing so would introduce a real manageability problem. It is more likely that one security policy will be implemented across the board for all applications.

- **Manageability.** This type of partitioning can have a drastic effect on manageability. First of all, there are a number of semi-autonomous applications that all have to be configured to work correctly with each other. Then, each of the individual applications (and, potentially, the server it runs on) needs to be managed both separately and collectively. Potentially, this problem gets worse every time new functional requirements are introduced: if the requirements are identified as belonging to a new subset of the system functionality, a new application is added to the managed set.

- **Maintainability.** On the face of it, the system should be more maintainable. Each application supports a self-contained subset of the application functionality, so it should be easier to identify and fix any bugs in those applications. Unfortunately, these applications need to collaborate to implement much of the overall system functionality, which means that a bug may not be nicely confined to a single application. It also means that the applications need to communicate with each other – they're not really all that autonomous after all. The ideal mechanism for this would be through a well-defined interface exposed by each of the applications, accessed through some form of message bus or remote invocation (the applications are designed to be deployed as separate processes or onto separate servers, remember). In practice, however, a number of systems of this type used the database to interact, with an application reading from and writing to tables 'owned' by other applications. The primary motivations for this were ease of development and improved performance, but this came at the expense of breaking the partitioning principle that spawned this architectural style in the first place.

- **Flexibility.** Flexibility is potentially improved by this type of architecture. If a set of new functional requirements is to be implemented in a new application, that application can potentially be introduced without any disruption to the other applications. This will be the case if the new application is completely isolated from the others (i.e. it doesn't need to collaborate with them at all) or if it has only a one-way dependency on them (see 'Principles' in Chapter 9).

- **Portability.** This type of partitioning has no real impact one way or another on the portability of the system.

- **Cost.** There is no significant cost impact of adopting this architecture; there is no reason why producing a system partitioned in this way should be particularly more or less expensive than any other type of partitioning. However, as we have seen, there are several serious problems that need to be solved if this architecture is to be used, and these solutions could be very expensive:

  - Probably the best way to improve availability is to introduce some form of redundancy or replication (see 'Principles' in Chapter 7). Let's say we deploy each application to two servers (or server processes), the additional server to take over if the other one fails as described in the ACTIVE–REDUNDANT ELEMENTS pattern. We now have double the management problem as we have two servers for each type of application. We also have a potentially complex routing and collaboration problem – how do we ensure that the applications continue to collaborate correctly if one fails and the backup takes over?

  - Probably the best way to improve performance is to allow the various applications to work asynchronously most of the time and only synchronize them when we really need them to work together (perhaps the shopping application needs to wait until the registration/personalization system has written some details to a particular table in the database). This is achievable but can massively increase the complexity of the overall application. This increase in complexity is expensive to design, develop and test, and can reduce the maintainability and, potentially, the flexibility of the overall system.

  - There is no real way to improve the manageability of the system. Whichever way you look at it, this system is implemented over a number of different applications (and servers or server processes) that all have a unique role and characteristics. Management becomes increasingly complex the more functionality the system supports.

So, we have a system that conforms to some 'good' software engineering principles due to being partitioned into semi-autonomous applications. The applications are each focused on their own concerns, reducing the complexity of each part and dependencies between the different applications can be minimized.

The situation described reflects the thoughts and concerns of those tasked with developing the GlobalTech system. It requires a product catalogue, registration and personalization, online ordering for retailers, various information-based applications such as the retail outlet finder, and online troubleshooting. Each of these has its own concerns and must be logically separated to some degree. As part of the separation, each could be implemented on its own hardware. However, they must all combine at different times and in various ways to delivers a 'seamless' experience for the user.

The partitioning principles discussed above only really address the logical development of the software and not its deployment. When we consider deployment of the applications a number of pretty serious disadvantages emerge. How can we achieve a similar logical partitioning without encountering the problems in deployment?

Adopt an APPLICATION SERVER ARCHITECTURE: group all core system functionality in a single application. Internally partition the application according to the preferred logical architecture.

If we had decided to adopt the 'collaborating semi-autonomous applications' architecture outlined above for the GlobalTech system, we would have ended up with a complex architecture consisting of seven or so separate applications. Adopting an APPLICATION SERVER ARCHITECTURE means that we lump all this complexity into a single application, as in Figure 6.2.

By adopting this architecture we are trading off high-level simplicity (we now only have one application to worry about) against lower-level complexity (the application is going to be more complex than any of the separate applications would have been). However, as we discussed in Chapter 2, it is this high-level view that, as system architects, we are most interested in. That isn't to say we will completely discount or ignore the lower-level complexity; we will consider the logical architecture of the application in a moment.

Despite the seeming simplicity of this architecture, we still have a number of choices to make about the implementation of the application. We have to decide the technology platform and mechanisms to be used. Given the complexity of the requirements (including the need for long-lived sessions and different types of security), we can quickly discount using a set of CGI scripts. It is certainly possible to build large systems using CGI but the complexity of developing, testing, configuring and managing the scripts, not to mention the issues of performance and scalability, make it a very impractical solution.

Figure 6.2   GlobalTech Application Server Architecture.

If we're going to develop the system in Java we could go for a basic solution using JSP and Servlets. The web server may come with an integrated Servlet/JSP container or we can choose a standalone one such as Tomcat or Resin. Alternatively we could choose a full-blown J2EE application server such as BEA WebLogic, IBM WebSphere, JBoss, or ATG Dynamo, each of which provides us with a container for EJBs and other J2EE technologies, such as JMS. We might also wish to take advantage of component frameworks for functionality such as e-commerce, personalization and fulfillment that can run in some of these application servers.

Alternatively, we could even decide to build the application from scratch, although having to build our own server page implementation, communications protocols, database connectivity, etc., probably means we would spend more time and money doing this than if we adopted a JSP container or J2EE application server.

If we are going to use Microsoft technology for the system, the de facto choice for implementing the application is .NET. Again, we would start from a base of dynamic server pages implemented using ASP.NET to generate HTML or XML web services. The .NET platform provides a transactional component model in Enterprise Services and asynchronous interaction using MSMQ. Using .NET allows developers to choose a language which matches their skills, so that the business logic could still be developed by developers using Visual Basic .NET while other parts use C#. The application could be developed directly on the .NET platform or we could buy additional servers, such as Microsoft Commerce Server which would deliver some or all of the functionality needed.

Of course, there are other technologies than Java or .NET to choose from. There are application servers for Perl, Smalltalk, C(++) and others and we could probably choose to implement the GlobalTech Application in any of these. It really isn't the purpose of this book to try to make language or specific technology recommenda-tions – different technologies will suit different requirements (both functional and non-functional), organizational politics or strategies, budgets, skill sets, etc. To be specific in our example, we will choose to implement the GlobalTech Application using a J2EE application server. This gives us a number of standardized (within the scope of the Java language) APIs we can take advantage of, as well as a defined component model and some degree of vendor independence. This isn't to say that we'll ignore .NET (the other real contender in terms of corporate strategy and read-ily available skills) – the discussion of the other patterns will include .NET-specific implementation advantages or issues.

Choosing to implement the application in some form of application server still requires us to define the software architecture of the GlobalTech system. We can apply the principles of partitioning to the application architecture to partition the software logically and separate concerns (see Figure 6.3).

For now at least, that is about all we're going to say about the internal structure of the GlobalTech Application. There are many ways we could possibly structure the application and our choice is just as likely to be driven by a particular implementation technology (such as J2EE or .NET) or by the requirements we have to implement, as it is by some general software engineering principles we want to employ. Resources such as [Bass *et al*. 1998], [Alur *et al*. 2000], [Buschmann *et al*. 1996] and [Fowler 2003b] deal with some of the issues of creating the software architecture and the common software patterns found within such an architecture – some of which are platform-specific. We're more concerned with the bigger picture of the system architecture. Adopting an APPLICATION SERVER ARCHITECTURE means that we place the core software of the system in a single application 'box'.

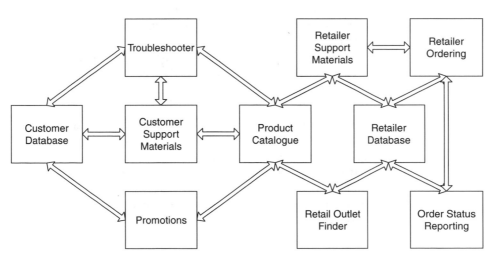

Figure 6.3 Logical partitioning of the GlobalTech Application.

Impact of the Pattern on Non-functional Characteristics

Availability

Availability isn't improved over the 'collaborating semi-autonomous applications'. As discussed previously, the fact that some applications could continue to function when others have failed or been taken down is of dubious benefit. However, the availability of the APPLICATION SERVER ARCHITECTURE is really no worse.

Performance

Performance is likely to be significantly improved. Whereas we had all the semi-autonomous applications collaborating (using some form of inter-process or inter-server communication, possibly via the database) to render pages or perform complex functions, now we have a single application, although parts of this may still require inter-process communication depending on implementation choices.

Scalability

The application of this pattern does not in itself improve the scalability of the system. However, as we shall see in Chapter 7, an APPLICATION SERVER ARCHITECTURE lays the foundation for a highly-scalable system.

Security

Security is marginally improved due to having only one application and one database to worry about securing.

Manageability

Manageability is significantly improved: whereas we had many applications to manage, now we only have one. Even when we add more complexity to the architecture to achieve scalability, etc., we shall see that an APPLICATION SERVER ARCHITECTURE lays the foundation for a more manageable system.

Maintainability

Because all the logically separate software 'modules' are part of the same application, we don't have to worry about complex communication mechanisms. However, we have not lost the benefits of having well-defined sets of functionality which can, potentially, help to isolate bugs. On the whole, maintainability is improved.

Flexibility

This type of system architecture is not as flexible as the 'collaborating semi-autonomous applications architecture'. Whilst we have a similar partitioning, which gives us some degree of flexibility, we have abandoned the semi-autonomous nature that caused us performance, management and maintenance headaches. This means that we can't just add new functionality without having a negative impact on the existing system.

Portability

Unaffected by this pattern.

Cost

As we've already discussed, an APPLICATION SERVER ARCHITECTURE provides a foundation where manageability, performance, availability and scalability can be addressed more easily (and, hence, more cheaply). Whether it is actually cheaper to adopt an APPLICATION SERVER ARCHITECTURE than the 'collaborating semi-autonomous applications' approach is debatable. Certainly, running the application in the .NET framework or a J2EE application server can potentially reduce costs; the cost of purchasing the infrastructure can easily be offset against the cost of building all the functionality provided from scratch. Even if we were to build the 'collaborating semi-autonomous applications' using J2EE servers, we would need many more server instances which can potentially affect license costs.

The idea that using .NET or a J2EE application server can allow the development team to 'focus on the business logic' is pretty sound. However there are two important caveats to this. Firstly, the development team needs to be very experienced with the technology in order to focus on the 'business logic'. If not they will spend a lot of time trying to figure out how the framework actually interacts with their code and components. Secondly, the adoption of .NET or a J2EE application server does not mean that the development team can completely ignore the infrastructure. Both these types of framework need significant configuration management and ongoing support in order to get the best from them.

Moving On

Having decided on the starting point for our architecture, we shall now embellish it slightly with another fundamental pattern: PERIPHERAL SPECIALIST ELEMENTS. This will give us the basic shape for our architecture and provide the foundation on which we will build when we develop the system for performance, control and evolution.

PERIPHERAL SPECIALIST ELEMENTS

By adopting an APPLICATION SERVER ARCHITECTURE we have decided to lump all the system software into a single application. But we haven't felt the need to 'fold in' the web server or the database software. Why choose to exclude these system elements from our reductionist approach? What about other software elements that may make up our overall system, such as mail servers and search engines?

BOX 6.1 Application servers: The new operating systems?

Almost all Internet technology systems built around an APPLICATION SERVER ARCHITECTURE will employ a third-party platform in the role of the application server. This platform could be Microsoft's .NET Framework running on one of the Windows family of servers. Alternatively it could be one of many implementations of J2EE, such as IBM WebSphere, BEA WebLogic, JBoss, ATG Dynamo or the SunOne family of servers, running on Solaris, Windows or Linux. In each case, the application server offers a consistent set of functionality with which to create your application, including transaction control, a security model, asynchronous messaging, a web component model, remote procedure calls, thread handling, data management, web service support and internationalization support. Each application server builds on the functionality provided by the underlying operating system and adds its own functionality to fill in any gaps. They build on the operating system's resource access and networking capabilities to provide consistent wrappers around standard functionality, usually in the shape of a class library to be used with an object-oriented development environment such as Java or C#. Examples of such functionality include:

- File and network access
- Process control and thread scheduling
- Security model and access to the security subsystem
- GUI libraries
- Internationalization

In addition to wrapping the underlying platform, they provide additional code to 'add value' by extending the underlying functionality and providing useful abstractions, such as:

- Simplified data access and persistence
- Transaction control (often declarative rather than programmatic)
- Asynchronous messaging
- Remote procedure calls based on distributed objects
- Event management
- A component model
- XML and XSLT support
- Web lifecycle and parameter management
- Web service support

This means that a single environment can provide a comprehensive platform for application development.

Should we integrate all software elements into the application server, leaving us with a single, internally-partitioned application that implements all system functionality?

The term 'outsourcing' is widely used in business circles. The idea is essentially to strip out any specialist activity leaving a company to focus on its 'core business'. Outsourcing has had somewhat of a bad press since many businesses have used it as a way of cutting costs by selling service and supply contracts to the lowest bidder and ditching large numbers of employees in the process. However, the principle is a sound one which is commonly found in most business sectors. For example, very few online retailers would consider having their own distribution function that ships their goods to the customer. Instead, they will engage a distribution company such as UPS or Bertlesmann to deliver the items they sell. This means that the distribution companies become very efficient at distribution while the online retailers focus on selling goods online. The 'jack of all trades' is frequently master of none, and companies that insist on doing everything themselves will usually do at least one thing poorly, if not many.

In the APPLICATION SERVER ARCHITECTURE pattern we describe an architecture where the 'core business' of the system is lumped together in a single application. However, we retain the web server and database as separate elements because they fulfil specialist activities: the web server is extremely good at handling HTTP requests and responses; and the database at storing and retrieving data. In both these cases there are commercial and freely-available products to which we can choose to outsource this specialist functionality.

In the GlobalTech system, there are a couple of other specialist pieces of functionality that could be implemented using 'off-the-shelf' software:

- Sending emails. Rather than implementing our own mail server we could adopt a freely-available SMTP server.

- Searching. Although we could implement our own specific search functionality we might prefer to adopt a general search engine to perform indexing and retrieval for us.

There are also several areas of GlobalTech functionality that, whilst being specific to GlobalTech and so unlikely to be implemented using off-the-shelf software, can be considered 'specialist' or 'extraordinary':

- The daily creation of 'personalized' emails to a group of users. The target group is dynamically determined each time the process is run. One day it might be every user registered, another it might be every user that has logged in during the past month, and on yet another it might be every user that has purchased a particular type of product.

- Update of the dealer catalogue. Certain elements of the product catalogue information (relating to lead times and pricing bands) are dealer-specific. This information is updated in GlobalTech's supply-chain management system and then sent out to other systems as one or more messages.

- Update of the non-dealer product catalogue information, retailer database and retail outlet finder. The raw data for these changes is deposited as a set of files on the servers housing the database. Every so often, daemon processes on the application servers will wake up and look for update files. If an update file is found, its contents will be processed and changes will be made to the database.

These functions can be considered outside the 'core business' of the application for a variety of reasons:

- They are not directly accessible by the system's users: each of these functions is invoked by some form of 'system event', not in response to a user request.
- They run for a limited time and/or asynchronously.
- They interface with the 'outside world' in unusual ways.

Each of them could be tightly integrated into the application, along with the other functionality, but this potentially gives rise to a number of problems:

- **Availability.** Because each of these functions interfaces with the outside world, they are just as likely to be updated due to a change in the outside world as they are due to a change in the functional requirements. If they are implemented as part of the core application we may end up having to take the application server down for maintenance even when the changes made do not in any way affect the functions that fulfil user requests.
- **Performance.** Each of these functions is fairly intensive, involving complex querying or update of the database. During the period of operation, the performance of the application could be severely hit as resources are used for information update or email production rather than fulfilling user requests.
- **Security.** The update functions need specialist security arrangements. In the case of the dealer catalogue, we want to ensure that GlobalTech's supply-chain management system is the only possible source of update messages. Similarly, we want to be certain that the files used to update the product catalogue, retailer database and outlet finder only come from authorized sources. In both cases, the consequences of 'spoof' messages or files being processed could be pretty dire.
- **Manageability.** The management of these functions is more complex than that of the 'standard' functions in the main application. Whereas the core functionality is largely self-contained, the specialist services will tend to have more connection to external data and functionality. Any problem with these connections needs to be highlighted. Also, the services tend to run at particular times and so they require a different type of monitoring than the continuously functional 'core'.

So we can see that there is often a case for placing the 'core business' functionality in a single application and treating specialist or extraordinary functionality separately.

Separate 'extraordinary' functionality from the core application and implement it in specialist or dedicated elements. Place these elements at the periphery of the application – integrated with it but executed, maintained, secured and managed independently from it.

If we evolve the GlobalTech APPLICATION SERVER ARCHITECTURE to split out PERIPHERAL SPECIALIST ELEMENTS from the main application, we get the architecture in Figure 6.4.

Splitting out the specialist behaviour like this raises some interesting implementation questions. The Search Engine and the SMTP Server are likely to be standalone applications; we don't need to worry about how to run them. However, we need to decide how the bespoke specialist applications are to run in the same way we needed to decide how to run the core application. We could choose to run each specialist application in its own application server (especially if we have chosen an application server to run the core application), but this might be overkill in some cases. The Dealer Update Application, with its message-based interface to an external supply-chain management system, may well benefit from running in an application server with built-in message support, but it could be implemented as a simple parse-and-update program run by a scheduler. The Personalized Email Application could possibly run in the same way, but the requirement is for an application that can be instructed to select different groups of users and send them different types of emails. This means we need the option to interact with the application before it generates a group of emails. If the rules for selecting a group and emailing them are very straightforward, we may decide to implement it as a program that reads a configuration when it is run by the scheduler. If defining groups and emails

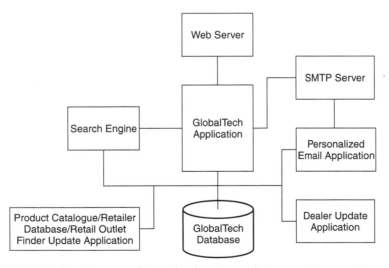

Figure 6.4 Logical architecture of GlobalTech system with PERIPHERAL SPECIALIST SERVERS.

turns out to be even 'reasonably' complicated, it is more likely that it is going to need to be run inside some form of application server.

Another implementation question is where to deploy these specialist applications. If the Search Engine has a remote interface, it could potentially be hosted on a separate hardware server. If it doesn't, or if the amount of data that a search might generate is particularly large, we will want to host it on the same server as the core application.

War Story

One leading search engine product, used on a recent project, did not support a true remote API. If it was to operate as a standalone server it could only be accessed using HTTP, returning results as a text document (although one format that could be used was XML). If we wanted to program using a 'proper' API, we had to bind the product's libraries directly into the core application.

There is no problem hosting the SMTP Server on a separate hardware server as SMTP is a remote protocol. It is probably desirable to do so because we can ensure the hardware is optimized for storing and sending emails: not much processor power or memory (relatively speaking) but lots of disk space and a very high bandwidth connection to the public Internet.

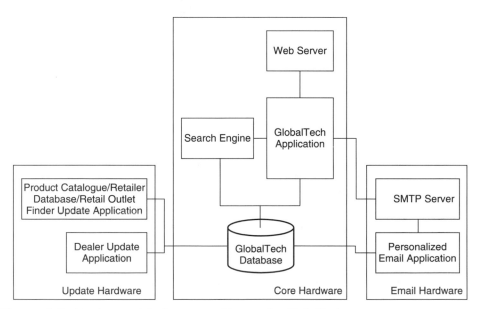

Figure 6.5 Fundamental deployment architecture for GlobalTech system.

None of the bespoke specialist applications actually needs to communicate directly with the core application (as long as the application is written to take account of data sets that may be updated 'underneath' it). As long as they can communicate with the database, we can deploy them to separate hardware servers if we can justify the cost. Given that the two update applications will run periodically we will host them on a single server. To maximize the performance of the Personalized Email Application we will host it on the same server as the SMTP Server – and make the hardware a little more general-purpose than if it were hosting the SMTP Server alone (see Figure 6.5).

Impact of the Pattern on Non-functional Characteristics

Availability	On the whole, the availability of the core application is improved due to splitting out specialist functionality. If the Dealer Update Application fails, the core application can continue to function (assuming the failure of the update doesn't render the dealer data completely invalid).
Performance	Overall system performance is potentially improved as PERIPHERAL SPECIALIST ELEMENTS are often introduced to carry out a task that is particularly expensive or complex and so would lead to (probably unpredictable) performance degradation if they were run as part of the core application. The performance of the specialist elements will also be improved if they are hosted on their own dedicated hardware rather than sharing with the core application.
Scalability	The scalability of the overall system is largely unaltered, but the separation of extraordinary functionality allows it to be scaled independently from the core system elements.
Security	As it introduces more and different elements into the system, the use of PERIPHERAL SPECIALIST ELEMENTS can make security more of a challenge. However, by separating these elements from the mainstream their security can be individually tailored.
Manageability	Manageability of the extraordinary functionality is improved because each specialist application can be managed appropriately. However, manageability of the system as a whole is negatively impacted because different management procedures and techniques have to be introduced for each application.
Maintainability	The use of PERIPHERAL SPECIALIST ELEMENTS can improve the maintainability of the system as any problem with the specialist functionality is isolated in its own application.
Flexibility	PERIPHERAL SPECIALIST ELEMENTS frequently deliver additional, non-core, functionality in a flexible manner.

Portability	Portability is largely unaffected when we consider the main application and the bespoke specialist servers we have built. Unless we choose to implement them in different technologies, porting the core application and specialist servers is likely to be as easy or as difficult as porting one application with both core and specialist functionality. Choosing to implement specialist functionality using off-the-shelf products (commercial or non-commercial) can affect portability. An SMTP server is likely to be available for many operating systems and there are a number of different SMTP server products to choose from so portability is improved. On the other hand, if we choose a proprietary search engine technology we may become tied to that vendor and the operating systems they support.
Cost	On the face of it, choosing to split out specialist behaviour like this will increase our costs: we will probably increase the number of hardware servers and we have increased our maintainability problem (a major source of ongoing cost). However, we have to trade this off against potential savings: use of off-the-shelf products (commercial or non-commercial) can save money compared to developing the functionality ourselves. Also, adding separate hardware servers isn't necessarily more expensive. If we were to host all applications on a single server, it would have to be very powerful. By placing the specialist applications on optimized hardware (and reducing the capacity of the Core Hardware accordingly) we may not spend much more money than buying a single big server – maybe we can even reduce the hardware budget.

Moving On

All of the elements introduced so far are going to be prone to failure or will need taking out of service for maintenance. We really need to start thinking about improving the availability and scalability of both the core and specialist applications (and the hardware they run on). Patterns such as ACTIVE-REDUNDANT ELEMENTS and LOAD-BALANCED ELEMENTS will address both of these characteristics. Securing these new elements should also be a priority which leads us to consider introducing a DEMILITARIZED ZONE and, possibly, KNOWN PARTNERS.

What makes these Patterns Fundamental?

In the next three chapters we will explore patterns that improve on system performance, system control and system evolution. What is so special about the APPLICATION

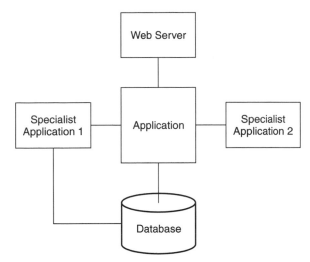

Figure 6.6 Spatial configuration defined by the fundamental patterns.

SERVER ARCHITECTURE and PERIPHERAL SPECIALIST ELEMENTS patterns that they deserve their own chapter?

In the opening of this chapter we briefly talked about getting the shape of the architecture right, picking a good starting point from which to evolve the detail of the architecture. If you look at the architecture of many Internet technology systems you'll see that the core of the architecture is built around these patterns. No matter how much complexity is added to improve performance, security, manageability, etc., these systems have a core that looks something like Figure 6.6.

The exact nature, number, and interconnectedness of the specialist servers will be different for each system, but the basic shape, what Alexander might call the 'spatial configuration', is the same.

So, these patterns provide a starting point for the system architecture, but is it a good point from which to start? Well, it certainly provides us with a more consistent base than the 'collaborating semi-autonomous applications' architecture posited earlier on, and we shall see that the APPLICATION SERVER ARCHITECTURE and PERIPHERAL SPECIALIST ELEMENTS underpin many of the patterns that significantly improve the non-functional characteristics we're concerned about.

Summary

In this chapter, we have described two patterns that we believe are core to all high capability Internet technology systems. These patterns provide a basic 'shape' for such systems and underpin many of the other patterns described in the rest of the book.

CHAPTER

7

System Performance Patterns

I Feel the Need, the Need for Speed

Users of Internet systems can be extremely unforgiving, with a very low tolerance of systems that are slow, unreliable or unavailable. Given that the Internet itself can be unpredictably slow and unreliable, systems that use it to deliver information and services often have to be especially fast and reliable.

When a user navigates to a web page, they expect that page to appear in their browser in a reasonable time (see Box 7.1). It doesn't matter to them whether the failure to appear is because the server was unavailable due to excessive load, due to a server error, or because the server was just too slow to deliver the page before the user got bored of waiting – as far as the user is concerned, the page wasn't there. This is the nature of system performance – a system has to have the right combination of availability, scalability and performance in order to ensure that the user always gets a quick response regardless of the state of the system (normal, failing, or in maintenance) and the number of other users accessing it.

The consequences of poor system performance can be very severe. In terms of a public Internet system, poor performance can result in users simply switching to a competitor's site. At best, this means that you lose the user for that session (and they

BOX 7.1 What is reasonable?

What constitutes a 'reasonable time' is subject to much debate and research. As a rule of thumb we tend to use the following figures:

- Less than 3 seconds for a landing page (one that is normally navigated to directly)
- Less than 5 seconds for a page navigated to from another page in the site
- Less than 3 seconds for a 'simple' form submit (e.g. login)
- Less than 10 seconds for a 'complex' form submit (e.g. user registration, site search)
- Less than 20 seconds for a 'transaction' (e.g. order placement)

Of course, these figures will apply differently to pages in your application that provide a service specific to your system – a generic search engine couldn't get away with a response time of 10 seconds for a search. Whatever the exact figures, though, the principle remains the same; the end-to-end response times expected by users are relatively low and a large proportion of that time can be due to the latency of the network – over which we have no control.

Another large proportion of the download time is due to the 'weight' of the page. The weight is essentially the size of the raw HTML produced by the application server plus the size of all the images on the page. Even ignoring latency, and assuming an ideal connection, a page with a total weight of 30 kilobytes will take around 5 seconds to download on a 56K modem. This means that, in addition to ensuring page weights are kept well below 30 KB for landing pages, the end-to-end response time for the application server, even under full load, needs to be less than 0.5 seconds for most pages.

may have been trying to place an order or to find out important information about your company). At worst, you lose the user forever to the competitor.

System performance is just as much of a challenge for extranet systems. Just because a user has a direct relationship with your organization doesn't mean they will tolerate poor performance. Inability to interact with you online will force the user to revert to their traditional communication channels – such as faxes and call centres – often negating the benefits sought by launching an online application.

This level of sensitivity to performance can be something of a culture shock for designers and developers brought up to develop internal corporate systems. We're not saying here that corporate systems are necessarily slow or unreliable – simply that the captive nature of the audience tends to have certain consequences for the form of the delivered systems. The non-functional characteristics of internal corporate systems tend to be more lax:

- Less than 100% availability is the norm, with system downtime planned for and expected. At one end of the spectrum the system might actually be unavailable more than it is available with user access being prevented from the evening each day to early the following morning whilst various forms of batch job and maintenance work are carried out overnight. At the other end of the spectrum, users can be informed of *ad hoc* downtime and plan their interaction with the system accordingly. Very few users in a corporate environment will not have seen emails stating that 'XYZ system will be unavailable between 8 pm Friday and 6 am Monday as it is being upgraded'.

- The need for scalability is far more limited. For any given system, the number of users authorized to use it can be limited and there is low probability that a sudden and significant increase in the number of users supported will be required. Even if that was to happen, the increase is likely to be planned for, enabling the necessary scalability work to be carried out before the new users are given access to the system.

- As the architect of an internal system, you will probably have far more control over the various parts of it. Steps can be taken to improve perceived performance, from mandating minimum levels of client hardware and software or upgrading bandwidth at network 'hotspots'. For a public Internet system, if the 'hotspot' is outside the organizational boundary, there is usually little you can do.

- The need for performance does not significantly decrease but users will accept a level of performance reasonable for the task they're doing. If they know what they want to do is complex then they will live with an 'hourglass icon' for a number of minutes if necessary.

In addition to this more relaxed view of system performance, the users of a corporate system will also have an understanding, and be affected by, the cost/benefit tradeoff of any improvements. Even if they are frustrated by a system with poor performance, they may not want their organization to spend the money to improve it if that money means a lack of funds in other areas.

The users of an extranet or public Internet system will have no such leniency towards their system. The bottom line is that Internet systems must perform or die. The patterns in this chapter address some of the common availability, scalability and performance issues encountered in terms of system architecture.

Principles

There are two important principles that underpin the system performance patterns: redundancy and functionally-identical elements. Both of these are primarily concerned with enhancing availability and scalability rather than end-to-end performance but they provide a robust underpinning for the patterns aimed at enhancing the raw speed of the system.

Redundancy

The principle of redundancy is very simple: add more capacity than you normally need, then use this capacity in abnormal situations such as when things fail or when there is more load on the system than usual.

Redundancy can be introduced into almost every aspect of system architecture. Two prominent forms of redundancy are duplication and over-capacity, which are applied in different cases. As an example of redundancy through duplication, we might use two switches for external traffic – one sitting unused until the other either fails or is taken out of service for maintenance. As an example of over-capacity, we might choose an Internet connection with more bandwidth than we would normally need in order to cope when more users access the system than expected. In grander terms, we might even introduce a redundant installation of the entire system to protect against the complete failure of the system. This latter option is usually only applicable when the system is truly mission-critical to the organization.

Of course, there is a downside to the benefits provided by redundancy: additional cost. By definition, the extra capacity introduced won't normally be required but does need to be paid for. For each element of redundancy introduced there is a cost/benefit decision to be made.

Functionally-Identical Elements

A fundamental assumption of introducing redundancy through duplication is that the duplicate elements are functionally identical to each other – they all do exactly the same job. However, this isn't to say that they must exhibit the same non-functional characteristics as each other. For example, suppose we choose a very expensive switch that has proven to be very reliable in other systems and is very quick to repair in the unusual event that it does fail. If we duplicate this with an identical switch we have doubled our cost and the fact that the switch is extremely reliable means that the duplicate is hardly ever going to be used (perhaps it never will be used). Do we really need a second, highly-reliable switch to be used only in the short and infrequent times the original one fails? A cheaper solution might be to purchase a second switch that has nowhere near the stated reliability of the original but performs exactly the same switching function. As it is going to be used only very rarely and for a short period of time, the lower reliability should not be a problem and we can save ourselves a lot of money.

On the other hand, if we are implementing an online trading system we may decide to duplicate the whole system in a totally separate (and physically remote) data centre. If some form of disaster strikes we can switch over to the back-up system and continue trading. Because we have no idea how long the primary system will be out of action, we probably want to ensure the backup system has the same capacity as the original. Given the value of the business going through the system, saving a few million pounds on a lower capacity back-up system may prove to be a false economy if the system needs to be used for a matter of days or weeks and it is going to struggle with the volume of trades we normally have to settle.

When we add redundancy through the use of duplication we need to be sure that the duplicate elements are all functionally identical, but we have the option of varying the non-functional characteristics based on the circumstances.

ACTIVE–REDUNDANT ELEMENTS

We have all grown fairly used to the presence of electricity in our lives. However, the supply of electricity is not 100% guaranteed. In bad weather, power lines may come down, cutting off power to whole communities. If power is lost to your home for a few hours, it may mean that you have to use a torch to find your way around. If power is lost for longer, you may lose the contents of your freezer as it gradually warms up. These impacts are not particularly desirable but they do not constitute a disaster. On the other hand, if the power used in a hospital for a life support system fails then it is a serious issue. For this reason, the hospital will maintain some form of backup system, such as a generator, that can take over when the mains power fails.[1]

There is always a possibility that part of your system may be taken out of action. How do we ensure that the system as a whole continues to function?

The GlobalTech web site will serve over 100 countries around the world and hence will be in use round the clock. The site is intended to augment, and in some cases totally replace, the business-critical functions of customer service and retailer ordering. As a result, extended periods of downtime are not acceptable. This is a fairly typical requirement for large-scale Internet technology systems.

When defining the required characteristics of the system, it is determined that there should be no more than 90 seconds of downtime per day, on average (not including the planned maintenance downtime of one hour per month and four hours per quarter set aside for upgrades). This equates to a minimum of 99.9% availability. However, no system is immune to failure – whether in hardware or software – and this availability has to be achieved even in the event of such failure. As discussed earlier in the book, hardware components tend to have a reliability rating expressed as a mean time between failure (MTBF). If any of the principal components in the system – CPU, memory, cooling fans, power supply, hard drive, motherboard, network card – fails then the whole system is rendered inoperable. There is a high likelihood that any given system will fail sometime within the lowest

---

[1] It was brought home to one of the authors just how used to electricity we are when he was on holiday in New York during the blackout of August 2003. Being unable to get cash out of an ATM, or use your credit card, so you can buy food from one of very few shops remaining open, is a scarily debilitating experience.

MTBF of any of its components. Once you go beyond the lowest MTBF, you could view the system as 'living on borrowed time'.

The system needs to have high availability but it also needs to be maintained and upgraded over time. Such maintenance typically requires bringing the system down, performing the maintenance/upgrade, and then bringing it back up again. As far as the users of the system are concerned, there is no difference between the system coming down for maintenance and it falling over due to a hardware failure. In both cases, the system is not there when they want it.

Provide alternative capacity for your critical system elements by duplicating those elements. Redirect users to the duplicate should the active element become unavailable.

This solution is a direct application of the principles of redundancy and functionally-identical elements. In the case of ACTIVE–REDUNDANT ELEMENTS we typically introduce one duplicate of the original. The original is the active element – it performs the role of the element in normal circumstances. In the event of the active element failing or needing to be taken out of service for maintenance, the duplicate – redundant – element takes over the role.

So, how can we apply this pattern to the initial GlobalTech architecture identified in Chapter 6? The simplest approach would be to introduce a redundant version of the core hardware and the software elements it hosts. However, we now have another problem: how do we introduce the redundant server in the event of failure? At the most basic level, an administrator could physically swap in the redundant hardware server. However, this is a very inefficient, and frequently impractical, solution. A better solution is to route the inbound network traffic from clients to whichever server is currently in service. To achieve this, we introduce a switch that can route inbound traffic to either server. The switch is configured such that it usually directs traffic to the active server but it automatically directs traffic to the redundant server in the event of the active server failing. The switch configuration can also be altered to move traffic temporarily from the active server to the redundant server if we want to upgrade or maintain the active server (see the DYNAMICALLY-ADJUSTABLE CONFIGURATION pattern). In order to ensure the availability of the switch, we also introduce it as a pair of ACTIVE–REDUNDANT ELEMENTS, as in Figure 7.1.

In the diagram, System Software represents the web server, the GlobalTech Application, the search engine and the GlobalTech database shown in Figure 6.5. This raises the question of whether we should also introduce ACTIVE–REDUNDANT ELEMENTS for each of the PERIPHERAL SPECIALIST ELEMENTS. If we want to have the best possible overall availability for the system, the answer is that we probably should. However, we have a bit more flexibility here.

The update applications (and the hardware they run on) are completely under our control and don't interact with the end user at all. To save the cost of additional hardware (plus the negative impact on some of the other non-functional characteristics described below) we may decide that this isn't necessary. The update applications only run for some of the time anyway so we have time to perform maintenance and failure will just cause the update to stall until the application is brought back into service.

The Personalized Email application and the SMTP server do interact directly with the user. Whilst the users may not be too sorry to receive their emails late or not at all, they will be less happy if the promised confirmation email fails to be sent when they register (they may think they need to go through the registration process again which would result in multiple profiles per user, not a good situation for marketing or customer support). So we decide to introduce ACTIVE–REDUNDANT ELEMENTS for the Email Hardware and the software elements it hosts (not shown in Figure 7.1).

Another question raised by the diagram is how the active–redundant switches are switched between if one fails. At the top of the diagram is the System Entry Point. Usually this is the network connection to the outside world provided by the hosting organization (which may be an internal organization). Most hosting organizations will allow two external switches to be identified: one 'primary' (the active switch) and one 'secondary' (the redundant switch). In the event that a connection cannot be made to the primary switch, data will be routed to the secondary switch.

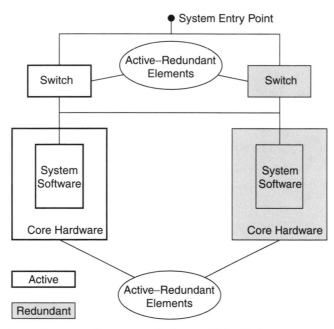

Figure 7.1 ACTIVE–REDUNDANT ELEMENTS applied to the GlobalTech system.

This is a fairly typical implementation of the failover mechanism between ACTIVE–REDUNDANT ELEMENTS: both are registered with the element or elements that interact with them and it is up to that element to work with the redundant element if the active one is unavailable for some reason. In this case we need to decide whether the redundant element now becomes the active one (and the previously active element becomes the redundant one when it is brought back into service), or whether the interacting element uses the redundant one for a time before trying to see whether it can connect back to the active element. In either case, it is up to all the elements that interact with the active–redundant pair to implement the same strategy for deciding which element to work with and for how long.

An alternative implementation is to make the ACTIVE–REDUNDANT ELEMENTS themselves responsible for failover. In this case, the redundant element monitors the state of the active element and takes its place if it fails or is taken out of service. This is a simpler solution for elements that interact with the ACTIVE–REDUNDANT ELEMENTS; they are completely unaware that there is actually a pair of these elements. However, it makes the ACTIVE–REDUNDANT ELEMENTS themselves much more complex to implement.

Impact of the Pattern on Non-functional Characteristics

Availability	Availability of the system is improved due to the presence of a redundant element that can take over in the event the active element fails or has to be taken out of service for maintenance.
Performance	There will be a very small (possibly insignificant) negative impact on performance due to the introduction of the 'failover' mechanism that switches in the redundant element should the active one fail.
Scalability	Unaffected by this pattern.
Security	Security may be negatively impacted by the additional element and failover mechanism, both of which have to be secured.
Manageability	Manageability is negatively impacted as one element has been replaced by two and the failover mechanism also has to be managed.
Maintainability	Unaffected by this pattern.
Flexibility	Unaffected by this pattern.
Portability	Unaffected by this pattern.

Cost   The impact on cost can be significant: where we once had a single element, we now have two (plus the cost of implementing the failover mechanism). If the elements are identical, we have basically doubled the cost of introducing that element. We can mitigate this by introducing a cheaper version of the element as the redundant one (see the functionally-identical elements principle) but this restricts our implementation choices: we would definitely want to switch back to the active element as soon as it is introduced back into service. See the 'Costing the GlobalTech system' section for an illustration of cost.

Moving On

In some cases you will be able to specify a cheaper, lower-performing system element to provide redundant failover. However, at times of peak load it would be good if this spare capacity was available to handle some of the traffic. Sharing the traffic between the active and redundant elements would make the system more scalable while still offering the possibility of either element supporting the users should the other one fail or be taken out of service. As the previously redundant server is now performing useful work all of the time – rather than just a small percentage of the time – the cost/benefit figures for the project also start to look better.

If the active element is maintaining some form of session state, we will need to think about introducing the SESSION FAILOVER pattern in order to have that state available on the redundant element should we have to failover to it.

We also have to worry about the persistent data in the system. By duplicating the system software we have also duplicated the database – which causes us a problem when the active database is updated but the redundant one isn't (when we failover to the redundant system software, the data will be out-of-date). We will probably need to apply the COMMON PERSISTENT STORE and DATA REPLICATION patterns to get around this.

LOAD-BALANCED ELEMENTS

Ants are remarkable creatures. A group of ants can work together to transport large amounts of food across significant distances. If an individual piece of food is too large for a single ant to carry, many ants will join forces to move it. There is no reliance on one or more 'super ants' that bring extra carrying capacity, the load is shared equally – the number of ants required is proportional to the weight of the load being carried. If the weight grows heavier, simply add more ants. If one ant drops out, the rest either take up the slack or another ant can be summoned to take over.

Applying the ACTIVE–REDUNDANT ELEMENTS pattern solves some availability issues but presents other problems around matching capacity to load as either capacity decreases (switching to the redundant element) or load increases (potentially beyond the capacity of the active server).

How can the system continue to function when elements become unavailable and when system load increases beyond the capacity of a single element?

In the ACTIVE–REDUNDANT ELEMENTS pattern, one element processes the entire system load in steady state. Whether due to failure or maintenance, the redundant element is occasionally switched in. When it is, other patterns and strategies can be applied to ease the process of failover. This is fine whilst the system load remains well within the capacity of both the active and redundant elements (remember we may decide to choose a lower-capacity redundant element for reasons of cost) but leaves us nowhere to go when that capacity is exceeded. In this event, the system could fail or simply become unavailable to the excess users until we can purchase or implement a larger capacity element.

The requirement for the GlobalTech system is to support a peak of 3000 consumer and 700 retailer users at the outset. Given the complexity of the GlobalTech Application, this translates to one *very* big server which will cost a lot of money to buy. Doubling this cost to introduce a redundant element is probably not feasible so we might opt for a lower-capacity redundant version. Let's say we want one that is only a fifth to a quarter of the cost. This may translate to 20–25% of the capacity so perhaps it can handle 600 consumer and 100 retail users. In the event of failure or maintenance, the system performance under predicted average load (2000 consumer and 500 retail users) is going to be very poor, possibly rendering the system totally unusable even under moderate load.

In terms of system failure, we may be willing to take the risk that it will occur at a time of low load. After all, there is a finite possibility that such a failure may never happen. However, the need for maintenance on the active server is a certainty – like death and taxes. At these times, the redundant server will have to shoulder the burden, regardless of the level of load. If it were possible to determine a time slot in which low user load is guaranteed, it would be feasible to schedule all maintenance for that time. For a purely national-based system, such a time slot may occur in the middle of the night. However, given the global nature of GlobalTech's customer base, it is impossible to define a time slot in which low system loading can be guaranteed.

If we wished to persevere with the ACTIVE–REDUNDANT ELEMENTS pattern, we could restrict the number of users allowed to access the redundant element to a level it can happily deal with (see the CONNECTION LIMITATION pattern), but this means that the system is effectively unavailable to the remainder. Having a system that is only available to a small proportion of the users that want to access it may not be satisfactory.

Neither of these approaches deals with the scalability issue. Even if we can live with a reduced-capacity redundant server, we have an active server that only caters for the initial expected user load. If we want some long-term or progressive scalability we need to over-specify the active server, further increasing its cost and further increasing the gulf between the active and redundant elements.

What is needed is a way to make the scaling of the system easier and more linear, whether that scaling is up or down.

Use multiple elements of similar capability and balance the load continuously across them to achieve the required throughput and response. To increase capacity, add further elements to the load-balanced set.

The main problem with the use of ACTIVE–REDUNDANT ELEMENTS is that the redundant element only has value as a backup. While the active element is operational, the redundant element adds no value and so its cost is entirely 'overhead'. However, by balancing user load continuously across all available elements, rather than simply switching in a redundant element when the active element fails, the capacity of all elements is used all of the time. In this case, it makes much more sense to have a roughly equal set of elements as each will serve as many users as it is capable of serving. With more roughly equal elements, the loss of one element will not imbalance the system as it would do if we were using ACTIVE–REDUNDANT ELEMENTS with a reduced-capacity redundant element. Hence, we try to ensure that we replace a combination of one high-powered active element and one low-powered redundant element with a number of medium-powered LOAD-BALANCED ELEMENTS to achieve better levels of performance at a roughly similar cost.

The principal way in which GlobalTech can benefit from the application of LOAD-BALANCED ELEMENTS is to balance the load across the Core Hardware servers and to have a number of load-balanced instances of the system software on each hardware server, as shown in Figure 7.2.

The servers are fronted by a load balancer that continuously spreads traffic across all available servers depending on the individual server load. When capacity is to be added or removed, the load balancer can be dynamically reconfigured (see the DYNAMICALLY-ADJUSTABLE CONFIGURATION pattern) to add or remove the relevant server from its list. The load balancer uses a load-balancing algorithm to decide how to spread the load between the servers. The simplest algorithm is 'round robin' which simply passes a new request to each element in turn regardless of how loaded the element actually is. Other load-balancing algorithms use more sophisticated models of server capacity or actual load (by querying the server periodically about how much capacity it is using). These algorithms are either reasonably complex or else need state to be maintained (round-robin or capacity-modelled), hence the load balancer is usually implemented as a separate element rather than the load-balancing algorithm being integrated into the elements that interact with the LOAD-BALANCED ELEMENTS. One exception to this is that there are products that combine switching with simple load-balancing capabilities.

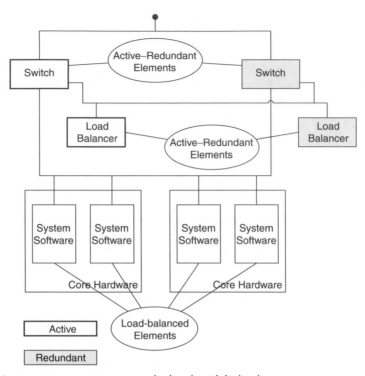

Figure 7.2 LOAD-BALANCED ELEMENTS applied to the GlobalTech system.

In order to improve the availability of the load balancer we would introduce an active–redundant pair. This degree of redundancy is inexpensive and we always have to make a choice when adding a new element to the architecture whether to have a single point of failure or to introduce redundancy.

We could simply have one instance of the system software on each of the two hardware servers. However this means we halve the capacity of the system if one server (hardware or software) fails or is taken out of service. With four software servers we only lose one-quarter capacity in the event of software failure or maintenance. Losing a hardware server still halves capacity but this is likely to be a far less common event (hardware servers are often built with fault-tolerant components, such as RAID hard disks, which makes losing an entire server very unlikely and many forms of maintenance can be carried out while the server is still up and running) than losing a software server. In practice, this hardware/software combination probably doesn't give the level of availability we want for GlobalTech. Something like four hardware servers, each running one or two software servers, would be more typical (see the 'How many servers do you need?' and 'Costing the GlobalTech system' sections). However, to keep the example relatively simple, we'll stick with four software servers and two hardware servers.

The use of servers with identical non-functional characteristics allows us to specify identical hardware and software for the servers. This improves the maintainability of the system as there is only one type of server that administrators need to know about. There is a single set of patches and fixes that must be monitored and applied. Also, any sub-elements, such as hard disks, are interchangeable between servers, reducing the level of spare elements that need to be held. The benefit can also be seen in terms of adding or replacing capacity. If a new server is needed, you can use a hardware and software configuration identical to the existing ones. This allows you to use mechanisms to snapshot a particular server configuration and then automatically build a server based on this configuration, such as JumpStart (Sun) or Ghost (Windows).

Applying the LOAD-BALANCED ELEMENTS pattern to the GlobalTech system has many advantages. However, it also has some downsides due to the increase in the number and type of elements now in use as part of the system. In this new context, there can be a negative impact on security as there are more elements to attack and it is more of a challenge keeping each element up to date with security measures (patches, fixes, etc.). An increase in the number and diversity of system elements also makes the system less manageable.

In the situation where you are using a multi-tier architecture, you can apply the LOAD-BALANCED ELEMENTS pattern for the servers of each physical tier (see the DEDICATED WEB AND APPLICATION SERVERS pattern).

Impact of the Pattern on Non-functional Characteristics

Availability	Availability is improved. As with ACTIVE–REDUNDANT ELEMENTS, loss of an element due to failure or maintenance does not mean the system ceases to function. However, the reduction in capacity of the system is determined by the proportion of load the element takes, not the capacity of the redundant element. In cases where we would have to have a much lower capacity redundant element for reasons of cost, LOAD-BALANCED ELEMENTS are likely to provide better capacity. Unlike ACTIVE–REDUNDANT ELEMENTS, LOAD-BALANCED ELEMENTS can also cope with multiple failures or failure during maintenance.
Performance	Performance is negatively impacted as the load balancer needs to determine the element to which it should forward a request.

Scalability	Scalability is greatly improved. With ACTIVE–REDUNDANT ELEMENTS we can only scale the system by increasing the capacity of the active element (possibly only by replacing it). Using LOAD-BALANCED ELEMENTS, we can increase the capacity of the system by adding new elements to the load-balanced set. The load balancer will ensure they receive their 'fair share' of requests and the system is scaled.
Security	Security is negatively impacted due to the introduction of additional elements that need to be protected.
Manageability	There is a great negative impact on manageability. We now have a number of additional elements to manage and that number can grow according to our scalability needs.
Maintainability	Unaffected by this pattern.
Flexibility	Unaffected by this pattern.
Portability	Unaffected by this pattern.
Cost	Cost may not be too severely impacted. Depending on the type of hardware, the cost of buying a large number of medium-capacity servers may actually be lower than the cost of buying one high-capacity and one low capacity (redundant) server. It may be a bit more expensive, but it is rare that it is a lot more expensive. The cost of the load balancer needs to be added to the cost of the system (see the 'Costing the GlobalTech system' section).

Moving On

So, we now have a well-balanced system that can deliver application functionality in the face of failure or the need for maintenance and that can scale up relatively quickly and easily. However, as with ACTIVE–REDUNDANT ELEMENTS, we need to worry about session and persistent data; SESSION FAILOVER and COMMON PERSISTENT STORE help us here.

BOX 7.2 ACTIVE–REDUNDANT ELEMENTS vs LOAD-BALANCED ELEMENTS

ACTIVE–REDUNDANT ELEMENTS and LOAD-BALANCED ELEMENTS both offer solutions to the problem of maintaining system availability in the face of failure or the need for maintenance. LOAD-BALANCED ELEMENTS offers the additional advantage of being more scalable but at the expense of additional complexity. The

GlobalTech architecture we have evolved to this point has elements of both types. Why would we choose one over the other in a particular situation?

Sometimes we will have no choice. In the case of the outermost switch, we can only apply LOAD-BALANCED ELEMENTS if the hosting organization provides an external load balancer. Otherwise we must deploy a pair of ACTIVE–REDUNDANT ELEMENTS. However, it is rare not to have a choice so we need to consider the following questions:

- What is the capacity of the element? If an element only just provides the peak capability we require initially, scalability is going to be a problem and we should seriously consider LOAD-BALANCED ELEMENTS. If it can easily cope with even our long-term predictions, ACTIVE–REDUNDANT ELEMENTS is a possibility.

- How expensive is the element? If it is cheap to buy even a high-capacity version, we don't save significantly by applying LOAD-BALANCED ELEMENTS. The cost of the load balancer may even make it cheaper to buy an active–redundant pair.

- How reliable is the element: how easy is it to maintain? If it is very reliable, we can worry less about what happens when it fails. Similarly, if maintenance is a very simple operation (or one that can be done while the element is still in operation), we don't have to worry about multiple failures or failure of the redundant element during maintenance.

- What is the impact of failure? If failure impacts the system in only a minor way (e.g. we slightly delay sending registration confirmation details), we may decide that ACTIVE–REDUNDANT ELEMENTS is good enough.

If the answers to these questions are 'higher than we need', 'very cheap', 'extremely reliable and easy to maintain', and 'not very high' respectively, we certainly want to apply ACTIVE–REDUNDANT ELEMENTS. Even if the answer to the last question is 'very high' we will probably deploy active–redundant pairs if the answers to the first three (or even two out of those three) are favourable.

This is why the switches and the load balancers in the GlobalTech architecture are active–redundant pairs: switches generally have very high capacity, are not that expensive in the grand scheme of things, and are usually very reliable and easy to maintain. The application (part of the system software) on the other hand is unlikely to cater for in excess of 8000 consumer users and 2000 retail users unless it is running on an enormous server. It is also likely to be one of the most expensive elements to deploy in the system (application server, database and web server software licenses, plus hardware to run them on) and the application server is likely to need regular maintenance for bug fixes and version upgrades even if it proves to be very reliable. Hence, LOAD-BALANCED ELEMENTS is a much better solution.

SESSION FAILOVER

The world was a far more frustrating place in the days before customer relationship management (CRM) software and good call centre systems. You would call up a large utility firm, armed with your account number, to change your address. You would inform the person answering the call that this was your intended purpose and supply them with your name and account number. After a short delay they would tell you that you needed to speak to someone in retail sales and that they would put you through. A couple of minutes of piped music would end with a happy voice asking you for your name and account number. Once you had again provided this information and told them that you wanted to change the address for your account, you would be told that what you really needed was the account alteration department. They would take the details of your current address and then offer to put you through. Your hopes are raised when, after a few more minutes of piped music, the music stops and a voice cuts in 'I'm sorry, this call could not be completed at present. Please try again later.' You call back to complete your change but you are told that the system has no record of your call and that you will have to start again. You ring off and call up another company to move your account...

There are lots of frustrating aspects to this interaction. One of them is the fact that you provide some information, which is lost when the call is interrupted. You would like to think that you could continue from where you left off. The fact that you had to give the same information several times suggests that there is no real cohesion between the different parts of the organization you are talking to. This kind of problem is largely unacceptable in these days of CRM systems. In the impatient world of Internet interaction, you need to do better.

If users interact with a server and build up state on that server, they will be unhappy if the state is lost when the server becomes unavailable. How do we ensure state is preserved in the event of server failure?

On the face of it, applying ACTIVE–REDUNDANT ELEMENTS or LOAD-BALANCED ELEMENTS to application functionality addresses the issue of providing continuous service. However, for certain types of interaction, those that involve the user supplying information, this information (or state) is built up on the server as the user progresses. The ACTIVE–REDUNDANT ELEMENTS or LOAD-BALANCED ELEMENTS patterns are primarily concerned with the consistent provision of functionality and not the preservation of information. The GlobalTech web site has many functions that require state to be maintained between individual browser requests. Some of these include:

- The Outlet Finder, which allows users to refine searches using only the results of previous searches
- The Shopping Basket, to which the user adds items over time before ordering the items
- Retailer Ordering, in which the user follows a multi-stage process to create and place an order

Such an ongoing interaction is termed a 'user session' and the state accumulated is 'session state'. It requires that switches can support 'sticky sessions' – they recognize that a series of user requests is related and consistently direct the user to the same server.

However, whether due to failure or maintenance, that server may become unavailable during the course of a session. The overall availability of the system is maintained by bringing in a redundant server or switching user requests to a different server in the load-balanced pool, but the individual user interaction with the server is interrupted. If the user's session state was held solely by that server, the state is lost when the server goes out of service. The server that takes over processing the user's requests knows nothing about the user or their session state. As far as this server is concerned, the user session is new; as far as that user is concerned, the system has failed.

The maintenance of session state in web-based systems is complicated somewhat by the stateless nature of HTTP. Each HTTP connection is essentially discrete, regardless of whether it comes from the same web browser. There is no way of associating two requests using the basic HTTP protocol. This was identified early in the life of the interactive Internet as being a severe limitation to client–server interaction. Hence, people came up with several ways of associating HTTP requests from the same client:

- The web server returns a small name/value pair, called a cookie, to the client. Each time the client accesses the web server, it submits all cookies that originated from that web server. The functional elements can work with the web server in using one or more cookies to maintain user information between requests.

- All of the hyperlinks in each page can have user information added to them (usually termed 'URL re-writing'). This information then forms part of the address for the next request and so can be extracted by the web server and provided to the functional elements.

- Hidden fields can be created in the HTML forms being sent back to the client. These hidden fields are not displayed to the user but they can contain data and are re-submitted to the web server when the user submits the rest of the form. Again, the web server can extract this information and provide it to the functional elements.

All of these mechanisms are fine as far as they go – they can all maintain a modicum of session state and pass it to the server with each request, relieving the server of the need to maintain the state. However, they all suffer from limitations. Passing user data back and forth between client and server is a security risk. Also, if large amounts of data must be maintained for complex interactions – such as the Retailer Ordering functionality in the GlobalTech example – it soon becomes unwieldy and may even have a negative impact on performance. Cookies present a particular issue as many users cannot or will not allow cookies to be stored in their browsers. Some better mechanism is required for maintaining session state during failover.

A common implementation of this 'better mechanism' is to hold all session state information in memory on the server. An identifier (the 'session id') is supplied to the client by the server and relates client requests to the in-memory state. This session id is passed back to the server by the client using one of the three techniques described above. However, a major drawback with this approach is that the session information is lost if the server fails.

Implement a mechanism that holds session information whilst the user is interacting with the system and makes this information available to the duplicate servers in the system.

In the event that a duplicate server is switched in, it can retrieve all the session information associated with a particular user and the session can continue as if no change had occurred. As a result, the user will see no perceptible interruption in the interaction.

To save the session state and make it available to other system elements, we introduce a session backup server to the GlobalTech architecture. As with the other elements of the system, the session backup server consists of two ACTIVE–REDUNDANT ELEMENTS with a switching mechanism to fail over between them (see Figure 7.3).

All the system software servers save user session information to the Session Backup Server, every time the information is changed. The persistence mechanism

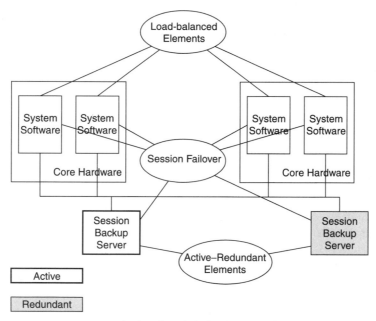

Figure 7.3 SESSION FAILOVER applied to the GlobalTech system.[2]

---

[2] The network switches and load balancers are still included in the architecture, but have been omitted from the diagram.

is a simple object serialization that relates a session identifier to a serialized state object [Anderson and Dyson 1998]. If any server goes down, its users can be routed to another server. When any server receives a request that contains a session identifier – indicating this is not a new user – that it doesn't recognize, it queries the session backup server to see if there is a persisted session available. If there is a persisted session object, the server de-serializes the state object and continues to process the request in the context of the session loaded.

This is a simple and passive form of failover – the session is only failed over if the user makes a request while the server is unavailable. An alternative implementation would be for the session backup server to detect that the server has become unavailable and force other elements to load all the persisted sessions. This is much more complex but can be useful if the form of user interaction isn't a simple request–response, such as if a user request might require the system to interact with a number of back-end systems or web services over a period of time.

SESSION FAILOVER is becoming a standard part of the major distributed platforms and applications. For example, ASP.NET provides several built-in session state management options. By simply changing the configuration file, you have a choice of persisting your session state to an instance of an SQL Server database or a dedicated state server process. Many of the J2EE application servers also offer at least passive SESSION FAILOVER mechanisms.

Obviously, there are some drawbacks to implementing SESSION FAILOVER. The main issue is performance. Every load or save of session state incurs at least an extra network hop. As the system elements are likely to be running in a stateless way (as they are using HTTP), this will probably mean two accesses to the persisted state per interaction – one to load it at the start of the interaction and another to save it at the end. You may also have the overhead of writing code to retrieve and store your session state, although careful choice of platform can provide this functionality for little or no effort on the developer's part.

Once again, we have introduced more system elements – the load-balanced session backup servers. These will reduce the manageability of the system and potentially reduce the level of security, as discussed in LOAD-BALANCED ELEMENTS.

Impact of the Pattern on Non-functional Characteristics

Availability	Availability is improved as the user's session state is maintained even if the requests need to be directed to a new server due to the loss of the one that had been maintaining that state.
Performance	Performance is likely to be negatively impacted due to the need to periodically save the user's session state.
Scalability	Unaffected by this pattern.

Security	We have introduced some new system elements – the session backup server and its redundant pair – that need to be secured. We also have a mechanism that saves the state information in some way. We have to ensure that sensitive information is not stored as part of the state or is obscured in some way (see INFORMATION OBSCURITY).
Manageability	Manageability is negatively impacted due to the introduction of a new mechanism and associated elements that all have to be managed.
Maintainability	Maintainability can be marginally improved as it is possible to retrieve information about the state of user sessions in the event of system failure.
Flexibility	Unaffected by this pattern.
Portability	Unaffected by this pattern.
Cost	The cost is most likely to be affected by whether dedicated session backup servers (both software and hardware elements) are purchased. This maximizes availability but incurs significant expense. Alternatively we could run the session backup servers on other hardware servers (such as the Core Hardware in the GlobalTech example) and save some expense, but with a slight decrease in availability.

Moving On

The SESSION FAILOVER pattern improves the overall availability of a system that employs ACTIVE–REDUNDANT ELEMENTS and LOAD-BALANCED ELEMENTS. However, we still have a slightly monolithic view of the system software. The web server, application server and database are all lumped together into a single 'software stack'. In the event of failure of the Core Hardware server, we will lose half our capacity to serve requests, regardless of the type of request. This is addressed by DEDICATED WEB AND APPLICATION SERVERS. We have also yet to address the issue of a duplicate database, tackled by the COMMON PERSISTENT STORE and DATA REPLICATION patterns.

DEDICATED WEB AND APPLICATION SERVERS

Let's return to the detail of the APPLICATION SERVER ARCHITECTURE (see Figure 7.4).

In the previous patterns we have abstracted this software stack as 'system software' while we look at how to tackle the availability and scalability of the system as a whole. However, these are the elements that make up the core of the system and so their availability, how well they scale, and their performance will have the most significant effect on the availability, scalability and performance of the system.

Figure 7.4 APPLICATION SERVER ARCHITECTURE for the GlobalTech system.

One of the problems with treating these elements collectively as the 'system software' is that they have very different characteristics and roles in the system. The web server is concerned with handling web requests, the GlobalTech Application with delivering business functionality, and the GlobalTech database with holding persistent information and handling queries. Can we further improve the non-functional characteristics of the system by treating these elements individually rather than collectively?

How can we independently scale, tune and improve the availability of the 'web' and 'application' elements of the system?

Users will principally interact with GlobalTech through an HTML interface. As with most corporate sites, we have a page template that incorporates the company logo, a set of navigation elements and some copyright notices, as well as the main content of the page. In order to display a particular page, the user's browser will make a number of requests to the system. The first will be the request for the page which will result in the page elements being assembled and any associated functionality being executed (perhaps a query for the detailed information about a particular product, plus some targeted information about other products of interest). This will result in an HTML page being assembled and returned to the browser, which will then make a number of requests for all the images in the page.

From the users' perspective, they have not navigated to that page until all the individual browser requests (perhaps as many as 30–50) have been completed. However, only the first of these involves the GlobalTech Application in any way, the rest can simply be handled by the web server.

So the web server needs to be good at handling a much larger number of requests than the GlobalTech Application. It also needs to be very good at shifting (potentially large) quantities of data between the network interface and the disk as it serves up images and other binary assets, such as documents and executables. The application on the other hand needs to be good at performing complex processing operations that result in a fairly small amount of data (the HTML page) being produced. With the current architecture, the Core Hardware server needs to be very powerful (lots of disk space, CPU power and memory) to support both types of software element effectively.

In scalability terms, we may find that we need to add more instances of the GlobalTech Application as more customers use the system. However, we may find that only 30% of web server processing capacity is being used due to the complexity of the functionality (even handling 30–50 requests per page is far less demanding than processing retailer orders). With the system software approach, where all core elements are hosted on the same piece of hardware, we will have to add more web server capacity even though we do not need it.

Finally, even though we have improved the overall availability of the system through the application of LOAD-BALANCED ELEMENTS for the system software, we cannot vary the availability of the web servers and the GlobalTech Application. If the web server on a particular Core Hardware server fails, the corresponding GlobalTech Application will receive no requests. It is sitting idle while the remaining application instances have to shoulder its load until the web server is brought back into service. This is a waste of a perfectly functional application instance.

Deploy the web server and application server software onto dedicated hardware servers that are optimized to support these different types of functionality.

We split out the web server software elements onto separate dedicated hardware servers (see Figure 7.5).

The web servers are deployed as a set of three LOAD-BALANCED ELEMENTS with the outermost switch collaborating with the web load balancer to choose the web server to which to forward requests. A second load balancer is also introduced between the web servers and the system software (now just consisting of the GlobalTech Application and database).

This use of two different load balancers gives us the ability to tune the availability and scalability of the web and application elements independently. In the GlobalTech system, we have three web servers which can all be hosted on fairly modest hardware; tuning these servers for disk access and I/O rather than raw processing power means that the web servers are collectively able to handle up to 7500 simultaneous users (see the 'Costing the GlobalTech system' section). This is more than enough to handle the estimated peak load at the outset of 3700 concurrent web sessions (3000 consumers and 700 retailers) but avoids dropping to a capacity of 2500 in the event of the failure of a single hardware server. Each system software instance is only likely

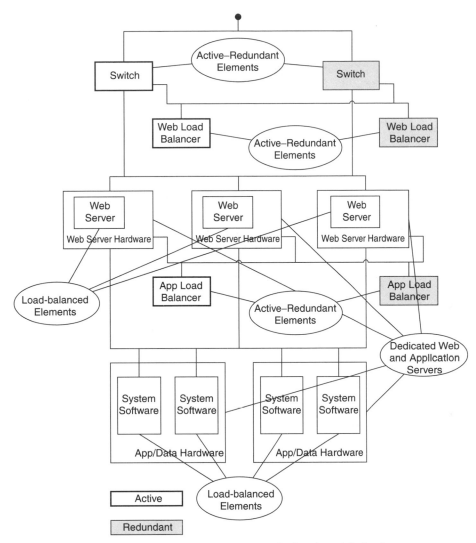

Figure 7.5 DEDICATED WEB AND APPLICATION SERVERS applied to the GlobalTech system.

to be able to handle around 800 consumer and 200 retail users, so we are going to need to add further instances long before the web servers run out of capacity. This is possible due to having DEDICATED WEB AND APPLICATION SERVERS – we can add more instances to the load-balanced pool of system software instances without changing the configuration of the web servers.

The use of two types of load balancer also improves availability. The loss of one or more web servers does not affect any particular system software instance.

Given the fact that the web servers have a greater relative capacity than the system software, we can probably cope with the loss of one web server with no effect to overall system capacity.

The effect on performance is more complicated. A concern that is often raised about this type of architecture is that we have introduced a network 'gap' between the web servers and the system software. Taking into account the use of a load balancer, doesn't this introduce a large performance hit between receiving a page request and passing it on to the GlobalTech Application? This is true but we can compensate for this performance hit through the use of specialist hardware. We can place the binary web assets on the web server hardware so requests for images, etc. do not go further than the web server. We can tune the Web Hardware servers for serving HTTP requests, which includes very efficient I/O processing both for network and disk access and good caching of binary web assets. We can also tune the application/data hardware servers for processing functional requests thereby improving the performance of responding to these requests. This improvement should outweigh the impact of introducing the network gap. Performance of multi-tiered systems is considered in more detail in 'Why tiers are not a catastrophe'.

Impact of the Pattern on Non-functional Characteristics

Availability	Availability is improved due to the separation of the web servers from the rest of the system software – a web server can fail without having a negative impact on any particular system software instance as it did in previous versions of the architecture.
Performance	Performance can be improved depending on the degree to which the web and application/data hardware servers can be optimized. This will depend on the type of application and its interface – sites with lots of graphics or large binary assets to be downloaded, or particularly complex application functionality, are likely to benefit most from the split.
Scalability	Scalability is improved due to the ability to independently scale the web server and system software load-balanced pools.
Security	Security is negatively impacted as there are now a number of new elements that need to be secured. However, DEDICATED WEB AND APPLICATION SERVERS does provide the foundation for the DEMILITARIZED ZONE security pattern.
Manageability	Manageability is negatively impacted due to the need to separately manage the web servers and system software, plus the additional load balancers.

Maintainability	Maintainability is potentially improved as problems specific to the web servers will be isolated on those machines. Equally, the web servers and the system software stack can be fixed independently if necessary.
Flexibility	Unaffected by this pattern.
Portability	Unaffected by this pattern.
Cost	The introduction of a number of new hardware servers may initially have a negative impact on cost depending on the size of the servers required. However, the use of optimized or specialist hardware should prove cheaper in the long run – scaling the system doesn't necessarily require new hardware of all types to be purchased (see the 'Costing the GlobalTech system' section).

Moving On

Having split the web servers and application/database system software into separate tiers we will now look at splitting out the database in COMMON PERSISTENT STORE and DATA REPLICATION. This pattern also provides the foundation for a fundamental security pattern, DEMILITARIZED ZONE.

COMMON PERSISTENT STORE

The Singleton pattern [Gamma *et al.* 1995] is probably one of the most misunderstood of all patterns. However, if people were not so interested in it, there would be less debate surrounding it. The most common interpretation of the Singleton pattern is that it provides a single point of access to shared functionality and its associated data. Why is this so important? Well, the main reason is that any information system needs to share things. There are different approaches to sharing data, depending on the role of this data in the system. One approach is for each component to maintain its own copy of the data it needs. However, if this data represents some updatable part of the system model, such as a customer record, the possibility arises that one component's copy can become out of step with that of another component if one of these locally-held customer records is updated. Most systems contain data that must be consistent regardless of the location from which it is viewed.

If the system employs multiple elements to deliver a particular part of the system functionality, how do we ensure that those elements present a consistent view of the data in the system?

So far, we have concentrated very much on the functionality of the system and how to keep that functionality available with acceptable performance in the face of failure or the need for maintenance. What we now need to address is the system data.

If we build a monolithic system consisting of a single server, there are few issues surrounding such persistent data access. All users access the same server and this server holds the system data, hence all users access the same system data. However, applying LOAD-BALANCED ELEMENTS to improve the availability of the system introduces problems in terms of the consistency of dynamic application data. If a user interacts with one element in the system at one time and then interacts later with another element providing the same functionality, they will expect the same dynamic application data to be reflected in both interactions. For example, if you go to an online bookstore to place an order, that order may be handled by application server A. If you return a few hours later to check on the progress of your order that interaction may be handled by application server B. If all persistent data access is local to each application server, then server B will know nothing of the order you placed on server A. This is obviously not acceptable.

In the GlobalTech system we have a lot of types of data that may change through users interacting with the system. Customer profiles, customer orders, retailer profiles and retailer orders are all going to be created and maintained by the users of the system and so this data needs to be consistent across all the servers that the user may interact with. We could look at propagating changes from the server on which the user creates or changes data to the other servers in the load-balanced pool (in a form of DATA REPLICATION) but this is a complex and difficult process; it requires every system software instance to be able to access the database of every other system software instance to ensure they are all up-to-date. Instead we need a single consistent data set that all servers access and update.

Store all application data in a single COMMON PERSISTENT STORE and have all the servers access it.

In the GlobalTech system, the COMMON PERSISTENT STORE is implemented as a database management system running on its own hardware server (see Figure 7.6).

The COMMON PERSISTENT STORE is the single location in which the application's data is stored and from which it is retrieved. Any changes made to the data by one GlobalTech Application will be visible to the others as they all retrieve their data from the same location.

Although the most common implementation of COMMON PERSISTENT STORE for the types of application we are interested in is a database management system (DBMS), there are other options. The session backup server is essentially a COMMON PERSISTENT STORE: all the GlobalTech Application instances save their session state to the server using a simple serialization mechanism. This is possible because there is no chance that different users interacting with different instances could possibly want to change the same data (because that data represents the state of their own session). In the

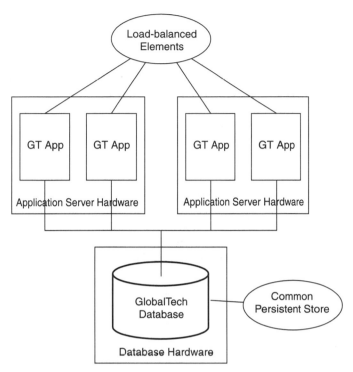

Figure 7.6 Common Persistent Store applied to the GlobalTech system.

case of the profiles and orders of the GlobalTech system, there is definitely a chance that the same data may be being changed by different users and so we need some form of locking and transactional update, which is provided by most DBMSs.

Although it is essential to apply this pattern in order to ensure the consistency of data in a system implemented using a number of load-balanced applications, there are a couple of serious issues with it. Availability is severely impacted. Where Active–Redundant Elements and Load-Balanced Elements improved availability by introducing duplication of each type of system element, Common Persistent Store removes duplication of databases to achieve consistency. So the database now becomes a single point of failure for the system; if it fails or needs to be maintained, the system stops working.

Performance can also be seriously affected. By splitting the database out onto its own server we have introduced a 'network gap' between the application and the database. The negative impact on performance of this gap is likely to be much more significant than the gap between Dedicated Web and Application Servers. Whereas web servers simply forward requests for dynamic pages to the application, the amount of traffic between the GlobalTech Application and the database is significant. A single page request can lead to a large number of database queries (perhaps the page shows the details of a product, plus a list of 'other products of interest' based on the user's profile) or a large amount of data to be returned. All these queries and the resultant data have to pass across the network gap.

Impact of the Pattern on Non-functional Characteristics

Availability	Severely negatively impacted by the introduction of the COMMON PERSISTENT STORE as a single point of failure.
Performance	Potentially there is a negative impact on performance by the introduction of a network gap. This can be somewhat mitigated by optimizing the Database Hardware server but the degree of traffic between the application and the database is likely to outweigh the benefits of this optimization.
Scalability	Because the COMMON PERSISTENT STORE is the only element of its type in the system, and one that is likely to be involved in most, if not all, user requests, it becomes a bottleneck for scalability. If it reaches the limits of its capacity, we can only replace it with a higher-capacity element.
Security	Although we have introduced another element to the system, security is potentially improved as we can take security measures to protect the persistent data – something we particularly care about.
Manageability	Manageability is negatively impacted by the addition of yet another hardware server and its corresponding software element.
Maintainability	Maintainability is potentially improved as problems specific to the COMMON PERSISTENT STORE are isolated to its server. However, we have an issue of availability if the Database Hardware Server or the database cannot be maintained while they are in service.
Flexibility	Unaffected by this pattern.
Portability	Unaffected by this pattern.
Cost	Cost is potentially greatly increased. When we had one database per application, it only required a relatively small amount of resource to function – the memory and CPU utilization will have been dominated by the application. Now we have a single hardware server that has to support a software element processing all queries from all applications, it will need to be a substantial server. Any saving made by being able to further optimize the Application Server Hardware is likely to be small in comparison.

Moving On

This pattern is really applied as a matter of necessity – most applications update persistent data and it must be consistent across all servers. However, its application brings a number of liabilities that must be addressed:

- Lack of availability – addressed by DATA REPLICATION
- Lack of performance – addressed by LOCAL CACHE and SEPARATE SYSTEM-MANAGED DATA
- Lack of scalability – addressed by EXPANDABLE HARDWARE

Why Tiers are not a Catastrophe

Some time ago, one of the authors was explaining J2EE architecture to a very bright guy as part of a knowledge transfer exercise. As the explanation of the overall application cycle, the creation of EJBs, the use of the naming service and so on progressed, he looked perturbed and slightly puzzled. Expanding on the description, it clicked with him (despite the poor explanation) that the servlets and EJBs were actually in separate tiers on different sides of a network boundary. 'Ach', he exclaimed, 'Is a catastrophe!'

This was not what had been expected. Surely the whole industry was aware of the benefits of N-tier systems. Why, the use of multiple tiers was part of the jigsaw that gave you lots of really good stuff like scalability, availability, manageability, etc. However, there was a moment of vertigo – was the author missing something blindingly obvious? Had he succumbed to 'Markitecture'?

Seeds of the Catastrophe

The first point to make here is that we are talking about separating an application's functionality across multiple physical tiers. This is distinct from splitting the functionality between multiple logical layers. You can have all the layers of a layered architecture on the same machine (think, for example, of the TCP/IP stack) without compromising the partitioning and loose coupling provided by a layered architecture. However, splitting functionality across physical tiers has some major implications.

It is blindingly obvious that multiple physical tiers in your system will slow down end-to-end communication. We spend lots of time discussing and promoting the patterns and good practices for distributed development. Most of these patterns revolve around reducing the number of distributed calls and passing more information per call. The reason for doing this is that distributed calls are slow – very slow – very, very slow. Distributed calls are several orders of magnitude slower than in-memory calls, or even cross-process calls on the same machine. Hence, for good distributed design they should be avoided if possible (caching strategies) and minimized if not (application of patterns such as Combined Method [Henney 2000]).

So, here we are, on the one hand preaching that you should minimize distribution while on the other using the classic three-tier layout (in Figure 7.7, each line between the servers indicates one of these 'orders of magnitude' cross-machine calls). How can this make sense given the hugely detrimental effect this will have on performance? I know that we have stated that no single non-functional characteristic should necessarily dominate an architect's thinking, but how can you justify such a huge downside? What is there to gain from splitting the functionality in this way?

The Terminology Trap

As the authors considered this issue, it gradually dawned on them that there was a terminology issue causing a lot of confusion. If you read various distributed system, J2EE and .NET books and articles, you will come across the following terms:

- Web server – The software that receives and processes HTTP calls from the client; also refers to the machine on which this runs if it has no other software running on it.

- Application server – The software that provides the virtual platform in which the software components of the application run; also refers to the machine on which this runs if it has no other software running on it.

- Tier – A dangerous word. It can mean either a set of physically separate servers that perform the same role and contain the same functionality (e.g. the database tier) or it can mean a set of functionality separated by a boundary, which *could* be a network boundary (e.g. the EJB tier).

- Web tier – Used in J2EE to mean the container in which software components related to web user interfaces (i.e. servlets and JSPs) run.

- EJB tier – Used in J2EE to mean the container in which business components run.

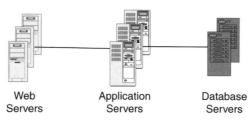

| Web Servers | Application Servers | Database Servers |

Figure 7.7   Classic 'three-tier' hardware layout.

The key issue here is the ambiguity of the term 'tier'. To some people, a tier is distinct from a layer because a tier represents a network boundary between two machines. This is distinct from a logical layer which carries no implication of distribution at all. Hence, at first sight, the use of the terms web tier and EJB tier indicates that there is a distribution boundary between them. Indeed, closer inspection reveals that the interface between the two must use J2EE's Remote Method Invocation (RMI) semantics implying that there is a likelihood that they will run in separate processes if not on separate machines.

This is where the potential 'catastrophe' appears. You have a web server (which can, and frequently does, house a servlet container) and an application server that is EJB-centric. Doesn't it make sense that the web tier components are housed on the web server and that the EJB tier components are housed on the application server? After all, there is an RMI interface between them.

Imagine that the web components and business components are indeed on separate physical tiers. Further to this, imagine that we have applied the DEMILITARIZED ZONE pattern so that there is a choke point between the web servers and application servers. This would lead to a high overhead for any RMI call between the web tier and the EJB tier. If your web tier components make lots of calls on your EJB tier components then a lot of high-latency calls would be made for every user request, slowing down your application significantly. For most distributed systems, this would indeed be a 'catastrophe'.

Despite the use of the term 'tier' and the RMI interface between the J2EE web tier and EJB tier, most J2EE applications will deploy the web software components and EJB software components onto the same physical tier – the one housing the application servers. In later versions of J2EE (1.3 and beyond, which include EJB 2.0), the interfaces between the two 'tiers' may be defined using EJB Local interface semantics which removes the possibility that they are remote from each other.

The application server software provides a servlet container as well as an EJB container and the different types of component are deployed into each container. However, when a call is made between a web software component and an EJB software component, that call never leaves the application server. The application servers are designed to optimize such internal RMI calls so that they incur a minimum of overhead. This reduces the concern about the overheads associated with this 'pseudo-remote' boundary. The actual physical layout in this case is shown in Figure 7.8.

From Two-Tier to N-Tier

So, why have a separate physical tier of web servers at all? If all our 'intelligent' web processing is taking place on the application server, then why use a tier of dedicated web servers? There are various reasons why you might want to do this, as discussed in DEDICATED WEB AND APPLICATION SERVERS, but the main reasons are generally that you can place the web server tier outside the organization in a DEMILITARIZED ZONE

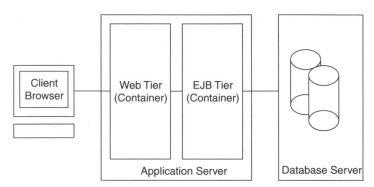

Figure 7.8 Physical deployment of application tiers across hardware tiers.

and that you can scale and tune the web server elements and application server elements independently. In this case, your architecture will end up looking like that in Figure 7.9. If you don't need to scale or tune independently or you are not using a DEMILITARIZED ZONE then you don't need a separate tier of web servers. However, if you don't have such requirements then you are not likely to be creating the sort of systems we are discussing in this book.

An important aspect of this architecture is that the web servers are simply serving static content (HTML pages, images, etc.). Any dynamic functionality that would involve a servlet, for example, will be tunnelled through to the application server tier where the servlet will run. The results of running that servlet (or JSP or ASP.NET page) will then be tunnelled back to the web server and on to the client. This tunnelling can be achieved through standard web server-side redirection or using specialist proxies supplied by the application server vendors.

One thing to clarify here is that the question of whether you have separate Web and Application Servers is entirely independent of the question of whether you use EJBs or other transactional components (e.g. .NET Enterprise Services) to house your business logic. There has been much discussion over the past few years about 'transactional components on the middle tier' as EJBs and Microsoft's MTS/COM+ were launched and promoted. Again, the key to this is the terminology: the 'middle

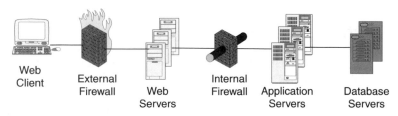

Figure 7.9 Introduction of firewalls between hardware tiers.

tier' is the EJB container (or equivalent) shown in Figure 7.8. There was much muddled thinking and marketing about such transactional components giving you improved scalability, when most of the scalability benefits came about due to the associated programming models. You may decide to use transactional components as they have benefits in terms of declarative security, declarative transactions, object pooling and lifecycle management. However, if you have little transactional business logic, you may decide to implement your business logic in standard Java or C# classes that are called directly from servlets, JSPs or ASP.NET pages. In this case, there is no 'middle tier', simply the web tier talking directly to the database. This should not be confused with traditional two-tier computing where most of the business logic is on the client, but if you create your web components badly you can soon rediscover a lot of the downsides of this model!

In our terms, all we are concerned about is the scaling of the application server tier. How you decide to partition and implement your business and presentation logic inside this tier is largely immaterial from the system perspective as long as it does not cause any problematic dependencies outside the tier or limit the ability to scale by adding more elements in parallel.

One Size does not Fit All

Having spent the last few minutes emphasizing that most people do not separate their presentation processing from their business logic, there are some cases where you might want to do this:

■ Some or all of your business processing is encapsulated in shared services (particularly web services) and so must be accessed across a boundary between processes or machines (known as a remoting boundary).

■ You have a set of security zones in which different processing runs.

■ There is a particular reason why you want to split out the transactional component tier (you might want to avoid application server license costs by running some of your servlets and JSPs on a different server tier that can scale independently).

In these cases, you will have to make remote calls to access your business logic and take the associated performance hit. However, these situations demonstrate a tradeoff where another non-functional characteristic is improved at the expense of performance (flexibility in the first case, security in the second and cost in the third).

Access to external data sources and functionality is also frequently remote. One consequence of applying COMMON PERSISTENT STORE is that the database is now remote from the business and presentation processing. If PERIPHERAL SPECIALIST ELEMENTS provide access to external data and functionality, some of these elements often need to be housed on their own servers, leading to another network hop. You could end up with an integration tier in your system architecture diagrams – which may or may not include your system database depending on your point of view – so you may end up with more than three physical tiers in your architecture.

In summary, you need to be careful of your terminology and don't be afraid to ask questions such as 'what is the purpose of that tier of servers?' and 'where, precisely, is the remoting boundary in this part of the system?'

DATA REPLICATION

In the COMMON PERSISTENT STORE pattern we looked at how we should centralize the store to provide essential consistency of information to all instances of the application with which the user might interact. This presents us with something of a paradox:

To deliver high availability we must introduce some level of duplication of system elements. However, if those elements store data, no inconsistency can be tolerated between them. How can this inconsistency be prevented?

The critical issue introduced by COMMON PERSISTENT STORE is that it becomes a single point of failure in the system. The obvious solution to this is to apply ACTIVE–REDUNDANT ELEMENTS or LOAD-BALANCED ELEMENTS to the store in order to provide high availability in the same way that we have done for web servers, application servers, routers and load balancers. However, all of the preceding system elements are largely functional in nature and only deal with data in a transient way. Even then, we saw in the SESSION FAILOVER pattern that there were issues with the handling of transient, user-specific data (held in the form of session state) when one element had to failover to another.

In the case of session state, inconsistency between servers means that user sessions are terminated prematurely. In the case of persistent data, the consequences may be more insidious – such as an incorrect price or stock level being used. This is still a failure of the system, and potentially one that can cause data corruption as well as dissatisfied users. This is definitely an issue for the GlobalTech system as it uses a COMMON PERSISTENT STORE to hold all persistent data, including catalogue data, retailer information, user registration data, and order data. What we really need is a COMMON PERSISTENT STORE that has some internal duplication to improve availability.

Deploy the COMMON PERSISTENT STORE as a pair of ACTIVE–REDUNDANT ELEMENTS. Implement a mechanism that replicates the data between them and ensures the transaction is not completed until the data is available on both the active and redundant elements.

This is quite easy to say but can be quite difficult to achieve in practice. One such mechanism would be the replication features built into the database management software as part of its clustering capability. This places the responsibility for the consistency of the data firmly in the hands of the database vendor. For the GlobalTech system we have opted for a DBMS that supports clustering and data replication (see Figure 7.10).

In implementing this kind of DATA REPLICATION, it is absolutely critical that the GlobalTech Application instances see only one persistent store. If we leave it up to each application instance to choose which database it should talk to based on the kind of failover mechanisms discussed in ACTIVE–REDUNDANT ELEMENTS, we risk the situation where two different application instances are talking to two different databases; which raises the spectre of inconsistency once again.

In this case it is usually better that the ACTIVE–REDUNDANT ELEMENTS collaborate to make the failover invisible, either by monitoring each other or by having some token in the replication mechanism that indicates which element is active and which is redundant.

There are alternatives to using a replicated database but they tend to be less sophisticated, which leads to more problems with management and maintainability

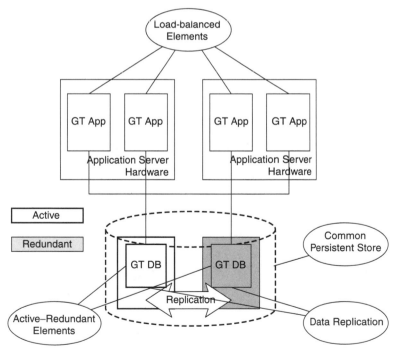

Figure 7.10 DATA REPLICATION applied to the GlobalTech system.

and/or poorer availability. For example, if the data is stored in a number of small files (either because serialization is used for persistence or because the database technology uses fragmented files), they can be replicated across to the redundant server as part of the transaction using a simple file-synchronization process. Another approach is simply to have the application's persistence mechanism write everything twice, once to each of the active and redundant elements.

Another place we should consider applying DATA REPLICATION is to the session backup servers (not shown in Figure 7.10). Although these are not a single point of failure for the system as a whole, they are a single point of failure for SESSION FAILOVER. If the active session backup server fails, the redundant one will be available to have new or updated session state persisted to it, but the state stored on the failed backup server will be lost.

If we were concerned only with consumer users we may decide this is acceptable as it is only really a problem should the active session backup server fail very closely followed by an application instance. If this unusual circumstance resulted in a handful of users losing some changes they were making to their profile or their shopping basket losing some purchases, we may decide to live with it (unfortunate for those users but the cost of solving such a rare problem probably couldn't be justified). However we use the same mechanism to support the construction of retail user orders. These may take a long time to put together and are worth a lot of money to GlobalTech.

So we decide to go for a belt-and-braces solution by implementing DATA REPLICATION for the session backup servers as well. However, we don't need to significantly change our serialization mechanism; each application instance writes out its state to both the active and the redundant session backup servers before it continues processing the request.

Impact of the Pattern on Non-functional Characteristics

Availability	Availability is improved by replacing the single point of failure with a pair of ACTIVE–REDUNDANT ELEMENTS.
Performance	There is a significant negative impact on performance for any operation that involves writing data to the database.
Scalability	Unaffected by this pattern.
Security	As long as the security mechanisms work in the same way for a pair of ACTIVE–REDUNDANT ELEMENTS as they do for a single server, security is unaffected.
Manageability	Manageability will be negatively impacted due to the need to manage the active–redundant pair of elements and the DATA REPLICATION mechanism.

Maintainability	Maintainability should be unaffected unless there are problems with the DATA REPLICATION mechanism itself, in which case there may be some uncertainty as to the state of the data set the application is using!
Flexibility	Unaffected by this pattern.
Portability	DATA REPLICATION is often implemented using proprietary mechanisms that have their own non-functional characteristics. If the database is accessed using SQL, potentially it can be swapped with another SQL-compliant database, but the new database may not have a DATA REPLICATION mechanism or it might work in a very different way.
Cost	The simplest way to implement such a complex mechanism as DATA REPLICATION is to buy a persistent storage product that supports it. This can be very expensive, particularly when compared with other products that don't support DATA REPLICATION but otherwise meet all the functional and non-functional requirements for the system. Bespoke solutions can be developed but these are usually reasonably complex and so take time and money to develop and maintain.

Moving On

One way to improve the performance and reduce the complexity of this pattern is to apply SEPARATE SYSTEM-MANAGED DATA. Implementing a LOCAL CACHE for the application instances can also reduce the load on the persistent store which frees more resource for it to replicate its data. Use of CONNECTION LIMITATION can also reduce the strain on the persistent store.

How many Servers do you Need?

One of the key questions when specifying a system is how many servers you need. The answer to this question will depend on the style of application and where you deploy the different components. Assuming that you have decided to apply DEDICATED WEB AND APPLICATION SERVERS, you will need to do two sets of calculations – one for the web load and the other for the application processing load.

The web load can be considered in terms of:

- Processor usage per concurrent user
- Maximum concurrent connections per web server
- Response time per request for binary assets

If your web server vendor cannot provide suitable figures, processor and memory usage can be determined empirically using standard system profiling tools during load testing. The same mechanism can be used to test limits on concurrent users. The web logs can be a good source of information when the system is loaded. From these you can determine the request response times and see if the number of errors increases with increased load. All of these metrics are useful to monitor on an ongoing basis, with the response time and pending connection queue giving the best indication of when you need to increase the amount of capacity.

Obviously, the precise capabilities of a particular web server cannot be predicted here. It may be that the vendor can give you precise scaling information or metrics for user sessions per server. If they cannot (or even if they can) you can perform your own rough load tests as part of the initial architectural investigation for the project.

Prediction of the number and size of application servers required can be more difficult. Again, there are useful metrics that can be sought from vendors or determined during evaluation:

- Minimum memory usage per server
- Memory required for a 'block' of user sessions (usually somewhere between 100 and 500 users)
- Maximum number of concurrent user requests
- Response time per page request
- Average CPU usage per block of users

Experience tells us that memory and processor capacity are the two key resources. In estimating for application servers we often use the following rules of thumb:[3]

- A single web server can handle requests for roughly 2500 simultaneous user sessions (regardless of whether the user is a consumer or a retail user – there is no difference to the web server) given dedicated use of a single processor and 1 GB memory.
- A single instance of the application running inside an application server can comfortably handle roughly 800 consumer and 200 retail user sessions given a dedicated processor and 2 GB memory. It can handle up to 1000 consumer and 250 retail user sessions with only a small degradation in performance.

---

[3] These numbers are based on using particular products for the web server, application server and database, and a particular hardware vendor, as well as an assumed level of complexity for this type of system. We do not want to recommend any vendor or product as what is appropriate to your particular project will depend on many factors. What we want to emphasize here are the relative costs of each of the different configurations. We should also point out that this methodology of using CPU and memory to determine capacity is only useful for very rough estimates, but it is good enough for this worked example.

- The database needs one processor and 2 GB memory to handle requests for every 1000 consumer and 250 retail user sessions. It scales roughly linearly.

It is probably worth mentioning that the application of the metrics and principles described here usually gives rise to a particular 'shape' of system. If you consider a system that needs to service 7500 users as a peak load, this would suggest a configuration of three web servers, six application servers and a two-server database cluster, giving the kite shape in Figure 7.11.

This kite shape has been derived from empirical evidence across many high volume Internet-facing projects that have applied the DEDICATED WEB AND APPLICATION SERVERS pattern. The relationship between the tiers and the number of boxes is common currency amongst architects familiar with this type of system and it is the de facto layout for systems.

A common variation is the inverted triangle shown in Figure 7.12. In this case, the functionality provided by the application servers is less central to the system as a whole. There are many system users that need servicing, hence the larger number of web servers, but their needs are mostly met by content retrieval and generation without recourse to much business logic.

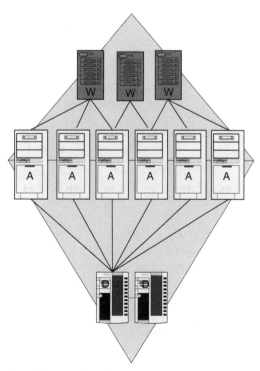

Figure 7.11 'Kite' shape layout of hardware servers.

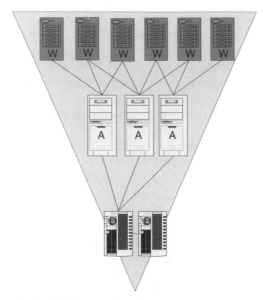

Figure 7.12 'Inverted triangle' layout of hardware servers.

The question arises over what to do when you are applying new technology, or specifying systems that fall outside the high-volume Internet-facing model. An example of this occurred in the early days of .NET on a particular project. This project applied the DEDICATED WEB AND APPLICATION SERVERS pattern, but there were complicating factors:

- The physical architecture was to be shared between multiple projects with different characteristics (some had little application tier processing).

- There were no metrics for application and web servers using .NET. You could assume that it would be similar to J2EE, but there were no guarantees.

In the face of such uncertainty, an initial architecture of three dual-processor Windows 2000 servers per tier was adopted. As each application completed its load test cycle, the metrics derived from this could be combined with those of other applications to indicate which tier required additional server resource.

As new technologies emerge and different application variations are required, the precise specification and number of servers will vary. This is particularly true of the application servers given the fluid nature of business logic and its comparative uniqueness to a business sector (or even a specific business). Hence, it is usually far more difficult to predict the ongoing requirements for the business layer. The requirements may even change over the life of the application as the application server software is upgraded. Such an upgrade may require a change to the underlying hardware or the system software (e.g. the operating system or the virtual platform, such as J2EE) that the application server uses. If the business layer is on its own set of servers, then these servers can be scaled, configured or replaced in isolation from the presentation layer and database servers as requirements change.

Costing the GlobalTech System

Let's consider how the costs differ between the various possible configurations for the GlobalTech system hardware.[4]

ACTIVE–REDUNDANT ELEMENTS

The first configuration used ACTIVE–REDUNDANT ELEMENTS for the complete system software. To cater for the initial peak of 3000 consumer and 700 retail users we need the following:

	CPU	Memory (GB)
Web Server	2	2
Application Server	3	6
Database	3	6
Total	8	14

This assumes that the application scales linearly (possibly true up to a point, but we're likely to be stretching it with 3700 users of mixed type) and we can seamlessly dedicate multiple processors to a single software server. Based on the list prices of a major hardware vendor, the cost of a server with this specification is $85 000 (the absolute cost for the server is not particularly of interest, just the relative costs of different types of server from the same vendor). And this is just for the active server, if we specify a redundant server that is 20–25% of the cost of the active server we can get one with four processors and 8 GB memory for $18 000. This means the capacity of the redundant server is limited to around 800 consumers and 200 retail users on average, with a peak of 1000/250 users. This is half-capacity on average and a third of our required peak capacity.

So the total cost for a version of the system in which the central elements are configured as ACTIVE–REDUNDANT ELEMENTS is $103 000, and it only copes with the initial average and peak loads. To cope with the required expansion to an average of 7000/1200 users (8000/2000 peak) we would require:

---

[4] The capacity calculations here are based on the figures in the 'How many servers do you need?' section. Please refer back to these figures if you want to perform the calculations yourself.

	CPU	Memory (GB)
Web Server	4	4
Application Server	8	16
Database	8	16
Total	20	36

This capacity would require a completely new active server costing a whopping $700 000. The 'good' news is that we could then use our old active server as the redundant server in the new system. Even then, we have a real problem creating a temporary system capable of supporting 20 000 consumer users.

LOAD-BALANCED ELEMENTS

Let's compare an equivalent system configuration based on LOAD-BALANCED ELEMENTS. Sticking with the example configuration in the pattern, we require two hardware servers of the following capacity to handle the initial average and peak loads:

	CPU	Memory (GB)
Web Server	1	1
Application Server	2	4
Database	2	4
Total	5	9

Unfortunately, it is not usually possible to buy a five-processor machine; we'd have to buy one with four or six processors. Using the same hardware vendor as before we can buy two servers with six CPUs for $60 000 each – a total of $120 000. However, as we said in the pattern description, we are likely to use four hardware servers so that we don't go down to half capacity in the event of hardware server failure. In this case we need four of the following servers:

	CPU	Memory (GB)
Web Server	1	1
Application Server	1	2
Database	1	2
Total	3	5

Again, each hardware server will have to have four processors rather than three but, even so, each server can be bought for $30 000 giving a total of $120 000 for four of these servers. Compared with the ACTIVE–REDUNDANT ELEMENTS configuration we will spend an additional $17 000 but we have much better capability in the event of hardware failure. Of course, we might argue that we could get away with only three servers (given we have to install four CPUs in each), saving $30 000. In this case we will lose 33% of our capacity if one of three servers fails as opposed to 25% if one of four fails, and our objective for having four servers was to improve availability in the event of failure. This kind of decision requires a more detailed cost/benefit analysis.

The real benefit of using LOAD-BALANCED ELEMENTS comes when we need to expand to cater for 8000/2000 peak load users; we simply need to add a further four servers. We can even temporarily expand to cater for 20 000 retail users by hiring a further two or three servers for the period of the product launch.

DEDICATED WEB AND APPLICATION SERVERS

In the DEDICATED WEB AND APPLICATION SERVERS configuration we need two web servers each with a single CPU and 1GB of memory. Such a machine can be bought for $8000. However, we only need two of them to cater for the initial peak load of 3700 users of both types (and they will easily cope with that as each one can handle 2500 users), giving a total cost of $16 000. We can also get away with a two-processor 4GB machine for the application/database hardware. These are much cheaper, costing $20 000 each. In order to expand to the 8000/2000 peak we need to add two web hardware servers and four application/database servers.

COMMON PERSISTENT STORE AND DATA REPLICATION

The COMMON PERSISTENT STORE configuration introduces one big cost: the database server. Because all the database capacity has to be in a single machine, we are back in the range of high-end machines that we can populate with a large number of CPUs. To support the initial peak of 3000/700 users we need three processors and 6 GB memory which equates to one of the four-processor machines that came in at $30 000. However, we can save on the application servers. If we stick with four servers, we need four machines with one processor and 2 GB memory. This takes us into the web server specification territory and a cost of $12 000. So the total cost is again lower: $30 000 for the database server, $16 000 for the web servers and $48 000 for the application servers, giving a total of $94 000.

The COMMON PERSISTENT STORE looks less good when we have to cater for 8000/2000 users. In this case we need database hardware with eight CPUs and 16 GB memory which comes with a price tag of $85 000 (and we have to scrap or re-purpose the old server). We also need two more web servers and four more application servers, giving a total upgrade cost of $149 000.

Finally, in order to get full active–redundant DATA REPLICATION, we need to specify a redundant database server, doubling the cost (although we may consider specifying a lower-powered redundant server).

Summary

Throughout this discussion we have ignored the cost of rack space (which can be very expensive if hosted in a managed data centre). We've also ignored the cost of the hardware servers for the PERIPHERAL SPECIALIST ELEMENTS. The table below summarizes the rough costs, in thousands of dollars, of each of the configurations considered above (the cost for the initial requirements is followed by the additional cost for expanding up to full capacity):

	Web Servers	Application servers	Database Servers	Switches	Load balancers	Total
Active–Redundant		103/600		2/0		105/700
Load-Balanced		120/120		2/0	4/0	126/120
Dedicated Web and Application Servers	16/16	80/80		2/0	8/0	106/96
Common Persistent Store	16/16	48/48	30/85	2/0	8/0	104/149
Data Replication	16/16	48/48	60/170	2/0	8/0	134/234

CONNECTION LIMITATION

One of the classic problems in the sphere of resource utilization is the problem of the dining philosophers. If you are not familiar with this problem, it consists of a set of philosophers seated round a table. The table is laid with one fork per philosopher, each placed between two philosophers. In order to eat their food, each philosopher needs two forks. However, if each philosopher starts by picking up one fork, there are no forks left, so no philosopher can acquire two forks unless another puts one down. If all the philosophers carry out the same actions (putting down and picking up forks in the same sequence) then there is no way that one of them can ever acquire two forks. The reason the problem requires philosophers is presumably that they should be able think their way out of the tricky situation. However, it may just be that they are more philosophical about the fact that they are becoming hungrier and hungrier.

Sometimes you have more users than you can comfortably service, which degrades the service for all users. How do we ensure that all the users we service receive a minimum level of service?

Part of producing a system with acceptable performance is the ability to respond to a particular user request within a given time. As discussed earlier in the book, performance is frequently measured in terms of roundtrip response times between the client and the server. If the system cannot respond in an acceptable time, customers will be left waiting for a response. The system will feel very sluggish and may even appear to have 'hung'. When performance is this poor, the system may as well not be available.

Usually, the reason why a system cannot respond in an acceptable time is because there is some resource – be that bandwidth, memory, processor power or database connections – that is not available to the processing component when it needs it. As a simple example, assume an application server with 2 GB of memory that can comfortably host 800 simultaneous user sessions. If 600 users connect to the system at one time, everyone will have enough memory. If 1000 users connect, the system will start to struggle; if 1200 users connect there will not be enough memory to go round. In response to this extra demand, the system will start paging user data back and forth between memory and disk (using virtual memory). This paging will slow down the performance of the server as it involves more disk I/O and associated processor capacity. As a result, roundtrip times to the server and hence the perceived performance will worsen. If the system runs out of virtual memory, memory allocation may fail or pause until memory from another user is freed up. This can cause processing errors, timeouts and even slower roundtrip times. The amount of memory required by a particular user will ebb and flow as the session proceeds. At a point where a user session requires more memory, it may have to pause waiting for more memory to come available. This waiting for resource causes poor performance.

In the GlobalTech system we have a set of web servers that we believe can comfortably handle around 7500 simultaneous users (of either type). However, we only have enough application instances to serve around 4000 consumer users and 800 retail users. We have the option of adding more servers to scale the application but this takes time and we don't see it as being necessary at the moment (or worth the cost). However, suppose something unexpected happens (like a range of GlobalTech products win a major design award, for example) and 7500 users do all turn up at the same time: the web servers will cope but the application servers will struggle and everyone will experience poor performance.

In terms of the philosophers, if they spend all their time fighting over who gets to use the forks, they all starve.

Limit the number of users that can connect to the system, or requests that can connect to a system element, at any one time to avoid resource contention and the associated poor performance.

For the GlobalTech Application, we may decide to apply the CONNECTION LIMITATION pattern to restrict the number of users we allow to access the system at any one time. Given that only the application instances really know what a 'user session' is, we need to set the limits there; in the case of our current architecture we need to configure a limit of around 1000 user sessions per application instance. This has the added benefit that if an application instance fails, we won't overload the remaining servers if they are already at peak capacity. The exact choice of limit will be down to our policy on exceptional circumstances: do we want to ensure that we give as many people as possible access to the system, even if they experience a small amount of performance degradation, or are we strict in only allowing users to access the system in numbers that won't overload it?

We also have to decide what to do with users we don't allow to access the system. For GlobalTech, we will implement a static 'holding page' that explains the system is unavailable because it is so popular. If a user is refused connection by an application server, the web server will return this page instead. The user may try to access the system again quite quickly, by which time one of the existing customers may have ended their session. If not, they will again be frustrated. This is far from an ideal situation since this customer may go elsewhere. However, all of the other customers being served should be seeing the required level of system performance. If we were to let the extra users through, potentially everyone's performance would suffer and we may lose many more customers.

We can also use the CONNECTION LIMITATION pattern in other parts of the system. We may limit the number of concurrent connections between the web servers and the application instances in order to keep throughput consistent. However, in this case, the connections that are not being serviced will be queued, waiting to be processed rather than rejected. This will reduce the amount of resource contention on the application server – meaning that performance should not degrade – but will ensure that all connections are serviced in a fair way. The same type of connection limitation is commonly used between the application server and the database server.

Impact of the Pattern on Non-functional Characteristics

Availability	Availability is negatively impacted as we reject any requests over a set limit. However, this is availability from the user's point of view rather than system availability – some users are still able to access the system even though others can't.
Performance	We can guarantee a level of performance regardless of the demand for the system.
Scalability	Perhaps strangely, scalability is improved by limiting the number of connections to the system or a particular system element. Our view of scalability is that it defines the system's ability to cope with increased load without degrading performance significantly. By imposing the CONNECTION LIMITATION pattern we can ensure good scalability up to that limit and then prevent degradation due to overloading.

Security	Unaffected by this pattern.
Manageability	There is a slight negative impact on manageability due to the need to manage the connection limit.
Maintainability	Unaffected by this pattern.
Flexibility	Unaffected by this pattern.
Portability	Unaffected by this pattern.
Cost	The cost of implementing a connection limit is pretty low. A number of products support this concept as standard but even a bespoke implementation is not that big a job.

Moving On

RESOURCE POOLING provides a mechanism for ensuring that the best use is made of limited resources, including those limited by CONNECTION LIMITATION. A LOCAL CACHE of persistent stores can reduce the need to limit connections as a request may be able to work with the data in the cache rather than going to the database.

RESOURCE POOLING

The rental of videos and DVDs is a large and widespread business. People want to watch a variety of films but they cannot justify spending £18 to buy every film that looks interesting as they will probably only want to watch the film once or twice (unless they have a very serious interest in films). Instead, they can rent the DVD for a fraction of the cost and then hand it back to be rented out again. This works well for the consumer, as they only pay for the small time they have the film, and also for the rental company as they can rent the same DVD over and over again to cover the cost of buying and maintaining it. In any distributed computer system (and many non-distributed ones), you will find similar examples of resources that are relatively expensive or scarce but to which you do not need continuous access.

How do we maximize the utilization of limited or expensive resources?

Internet systems typically use resources that are expensive to obtain. The classic example here is the database connection. Database licenses tend to limit the number of concurrent connections. The more concurrent connections your database can satisfy, the more expensive the license. In the GlobalTech system, we may potentially have 3700 concurrent users at peak load even from the outset (3000 consumers and 700 retailers). If every process that services one of these users requires a database connection to do its work, then this means we need a 3700-user license (even from here, you can hear the whoops of joy from the database salesman). Although this gives us the required performance, it also gives us a mighty budget headache.

One thing to notice about the system is that on closer inspection, each process does not need the database connection for the whole time it is processing a user request. Typically, a request will either generate output for the user or take input from the user. In the case of generating output, the database connection is needed at the start to obtain the data to be turned into output (e.g. to be represented as HTML). In the case of input, the process will check the input data, maybe perform some calculations and then use the database connection at the end to store the data sent by the user (e.g. a new customer address record). In both of these cases, the database connection is only required for a small fraction of the time taken by the user request.

It would be good to share the database connection and release it when we are not using it. However, the process of creation and destruction of database connections is relatively expensive. If you have to create a database connection as part of your processing, it will have a large impact on the time it takes to process.

Implement a pool of resources from which it is relatively inexpensive to acquire such resources and to which they can quickly be released when no longer required.

Most application servers (and some web servers) now provide the capability to pool database connections. This may involve setting a flag on a connection string (as in ADO.NET) or it may be inherent in the way that database connections are obtained (often the case in J2EE). In either case, a pool of connections is created when the application starts on a particular server. All processes or threads running as part of that application obtain connections from the pool as they need them and return them as soon as they have done with them. As the act of acquiring a connection from the pool has a relatively low overhead, there is no incentive to keep hold of the connection for the duration of the request.

By pooling resources, it is possible to serve the same number of concurrent users from a smaller pool of resources. In the GlobalTech system, we figure (based on code inspection and testing) that a connection is only required, on average, for 20% of a request. This means that we should be able to survive with about 3700/5 connections, i.e. we need a database license for about 750 concurrent users.

We have used database connections as the example here, but there are many other types of resource that can be pooled, such as connections between web server and application server or connections to other data sources like ERP systems. You can create your own pools and pooling mechanisms, or you can use a pre-built pool that conforms to a standard pooling architecture such as the J2EE Connector architecture or COM+ resource dispenser.

The use of resource pooling gets over some of the issues associated with the CONNECTION LIMITATION pattern. As the resources can be shared between more users, there is less of a chance that some users will be unable to use the system. As more users are supported by fewer resources but with the same level of performance, the scalability characteristics of the system elements that use the pools are improved. However, the pools must be configured and maintained. This adds to the manageability overhead associated with the system.

Impact of the Pattern on System Characteristics

Availability	Unaffected by this pattern.
Performance	Performance is improved due to the reuse of limited resources that can be expensive to create or initialize.
Scalability	Sharing of valuable resources enables more users to connect to the system than otherwise could.
Security	Unaffected by this pattern.
Manageability	There is a slight negative impact on manageability due to the need to manage the resource pool.
Maintainability	Unaffected by this pattern.
Flexibility	Unaffected by this pattern.
Portability	Unaffected by this pattern.
Cost	Many products support resource pooling as standard and bespoke implementation is not a significant investment.

Moving On

We often use CONNECTION LIMITATION and RESOURCE POOLING when we have to connect to a persistent store over a network. Limiting the connections reduces the load on the store and we can pool connections to the database that are likely to be expensive to initialize. However, using a LOCAL CACHE can reduce the number of times we need to connect to the database.

LOCAL CACHE

If I work for a small company with a single office, it is relatively simple to create a list of my customers. All of the records and people I need to access to gain this information are in one office. If the company grows so that it has 15 sales offices in different countries, creating that customer list suddenly becomes a lot harder. If I maintain a single set of records, there will be a large amount of overhead as the other 14 offices need to access this data through emails and phone calls. You come across the same issue when you distribute your application data across multiple servers.

How can we speed up access to information distributed across multiple servers?

In implementing the COMMON PERSISTENT STORE pattern we have housed the GlobalTech database on its own hardware server. As discussed in that pattern, this introduces a performance problem as all queries and resultant data have to travel over the network connection between each application instance and the database.

In some cases, this is completely unavoidable. For example, when a retail user is constructing an order, they will build the order over time as part of a session and, once they confirm that order, it will be written to the database for further processing. It must be written to the COMMON PERSISTENT STORE because a second user may want to access the order details soon after it is confirmed.

In other cases, however, we could avoid connecting to the remote database. The product details that are used as part of the order construction process should not change during that process; in fact, none of the catalogue information should change whilst an order is being constructed. So if we have to read in the details of a product because a user wants to add it to the order, we can safely reuse those details if the user wants to access them again – there is no need to contact the database again. In fact, those details could be used by any user of the system that wants to place an order, until the point where we decide we actually need to change them.

We could take this approach to lots of different types of data: the product catalogue, the retail outlet finder, the customer support materials, etc. All of these will be updated but only very infrequently compared to the frequency with which users are likely to access the data.

Identify information that changes infrequently, compared to the frequency with which it is accessed, and cache it locally to where it is used.

The types of information identified above are the most obvious candidates for caching. In the case of the GlobalTech Application, we don't want to implement a number of specific caches for all different types of data so we implement a single object cache local to the application instances. We mark object types (ProductDetails, SupportMaterial, etc.) as being 'cacheable' and, every time we need to read a particular object we check whether it is in the cache. If it is, we use the locally held details, if not we read the details in and add the object to the cache. If we hide this cache behind the regular database access interface, we can even make the cache invisible to the application – it uses the interface to retrieve the data and is unaware of where the details actually come from.

We already have a type of LOCAL CACHE in the GlobalTech system, introduced as part of DEDICATED WEB AND APPLICATION SERVERS. Logically, the binary assets for the site (the site 'furniture' images, the product detail images, the customer support downloads, etc.) belong in the GlobalTech database – they are part of the data the application uses to deliver the system functionality. However, storing large binary objects in a general-purpose database can have a massive negative impact on database performance when they are retrieved. This performance hit is compounded by the need for the web server to pass every request for a binary asset back to an application instance – the application is involved in responding to every single HTTP request rather than just those that require a dynamic page to be constructed.

Instead we store the binary assets on the web server and simply store their relative URLs in the database. This way, the web server can serve binary assets to the user from their local storage without involving the GlobalTech Application or database in any way.

There are many ways to implement LOCAL CACHE and a number of algorithms for determining the characteristics and 'efficiency' of the cache. If the size of the 'cacheable' data is relatively small, the simplest thing is to load it all into memory as part of the application's initialization process. All we need to do then is provide a mechanism to invalidate and reload the cache if any of the data changes. This is a pretty blunt instrument but extremely effective.

A more sophisticated cache allows us to cache 'the most frequently used data' rather than every possible cacheable object. This is particularly useful if we can't fit all the cacheable data into the cache at once and is adaptable to any changes in use in the system. The details of a new product, for example, might be infrequently accessed before its official launch, and then become very frequently accessed after that.

At an even higher level of sophistication, we can cache data that the user changes. If the system uses a lot of 'personalization' techniques, it might be a good idea to cache user profiles. However, we need a sophisticated invalidation mechanism to make sure that any changes the user makes to the profile are immediately reflected in the caches of all application instances.

Impact of the Pattern on Non-functional Characteristics

Availability	Potentially there is a minor improvement in availability. If the COMMON PERSISTENT STORE fails, some data is still available in the LOCAL CACHE. However, only a subset of functionality is likely to remain available; functions such as ordering require access to the persistent store, not merely to a cache.
Performance	Performance is improved by the local availability of data or assets that would otherwise have to be retrieved from a remote store.
Scalability	Unaffected by this pattern.
Security	We need to consider the type of information being held in the LOCAL CACHE. If the information is sensitive, introduction of the cache has a negative impact on security as we have to protect the cache as well as the persistent store.
Manageability	There is a negative impact on manageability as we have to manage the cache and any caching parameters that can be 'tuned'.
Maintainability	Unaffected by this pattern.
Flexibility	Unaffected by this pattern.
Portability	Unaffected by this pattern.

Cost   The cost of implementing a LOCAL CACHE depends on its
                        sophistication. It is relatively easy to build and maintain a
                        very simple cache and the cost is minimal. However, an
                        adaptive cache that holds frequently updated information is
                        harder to build and products that perform this function can
                        be expensive to buy.

Moving On

The identification of cacheable data and the implementation of the cache is eased by
the application of SEPARATE SYSTEM-MANAGED DATA. If the cache is to hold sensitive
data, we may need to apply some form of INFORMATION OBSCURITY to it. OFFLINE
REPORTING employs a similar principle to achieve a very different effect: by caching
data locally to a reporting and analysis tool, we can avoid adversely affecting the
performance of the running application.

OFFLINE REPORTING

You are driving along the road, heading for home. You have travelled far and you
are looking forward to a rest as familiar roads start to lead you home. Then, in
the distance you see it. A group of stationary cars next to a set of people clad in
Day-Glo clothing and carrying clipboards – a traffic census. Now, you know that
the highways agency needs information about traffic flow and car journeys. Without
this information, new roads would be built in the wrong places and much needed
repair work would only occur once the damage had been done. However, you will
now have to stop – to bring your personal journey to a grinding halt – to provide
this information. Why you? Why now? As your car comes to a halt at the end of the
line of traffic, you slump forward on your steering wheel, convinced that there must
be a better way of doing things.

How can we extract important information from a system without significantly impacting the ability of that system to do its job?

As the GlobalTech system runs, it gathers lots of information that is useful
throughout the organization. The marketing department is interested in sales records
and information on what products customers browsed at the same time, as the basis
of future promotions. The support department is interested in which solutions were
viewed the most and the combinations of keywords used most frequently in the site
search engine.

This information is likely to be critical (or at least very influential) to the ongoing
success of the system. If we know how the users use the system, we can focus

our efforts to improve it in the right areas. In the case of sales, this might help us provide more relevant and targeted promotions, which could improve our level of sales without significantly altering the cost of sale. In the case of support, we can make the self-service customer support area easier to use, which should result in a reduction in calls to the support centres and hence a cost saving. Being able to analyse the way the users use the system can have a direct affect on GlobalTech's bottom line.

However, the information required by the marketing and support departments is in the live, running database. As the system is used by lots of users, the dataset in the database becomes very large. In order to generate useful reports for marketing and support we have to do a lot of sophisticated and complex processing. This is likely to drain significant capacity from the GlobalTech database whenever the reporting process is run, which can affect the performance perceived by users unlucky enough to be using the system during the process. It would be very unfortunate if a process designed to help improve the system caused some of the users to have bad experiences of the system.

Periodically snapshot data that needs to be analysed. Export this snapshot from the live system environment so that any reporting can be carried out 'offline'.

There are three prime areas for offline reporting in the GlobalTech system:

- The customer database, which contains information on the behaviour of customers, such as the pages they viewed and the purchases they made. A snapshot is taken of this dynamic subset of the data and is imported into a database instance running on the marketing and support departments' intranets. Reports can be run and queries can be made against this snapshot.

- The retailer ordering database, which contains figures of interest to the marketing department. A snapshot can be loaded into a back-office database for report generation.

- The order status reporting system. Information can be generated, for customers who have their order status reported offline, from a snapshot of the data rather than having it extracted directly from the live system.

Implementing the snapshot and export mechanism is not a trivial operation. Most database products support some form of export but not all of these can be tailored to export only the sets of data that we are interested in, and others cannot be run without preventing access to the database. For the GlobalTech system we will implement a bespoke snapshot mechanism for each of the three areas of interest. Implementing three separate mechanisms means we can run the snapshots at different times. The queries required to generate the snapshots will have a negative impact on the database, but nowhere near as big an impact as running the reporting against it. We can also parameterize the snapshot mechanisms as much as we like, for example specifying that we're only interested in how users view certain areas of the site, or the profiles of new customers.

Implementing the export mechanism can be as simple as using FTP or SCP to move the snapshot data file out of the live environment into the corporate environment (and then into whatever back-office systems will perform the analysis). We have to be careful here that we don't compromise security by allowing just anybody to access the data. However, it is certainly more secure to require people within the corporate environment to pull snapshot data from the live environment than to open up a channel from the live environment to the corporate one. Such a channel could be exploited by anyone who manages to compromise the Internet system to gain access to the corporate environment.

Impact of the Pattern on Non-functional Characteristics

Availability	Unaffected by this pattern.
Performance	Performance is improved as we have isolated an essential but 'expensive' process from the live system.
Scalability	Unaffected by this pattern.
Security	Security is potentially negatively impacted as we create snapshots of, possibly sensitive, data. These snapshots need to be protected from anyone who should not have access to them. We also have to be careful that our export mechanism does not leave security holes that could be used to gain access to the corporate environment.
Manageability	Manageability is negatively impacted due to the introduction of new mechanisms and system access points that have to be managed.
Maintainability	Unaffected by this pattern.
Flexibility	Unaffected by this pattern.
Portability	Unaffected by this pattern.
Cost	The implementation cost really depends on the sophistication of the snapshot and export mechanisms. If we don't mind exporting the whole database in a single, unparameterized snapshot and the database product supports snapshots being taken whilst it is still running, this should be a simple and cheap mechanism to implement. If we want to be more selective about what we snapshot and how we export it, we will need to build a bespoke solution, which could be reasonably expensive to build and maintain.

Moving On

OFFLINE REPORTING provides information about the system that could be fed into the SYSTEM OVERVIEW to give us a picture of trends in using the system and how they relate to its 'health'.

SEPARATE SYSTEM-MANAGED DATA may make it easier to create the snapshots as we are only interested in data created and modified by users or as a consequence of their actions. If we store all data in the same database, we may take snapshots of the data that we own and modify, which is pointless.

If the export mechanism makes use of the public Internet, we may wish to set up SECURE CHANNELS, or even KNOWN PARTNERS, to make sure the data cannot be intercepted when it is exported. We might also want to use INFORMATION OBSCURITY to hide sensitive information held in the snapshot in case an unauthorized person gains access.

War Story

One of the authors worked on a system that used the concept of OFFLINE REPORTING in reverse. This retail system required information on products to display to the user. The product data was held on a mainframe that formed a central part of the retailer's business systems. The idea of giving the new Internet-based system access to the mainframe data was scary enough for the mainframe folks. The idea that processor time would be gobbled up for free-text searches really killed direct access to the mainframe as a possible solution very early in the design cycle.

The answer here was to extract product data on a regular basis and to load this data into a smaller database – in this case, Microsoft SQL Server. A full text index could be generated on this database as part of the import. This database formed part of the Internet system, as did the servers on which it ran. It was therefore entirely up to the creators of the Internet system to decide what sort of tradeoff between performance and money was involved when specifying the hardware to underpin this service.

Other Patterns

System performance is naturally in tension with the control of the system. There are clear examples of this in the way that many of the system performance patterns, such as LOAD-BALANCED ELEMENTS, DEDICATED WEB AND APPLICATION SERVERS and COMMON PERSISTENT STORE, gain much of their benefit by increasing the number of elements in the system which means that there are more elements to configure as part of a SYSTEM OVERVIEW and more information generated from CONTINUAL STATUS REPORTING (hence more network traffic). Similarly, the addition of security measures such as Secure Channels and Information Obscurity slow down the overall performance of those parts of the system to which they are applied. This is why you will usually apply a mixture of control and performance patterns, as the latter help to offset the negative impacts on performance of the former. The only clear place where a performance pattern reinforces a control pattern is the way that Dedicated Web and Application Servers is pretty much a prerequisite for a Demilitarized Zone.

There is also a natural tension between many system evolution patterns and performance patterns. The overheads introduced by a Virtual Platform or Dynamically-Discoverable Elements will slow down the system, so it is common to apply system performance patterns to compensate for this. Conversely, there is some degree of reinforcement as Expandable Hardware and Dynamically-Discoverable Elements complement performance patterns, such as Load-Balanced Elements, that help to improve the scalability of the system. Similarly, the application of Separate System-Managed Data can help to reduce the amount of data that has to be kept synchronized by Data Replication.

In the next chapter we will look at patterns that help to make the system more controllable.

CHAPTER

8

System Control Patterns

Dangerous (*adj.*): Speed Without Control[1]

As soon as a system enters operation, it must be under the complete control of the organization that owns it. Such control is just as important as the performance of the system – if we can't find out information about the running system and then modify the system's characteristics in response to that information, or if users can't access the functionality they require (or, worse, if they can access functionality they shouldn't be able to) then the system is out of control. At best, lack of control will limit the business value of the system. A lack of technical information, such as how much memory is available to the various processes at a particular point in time, means that we can't be confident about how stable the system is. If it starts to run low on memory, we won't know until processes start to fail or the performance of the system degrades substantially.

A lack of business-related information, such as how many users take up a particular promotion or how many orders are placed per day, impairs the ability of

---

[1] Our spurious definition is inspired by the famous racing driver Mario Andretti who is quoted as saying 'If everything seems under control, you're just not going fast enough.'

a business to make decisions about the success of the system or how it should evolve to meet customer needs.

At worst, lack of control can be dangerous. Unauthorized access to sensitive information can have all sorts of consequences – most of them bad.

As architects, our architecture needs to deliver complete control to the organization responsible for running it on a day-to-day basis. In this chapter, we will look at a number of patterns that primarily deal with enhancing the manageability and security of the system.

Terminology

When discussing complex topics, it is important to get our terminology consistent and to understand what we mean by different terms. Throughout this chapter, we discuss various issues around system management and security and we use certain terms that are open to differing interpretations – logging, reporting agent, monitoring, monitoring agent, alerting, alerting agent, firewall, hacker and cracker. If you are uncertain of any of these terms, or you think you may have a different definition from ours then please check our definition in the glossary to avoid confusion.

CONTINUAL STATUS REPORTING

While your Internet technology system is working well, everyone is happy. However, when something does go wrong, things can deteriorate very quickly. In order to fix the system, you need to know which element or elements have failed and to what degree. Once the system is running again, you need to consider measures to avoid such a failure happening again. This then leads to the question of why the element failed – was it a sudden, catastrophic failure or did the element finally collapse due to consistent over-work? If the element was overloaded you can replace it with a higher-specification element as soon as practical. Even better, if you knew that an element was becoming overloaded you could arrange for it to be replaced before it failed or even before it hit maximum capacity.

To control your system effectively you need to be armed with information at regular intervals about what each system element is doing. How do you obtain this information?

Any high-capability Internet technology system has many elements. Those elements, and the interactions between them, form a relatively complex machine that has been designed to deliver the required level of performance, scalability, availability and other non-functional characteristics. As part of this design, the system may be able to withstand the failure of any particular system element. However, such a failure will lead to higher levels of load on the remaining system elements and so may have a negative impact on their performance and hence the performance of the system as a whole. Also, a system containing the failed element no longer has the same level of availability as it would have with the element functioning. Should another element of the same type fail before the first one is replaced, your system may become unavailable for some or all of your users.

The simple answer is to replace failed elements. If you are driving a car and one of the spark-plugs fails, you will immediately notice a reduction in performance. The car will not accelerate as well as it did before, you will hear and feel that the tick-over of the engine has become uneven and you take the car in to be repaired. In the same way, the failure of an element in an Internet technology system (the 'car') may be noticed by the users (the 'drivers'). However, the user of the system is not the owner of the machine and is not responsible for fixing it. This responsibility lies with the operations team who must ensure that the system continues to perform to the required level after deployment. The operations team needs to know when an element has failed in order to replace it. It would also be very useful for them to know that certain elements are operating at, or near, capacity so that they can plan for an upgrade. In the longer term, it would be useful for them to be able to examine how the load on elements changes over time as system usage ebbs and flows.

The GlobalTech system, as evolved through application of the system performance patterns, has many elements in it. Figure 8.1 shows a simplified view of the system with the switches and load balancers omitted for ease of representation. This still leaves 11 major elements which could fail (discounting web server and data access server hardware). Failure of one of the business tier hardware servers would take out two of the application servers – doubling the load on the remaining two servers. If this happens at a time of light system load, it may not even be noticed by the users of the system. However, as load increases, the two remaining application servers (and their underlying hardware) are pushed towards maximum capacity, severely impacting performance for many system users. At this point, a crisis has arisen that could have been avoided had the operations team known as soon as the business tier server failed since it could have been repaired or replaced before a time of peak load.

When you are developing an Internet technology system, you have many means by which you can examine what is going on in the system and its elements. These mechanisms range from software debuggers that allow you to stop program execution and examine the state of a software component, to graphical system monitors to which you can refer as the system runs, and low-level techniques such as network traffic monitoring that shows data flows back and forth. All of these are valid techniques in development but they do not transfer well into the staging and live environments or even into system testing.

One obvious issue is that most of these mechanisms are very intrusive – you would not want a developer to be able to stop application execution in a debugger on the live system. Similarly, security policies pertaining to the live system may well prevent you from running a network capture utility as you would then be able to

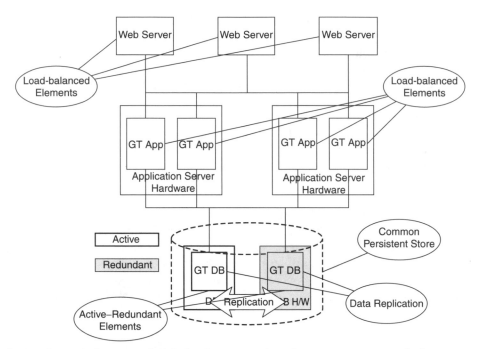

Figure 8.1 Architecture of GlobalTech system with performance patterns applied (simplified diagram).

pick up any traffic on the network, even if it was not for your application. The use of a graphical system monitor would require you to log into the target system. This may be possible in the test environment but it would remain the preserve of administrators in the live environment.

Even if you could use an interactive system monitoring tool in the live environment, it would be of limited use when tracking down transient problems as you cannot sit and watch it all the time just waiting for a problem to occur. Due to large variations in the level of use of Internet systems and the unpredictability of this usage, it is difficult to predict which system elements may be subjected to undue strain. Hence, you cannot reasonably decide to monitor just one or two elements as the main strain may be on other elements. In reality, you would not sit and watch interactive monitors to detect variations in system behaviour. Instead you would use an automated means of obtaining the status of various system elements. However, you are still faced with the same issue – namely that you cannot definitively predict which elements will be the most stressed or likely to break and hence need status monitoring. It costs time, effort and potentially money to set up status reporting for every element in the system. If most elements work normally for most of the time, you will have wasted much of that effort. The same argument holds for having system elements produce a lot of status information. Much of this information may never be required if the element works consistently and at low capacity. However, if you do not harvest enough information, you may not be able to determine the cause of failure when an element breaks. Again, setting up the reporting of more status information will usually cost more in terms of time and money. Reporting lots of information also has a negative effect on the performance of the system as a whole since the act of reporting and the hard disk and network traffic generated imposes an overhead on the system. The generation of too much information can even have a negative effect on diagnosis as the true cause may be hidden underneath a sea of detail.

To address the issue of overhead, you may have each system element record its own status information as it goes. This reduces the network traffic overhead of reporting to remote locations, but it means that the information is not easily accessible. This would work if the status information was being gathered solely for the analysis of trends, but it does not address problem detection or failure alerting applications.

Define a reporting interface or protocol for every type of system element that can seriously affect the operational health of the overall system (usually all, or nearly all, of them). Have each individual system element continuously report its status according to its type. Log some or all of the data generated so that it is available for subsequent offline analysis.

You must answer the following questions for the system:

S1. Which elements would cause the most impact in terms of availability and performance should they fail?

S2. Which elements would be a bottleneck for performance and scalability should they approach maximum capacity?

S3. Are any elements particularly unreliable?

S4. To where will elements report their status?

S5. What should be the format of the status information and how will elements transmit it?

S6. How much load (processor, memory, network traffic, etc.) will the suggested level of monitoring generate? Do you need more capacity in parts of the system to cope with this?

For each system element from which you need status reports, you also need to answer the following questions:

E1. What information do you need to know about the element?

E2. Does the element have a built-in capability for reporting its status to the required location using the required mechanism? If not, how can this be added?

E3.   What conditions or thresholds are important for this element in terms of excessive load or imminent failure?

E4.   How often should the element report its status?

Some of the answers to these questions are intertwined with each other so you may not be able to perform a traditional 'waterfall' analysis by deciding how the status reporting should work in system terms and then imposing it on the elements.

All system elements should report their status to some degree as any overload or failure should be detected and corrected over time. However, you can use the answers to questions S1, S2 and S3 to determine which elements may need to report their status either more regularly or more fully. These decisions will affect the answers to E1 and E4 for particular system elements: if an element is more critical to the operation of the system, you will want to report on it more frequently to help respond to its failure; you may also want more depth of information from it in order to precisely diagnose any problem.

The answers to questions E1 and E4 deserve special attention. In an ideal world, all system elements would send status information to the processing location as frequently and fully as possible. However, the act of notification will take up resources such as network bandwidth and memory/processor capacity on the device notifying its status. Hence, a compromise must be made so that different parts of the system report different amounts of information at different rates depending on how critical they are to the system.

The amount of information you want from an element (question E1) may be far less than it is capable of reporting. The types of information generated by system elements can be broadly classified as follows:

- Status information: the element is running correctly; the network card is running at 100 Mbps; all disks in the RAID array are working OK.
- Usage information: the number of concurrent user requests; the level of memory usage; the amount of data passed through a network interface.
- Execution information: the user thread has entered a particular method on a software component; an HTTP connection has been made to the web server; an SSL connection has been established with the content switch.

In each case, a reporting agent must be used to generate and propagate the information. The reporting agent could form part of the system element on which it is reporting, for example the web log generated by a web server or a reporting module embedded in a network switch. In the absence of a built-in reporting agent, you can introduce a reporting agent that is a separate software entity. This will poll the status or usage of a system element and generate appropriate logging information.

For example, a dedicated network router will have dozens of system parameters that can be reported, but you will most likely be interested in at most a dozen of them (the 'liveness' of each network interface, the number of packets passed through each network interface, the number of bad packets dropped, etc.). You will want the most status information from the most complex elements in the system – particularly custom-built software components – as these will have more complex failure modes that need to be detected and corrected.

Question E4 asks how frequently each element should report its status. The main factor that will affect the frequency of reporting is the use to which the information is put. If the information is required for operational monitoring so that problems can be detected and system elements repaired or replaced in real time then the system element must report its status fairly frequently. If the information is only gathered to plot historical trends, it can be reported less frequently. The frequency of reporting is discussed in the related patterns that build upon CONTINUAL STATUS REPORTING, notably OPERATIONAL MONITORING AND ALERTING and 3-CATEGORY LOGGING.

Given the amount of status information required and the frequency with which it is needed, questions S4 and S5 ask how it is represented and transmitted. The reporting agent will usually be responsible for propagating the element information to a monitoring agent. This propagation will usually be across a standard reporting protocol such as SNMP or CMIP (see Box 8.1). Almost all network-aware hardware devices (and many software systems) are able to report their status using SNMP or CMIP (or both). A quick examination of the elements in your system (asking question E2) should determine which is the better option based on its level of support. The reporting agent may push the information to the monitoring agent or the monitoring agent may pull the information from the reporting agent.

Where the reporting agent for a system element doesn't support a standardized protocol 'out of the box', it isn't necessary to implement it from scratch. Take the example of a web server generating HTTP log information into a file. A common technique is to implement an adaptor (often called a 'log-scraper') that extracts relevant information from the web log and creates status information from it. For simplicity, this element usually acts as a monitoring agent for the values it extracts but it can also pass the values on to a dedicated monitoring agent across a common reporting protocol.

Another possibility is to introduce or implement a general reporting agent for a system element that reports on the use of the element's resources such as memory, processor and disk space. Whilst this doesn't give as sophisticated a picture as having the system element report its own status, it may be sufficient for reporting failures or bottlenecks.

The final question to address is S6 – if you are loading the system more, in order to generate, transmit and process status information, can you afford to upgrade the affected system elements to reduce the negative impact on system performance? The processing is usually less of an issue as this will usually take place on a machine that is specifically tasked with monitoring and control of the system. On the other hand,

BOX 8.1 | SNMP and system control

Simple Network Management Protocol (SNMP) is the *de facto* standard for the monitoring and management of networks, servers and software applications. If you are looking to implement OPERATIONAL MONITORING AND ALERTING, SNMP is usually a good place to start. Almost every piece of hardware you buy has the built-in capability to provide SNMP information, but what is that information?

Basically, SNMP works by defining a management information base (MIB). You can think of the MIB as a large tree root system similar to a file system. Each node in the MIB is either a container (similar to a directory) or a leaf node (similar to a file). A leaf node represents some information about a particular device, such as the number of Ethernet frames sent by a network card. The container it resides in represents the hardware device it belongs to (in this case the network card) or a subset of that device's information. Software can be written to access the SNMP information that a device maintains and so retrieve the values associated with that device. Each piece of information can be accessed by a delimited name, for example the system name of a network host would be accessed through the name `iso.org.dod.internet.mgmt.mib-2.system.sysName` (just like a file on a file system but with a '.' as the delimiter). Each part of the name also has a numeric representation to make it easier to present to a machine, so the previous example would be equivalent to `1.3.6.1.2.1.1`. The value associated with an SNMP name can be a number, a string or one of several other formats. In the case of the system name, it is a string of up to 255 characters.

The software that accesses the SNMP data is usually a management console that is tasked with providing a SYSTEM OVERVIEW. This management console may obtain the information synchronously, by getting the values when required, or asynchronously, by listening for broadcast messages known as SNMP traps. Traps are generated when something happens that the management software should know about, such as a network card failing. The host operating system can be configured to generate an SNMP trap for this event that can be picked up and handled by the management console. SNMP also allows management software to write certain values as well as read them, so providing remote control for devices and software.

One obvious concern about the ability to read and write SNMP values is the potential misuse of this information. SNMP has a security model that allows an administrator to define particular communities with associated credentials. Any management software that wants to read or change information for a particular device must be able to provide appropriate credentials for the community in which the device resides.

There are other similar sources of management information in addition to SNMP. You may also encounter the Common Management Information Protocol (CMIP) and Web Based Enterprise Management (WBEM). Microsoft's Windows Management Instrumentation (WMI) is an implementation of WBEM that works on the Common Information Model (CIM), which is the equivalent of SNMP's MIB. Most management consoles will be able to manage devices and software that conform to either SNMP or WBEM. As an application writer, you can generate and consume SNMP or WBEM information and allow your software to be controlled from an appropriate management console.

there is no getting away from the need for the system element itself to generate status information and for it to be transmitted across the network.

The application of CONTINUAL STATUS REPORTING generates raw data on which higher-level functionality can be based. In OPERATIONAL MONITORING AND ALERTING, this information is used to determine when remedial action is required to address failures or overload in the system. The amount of information generated usually requires the application of the SYSTEM OVERVIEW pattern to make it manageable.

The GlobalTech support site has various system elements that must allow the operations team to monitor their health. These include:

- The routers that connect the demilitarized zone (DMZ) to the outside world.
- The firewall between the DMZ and the internal network.
- The network switches on the DMZ and the internal network.
- The hardware servers that house the web servers.
- The business tier servers called by the web servers.
- The database housing the support knowledge base.

All of these system elements should report their current state of health to some degree. In the GlobalTech system, we add status reporting capability to the important types of system element as follows:

- The web servers have the ability to continuously write their status to log files. A simple log-scraping program is run every 30 seconds to extract the number of user requests served, whether the request was for a dynamic page or a binary asset, and the time to serve each request. The log-scraping program makes this information available across SNMP.
- The application servers have a built-in SNMP interface. With a small modification to the application software we can ensure the servers report the number of requests for dynamic pages, the average time to serve each request, and the number of concurrent user sessions. We also report individual requests that take more than 30 seconds to serve, including detailed information on the request and the related session state information.
- The database server has a proprietary monitoring client used by the database administrator. We write a small proxy that intercepts information coming out of the database and extracts the high-level information about the number of queries run and the average time to return the result set.
- The switches and routers all support SNMP for indicating they are still alive.
- We run the 'top' command on every hardware server to monitor the server processes, reporting the CPU time and memory used by each process – this covers the load balancers as well as the other types of software server.

All of this information can be processed as part of OPERATIONAL MONITORING AND ALERTING.

Impact of the Pattern on Non-functional Characteristics

Availability	Availability is potentially improved as the generated information can be used to identify and predict element failure or overload.
Performance	Performance is negatively impacted because of the overhead of the continuous reporting.
Scalability	Unaffected by this pattern.
Security	There is potentially a negative impact on security as extended system information is available to any intruder who has the capability of monitoring network traffic.
Manageability	Manageability is improved because up-to-date information about each element's condition is continuously available.
Maintainability	Maintainability is potentially improved because management information can sometimes be useful in diagnosing a fault or problem. For example, requests for dynamic pages failing when the data access servers take more than 30 seconds to pass back the result set may indicate a pre-defined time-out in the database drivers used by the application servers.
Flexibility	Unaffected by this pattern.
Portability	Unaffected by this pattern.
Cost	The cost of introducing continuous reporting for every type of system element is always going to be significant whether the element supports reporting out of the box or not. This cost is justified because continuous status reporting is at the heart of a controllable system.

Moving On

Once the system elements are generating information about their health, we should use this information to help us maintain the system both reactively and proactively. The OPERATIONAL MONITORING AND ALERTING pattern addresses the use of CONTINUAL STATUS REPORTING to warn the operations team of impending problems whereas the SYSTEM OVERVIEW pattern tackles the reduction of the huge volume of status data into a picture of system health. The 3-CATEGORY LOGGING pattern provides a different type of information about the system's operation, focusing on the operations it is carrying out rather than its status.

OPERATIONAL MONITORING AND ALERTING

The load on public Internet technology systems is unpredictable and can vary based on some quite unexpected factors. When you architect the system, you will base the initial configuration on certain levels of use and you will factor in extra capacity to allow for the expected increases in load over the first 6 to 12 months of the life of the system. However, public Internet technology systems are quite complex, as is the environment in which they operate. Subtle changes in the way that the system is used can bring higher than anticipated levels of pressure to bear on particular system elements. Some system elements may fail (whether under load or not), negatively impacting the characteristics of the system. The system can generate a sea of data in which short- and long-term trends can be identified, but for a large-scale system navigating this sea presents a challenge. The operations team must be able to quickly identify the source of any problems that are building in the system in order to address them.

War Story

One of the authors was part of a project to build a new version of the web site for a well-known e-commerce dotcom (one that is still around today!). The go-live for the new system was scheduled for late Friday night as the weekend was one of their quietest times. On the Sunday evening, the system had been up and running for the whole weekend and was coping well with its load, a mixture of real users and simulated users; the simulation designed to reproduce the conditions of peak load. The system was coping reasonably well as the load climbed to 3500 simultaneous users – pretty much the maximum the system ever had to cope with. The load remained at around 3500 users for around an hour and then suddenly, at about 7.30 pm, the load started to increase massively – hitting 5000 in a matter of a couple of minutes (when the system really started to struggle). The team rapidly shut down all the simulated users but the load still grew, forcing the team to take the drastic measure of killing off a number of live user sessions and setting a maximum session limit of 4000. Once this limit was in place, the system started to recover. Emergency over, the team noticed that the technical room, which had been full of senior managers and board members watching the go-live, was now almost empty. Looking for someone to explain the situation to, the author wandered into the 'chill-out room'. There, all the managers and board members, plus many of the technical team, were watching a BBC documentary about the dotcom company and its rise to prominence ('Look, there you are on the table football'). Unfortunately, no-one had thought that such a high-profile television programme might actually make viewers think to go and visit the site just as we were running our load test.

How do we make it possible for human operators to spot potential problems in the large volume of information generated by status reporting from a complex or high-volume Internet-technology system?

A high-capability Internet technology system will consist of dozens of individual system elements such as web servers, application servers, database servers and network switches. The failure or saturation of any one of these system elements will negatively impact the non-functional characteristics of the system such as performance and scalability. To improve availability we often introduce duplicate elements, either as active–redundant pairs or as a load-balanced set.

Applying CONTINUAL STATUS REPORTING to the system will deliver the data required to spot unexpected load changes and element failures. The amount of information reported will increase as the number of elements in the system increases and the level of system use increases.

The architecture we have evolved ensures high levels of availability and scalability for the GlobalTech system. Load-balancing and replication are used to ensure that we can maintain availability in the face of the failure of an individual element. However, when an element fails, the non-functional characteristics will be negatively impacted.

For example, if one of the web servers fails, then the remaining web servers will continue to process the entire user load. However, the system will have a much reduced level of availability and performance will also worsen, as higher levels of user load were intended to be shared between three web servers. At peak times this may cause problems for GlobalTech as customers may be unable to access the support pages and will go back to using the phone support lines. Savings on telephone support is one of the major financial gains accruing from the implementation of the system. If the web users are thrown back onto the call centre, it will degrade the performance of the phone support system for the non-web users (making them unhappy). Additionally, the web users will be doubly unhappy to find that not only does the support web site not work, but they are currently 27th in a queue to talk to a GlobalTech support agent. Such failures in the system must be detected as soon as possible – long before the manager of the GlobalTech call centre phones the data centre asking what is going on with the web site. If the system operations team becomes aware of the failure of the web server, the failed element can be restarted, repaired or replaced to restore system capacity to the required level and the undesirable scenario can be avoided.

The example brings us back to the ability of the system operations team to successfully detect and address any problems in the system. However, the system will generate a lot of data. In Figure 8.1, there would be around 20 system elements reporting their status. In an ideal world, you could employ 20 operations staff round the clock to monitor the status of these elements. This is clearly impractical on grounds of cost and manageability. However, there are many parameters that can indicate immediate or potential problems in a system, and a large amount of generated data becomes increasingly difficult for a limited system operations team to process manually in a timely fashion (i.e. soon enough to avert system failure).

To help balance the amount of information generated with the number of operations staff available, we could restrict the number of system elements we monitor. But, in the type of architecture we are evolving, every element has a vital role to play and, consequently, can significantly affect the overall health of the system if it fails or is subject to excessive load. Cutting back on the number of elements monitored may cause a problem to go unnoticed until the point at which it has a critical impact on the running of the system (for example, if both web tier load balancers fail at the same time because we did not spot that the first one failed yesterday). We could also restrict the amount of information generated by the system elements. Again, this would make it easier to spot problems as there is less data to examine. However, although the limited set of data may indicate that there is a problem it may not give sufficient clues for the operations team to figure out what the nature of the problem is and so they may be unable to fix it until it becomes catastrophic.

To reduce the amount of network traffic and the amount of information to be processed, we could have system elements store their status information. This information could be analysed off-line or at set intervals which would make it easier to balance the workload of the operations team and so fewer team members might be needed. However, such intermittent monitoring does not give us the ability to react immediately to changes in use that might threaten the health of the system. This immediate response is important as system performance problems associated with the failure or saturation of system elements can have a direct cost implication in lost revenue, lost customers and lost reputation. The cost associated with implementing and maintaining any system monitoring solution must be balanced against these potential downside costs.

Use CONTINUAL STATUS REPORTING **to report the status of all system elements at an appropriate frequency. Implement an automated,** OPERATIONAL MONITORING AND ALERTING **process that watches for indicators of a failing system and warns the system operations team – allowing them to take preventative action if possible.**

Each system element should report health and usage information using an appropriate reporting agent following the CONTINUAL STATUS REPORTING pattern. Typically, the sort of information that should be reported includes:

- Whether the element is operating normally or malfunctioning.
- If the element is operating normally, an indication of the use of any limited resources (memory, processor, disk space, connections, etc.).

- The number of 'requests' (or 'transactions') handled in each reporting interval.

What constitutes a 'request' varies between system element types – for a network switch it is an HTTP request that needs routing, for a web server it is a request for a dynamic page to be assembled or for a static content page to be delivered.

The reporting agent must make the information available to an appropriate monitoring agent. This is commonly done over a standard protocol such as SNMP (as described in the CONTINUAL STATUS REPORTING pattern). Where a type of system element doesn't support a standardized protocol 'out of the box', it isn't necessary to implement it from scratch. A common technique for monitoring an element that supports simple, file-based logging is to implement a 'log-scraper' that extracts relevant information from a log and converts it into status information. For simplicity, this element usually monitors the values it extracts but it can also pass the values on to a dedicated monitoring agent.

One of the major considerations in implementing OPERATIONAL MONITORING AND ALERTING is to ensure that the implementation of CONTINUAL STATUS REPORTING for each system element produces information in the timeframe required for the monitoring and alerting to be effective. There are various considerations here:

- Rate of system state change. There is no point in reporting information more frequently than the state of a particular system element changes or is likely to change.

- Resolution mechanism. Given that the point of this pattern is to notify operations staff in time for them to apply remedial action, the rate of status reporting is related to the amount of time it takes to implement the remedial action. For example, if the remedial action involves sourcing and configuring a new server (which would take days) then there is no point in reporting the triggering status every 15 seconds.

- Impact of reporting on performance. Report information too frequently and performance will be affected by the amount of time spent monitoring and processing the information and the volume of information present in the network.

- Failure window. Report information too infrequently and serious problems could arise between reporting intervals. You can ask how long the system could reasonably survive if a particular system element fails. For example, if there is a single router to the outside world, it should be reporting its status every 30 seconds as any capacity issues or downtime will directly affect the user perception of the system. On the other hand, the status of one presentation tier server out of 20 will be less of an issue. This server could be down for five minutes without anyone really noticing. Hence you could have the presentation tier servers notify their status every four or five minutes.

What constitutes the right frequency really depends on the individual system and system element being considered.

The two principal issues addressed by OPERATIONAL MONITORING AND ALERTING are failure and saturation of system elements. In the case of failure, things are fairly black-and-white but this is not the case for saturation. If an individual element is subject to excessive load then this should be notified to the monitoring agent. If this excessive load is intermittent then the interval at which status is reported should be set to capture this saturation point so that it does not go unmissed. When system elements are deployed as LOAD-BALANCED ELEMENTS, the important monitoring metrics are not necessarily the status of an individual system element in the set, but of the set as a whole. As an example, consider the presentation tier hardware servers and the web servers that they house. The operations team will want to keep an eye on the aggregated loading across the whole set of servers. Once this reaches a consistent 60–70% it is time to warm up any extra capacity they may have in hand.

To apply OPERATIONAL MONITORING AND ALERTING to the GlobalTech system, we implement a monitoring and alerting system based on a system management application. Aspects of this implementation include:

- The reporting agents on each of the web servers will report user load and the time to serve each request. These are delivered to the system management application which will generate an alert should user load or response time exceed pre-defined thresholds for a sustained period.

- SNMP messages from the application servers are sent to the system management application. These messages are monitored for unexpected increases in the level of load, the amount of time to process a request and the number of concurrent users. Sustained increases of this type will generate an alert.

- Database information about the number of queries run and the average time to return the result set is sent to the system management application, which will generate an alert should these values exceed pre-defined thresholds for a sustained period.

- SNMP messages indicating normal operation are generated by all switches, routers, network cards, operating systems, application servers, databases, and web servers in the system and delivered to the management application. If such messages cease for a particular element, a critical alert is generated in the form of pager messages to members of the system operations team currently on duty (or on call). Any running instance of the graphical management console will display a dialog box requesting immediate action.

The alerts from the web servers, application servers and database will take the form of an email sent to the operations team and notification of a possible error on any running instance of the graphical management console.

The same system management application usually also provides the higher-level logical representation of the system described in the SYSTEM OVERVIEW pattern.

Impact of the Pattern on Non-functional Characteristics

Availability	The alerts can help the operations team prevent the system from becoming partially or wholly unavailable.
Performance	Performance is negatively impacted because a reasonably high level of continuous reporting is required on some system elements to support the required level of monitoring.
Scalability	Unaffected by this pattern.
Security	Unaffected by this pattern.
Manageability	Manageability is improved as there is no need to manually monitor the system.
Maintainability	Unaffected by this pattern.
Flexibility	Unaffected by this pattern.
Portability	Unaffected by this pattern.
Cost	Cost is increased, regardless of whether a specific management application is purchased or custom solutions are built. This cost is justified as it makes the system manageable for less money than employing many operations people.

Moving On

This pattern is usually implemented in combination with other monitoring patterns to provide a suite of information for different audiences. It uses some of the same high-level (usage and 'dead or alive') information from each system element as the SYSTEM OVERVIEW pattern. However, the timescales in OPERATIONAL MONITORING AND ALERTING are far more immediate. Another part of the system monitoring jigsaw is 3-CATEGORY LOGGING. This should be implemented alongside OPERATIONAL MONITORING AND ALERTING as 3-CATEGORY LOGGING provides background to the logical actions the system was performing at the point of any element failure.

There is little point in knowing of the impending doom of the system unless you can do something about it. Implementing DYNAMICALLY-ADJUSTABLE CONFIGURATION for major system elements and their parameters means that runtime information can be acted upon without the need for major maintenance.

3-Category Logging

The complexity of large-scale Internet technology systems and the pressure to keep the system running can easily lead to 'superstitious' techniques of system support. The problems that occur in the system can range from queues of discarded user sessions that are not cleaned up through to a critical system halt. In both cases, the symptoms can be noted and tracked, but the 'cure' is frequently simplistic – 'reboot the server and the problem goes away'.[2] As long as rebooting the server doesn't cause too much pain (which may well be the case for a load-balanced server) then this 'cure' just becomes a part of standard operations. The root of this phenomenon is that the team observing the problems does not have enough information to make an accurate diagnosis and so cannot identify and cure the real, underlying problem.

If the system fails, or performance degrades, how do we know what the various elements in the system were actually doing at the time?

Any Internet-technology system will be subject to full or partial failure at some point in its lifetime. During development, individual software components will be subjected to unit tests and the system as a whole will be subjected to integration testing. However, no amount of testing can ever guarantee that nothing will go wrong in production as it is impractical to test all possible interactions with a system. Even if you create an exhaustive suite of tests, they will usually be targeted at the expected use of the system and not any off-the-wall use that users may put the system to. An even more important factor for unpredicted events is the physical and platform environment on which the application is deployed. In the case of e-commerce systems, the production environment will usually consist of a set of powerful servers that cost a lot of money. Because of this, there is little chance that the testing and staging environments will precisely mirror the type and amount of hardware and software deployed in production. This means that there are potential race conditions and resource contention lurking in the production environment that will not occur in staging.

We need to determine the cause of failure so that we can take actions to prevent it. To diagnose any failure, information is needed about what the various system elements were doing at the time. In a multi-tiered, web-based environment, it is particularly tricky to trace a single path of execution from the initial HTTP request through to the back-end database access. There are many hardware and software components involved in satisfying such a request, any of which could be the source of the problem.

---

[2] One of the authors was recently on one of the much-vaunted 'next generation' passenger trains in the UK. It was late leaving the station and it was obvious from the actions of the staff onboard that there was a problem with the train. After a period of intense activity, the driver announced that all the lights and air conditioning were about to go off as they couldn't work out what was wrong and so had decided to 'reboot the train'.

The GlobalTech system uses CONTINUAL STATUS REPORTING to give an up-to-date picture of its health. OPERATIONAL MONITORING AND ALERTING will highlight the failure of system elements and any excessive load. However, if an application server goes down when it isn't under excessive load or resource-constrained we will have no idea what else might have caused the failure. Even if the application server was under excessive load when it failed, it is easy to jump to conclusions about why the failure occurred.

Any system that implements OPERATIONAL MONITORING AND ALERTING provides a lot of information about the system's health during normal execution. However, when a system element fails, the type of information reported as element status ('liveness', level of load, etc.) is of limited use in diagnosing the problem that caused the failure. We need to see what the system element was doing when the failure occurred in order to re-trace the sequence of events or activities that may have contributed to the failure. We may also need to know what other system elements were doing if the failed element was interacting with them at the time of its failure.

So, the simple solution is to generate a lot of diagnostic information. If all the system elements continually produce diagnostics indicating their current execution status we could successfully debug most hardware or software problems fairly quickly. However, the generation of diagnostic information decreases the performance of the system element and hence of the system as a whole. You could limit the diagnostic information generated if you knew what type of failure was anticipated. However, you do not know beforehand precisely what information may be needed.

You are faced with a similar problem in terms of deciding which system elements should be recording diagnostic information. You cannot know beforehand which elements of the system will fail, but recording diagnostic information for all elements in the system will take up a prohibitively large amount of storage space.

Implement a mechanism to log information about system events and system execution. This mechanism should log three categories of data:

- **debug – usually execution-trace information such as which methods have been called on a software component and with what parameters**
- **information – simple warnings about the system condition such as timeouts, missing data or uncommon code flows**
- **error – things that go very wrong such as failure to connect to a database or loss of connection between web server and load balancer**

The primary implementation of 3-CATEGORY LOGGING in the GlobalTech system is in the GlobalTech Application. As part of the software development process we introduce a logging convention in all software components, whether running in an application server or a web server. Every exception unexpectedly caught is logged as an error, as are unmet pre-conditions and post-conditions, and every method has a debug logging statement at the beginning that indicates the method called and the parameter values it was called with. Informational messages are reserved for known system events (such as scheduled processes or incoming messages).

For each category of log we implement three levels of logging (see Box 8.2): mild, moderate and severe. These levels control which information is written to the logs and in how much detail (for example, an exception that results in a server error will cause all of the stack trace to be written; a mild error will just log a summary of the exception).

The logs are implemented using a rolling archive system. Each log writes to a file for a period of time (we choose 24 hours for GlobalTech) before opening a new file and writing to that instead. We set a limit on the number of files that the system opens before it deletes existing files and replaces them. For GlobalTech we specify that no more than seven log files can exist at a time for each category of log, so we always have logs for the previous week of operation. If we wish to save a log for analysis we can use the OFFLINE REPORTING export mechanism to move it out of the production environment.

Because log files can happily chew away at disk space (which, in extreme cases, can fill up the disk space and cause the application to fail) we also use the status reporting mechanism to periodically report the use of disk space by the logs and set an alert level to warn us if the log files exceed a certain size.

To support the logging in the software components, the web server logging functionality is turned on. This gives a list of HTTP requests received and responses passed back that can be interwoven with the software component logs to try to determine which client call generated the error.

We also want database access logging as part of the overall solution, so we treat the database like a black box (the internal workings of the database are not our concern) and simply turn on its default error logging.

War Story

One of the authors worked on a project that encountered a problem with a set of integration servers that were configured as LOAD-BALANCED ELEMENTS. These integration servers were shared between projects and so they had a variety of software components installed on them. Intermittently the processor usage on one of the servers (not always the same one) would rise to 100% and stay there. The short-term solution was to re-start the server. This had no real negative impact on other applications using the server as it was effectively suffering a denial of service attack since it had almost no processor time available. Fortunately, the software components implemented a form of 3-CATEGORY LOGGING and the logging information gave a clue to the location of the problem. Consequently, logging around that component was increased until the problem occurred again. At that point, the project team had enough information to deduce that there was a bug in the database driver being used.

BOX 8.2 Categories and levels of logging

It is important to differentiate the categories of information logged at different times and in different environments:

- Error messages are generated when part of a system breaks. It could be that a network card has become disabled or, commonly, that a piece of software has behaved unexpectedly. Error messages are usually logged to a persistent store, such as a system log, database or management console. Error messages are generated in all environments – development, test and production.

- Debug messages tell the application developers something about the application at a particular instant in time, for example a debug message may state that a particular presentation tier client has called a remote method on one of the application servers. Each remote method could contain logging calls that would indicate when the method was called, its important parameter values, and when the method was exited. By correlating a set of debug messages with an error message, it is possible to identify what the system was doing when an error occurred. Obviously, messages of this type will generate a lot of log information, so this type of message is generally enabled in development but not in production environments. Some systems will refer to debug messages as *tracing*.

- Informational messages inform the reader of a particular occurrence in the system. An informational message does not usually represent an error. Indeed, it may form part of a positive log that provides an audit trail. As an example, if an interaction is performed with an external system, such as sending an XML document, it may be useful to keep a

log of the document identifier for later correlation.

These categories of information should not be confused with levels of information. Some logging systems don't make this distinction and assign a 'severity' level to the three categories, with error being the most severe and informational being the least. However, not all errors are severe and not all informational messages can be overlooked – they are each important to different people at different times in the system's lifecycle and operation.

When a system is in its normal state we probably want it to log most errors and any important informational messages (such as a successful import of the catalogue data or run of the personalization mailing for the GlobalTech system). However, we may want to ignore 'regular' errors, for example if we have a somewhat unreliable data feed that supplies non-critical information – errors that report the connection has been broken are not all that interesting as we expect them to happen as part of the normal operation of the system.

When we release a new part of the system, or are experiencing problems with an existing part, we probably want to look at all levels of debug information. During normal operation, however, we are probably not that interested in debug messages. We don't want to run the risk of 'over-logging', meaning we write out so much information that we quickly run out of space in which to store our logs. This will require us either to buy and install more storage or to overwrite old logs more frequently. Sometimes this may mean that you get rid of information you might otherwise find useful.

The point is that we often need to control the level of logging in each of the three categories of information, but these categories are not themselves levels. They are required at different times by different people and should be treated independently.

Impact of the Pattern on Non-functional Characteristics

Availability	Unaffected by this pattern.
Performance	Performance is negatively impacted because the logging mechanism introduces a processing overhead.
Scalability	Unaffected by this pattern.
Security	Unaffected by this pattern.
Manageability	Manageability is improved because the logged information can also be used by system managers to monitor system execution.
Maintainability	Maintainability is improved as the logging gives support and development engineers the information they need to track errors in the system or trace its execution.
Flexibility	Unaffected by this pattern.
Portability	Unaffected by this pattern.
Cost	Cost is increased as it will take time and effort to add and configure the logging for different system elements. This cost can be hard to quantify – it is fairly simple to implement a logging mechanism but a lot harder to ensure that all developers write their code to use it in the correct way. However this cost can be very quickly recouped as less time is spent on troubleshooting during the time the system is in production.

Moving On

It is almost guaranteed that the various system elements will log their information to different locations. You may see this as a benefit – error messages go to one place and debug messages go to another – but it can also be a problem to stitch together multiple sources of information to create a coherent picture of what the system was doing when a failure occurred and what sequence of cross-element events occurred in the run up to the failure. We need to apply the SYSTEM OVERVIEW pattern to generate a picture of what the whole system is doing at a particular time.

We will often want to change the categories of information being logged and the level of logging for those categories at runtime, perhaps in response to a change in the health of the system noted by the OPERATIONAL MONITORING AND ALERTING. We can use a DYNAMICALLY-ADJUSTABLE CONFIGURATION to alter the logging as and when we need to.

SYSTEM OVERVIEW

The operations team is having one of those meetings that nobody likes. The team manager has to explain to the board why the online system went down unexpectedly and so they need answers. Forensically, they have untangled the sequence of events. At 8.15 pm PST, one application server crashed due to a bug and the rest went down like dominoes. When the first application server went down, the loading on the other application servers immediately hit 100%, which gradually made each one less and less effective. The load balancer had worked very well – it overloaded the systems equally. Despite all of the system status information being generated, nobody knew that all of the application servers were running at around 85% of capacity (90% was the alerting threshold). As the generation of the usage figures involved a complex manual process (copying files and examining their contents), they are only checked retrospectively at the end of each week. At the end of last week when this figure was checked, the application server capacity figure was down at 60%. However, this week there had been a promotion in 40 countries for services available through the online site.

With a large number of system elements, each generating information, how do we assess the whole system's current health or identify long-term trends?

An Internet-technology system is rarely used exactly as predicted at its inception. The number of customers may be higher or lower than predicted and the profile of use may differ. As the load increases, either at peak times or at a steadily rising average level over a period of months, some system elements may approach their capacity. Even though the system has implemented OPERATIONAL MONITORING AND ALERTING on top of CONTINUAL STATUS REPORTING, this level of load may not necessarily be sufficient to trigger an alert. By the time it does trigger an alert, the level of load may be critical.

The picture is complicated as the system functionality is distributed across many system elements. Many elements are duplicated to improve availability. Each of these elements reports its status individually. However, there is a need to understand the overall picture. The information delivered to you may tell you that web server A is running at 80% capacity, from which you might assume that it needs an upgrade or that an additional web server host must be added. However, if web servers B and C are lightly loaded (which could be the case depending on the algorithm used by the load balancer) then the overall loading may still be well within limits. Conversely, customer patterns may point to the need for more capacity. If there are regular monthly peaks in system usage (caused, for example, by a regular 'end of month sale') then these peaks may steadily grow over time. If they grow at 10% every month you can predict when the peak is likely to exceed capacity. However, to make such judgements, you need historical usage data from which to extrapolate increasing (or decreasing) load.

The picture is further complicated since there is usually a need to reduce capacity (or decrease a particular non-functional quality such as availability) in order to upgrade a part of the system (e.g. you take a context switch out of service to add another blade to it, which leaves a single switch to take all of the load). Whether it is for upgrade or for routine maintenance, suitable times must be identified when such outages will cause least impact.

Finally, there is a huge amount of data generated by any non-trivial system. This must be turned into something understandable by the human operations team. This information can be generated by CONTINUAL STATUS REPORTING or as part of 3-CATEGORY LOGGING.

The GlobalTech system has implemented CONTINUAL STATUS REPORTING to generate system status information for its web servers, application servers, data access servers, load balancers, network switches and routers. This is used as the basis for OPERATIONAL MONITORING AND ALERTING that will generate an alert when there is a problem with the health of the system. The implementation of 3-CATEGORY LOGGING is such that individual events, such as software exceptions or blocked network packets, are logged either to individual system logs or to one of two central system log locations. System execution information is logged on individual file systems.

With all system elements in operation we have 26 streams of status data:

- three web servers, both software and hardware (six elements in total)
- four application server software instances running on two hardware servers (six elements in total)
- two database servers, both software and hardware (four elements in total)
- two load balancers for each tier of servers, web and application (four elements in total)
- two network switches for each segment (four elements in total)
- two routers where the external pipe comes into GlobalTech (two elements in total)

Each of these elements is reporting data on between four and 20 measurable characteristics.

The web servers record every client HTTP request in their web logs. Each hit will cause a record of somewhere in the region of 80 bytes to be created. Given the initial requirement of 2500 concurrent users (2000 consumer and 500 retailer), even if each user only views one page every 5 minutes, and every page only has 4 'extra' items (such as gif files) on it, this results in 6 million (5*20*24*2500) individual HTTP requests across the web server farm per day. These hits would generate 48 MB of logs per day distributed across multiple physical servers.

This 48 MB of logs would form part of the information recorded each day. There are two system log instances, three web servers, four application servers and two data access servers all recording information to their respective file systems (11 file systems with at least one and probably three to six log files). Bear in mind that these figures represent the average load at the start, not the peak load as the number of users ramps up over time.

All of this information is useful and is generated, processed and stored for the stated purposes. However, although this information is processed, for example to generate an alert if it exceeds a given value, it is not easily available for quick review ('at a glance') in times of system emergency. On the other hand, such a large sea of data makes it difficult to determine any long-term trends or patterns of behaviour that are affecting the system. All of the purposes to which it is turned are reactive rather than proactive. We need a view of the system's overall health that is consolidated across multiple element instances or across time, or both.

To make monitoring easier, we would like to standardize the monitoring of the system as much as possible. If all system elements are generating data in the same format then it is far easier to provide a view across this data. However, each system element may generate its own set of information and this may be delivered by a different mechanism than that used by other system elements. We must ensure that appropriate tools are used to gather the different types of information required.

Almost all of the status, event and execution information generated by the system is useful for long-term reporting as well as for operational response. Such long term reports are needed to help predict how the system may need to evolve over time. We want to be able to examine long-term trends in the system's health, but the sheer volume of data produced makes this a difficult data-mining job. There needs to be a structured and consistent way of representing this information so that it can be usefully viewed and interpreted by operations staff and management.

Provide a mechanism to aggregate the monitoring and logging information generated by CONTINUAL STATUS REPORTING and 3-CATEGORY LOGGING. Merge the information and abstract from it to give an overview of the system.

The overall result of SYSTEM OVERVIEW is to provide simplified status information (as generated by CONTINUAL STATUS REPORTING) for groups or combinations of system elements. The individual reporting agents will report their information into a central location. At this point you will be able to pick up the information, categorize it, filter it and then represent it to the user. The complexity of the implementation therefore depends on:

- The granularity of the system elements to be monitored.
- The amount of information from each element to be aggregated.
- The view of the information.

In theory, the granularity of the elements to be monitored could be anything coarser than 'all of the individual elements in the system'. In reality, the effectiveness of SYSTEM OVERVIEW relies on cutting down the amount of information to something that can be taken in 'at a glance', or at least over a coffee. For the sort of Internet technology system we are considering, you may well have one representation for each of the following:

- All the web servers
- All the application servers
- The servers in the database cluster
- The support infrastructure (routers, switches, etc.)
- Important external gateways

The level of information about each of these groups of system elements is the next thing to decide on. It could be as simple as a single flag indicating current status. The status could be *okay* (no monitoring limits have been exceeded); *risk* (one or more monitoring limits are close to being exceeded); and *broken* (one or more monitoring limits have been exceeded). The value of this flag is based on the current information from each of these groups of elements. This means that for each element being considered (and each of its sub-elements) you will have to determine what status values correspond to the different levels. You can then set these as trigger levels so that exceeding the threshold will cause the overall status to change.

In addition to the overall status, certain key indicators could be extracted and used as part of the SYSTEM OVERVIEW. This could be loading factors on the application servers, number of customer sessions, or whatever seems to make sense to the operations team.

The final part is to present the information to the operations team. This could be as simple as an email issued on a regular basis (once a day, at the start of a shift, hourly). Alternatively, if you have a management console, you could use its event correlation services to merge and display the data arriving. For example, you may use the GlancePlus service of HP OpenView to map the data into a user interface showing the system elements and their current status.

You can apply SYSTEM OVERVIEW to status data and to log data generated by 3-CATEGORY LOGGING. As an example, take the log data generated by the web servers. This information is useful in several ways, the first of which is for problem identification and resolution. There could be repeated 404 (page not found) errors reported by the web servers which need to be identified and fixed. A log-scraper can easily identify these records and extract data on them. You will probably want different overviews to help provide quick clues to the source of any problem:

- The number of 404 errors for a particular resource across all web servers (for example a particular image). This would highlight a configuration problem with the application such as a missing resource or broken hyperlink. Such a configuration problem is likely to be across the application as a whole as opposed to a single server.

■ The number of 404 errors for each web server, regardless of which resource was being requested. If one server has far more errors than the others it may point to a fault on that particular server. Obviously, this figure must be normalized based on traffic (if one server handles more traffic it will potentially generate more errors on a pro-rata basis).

Similarly, you may want to collate information in different logs (web server, application server) based on user id or request identifier to determine error propagation through the system.

Log data may also be of interest to the commercial team as it provides one part of the jigsaw that describes how customers use the system. It can be used to determine the paths a customer takes through the system and so help interpret buying habits. This information needs to be collated across servers and over time (it does not matter whether different requests from a user were fielded by different servers – the overall set of requests that make up the session must be considered together). This can be done by retrieval and integration of the logs from the different servers using automated scripts, for example Unix shell scripts that trigger file transfers and then use tools such as sed, awk, grep, diff, uniq and sort to extract the required information. Alternatively, there are commercial tools available for Web log interpretation.

Another consideration when creating a SYSTEM OVERVIEW for trend analysis is what data to store. Obviously, storing raw status and log information collected over months from a complex system will take up large amounts of space. You may decide that it is better to store just the derived overview summaries and to discard the raw data. This limits the analysis you can do later but considered selection of the required summaries should make this less of an issue.

In terms of the problem of the GlobalTech system, each of the elements in the system reports its status using a technique suitable to that element as described in CONTINUAL STATUS REPORTING and the critical information is monitored as described in OPERATIONAL MONITORING AND ALERTING. For each type of coarse-grained system element (web server, application server, database server, support infrastructure) we abstract all the information into a single status flag: okay, risk, and broken. In addition we aggregate the number of simultaneous sessions across all the application servers and the request response times for dynamic pages (not for binary assets) across all web servers and application servers. A continuously running process on one of the management servers is responsible for extracting this SYSTEM OVERVIEW information which is then emailed to the operations team every 30 minutes.

The web logs are copied and consolidated by a process that runs on a regular basis. These logs are filtered to provide a set of views highlighting errors and usage patterns. These summaries are stored outside the system. The detailed information from which the summaries are generated is deleted after seven days. This gives the operations team long enough to investigate problems highlighted but keeps disk usage to a reasonable level.

Impact of the Pattern on Non-functional Characteristics

Availability	Unaffected by this pattern.
Performance	Although performance of the management function is negatively impacted by the introduction of an extra layer of communication, the performance of the system itself is unchanged.
Scalability	Scalability is improved indirectly as the need for extra capacity will be determined in good time and additional capacity can be added (finances permitting).
Security	Unaffected by this pattern.
Manageability	Manageability is improved because all system elements are considered as a single entity for monitoring.
Maintainability	Unaffected by this pattern.
Flexibility	Flexibility is improved as a new reporting agent or monitoring agent can be implemented under the abstracting layer without impacting existing agents.
Portability	Unaffected by this pattern.
Cost	Cost is increased by the creation (or purchase) of an additional layer. This cost may be quite substantial, depending on the degree of analysis and the number of different views we wish to generate.

Moving On

So far we have focussed on finding out what the system is doing. However, knowing about system problems is not much use if you cannot do anything about it. The DYNAMICALLY-ADJUSTABLE CONFIGURATION pattern addresses this issue.

DYNAMICALLY-ADJUSTABLE CONFIGURATION

Given a good estimate of anticipated usage, it is reasonably straightforward to architect an Internet technology system that can meet its original non-functional requirements. Monitoring the health of the system allows us to know (and possibly predict) how the system is currently coping with demand. However, knowing that the system is likely to crash in the next 15 minutes is not very useful unless you can do something about it.

If the system is reaching the limit of a non-functional characteristic, how can you react to this change in usage without interrupting system operation?

The demand placed on public Internet technology systems is unpredictable. It can be estimated when the system is created but it will fluctuate over time in response to commercial factors and publicity.

The non-functional characteristics of a system are based wholly or in part on settings applied to the various system elements. The system elements will behave differently for different values of these settings. To change the way that a system element behaves, and hence some of the impact it has on the non-functional characteristics of the system, you must change these values. If such values are hard-coded within the system element it cannot respond to unexpected changes in usage without being redeployed.

The timescale for such redeployment can vary from minutes to months depending on the type of system element involved. Additionally, such redeployment will usually require capacity to be reduced while elements are replaced. The consequences of failing to react to usage changes in an appropriate timescale can include system failure, poor performance and unscheduled downtime.

GlobalTech has applied CONTINUAL STATUS REPORTING in combination with the OPERATIONAL MONITORING AND ALERTING, 3-CATEGORY LOGGING and SYSTEM OVERVIEW patterns to give both immediate detailed information and longer-term summary information about the health of our system and any errors that are occurring within it. This alone does not give the operations team the ability to cope with the potential fluctuations in demand. Examining historical trends in system usage, it is clear that the retailer population in the set of GlobalTech users has different peaks and troughs to the consumer usage. At times of peak load, some retailer connections are rejected even though there is spare capacity on the consumer side of the system and vice versa. This sort of peak is usually transient, lasting a matter of hours rather than weeks, and so there is a small window in which any changes to retailer or consumer capacity would be useful.

Ideally our system would be self-repairing: if there is a large increase in user demand it should somehow re-configure itself to cope with that demand. But such self-repairing systems are extremely difficult to build and require the builder to predict most of the situations that are likely occur and to implement suitable remedies for all of those situations.

We can deduce a lot from the raw data produced by CONTINUAL STATUS REPORTING and 3-CATEGORY LOGGING and can identify potential remedies from these diagnoses. For example, a slow database caused by too many queries being run simultaneously can be cured by limiting access (CONNECTION LIMITATION) to system functionality that causes queries to be run, limiting the number of simultaneous queries allowed on the database, or beefing up the data access server hardware. But we need to be able to implement those remedies in a timely manner such that they can prevent problems occurring (or mitigate the after-effects of a problem that has occurred).

We could implement remedies fairly quickly by taking part of the system out of service, introducing the remedy to that part then bringing it back into service (this works well with a system that is architected for high availability). But such an approach often exacerbates the problem it is trying to resolve. For example, if the system needs to be configured to cope with a higher number of users browsing around the system, taking one of the application servers out of service to set it up for more browsing (and, by implication, fewer transactional) users places additional load on the remaining servers – possibly leading to catastrophic failure.

If the non-functional characteristics of a system are based wholly or in part on a set of built-in limits or settings then it cannot respond to unexpected changes in usage without being redeployed. Such redeployment could take weeks or months. Conversely, each system element could read its configuration information from a location that can be changed by the operations team but this will make each system element slower to initialize and more complex to implement and maintain.

A system element will be more flexible if it reads its configuration information from an external source but if it reads the information only on startup then it must be reset or rebooted for any change to take effect. Such a restart will reduce system capacity until the system element has restarted. Conversely, a system element that is entirely dynamic will be trickier to implement as it must re-assign its resources while still servicing requests. Such elements are likely to be more complex and contain more bugs.

A balance must be struck between the need for continual operation and the provision of a mechanism to adjust the way the system operates in a short timescale.

Identify key parameters that fundamentally affect the non-functional characteristics of the system. For each of these parameters, introduce a mechanism to allow elements to reload their configuration information at runtime.

The first step is to identify key parameters that fundamentally affect the non-functional characteristics of the system. These typically include:

- The number of simultaneous requests that can be made to a web server
- The number of simultaneous sessions that can be maintained by an application server
- The load-balancing algorithm used
- The number of simultaneous connections to a data access server
- The size of data caches
- Security keys

For each of these parameters, and any others identified for your system, introduce a mechanism for adjusting these values while the system continues to run.

The principle of adjusting system configuration at runtime is not unique to non-functional parameters. It is quite possible to use the same mechanisms to adjust the amount of functionality available or the look and feel of an application while it is running. However, not only is our focus on non-functional requirements, but applying this to non-functional requirements is probably its most useful application. The system will not fall over if a user cannot select a green background rather than a blue one, but it may do if the system runs out of cache space.

There are many variations on how application reconfiguration can be implemented. The two basic principles are push (the element is notified of the change asynchronously) and pull (the element reads the settings at an appropriate point). The settings could be stored in a variety of places (configuration file, database, system registry, distributed registry/repository, etc.). The precise location does not change the principle of the implementation.

The simplest implementation is probably just-in-time or on-demand pull, where the element reads the setting from a configuration location when it needs it. The setting is not cached for future use and any subsequent need for the value causes it to be re-read. This is a form of smart reference as described in the Proxy pattern [Gamma *et al.* 1995]. Obviously, this is quite inefficient for values that are needed frequently. Alternatively, the application may poll values on a regular basis and cache them between times. This is more efficient in terms of access to the storage location but it does reduce the responsiveness to changes (depending on the polling interval). For example, this type of on-demand pull approach to dynamic configuration changes is used by ASP.NET (see Box 8.3).

In some cases, some form of manual notification may be required for the element to re-read its configuration. For example, an administrator may select 'save' from a menu on a content switch (load balancer) after changing the list of available servers. This would change the server address values stored in the memory used by the content switch. The act of saving would not be complete until the changes had taken effect. This type of mechanism is used for various changes to hardware configuration such as changing (or adding) an IP address on a network card. A software example is the use of particular Unix signals (e.g. SIGHUP) to prompt a Unix daemon to re-load its configuration (see Box 8.4).

BOX 8.3 .NET configuration files

Most Internet systems are fronted by some form of server page, be they JSPs or ASPs. As the front end of the system, any downtime in these components may be directly noticed by the user. The latest generation of Microsoft ASP – ASP.NET – combines a simple configuration mechanism with the ability to update the configuration of a running component.

The configuration information for an ASP.NET component is contained in an XML file called web.config. The ASP.NET runtime checks to see if the timestamp on the configuration file has changed. If so, the next time a request is made for any dynamic web page in that component, the ASP.NET runtime re-reads the values from the file (such as appRequestQueueLimit, which defines the number of pending requests). This means that little or no downtime is required to apply the changes.

War Story

One of the authors worked on a project that needed to maintain a read-only database containing catalogue information derived from 'live' product information that originated outside the system. The catalogue database included a full text search index that allowed users to search for products by keyword. When this catalogue database needed to be refreshed, both the database and the full text search index needed to be rebuilt. The building of the full text search index took a reasonable amount of time. To avoid downtime, a second instance of the database was built and a new full text search index was built on it. Once the index was built and ready, system elements were diverted to the new database instance simply by changing the database connection string in their configuration files.

In the case of asynchronous notification of change, the element must cache the value internally (it may initially explicitly read this value from the configuration source). For a notification to be asynchronously triggered, an element must provide some form of entry point to which notifications can be delivered as defined in the Observer [Gamma *et al.* 1995] and Publisher–Subscriber [Buschmann *et al.* 1996] patterns. For a software component, this could be a remote procedure call interface, the arrival of a message on a queue or some form of system-level notification. In hardware terms, the change could be an SNMP broadcast that is picked up and implemented by the relevant monitoring agent.

BOX 8.4 DNS and BIND (with due respect to Liu and Ablitz)

Aside from the underlying network connectivity, the Domain Name System (DNS) is the one thing whose absence would cause the Internet as we know it to grind to a halt. As such, it must be able to run with very little downtime. At the same time, it needs to be configurable – not least so that you can add new entries to its cache of names and addresses.

The classic implementation of DNS is the BIND daemon, most commonly found in its Unix daemon variant. Unix name servers will start the BIND daemon which reads its configuration files (such as Zone files) on startup. If changes are required to the configuration, these changes are made to the files on disk and the BIND daemon is sent a SIGHUP signal by an administrator. This signal tells the daemon to re-read its configuration files and so to absorb the changes. Such action takes a fraction of the time required to stop and start the daemon itself.

The mechanism applied may be different for each system element. Some system elements may provide this sort of functionality out-of-the-box while you may explicitly build such a mechanism into a custom software component. Because of this, there is no standard way of making such changes. You might want to expend some time and effort in building a control panel through which you can alter the configuration – maybe as part of an interactive implementation of SYSTEM OVERVIEW – or you may decide that the frequency of change does not warrant this effort.

The principles behind DYNAMICALLY-ADJUSTABLE CONFIGURATION are not new; for example, they are discussed in the Configurable System pattern [Sommerlad 1999]. However DYNAMICALLY-ADJUSTABLE CONFIGURATION is very focused on the application of these principles to the non-functional behaviour of the system and places more emphasis on the need for some implementations to make such changes without restarting or resetting the system element.

Although the configuration change itself may be simple, combinations of other mechanisms used in the system may cause problems. Consider the presentation layer of a web application deployed across three servers as LOAD-BALANCED ELEMENTS implemented as a cluster. User sessions are stored in a session database according to SESSION FAILOVER. A cluster-specific mechanism (such as Microsoft's Application Center Server) can be used to replicate any configuration file changes across the cluster. However, as the changes are made, some users may be part way through a logical interaction with the system involving multiple page views. If the configuration change takes place part way through their interaction, indeterminate effects, or errors may ensue. The users of the system must be carefully shepherded so that users with ongoing sessions are continually directed to servers using the old configuration while new users can be redirected to servers using the new configuration. At a certain point, all users of the old configuration will end their interactions and the final server can be updated with the configuration change.

In order to be meaningfully applied, the system must implement CONTINUAL STATUS REPORTING and, potentially, 3-CATEGORY LOGGING to provide the information about the system's health that is required to inform the values set for configurable parameters. Conversely, the implementations of patterns such as 3-CATEGORY LOGGING can themselves use DYNAMICALLY-ADJUSTABLE CONFIGURATION. For example, it is standard practice to run error logging permanently but it can significantly reduce logging overhead for the majority of the time if you only run information and debug logging when they are required.

DYNAMICALLY-ADJUSTABLE CONFIGURATION is typically applied to software elements, however more complex hardware such as routers and switches usually have a set of configurable parameters that can be altered at runtime. If a system has been organized to provide a coherent SYSTEM OVERVIEW, the different types of configuration that are dynamically adjustable will also usually split out along these lines.

The Achilles heel of the GlobalTech system is its highly volatile user base. The use of a single system to service both business and consumer customers saves significant development and system management costs but makes the problems of high availability and good performance particularly difficult to solve.

Focussing on this problem, the GlobalTech team use CONNECTION LIMITATION and introduce two points at which to throttle the number of user requests – at the web servers and at the application servers (limiting the number of HTTP requests and simultaneous sessions respectively). These limitations are split between business and consumer users – there is a limit for each different type of user that can be altered independently. These limits for requests and sessions are made configurable at runtime so that they can be altered on the fly.

With these four DYNAMICALLY-ADJUSTABLE CONFIGURATION limits, the GlobalTech system management team have a large degree of flexibility to deal with expected and unexpected surges in user load. If there is an unexpected surge in retailer demand (perhaps due to unforeseen competition in the market) the limits for business users can be increased at the expense of consumer users. If there is a planned product launch, the retailers can be notified in advance that preference will be given to consumers for the period of the launch. Should response to the launch be unexpectedly high, further restrictions can be placed on retailers; should demand be low, restrictions can be lifted.

Impact of the Pattern on Non-functional Characteristics

Availability	Unaffected by this pattern.
Performance	Performance is negatively impacted by the processing overhead if configuration changes are read using a 'pull-based' mechanism.
Scalability	Unaffected by this pattern.
Security	Unaffected by this pattern.
Manageability	Manageability is improved as the system's characteristics can be more easily altered to cope with unexpected conditions.
Maintainability	Unaffected by this pattern.
Flexibility	Unaffected by this pattern.
Portability	Unaffected by this pattern.
Cost	Cost is increased by the analysis effort required to identify the system parameters that can be altered to significantly affect the non-functional characteristics of the system and by the implementation of the dynamic reconfiguration mechanism for these parameters.

Moving On

The system is now very controllable – we know what is going on and we can change the way it behaves at runtime. However, a system is only fully under control if you can control access to it, and if you can control who is permitted to make changes to it and when those changes are made. Basically, a system that is not secure is not under control.

DEMILITARIZED ZONE

The Internet is renowned as a dangerous place in security terms. Many large organizations have been attacked by individual crackers or groups of crackers. Their motivation varies from profit, through vandalism and on to the simple joy of a new challenge ('I can pit my wits against you and win'). The larger the organization, or the more sensitive the data involved, the more of an attraction it is for the attacker to breach the security of the organization.

Internet technology systems, particularly those facing the public Internet, are regularly subject to attacks on their functionality, resources and information. How do we protect our systems from direct attacks?

Most Internet technology applications provide functionality that is vital to the business or daily life of their users. Alternatively, or additionally, they may contain some form of customer or company information that is quite sensitive. This functionality will be delivered using an APPLICATION SERVER ARCHITECTURE, with the data being held in a COMMON PERSISTENT STORE. The application may be delivered to the public, to business partners or to a variety of employees and contractors in the far-flung corners of a global organization. Each of these environments contains a potential security threat to the application's functionality and data. Statistics suggest that most attacks on computer systems originate within the organizations that use them rather than outside.

The risk of attack will vary based on the profile of the organization and the potential rewards for the attacker. However, even if you assess your organization as being of little interest to a serious Internet cracker, you will still need to take precautions. Most cars nowadays have some form of alarm or immobilizer system – usually fitted by the manufacturer. Such a system will not deter the serious criminal who will have a variety of countermeasures at their disposal. However, the system does serve to deter the casual criminal who will pass up your car for another that is not fitted with such an alarm (or will just lose interest and wander off). In this respect, Internet security is very much like the security associated with cars. Very few organizations require military-quality security for their corporate systems and data, however most organizations want to avoid being the victim of the 'petty cracker' or 'script kiddy'.

The Internet technology application must obviously be protected from penetration by crackers, but there is also a broader view. The application will usually need to access information and services that are internal to the organization. This suggests that there is some form of contiguous connection between the internal systems and the crackers that threaten the application. Hence there is also a need to protect any connected internal networks from a perceived threat, certainly if the source of that threat is external to the organization.

There is a balance to be struck between making the application accessible to legitimate users and protecting corporate systems and data from inappropriate use. In an ideal world, the application would require no authentication from the user and would make it easy to access all the information and functionality held by the organization. On the other hand, such information may well be sensitive, such as credit card numbers or medical records. The functionality may allow users to transfer money or obtain goods and services. Such data and functionality needs protecting in the same way that bank cashiers are protected from physical attack. Indeed, a competitor of GlobalTech recently had credit card numbers stolen from their application server as they were stored in a location accessible from the public Internet.

The GlobalTech system is typical of applications that must balance the forces described. The system holds customer profiling information, retailer order information and commercially-sensitive sales information, any of which could be stolen or corrupted by an attacker. This information will be shared with GlobalTech's corporate systems making them liable to attack as well. In addition to this, retailers

---

BOX 8.5 100% security

'Our system must be secure.'

'Security is our top priority.'

'We must protect our customers' data as part of the trust relationship we have with them.'

These and many other phrases will undoubtedly be used during the inception phase of any e-commerce project. However, security is no more of an absolute than any non-functional characteristic. Military systems will tend to rate security far higher than ease of use or richness of interface, but even they are regularly breached. It is a brave architect or designer who will guarantee 100% security for a system – especially for a high-profile e-commerce system.

As you have seen already, you cannot opt to have 100% of all non-functional characteristics in your system. It is almost impossible to have 100% availability due to practical limits

on the system architecture and the lack of a bottomless pit of money. And what does 100% performance mean?

In addition to the absolute limitations, there are tradeoffs to be made. Measures that improve one non-functional characteristic will in many cases affect the value of another non-functional characteristic. This is particularly true of security. Most security measures are based on trying to make it more difficult for attackers to access system data and functionality. The measures taken to secure a system will generally slow it down in one way or another. If the system is too highly protected, these security measures become serious 'speed bumps' on the road between your system and your customers. If you have too many speed bumps, you will soon have very few customers.

can order goods and services across the Internet. As this functionality is directly accessible from the outside world, it can be subject to direct attack. A breach of the security will potentially result in attackers being able to order goods and services at no cost. GlobalTech must take measures to protect this system data and functionality.

Provide a region of the system that is separate from both the external users and the internal data and functionality – commonly known as a DEMILITARIZED ZONE (DMZ). Restrict access to this region from the outside by means of limiting network traffic flow to certain physical servers. Use the same techniques to restrict access from servers in the DMZ to the internal systems.

Under this model, people outside the organization can only gain access to a set of web servers in the DMZ. Ideally these web servers are not responsible for any business functionality, since this makes it open to direct attack. Business functionality is delegated to application servers that can be shielded from the outside world. Hence it is best to use DEDICATED WEB AND APPLICATION SERVERS so that the application servers can be protected more than the web servers. The level of security on the exposed web servers can be increased and unnecessary services removed. Any attempts to access other servers from the outside will be denied by an external firewall, consisting of a combination of hardware and software firewall elements. As the number of servers exposed to the outside world is reduced, it means that there are fewer parts of the system that need a high level of security. In order to access those servers not directly exposed (and hence less securely configured), any attacker will have to breach several security elements that form part of the DMZ.

Network traffic within the DMZ and from the DMZ to the internal servers is limited by use of firewall software and hardware and router or switch filtering. A typical DMZ configuration, as used by GlobalTech, is shown in Figure 8.2.

The external router limits the network traffic from the outside world. It filters incoming traffic to ensure that packets carrying 'unfriendly' protocols are not carried into the organization. The external router can also ensure that traffic from the outside world is only allowed to access specific machines in the DMZ – traffic that attempts to access the corporate systems, or even the internal router, will be refused. This is sometimes referred to as a choke point. Traffic will be shepherded to the machines that make up the external face of the organization, such as the web servers. These machines will be built solely for the purpose of delivering web content and will be locked down to prevent other, unintended, access, as discussed in Box 8.6. The GlobalTech system only allows HTTP and FTP traffic into the organization, and even then such traffic is only allowed to the web servers. The external router drops any traffic that tries to reach the internal router, the firewall, or the external router itself. This rogue traffic is also logged at the firewall and notified to the system administrators in order to assist in the detection of potential intruders.

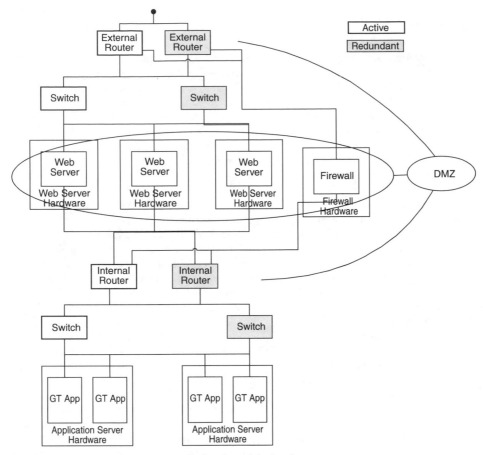

Figure 8.2 DEMILITARIZED ZONE applied to the GlobalTech system.

An internal router can then act as another choke point. Traffic through this router is limited to connections between the server in the DMZ and specific internal servers using a fixed set of protocols, which reduces the risk of attack on other internal systems. The use of an internal router helps to reduce the risk of attack should the external router be breached. Because of this threat, no traffic should be allowed directly from the external router to the internal router. The internal router used by GlobalTech allows inbound traffic only from the web servers, and even then it limits it to specific protocols (IIOP), specific hosts and specific port ranges. This means that any cracker who achieves a beachhead within the DMZ must either attack the internal router directly (and risk setting off alarms from the router) or they must be literate in IIOP to the degree that they could use it to gain access to one of the servers on the other side of the internal router.

As delivered, server-level operating systems provide a variety of useful services. However, services that are useful in a networked intranet environment can become a security threat when exposed to the outside world. A probing tool, such as SATAN/SANTA or SAINT, can quickly expose vulnerabilities in unsecured systems which can then be exploited by specific attacks. To reduce the chances of such a probe discovering weaknesses, systems that are exposed to potential attack should be hardened. This hardening takes the form of disabling or removing unwanted services, accounts and utilities. Examples of this would include the disabling of the telnet service on a Unix system, the disabling of the uucp account and the removal of any compilers that come as part of the standard build. In addition, hardened systems should have the latest security patches applied to them.

The process of hardening will generally consist of two stages. In the first stage, a base platform build will be defined. This will consist of just those packages and services that are required to run the components to be installed on the server together with the latest security patches. This will be bundled into some format that can be repeatedly installed (such as Sun Jumpstart) so that the server build is consistent and not prone to individual errors when being configured. The second part of hardening is that the hardened systems should be audited on a regular basis. Tools such as Nessus and Titan can be used to examine a Unix system, identify potential security vulnerabilities, and even automatically fix them. If a system has been hardened, then such tools can be run every day to re-close any security holes opened by crackers. Once the system is hardened, you may choose to install an intrusion detection system (IDS), such as Tripwire, to warn of potential attacks.

The characteristics of a hardened system will be different from those of a development system. Development systems tend to be very open, since this usually makes development easier. Those systems used in the QA or test environment should be hardened to the same degree as those in the live environment (as far as possible). This means that when the application or component is deployed onto the QA/test environment, any conflicts with security policy can be identified and addressed. It is no good waiting until your application is deployed in the live environment to discover that you cannot connect to your database because of firewall policy. It is usually part of the architect's job to ensure that suitable hardening takes place in QA/test to achieve this aim.

The whole operation of the routers and the traffic filtering may be controlled from a machine running specific firewall software. This makes it easier to apply consistent rules to the routers and to use statistical analysis to detect potential attacks. In some configurations, the firewall hardware itself acts as one or more of the choke points in the DMZ design. The firewall in the GlobalTech configuration acts as a clearing house for security alerts and as a management console for the DMZ. GlobalTech chose Firewall-1 software based on its track record and traditional association with Sun, on whose hardware it is deployed. The firewall software gets alerts from the two routers and provides a unified view of security in the DMZ. The firewall software also controls the configuration of the two routers to avoid inconsistencies creeping in between the three main parts of the 'firewall system'.

Applying a DMZ to a system is a good way of providing protection for the system. However, you must remember that protecting the platforms on which the system is built is only part of the solution. Security is an ongoing task – some people would say that security is more of a policy issue than a technical one. All protection mechanisms – such as a DMZ – must be backed up with appropriate procedures and processes to ensure that the level of security remains high (see Box 8.7). If there is a high level of concern about possible attacks on the system, an intrusion detection system (IDS) may also be used. An IDS monitors the traffic on the network or on specific hosts looking for suspicious activity. If the IDS identifies a pattern of network or host traffic that indicates an attack is underway it will notify the system administrators. An IDS may be used on the network between the two routers, on the internal network or both.

BOX 8.7 | Protection or response

In the security patterns we discuss, the focus is very much on the protection of the system and its data through strategies based around SECURE CHANNELS, INFORMATION OBSCURITY, KNOWN PARTNERS and a DEMILITARIZED ZONE. However, this is only part of the security picture. In [Schneier 2000], Bruce Schneier describes such protective measures as 'prophylactic' – in other words they are just protective measures trying to create a boundary between the system or data and the outside world. Despite our best efforts, this will never be enough to offer a conclusive security story. Schneier continues:

There are three parts to an effective set of countermeasures:

■ *Protection*
■ *Detection*
■ *Reaction*

...

Protection, detection and reaction countermeasures work in tandem.

We discuss briefly various detection mechanisms such as intrusion detection systems (IDS). Such mechanisms can plug into an OPERATIONAL MONITORING AND ALERTING infrastructure so that system administrators are informed of any attempted breach (or at least any that is detected). This provides us with a certain degree of detection. However, we have not discussed reaction and potential countermeasures – and nor do we intend to do so. Neither of the authors would pretend to be a security expert, we simply use it within the boundaries of our knowledge as part of the system architecture where it is required. In architecture terms, the focus tends to be on protection with detection enabled by architectural decisions but with reaction falling outside of the scope of the purely architectural. If you need more information on the processes and procedures involved in risk assessment, security audit, countermeasures and seriously secure systems then refer to material such as [Anderson 2001] or find yourself a good security consultant.

Impact of the Pattern on Non-functional Characteristics

Availability	Availability may be negatively impacted as the firewall becomes a single point of failure (standard procedure is for a firewall to 'fail closed', i.e. in the event of failure it will deny all connections to the protected systems).
Performance	There is a potential negative impact on performance due to the overhead of network traffic filtering and the necessity for physical separation between the web servers and the application servers as defined in DEDICATED WEB AND APPLICATION SERVERS (although splitting the servers may actually improve performance). If this has not already been done to improve another non-functional characteristic, it must be done to implement a DMZ and so will add multiple extra network hops for each user transaction.
Scalability	The scalability of the underlying application is unaffected. However, the additional elements (such as filtering routers and firewall software) must be able to scale to the desired number of users and concurrent connections.
Security	Security is improved because fewer systems are exposed to attack and multiple firewall artefacts must be breached to compromise security.
Manageability	Manageability is negatively impacted since the very restrictions that limit access to internal data may make it difficult to access the application from an internal monitor.
Maintainability	Unaffected by this pattern.
Flexibility	Unaffected by this pattern.
Portability	Unaffected by this pattern.
Cost	Cost is increased as extra elements must be procured to build the DMZ. These include not only the filtering routers, firewall software and firewall host, but also the extra network equipment, such as switches and cabling, used in the DMZ itself.

Moving On

A DMZ helps to defend the 'static' parts of the application. However, a DMZ provides limited protection for data in transit (it helps to prevent eavesdropping inside the DMZ but it does not protect traffic once it has passed outside the DMZ). To ensure the security of data as it passes between the system and the users you should implement Secure Channels. You can also apply Information Obscurity to protect data in storage.

You can improve the security of a DMZ by applying Information Obscurity to the configuration information of its individual elements. This makes it more difficult for an attacker to get a good idea of the topology, roles and relationships of different elements that make up the DMZ.

Information Obscurity

Fear is one of the major factors that held back the growth of consumer e-commerce for a long time. Stories of stolen credit card information and personal details have led to a great degree of mistrust of the level of security available on the Internet. People are still sometimes loathe to enter their credit card details to buy goods online in case these details are stolen from the legitimate vendor and used for fraudulent purposes. Interacting with many Internet technology systems, you provide a variety of information that you do not want shared with the world at large. There needs to be an implicit level of trust that the providers of such systems will take care of this information.

How do we ensure that sensitive data gathered and stored by our system is protected from unauthorized access?

A typical Internet technology system will use an Application Server Architecture and store its application data in a Common Persistent Store. As part of its normal operation, the system will gather information from users on many things ranging from their favourite movie star through to credit card details. This user information is typically stored in the Common Persistent Store, but it may also be retained temporarily in memory, in a cache, or in session state (which could be backed off to disk or to a state server). In addition to user information, the system will also need to access and manipulate its own configuration information, such as encryption keys, credentials, host names and so on.

Both user and system information may be of interest to any intruder. If the intruder is interested in user data, they may be able to monitor disk caches for interesting information. Alternatively, if they can find some credentials for the database, they could directly access whatever user information is stored in there. For a system that uses encryption in any form, the amount of protection delivered by the encryption relies on the security of the encryption keys (see Box 8.8 for more detail on the mechanics of encryption). If the intruder can easily find and identify the encryption keys used for particular purposes, then all benefit from the encryption is lost. Clearly, both user and system information must be protected in a suitable way.

There are two ways to secure sensitive information – lock it away where no-one can get hold of it or obscure the information such that it cannot be used even if it is stolen. Most systems will use a combination of locks and obscurity to protect information. The data in the database will be 'locked' as only users or processes (usually termed 'principals' in security literature) with appropriate credentials can access the information. The same will be true of data stored in a disk cache or in memory – only authorized principals will be able to access this information as it is secured by a combination of the operating system and access control lists or permission sets. Obviously, the effectiveness of such locks relies on the correct configuration of the access control and an effective administration process that will ensure that permissions are only changed with great care by principals authorized to make such changes. The administrators must also ensure that all known security patches are applied to the system to avoid holes in this overall security architecture. Given correct configuration and management, the obvious target for a cracker will be obtaining credentials they can use to 'legitimately' access the information they want. Such credentials could be directly or indirectly stored as part of an application's configuration information, e.g. a user name and password for the database may be stored as part of a database connection string. This information is basically the 'key' to the 'lock' which has been used to secure the data. If the key is stolen, the lock is ineffective. Hence, credentials (and any other system information that might be of use to a cracker) become part of the sensitive data that needs protection.

The other way to protect data is to obscure it, which for most data means encrypting it (see Box 8.8). The simplest approach would be to encrypt all data used and stored in the system. However, this suffers from multiple problems:

- Encryption and decryption are comparatively slow and, in general, the stronger the encryption mechanism used the slower it is to encrypt or decrypt. Hence, encrypting all the data in our system would have a serious impact on the performance of the system unless we were willing to make a large investment in dedicated encryption hardware to speed this up.

- In order to encrypt or decrypt, the application must have access to the encryption key or keys. These keys cannot themselves be encrypted as you still need a key to recover the keys! This is a similar issue to the protection of credentials for the 'locks' as discussed above. At some point, initial information is needed to start unlocking the protection around the data which means that this initial information is very sensitive and itself needs protecting. Definitely a case of *'quis custodiet ipsos custodes?'*.[3]

- All parts of the system that need to access encrypted data will need access to the encryption keys. This means that if all data is encrypted then all parts of the system must be encryption-aware (or interface with something that is) and the encryption keys must be made widely available – making them more vulnerable to being stolen.

---

[3] Who guards the guards?

BOX 8.8 Encryption, algorithms and keys

When data is encrypted, its original content (called the plaintext) is processed through an encryption algorithm to produce an obscured form (called the ciphertext). Early encryption used simple mechanisms such as substituting one letter for another based on a known mapping between the 'plaintext alphabet' and a 'ciphertext alphabet' (this dates from Roman times and is known as the Caesar cipher). Modern encryption algorithms are far more complex than this and so are more difficult to break. However, most algorithms are widely known as part of an effort to discover any vulnerability. This means that any attacker could, in theory, easily work out the plaintext from the ciphertext as the basic algorithms are predictable mathematical processes (even secret encryption algorithms can be broken, given enough processor power and sample ciphertext). To remove the predictability of the algorithms, they use a set of binary bits, known as an encryption key, as an 'unpredictable element' in the encryption process. Encrypting the same plaintext with the same algorithm but using a different key will produce different ciphertext.

As the key is what makes a particular piece of ciphertext unique, the keys themselves are sensitive information that may be of use to anyone wanting to subvert the use of encryption. Encryption can be two-way (you can decrypt the ciphertext at a later date to retrieve the original plaintext) or one-way (you cannot retrieve the plaintext from the ciphertext even if you have the key). If it is two-way, it can be either symmetrical (the same key is used for encryption and decryption) or asymmetrical (there are two paired keys – one that encrypts and another that decrypts). Using a two-way encryption mechanism, you can exchange information privately by encrypting it using a particular algorithm and key combination. To retrieve the plaintext from the ciphertext you will need the correct combination of algorithm and key (either the same key in the case of symmetrical encryption or the matching key in the case of asymmetrical encryption).

You will commonly hear people talk about 'public key cryptography'. This is based around two asymmetrical keys – one called the public key and the other the private key. As is suggested from the names, you make one key 'public' by handing it out to people who want to communicate with you and you keep the other key 'private' usually by lodging it in an encryption key management system on your computer (this is usually called 'importing' the key). Public key cryptography can be used to provide both privacy and data integrity. If someone wants to send you an encrypted message, they can create ciphertext based on the public key and send it to you. As you are the only one with the matching private key, only you can recover the plaintext of the message. This makes the message secret, but you cannot be sure who sent it as your public key is public! You can use the keys the other way round to ensure data integrity. If someone wants to send you a message and convince you that they sent it, they can calculate a unique number – called a hash – based on the document contents and then encrypt this with their private key. This encrypted value is called a 'digital signature' and is sent along with the message. When you receive the message and its digital signature, you can use the sender's public key to decrypt the hash and compare this to one freshly calculated from the document contents. If the two values match, you know that the message text has not been altered since the digital signature was created. Public keys are usually represented and distributed in the form of digital certificates as discussed in Box 8.10.

There are many algorithms that you can use for encryption depending on how secure you need to make your data. You can also make the same algorithm more secure by increasing the length of the key used (although this does not work in all cases [Schneier 2000]). The only problem is that the more complex the algorithm and the longer the key, the more time it takes to encrypt and decrypt the information. This means that the use of strong encryption is normally in tension with system performance, so some trade-off must be made between the two by the system architect.

That is as far as we will go with cryptography. If you are interested in more details, there are many good books dedicated to cryptography and computer security such as [Schneier 2000], [Schneier 1996] and [Anderson 2001].

Turning the question around, do we need system-wide encryption? Most of the data in the system, such as product catalogue information, is not of a sensitive nature. There is no benefit in encrypting information that is either of no use to a cracker or is made publicly available. Data can be classified into different levels of sensitivity and the level of obscurity (or the strength of the 'lock') can be made commensurate to its sensitivity.

Even then, other factors come into play. Consider a system that has a DEMILITARIZED ZONE. If it were to cache credit card details on the web servers, this data would undoubtedly need a strong level of encryption as the web servers are directly accessible from the outside world. On the other hand, if the same credit card data is stored in a well-configured database on a well-configured system that sits inside the internal router of the DMZ, does it warrant the same strong level of encryption? If encryption is still deemed necessary, a lower, and hence less onerous, level of encryption may be sufficiently prudent. However, this is not necessarily the best route. Using less powerful encryption would be good for performance, but would also add to the management overhead of maintaining multiple sets of encryption configuration and keys.

There are several types of sensitive information held on the GlobalTech system. The system holds all the information about orders placed by each retailer. Whilst this information is not going to be used for fraud, the big retailers would be very upset if their competitors, or the public at large, knew exactly what they were ordering, in what quantities, and how much they paid for each unit.

Perhaps less sensitive is the retailer profile which contains details of the account managers that deal with GlobalTech. Whilst this information isn't likely to cause any real problems if it is stolen or made public, it forms part of the 'trust relationship' between the retailer and GlobalTech. GlobalTech treats it as sensitive information simply because it doesn't want to have to explain to any retailer that details of its employees have been stolen from GlobalTech's system.

Grade the information held by the system for sensitivity. Obscure the more sensitive items of data using encryption and obfuscation techniques.

Following this principle, only part of the data held needs to be obscured as only part of it is sensitive. As an example, user ids are generally not considered sensitive (although they can give a cracker the first foot in the door) whilst passwords are definitely sensitive. Similarly, a customer's postcode is not in itself sensitive information unless it can be combined with a customer name or, even better, the name and credit card number. Almost every system would want customer credit card information to be hidden from prying eyes. The retrieval of a list of items purchased from an online store or an auction site could cause some unease for customers. Between these two examples, the retrieval of customer names from some of the less salubrious sites on the Internet or as part of a list of HIV-infected patients on a medical system would probably cause severe distress. Indeed, in many countries there are legal requirements for organizations to take due care in the management and protection of information gathered from customers and clients (see Box 8.9).

Obviously, the first task is to categorize the data held and used by the system based on considerations such as:

- The impact should that data be accessed by an unauthorized third party, for the user, for the company and for the relationship between the two.
- The incentive for a third party to find this data.
- The accessibility of the place where the data is stored.
- Whether this data can be used to compromise further data.
- The data protection rules governing this type of data.

BOX 8.9 Data protection and the law

In the UK, all information held electronically is subject to the Data Protection Act. Similar legislation exists for the whole of the European Union and must realistically spread throughout most of the civilized world as the Internet becomes a common, popular channel for buying and selling goods and services and exchanging information.

Under the terms of the UK Data Protection Act, you must make reasonable precautions to protect data related to any user of your system:

Appropriate technical and organizational measures shall be taken against unauthorized or unlawful processing of personal data and against accidental loss or destruction of, or damage to, personal data.

This means that the owners of the system may be legally liable if anyone breaks into the system and steals user information. As the architect of a system, you must ensure that the system conforms to any relevant data protection legislation. This is part of the due diligence with which you should perform your role.

Nobody is saying that every system must have 100% security even if this were possible (see Box 8.5). However, there is an expectation that you will weigh up security risks relating to the disclosure of user data as you are designing the system and the processes under which it will operate. If you take reasonable precautions based on the sensitivity of the data and the perceived level of risk, you are discharging your duties correctly. If you adopt a cavalier attitude towards user data, your IT director could end up in jail and you could end up out of work!

We cannot give any absolute advice in this area. The sensitivity of data will depend on the type of application and the organization for which it is being built. All we can advise is that you perform an audit of the data used by your application and make sure that you apply an appropriate level of security for each type of data based on your context. This audit should be repeated whenever the system architecture changes in a major way as the system evolves (e.g. the introduction of a DEMILITARIZED ZONE). Ideally you should make decisions about the sensitivity of the data independently of the decision on the obscurity mechanism to be applied. If you find that you have lots of data that needs obscuring to a high degree then the project sponsors need to be persuaded to make budget available to do this.

So, we need to determine which elements of any given data set are sensitive and then decide what type of protection they need. One place we can look for suitable examples of how to categorize and manage sensitive data are the operating systems on which our applications run. An obvious piece of data to protect is a user's password.

The first thing to note about the way that Unix and Windows handle user and password data is that they only encrypt a small part of the information. The rest of the information (for example, the user name, home directory, shell, and so on in the Unix/etc/passwd file) remains in clear text which means that it is far easier and faster to manipulate it than if it were encrypted. Only the sensitive part – the password itself – is encrypted (the level of encryption for passwords has increased markedly over time in Unix and even more markedly in Microsoft Windows, which was originally a single-user system).

The second thing to note is that a one-way algorithm is used to encrypt the sensitive information (the password) and the security subsystem never decrypts the password back into plain text. The password remains obscured throughout its use in the system – the only time that it is in plain text is when it is typed in by the user. In cases where we are using a piece of data to authenticate a user (it may be a password, pass phrase or the ubiquitous 'mother's maiden name'), it may be quite sufficient to store it in obscured form without the ability to retrieve the original plaintext.

Most sensitive user data is stored in a database. Small amounts of information can be encrypted and stored in character- or byte-based fields while larger amounts of ciphertext would be stored as BLOBs. Whether you store your encrypted data in the database or on the file system, you will need some metadata about it in order to identify the user with which it is associated (a primary key in the database or the file name on the file system). For custom software elements, you can use the encryption APIs provided in the Java and .NET worlds to manipulate encrypted data, although you need to be aware of some limitations built into cryptographic products exported from the USA which limit key lengths for 'foreign' implementations. Alternatively you can buy third-party cryptographic libraries that achieve the same purpose. If any part of your system is not enabled for encrypted data, you may need to build a custom adapter. One way of reducing the need for obscurity is to increase the number or strength of the 'locks' through which a cracker must pass in order to be able to access the data. You may find that it is easier in overall terms to implement a stronger DEMILITARIZED ZONE and use less encryption within the internal network than to make many parts of your application encryption-aware.

One thing to remember here is that INFORMATION OBSCURITY is concerned with the protection of information inside the application. Once it moves outside the application, or even onto the network between elements in the application, it is still potentially vulnerable. Hence, you often find that INFORMATION OBSCURITY is used in combination with SECURE CHANNELS so that data is protected both inside the system and in transit.

As noted earlier, it is not just user data that needs protecting but also the configuration information used by the application. In order to be flexible, information used by the application for its own purposes is often held externally (in configuration files for example). However, some of this configuration information, such as the encryption key, is itself sensitive information. The application needs the encryption key to access encrypted user data but you do not want an intruder to obtain it easily. Information-based security artefacts such as encryption keys are particularly sensitive as they can be stolen – copied – and you don't know that it's been copied if you don't spot the intrusion. To secure this type of data you could secure your external configuration file from unauthorized access. In addition, you could use an obscured name to identify the key in the configuration file. This makes it more difficult for an attacker to identify the correct information. If you are still not happy with the level of security (for example, the file could be accessed over the network if the system is configured incorrectly), you could move the sensitive data into a location that is only accessible to local principals, such as the Windows system registry. Alternatively, you can embed the information in a binary artefact, such as a compiled class or resource component, to make it more difficult to retrieve. In a late-bound environment such as Java or .NET, you might even want to obfuscate your bytecode or intermediate language to make it even less obvious which bit of data is the key.

Obviously, most of the considerations for the encryption key relate to the strength of the 'lock' protecting it. In the case of another sensitive piece of information, such as a database connection string containing credentials for that database, encryption can be used to obscure the contents of the string to help prevent the discovery and use of the embedded credentials. This encrypted information can then be placed in a suitable location which can be accessed by all parts of the system that need it.

> ### War Story
>
> One of the authors was involved in a programme of Internet technology projects that used the .NET platform. There was discussion across the programme about the security characteristics of the platform with respect to obscuring database connection strings that were needed by the different applications. All the projects used ASP.NET Web Forms as the basis for their applications and so the obvious choice was to use the XML-based web.config file to store the connection string. The architects across the programme took different approaches based on the security requirements of their applications.
>
> One project encrypted its connection string and stored it in the system registry so that it was only available on the local machine. This provided a high level of security but required the encryption key to be embedded in the application.
>
> At the other end of the scale, one project with a lower security requirement (and an internal user base) just stored the connection string in plain text in the web.config file. Although the web.config file is located in the application's virtual directory and so it was, in theory, accessible from the outside world, such access is disabled by default in the machine.config file that governs machine-wide configuration. The logic here was that if an attacker could get in with sufficient privilege to alter the machine.config file in order to allow them to download the application's web.config file then security was already compromised. Equally, if such a change was made by an errant administrator, such a rogue agent could potentially undermine all but the most stringent application security mechanisms, which could not be justified as part of the system architecture.

Once you have decided what is to be encrypted, you need to consider the impact on the rest of the system. The main issue with encryption is speed. Encryption and decryption on general-purpose computer systems requires the resource-intensive cryptographic algorithms to be run using the standard processor and memory. Although these resources are suitable for general application server usage, they are quite slow compared to what you would ideally want for cryptographic purposes. If you only require a small amount of cryptographic processing then this is usually OK. However, the more cryptographic processing you require, the more impact is caused by running it on sub-optimal hardware. One solution would be to upgrade all the systems to have faster processors (more on-board cache, etc.) and faster memory. However, this would increase the cost of each system notably. The alternative is to buy dedicated hardware that performs the encryption and decryption. Depending on the level and type of encryption required, this would probably be cheaper than upgrading the processor and memory. It would almost certainly be faster.

One final aspect to consider is infrastructure security as application security can be undermined by an insecurely configured infrastructure. To address this, INFORMATION OBSCURITY can also be used to help improve the security of the infrastructure. Some parts of the system already use obscurity, for example, when storing passwords. However, this can be undermined if a suitable password policy is not enforced. Other steps can be taken to make a system less vulnerable to attack such as using obscure hostnames rather than, say, 'dataserver', 'kerberos 1' or 'keymanager'. In some cases, you may hand the system over to a dedicated and professional operations team that will take on responsibility for this type of infrastructure security based on a minimal amount of guidance. Alternatively, there may be a lone system administrator who is not privy to the security requirements for each application and so will not necessarily get it right on their own. Unfortunately (for us and for you), overall system security belongs to the architect so, if the operations team is weak or inexperienced, you may sometimes need to get involved with specifying things down to the infrastructure level, such as password policy or obscured machine names.

After weighing the possible consequences of data disclosure against the risk of intrusion, we decided that the GlobalTech system does contain some data worth explicitly encrypting, in the form of the retailer order and profile information. There is no credit card information held by the system and the passwords used by registered public customers are encrypted anyway by the personalization and customization engine. The encryption used for the retailer information is not too strong as we don't want to have too much of a negative impact on system performance. The main intention is to make it difficult for any intruder to casually break this encryption. One point to note is that there is a single encryption key used for all retailer information – not one per retailer. There is little benefit (and much complexity) in the use of multiple keys as the application server software is authorized to view the data and has the decryption key. The authentication and authorization of each retailer is a separate matter (see KNOWN PARTNERS).

Impact of the Pattern on Non-functional Characteristics

Availability	Availability should not be negatively impacted, but care should be taken not to introduce single points of failure in the form of encryption key distribution and management services.
Performance	Performance is negatively impacted if an obscurity mechanism is introduced because of the processing overhead associated with the mechanism. This is particularly true of complex encryption algorithms with long key lengths.
Scalability	There should not be a negative impact on scalability, but any mechanisms used by the obscurity policy, such as encryption key distribution and management services, should themselves be scalable.

Security	Security is improved by data obscurity because, even in the event of an attack during which the attacker gains access to the file system, system memory and application database, any sensitive data is not usable by the attacker. Security is also improved by configuration obscurity as any attacker will find it more difficult to obtain the information they need to crack the system.
Manageability	Manageability is negatively impacted as additional resources will be needed for the encryption mechanism (such as key management).
Maintainability	Obfuscation techniques, in particular, can affect the maintainability of the system as the developers have to remember obscure names for the configuration files, etc.
Flexibility	Flexibility may be negatively impacted as you may need to maintain back-compatibility with existing encrypted data or obscured configuration.
Portability	Portability is negatively impacted as you must ensure that any new platform supports the encryption mechanisms you wish to use.
Cost	Cost is probably increased as the extra requirements of encryption may require either additional general capability to support software encryption or dedicated encryption hardware. You may also need to buy additional encryption software depending on what comes with your existing platforms and tools.

Moving On

The system is now protected by its Demilitarized Zone and the sensitive data it holds is obscured from intruders who break into the system. However, what about intruders who just watch the network? They could be inside or outside the organization, monitoring one of the many network segments on the Internet or between elements of the system itself. What is needed now is a way to secure data in transit by applying Secure Channels and, possibly, Known Partners.

SECURE CHANNELS

For many years, eavesdropping on electronic communications was the stuff of spy movies, or at least reserved for serious criminal investigations. Phone taps would be put in place by federal investigators, or James Bond would use a special device provided by 'Q' to intercept the latest satellite communication by a villain intent on destroying the world. With the advent of the public Internet, not only is it easier to access data passing over this network, but the amount and type of data being passed has expanded hugely. Companies will now entrust to the Internet, and to internal networks hosting Internet technology systems, the sort of business transaction they would previously only do using paper and a postal service; this leads to certain risks.

How do we ensure that data being passed across public or semi-public space is secure in transit?

Most large-scale Internet technology systems are intended for use across the Internet or across a 'semi-public' space such as a large corporate network. The systems will be based around an APPLICATION SERVER ARCHITECTURE and most of them will have adopted DEDICATED WEB AND APPLICATION SERVERS with some form of DEMILITARIZED ZONE for those exposed to the Internet or with stronger security requirements. The clients – be they web browsers or other applications that form part of a business-to-business chain – will contact the web servers across the public or 'semi-public' space to make use of the application's functionality and to pass data back and forth. If the web and application servers are separated, information will pass back and forth between them as business functionality is required. All of this information passing between clients, web servers and application servers could potentially fall prey to an eavesdropper. As some of this information could be sensitive, it presents us with a problem.

The Internet has witnessed a constant struggle between those who want information to be 'free' and those who would like to create a 'business Internet' that is well regulated and controlled. Regardless of their place on this spectrum, most people accept that as the Internet becomes a more widely-used medium, certain information that passes across it must be kept confidential, such as credit card details and medical records. Unfortunately the TCP/IP protocol family was never really designed to provide privacy or payload integrity. The main objective was to deliver the data encapsulated in the protocols in a reliable way. This lack of security features causes problems for many Internet technology systems. When exchanging goods and services for money or when delivering sensitive information to users, there needs to be a reasonable guarantee of confidentiality and integrity even though the traffic passes across the public Internet. We have no choice but to address this problem as we have chosen to use the Internet or a similar semi-public space as the transport between our system and the client. Having said this, only part of the data exchanged between clients and the system needs protecting. Much information delivered by Internet technology systems, such as product information, is public in nature and so any extra measures taken to protect such information is unnecessary – particularly if such measures slow the system down.

Faced with the lack of security features in TCP/IP, the only way that sensitive data can be hidden from a potential eavesdropper or from tampering is by restricting access to the channel or encrypting the contents of the packets being sent. Before the Internet, most communication security relied on denying unauthorized people access to the communication channel. As the phone networks were largely proprietary spaces, specialist knowledge, access and devices were needed to monitor information passing across them. The use of private networks, such as those used for EDI, compounded this as the potential eavesdropper would need to discover which particular channels in the overall network were being used and then gain access to them.

One of the principle strengths of TCP/IP is its ability to route round failure. In order to achieve this, routes are largely discovered dynamically. As such, it is difficult to determine precisely what route a stream of packets will take between points A and B. This use of dynamic routing makes it possible for eavesdroppers to cause traffic to be routed past their listening posts in preference to other routes. If this approach fails, attackers may be able to take over a router at one end of the conversation or the other and to monitor traffic that way. With the public Internet, there is no way of ensuring that all of your traffic goes along a 'secure route'.

The other alternative for keeping information safe in transit is to encrypt it. Although this can provide a high level of security, it has an obvious downside as any form of encryption will introduce significant overhead and so reduce system performance. There is also the question of how to set up encryption between two disparate organizations or between an organization and individuals. A third-party organization will not usually install specialist software to communicate with one business partner. Individuals will use a web browser as a client (or similar) and so you are limited to the capabilities of the browser. An individual is unlikely to want to install specialist encryption software to use your application no matter how much they like it. Basically, any setup overhead will greatly reduce the potential uptake of any Internet technology application.

The GlobalTech system must address these security issues. Retail customers will be asked to log into the system and prove their identity. The username and password combination should be protected from capture by a potential attacker as it passes across the Internet (even though such an attacker would probably cause more irritation than damage). Similarly, order information passed between retailers and the GlobalTech system will go over the Internet and should be protected not only from eavesdropping, but also from tampering. Even in the DEMILITARIZED ZONE, traffic between the web servers and application servers is somewhat insecure as elements in the DEMILITARIZED ZONE may be attacked from the outside, captured by an attacker and used as a base for monitoring traffic in the DEMILITARIZED ZONE.

Create secure channels that obscure sensitive data in transit using encryption and client–server authentication.

From the discussion so far, it should be obvious that we cannot control the route of the system's traffic across the Internet. Hence, the only way to provide confidentiality and integrity is to encrypt the traffic between client and server. To ensure that only the intended recipients can access the information in the message, the information can be encrypted before it is sent and then decrypted when it is received. The use of strong, end-to-end encryption will not prevent eavesdroppers from capturing the information as it passes their listening post. However, it should prevent them from understanding the information passed.

The most common mechanism for creating SECURE CHANNELS across the Internet is the Secure Sockets Layer (SSL). SSL capabilities are built into all major web browsers and also into popular development platforms such as J2EE and .NET. Any application that wishes to use these capabilities simply needs to obtain an SSL server certificate which authenticates the server to the client and can be used as the basis for secure session key exchange.

The GlobalTech system uses SSL between browsers and web servers to create SECURE CHANNELS (see Figure 8.3). Such channels are used to protect data in transmission in the following scenarios:

- Viewing of order status by retailers
- Placing of orders by retailers
- Logging in by public Internet customers
- Changing of details by retailers and public Internet customers

One issue to consider is that the increased security delivered by SECURE CHANNELS may conflict with other desired non-functional characteristics. One obvious conflict is between the use of SSL and performance. In theory, we could use SSL for all exchanges between client and server; in practice, this imposes far too much overhead on the exchange of non-sensitive information. Another less obvious conflict is between SSL and the application of LOAD-BALANCED ELEMENTS to the web servers in order to improve availability and scalability. When load-balancing is combined with SECURE CHANNELS it presents a problem as, if the client were to be routed to a different server than the one that began the SSL session, the new server would not possess the session key for that SSL exchange. One solution here is to pin a particular client to a particular server for the duration of its SSL exchange (sometimes termed server-affinity). However, this then has a negative impact on the availability and scalability characteristics of the solution. To use load-balancing and SECURE CHANNELS in combination it is best to use load-balancing hardware that understands secure channels and can itself participate in the secure channel on behalf of the server. GlobalTech decided to buy load-balancing content switches that contain dedicated hardware to process SSL so that the SSL session is between the client browser and the load balancer (as opposed to the client and the server). This solution avoids issues of server-affinity, but does open up a further security gap as unencrypted information is exchanged between the load balancer and the server.

To address this problem we introduce a totally new set of web servers and load balancers. Any traffic that enters the outermost switch will either arrive on port 80 (the default HTTP port) or port 443 (the default HTTPS – secure HTTP – port). Traffic on port 80 is switched to a standard web server via the standard load balancer. Traffic on port 443, however, can only go to a secure web server via a

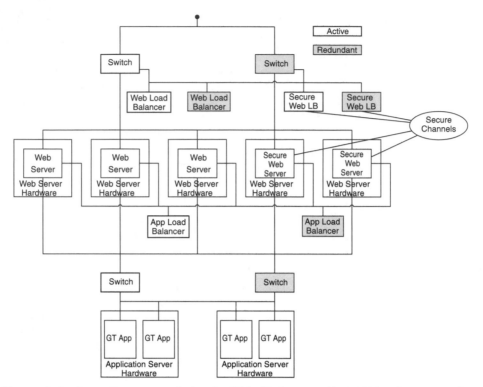

Figure 8.3   SECURE CHANNELS applied to the GlobalTech system (the DMZ has been omitted for clarity).

secure load balancer. The packets passed between the secure load balancer and the selected secure web server are still unencrypted but we have the opportunity to put in place additional security measures to harden the channel between the secure load balancer and the secure web server. This effectively extends the secure channel from the browser to the secure web server.

The use of SSL between the client and the web server is fairly standard and is the obvious place to apply SECURE CHANNELS (this applies for both B2C e-commerce and B2B e-commerce). However, this is not the only place that such security should be considered. Even if a site has been protected as described in the DEMILITARIZED ZONE pattern, it may be possible for an attacker to penetrate one of the routers or even a web server in the DMZ. From this vantage point they can potentially monitor traffic within the DMZ as it passes between the web servers and the application servers. If this traffic is not encrypted it is available to the eavesdropper. To avoid this possibility, you can set up a Virtual Private Network (VPN) between the web servers and the application servers. This VPN makes sure that data is encrypted as it passes through the DMZ, the firewall and the internal router. In the GlobalTech environment, such a VPN could be set up using IP Security Protocol (IPSec) peer-to-peer security between the two sets of servers. After assessing the sensitivity of the information passed back and forth, it is decided that the use of an internal VPN between web servers and application servers would be an unnecessary overhead.

So far, we have talked about synchronous secure channels between clients and web servers. However, there are other ways to implement secure channels. One option is to use an asynchronous messaging system and to encrypt the contents of the messages. Asynchronous operation gives us better performance and availability characteristics at the expense of more processing required to correlate messages and to recover from failure. In terms of Internet technology, we can use MIME-encoded email messages with encrypted payloads as a secure, asynchronous channel. Alternatively, we can use encrypted XML/SOAP messages as defined in the WS-Security specification. These messages can be delivered synchronously (HTTP), pseudo-asynchronously (one-way HTTP messages) or asynchronously (email). While the use of asynchronous messaging is generally useful, you may well need to write more custom code to support this unless you find some good products to help out.

Impact of the Pattern on Non-functional Characteristics

Availability	There is potentially a negative impact on availability if the obscurity mechanism causes server-affinity, which undermines effective failover.
Performance	Performance is negatively impacted by the processing overhead if you introduce an obscurity mechanism for data in transit.
Scalability	There is potentially a negative impact on scalability if the SECURE CHANNEL causes server-affinity, which undermines effective load-balancing.
Security	Security is improved because data that is captured in transit is not usable by the attacker.
Manageability	There is a slightly negative impact on manageability as there are now artefacts of the SECURE CHANNEL to be managed, such as SSL server certificates.
Maintainability	Unaffected by this pattern.
Flexibility	Unaffected by this pattern.
Portability	The choice of obscurity mechanism and its level of support on multiple platforms may have a negative impact on portability.
Cost	Cost is increased as you must obtain and maintain one or more server certificates for your SECURE CHANNEL. Also, you may need to increase the hardware specification of your web servers or buy dedicated encryption hardware to mitigate the associated performance overhead.

Moving On

We now have a way of communicating between client and server that hides sensitive traffic from potential eavesdroppers. However, we have no guarantee of authenticity of either client or server by applying SECURE CHANNELS on its own. For much e-commerce activity, it is very important that the client is sure that the server is genuine and that the server can guarantee the identity of the client (think 'million-dollar stock trades' to get a picture of why this is important). The KNOWN PARTNERS pattern addresses this particular problem.

Secure Sockets Layer and SSL Acceleration

The most widely accepted mechanism for creating secure channels over TCP/IP is to use the Secure Sockets Layer (SSL). Most e-commerce web sites use HTTP over SSL (HTTPS) as the means of passing sensitive information between the client browser and the web server it is talking to. When you access a page in an e-commerce application that asks you for your credit card information, you will see that the browser displays a padlock symbol in the status bar. This indicates that all traffic between client and server generated by that page will be passed over a secure channel (if you don't see the padlock, it is probably because the application uses framesets in which case only one frame contains the secure channel not the whole frameset).

Secure Sockets Layer

Let's look at how SSL works to better understand its benefits and limitations. In a typical encrypted exchange, two parties, Alice and Bob, wish to exchange information. As described in Box 8.8, they can use a shared, symmetric encryption key to pass information privately across a public space, such as the Internet. However, Eve, the eavesdropper trying to intercept the message, cannot decrypt the message even if she captures it as she does not possess the shared key. This is the basic privacy mechanism used by SSL.

In Internet terms, the roles of Bob and Alice are played by the web server and the browser or other client software. However, this presents us with a problem as usually the client and server do not know each other well enough to have established a shared key. The shared key cannot just be built into the web server and browser software otherwise everyone could decrypt everybody else's messages. Each SSL session uses a unique shared key, also called the 'session key'. What we need is a way for the web server and the client to exchange the session key.

The exchange of session keys is based on the use of digital certificates (see Box 8.10). The owner of the web server must obtain a server certificate that associates a given public key with the server's DNS name. Once the server certificate

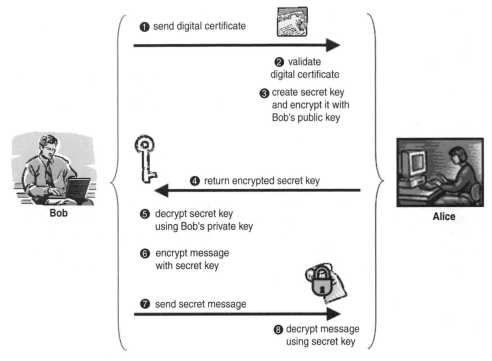

Figure 8.4 Secure key exchange.

has been installed on the web server, a client requests a secure channel by accessing a resource using a URL that starts with 'https:' rather than 'http:'.

This request causes the server to send the client its digital certificate together with a session key encrypted using the web server's private key (see the diagram). The client then checks the digital certificate to make sure it is issued by a trusted third party and that it matches the DNS name with which it is accessing the server. If the certificate looks valid, the client uses the public key in the certificate to decrypt the session key and then starts using the session key to exchange encrypted messages with the server. This exchange has done two things: the client now believes that the server is genuine, and the client and server now have a shared, secret key with which to exchange private messages – in this case the contents of HTTP POST requests. This key exchange can be extended to allow the client to authenticate itself with the server which is important for KNOWN PARTNERS, but is not essential for most SECURE CHANNELS across the Internet. For a more detailed description of how this whole exchange works, see [Anderson 2001].

You may at this point be wondering why we do not just use the public/private key pairs to encrypt the data passing back and forth. The answer is that the symmetrical session key and its associated algorithm are respectively shorter and quicker to run than those for public/private key encryption. Most machines do not currently have the necessary resources to encrypt the amount of data passing between a web client and a server in an appropriate time using public key cryptography. This is a trade-off between performance and security.

Because the session key is shorter and its algorithm simpler, ciphertext based on it is easier to crack than ciphertext based on public key cryptography. If the same session key is used all the time between a client and server, it becomes increasingly possible to work out the shared key using statistical analysis of the messages being passed (based on the number of times particular words appear in the language in which the messages are written). To counter this, the session key is changed on a regular basis using a mechanism similar to the initial exchange of the session key described earlier.

The SSL protocol is quite flexible in that it allows the client and the server to negotiate which specific protocols to use for the encryption (DES, RC4, etc.), key exchange (RSA, DSS, etc.) and integrity checking (SHA, MD5, etc.). In most cases you won't want to worry about this as the negotiation is automatic, but it is useful to know that you have the option to change the algorithms used if you need to. For more details on SSL, see [Netscape 1996].

SSL Acceleration

Processing SSL on the server is a high overhead as all traffic passing back and forth must be encrypted and decrypted. This process is resource-intensive and imposes a high overhead on general-purpose hardware. Such degradation in performance could be addressed by buying more powerful general-purpose hardware or by installing a specialist encryption card in each web server to help with cryptographic processing. However, this does not address the issue of load-balancing or failover of an SSL session.

To improve availability, many systems use LOAD-BALANCED ELEMENTS or ACTIVE–REDUNDANT ELEMENTS. When these elements are web servers running SSL sessions, this gives us a bit of a problem. If the user establishes an SSL session key with one server and is then directed to another server, how can they continue the secure session? The answer is to include the SSL capability in the load-balancing solution. Not only does this solve the problem of load balancing and SSL but, as such solutions are typically dedicated hardware, they can provide far higher cryptographic processing speeds than the server software.

The META group estimates that SSL accelerators are a cost-effective way to instantly improve some of the key non-functional characteristics of Internet technology applications, notably performance (up to 50% faster) and scalability (up to 47 times more connections per second can be supported). There are various solutions (try entering 'load balancing SSL' into Google for a selection of vendor whitepapers), but the best solution for performance is to decrypt on the router using dedicated hardware and then load-balance in plaintext. However, this means there is still a gap in encryption between the load balancer and the web server. This may be acceptable if you are simply offloading the SSL processing onto the SSL hardware in the content switch. However, if you need complete protection from eavesdropping in the DMZ, you still need to address this. To plug this gap you would also need to implement SSL connections between the SSL-aware load balancer and the web servers. It might be worth considering at this stage whether it would be better to balance the load for each session at the start of the session and require any sessions with failed servers to start again.

KNOWN PARTNERS

In any business endeavour, risk is generally a two-way thing. Much of the publicity around Internet security tends to focus on breaches of client security as holes in the web browser are exploited and on breaches of server security as crackers break into a system and vandalize it. What is not talked about as much is the creation of trust across the Internet. Without a reasonable level of trust, e-commerce would remain just another 'cool idea'.

How can we validate the identity of business partners so we can be sure they are who we think they are when we want to collaborate with them?

Internet technology protocols are designed to be easy to work with and to promote access to the data and functionality offered by Internet technology systems. Internet technology systems are based around an APPLICATION SERVER ARCHITECTURE and most of them adopt DEDICATED WEB AND APPLICATION SERVERS with some form of DEMILITARIZED ZONE to protect the functionality and data from direct attack. However, this still leaves the question of how to control access to the functionality and data offered by the system. We need to ensure that only authorized users can access certain parts of the functionality, particularly for high value transactions or where there is a need to definitively identify the client for audit purposes. This is particularly important when offering functionality across a public space such as the Internet.

For a secure partnership, the server must be able to identify the client. Identification of valid clients can be achieved quite simply using passwords. However, passwords are notoriously easy to break – even if they are passed across a SECURE CHANNEL.

If there is no guarantee of the identity of the partner with which you are trading, non-refutability becomes very difficult. In the case of GlobalTech, retailer ordering is particularly vulnerable to this. If someone could pose as a retailer, connect to the GlobalTech site and order hundreds of items, a serious disagreement may occur when the real retailer is notified of the impending order. The retailer will deny placing the order and GlobalTech will want to prove that the retailer did actually place the order – especially if GlobalTech has already ordered extra goods from their own suppliers in response to the order. GlobalTech needs to prevent unauthorized users from placing orders and ensure that clients are identified when orders are placed so that they are associated with the correct account.

Ideally, the mechanism should be sufficiently stringent and auditable that it could act as legal proof to indemnify GlobalTech in a court of law. However, if the mechanism is too difficult to implement and administer then customers will not use it. We would also want to try and avoid too much management overhead within the GlobalTech system.

Turning things around, the establishment of trust works both ways between client and server. The client must be able to definitively identify the server. Otherwise, it is possible (and sometimes relatively simple) for an attacker to place a fake server between the client and the real server. By attacking the local naming service, traffic for the real server can be routed to the fake server, allowing the fake server to obtain information from the client that the client thinks is safe from prying eyes due to it being encrypted.

Once the client thinks that a fake server is the real server, the fake server is able to breach the client's trust in many ways, such as persuading the client to download code that could compromise their system. Equally, the server may prompt the client for authentication information and store that information for a later attack on the real system. To ensure trust across a public space, measures must be taken that validate the identity of both partners in the transaction.

Ensure that access to system functionality and data is restricted to known partners who must authenticate themselves in a secure manner.

Before transmitting data, the client and server can exchange digital certificates (see Box 8.10). The client and server can use the public keys in each other's certificate to engage in the exchange of a shared session key in order to set up a SECURE CHANNEL. The secret key (plus additional data) is encrypted using the public key in the certificate and so can only be decrypted by the associated private key. If either of the participants is not the rightful owner of the certificate they provide, they will not (or should not) have the matching private key. This means that the exchange of the shared session key will fail.

BOX 8.10 Digital certificates

A digital certificate is a way of associating information about a person, system or organization (a 'principal') with a public encryption key. This association is very useful for authentication and for the message integrity, such as the creation of digital signatures (see Box 8.8). You can use the public key in the certificate to encrypt a message so that only the owner of the private key that matches the public key can read that message. Conversely, you can use the public key to decrypt some data encrypted with the private key, which provides a degree of assurance that the data came from the owner of the private key. Given that we are going to base privacy and data integrity on this mechanism, how do you prove the information in the certificate is correct?

A certificate is created by a trusted third party, or certification authority, which creates a digital document containing the information about the principal and the principal's public key. The third party then signs this document and the combination of the document and its associated digital signature becomes the digital certificate. Trusted third parties take a variety of forms including banks, government agencies and specialist companies such as Verisign and Thawte (try searching on Google for 'digital certificates' and 'trusted third parties' for more examples). One of the big questions is how such organizations know enough about a particular principal to provide any guarantee of their identity. There are various levels of certificate that relate to different types of verification that the certification authority can perform. This varies from simply validating an email address through to verifying company ownership.

Certificates take a number of forms depending on the principal information contained in them. For email, you can obtain a personal certificate that associates a public key with your email information. You can also obtain personal or organizational certificates to use as client or server certificates when creating a SECURE CHANNEL. As an example, consider the server certificate that GlobalTech would need to provide SECURE CHANNELS over HTTPS.

When a certification authority issues a digital certificate to a server, the owner of the server must prove that they have a right to the domain name that will be embedded in the certificate. The client can then compare the server domain name in the certificate with that being used to access the server. Any discrepancies between these two domain names indicate a potential security hazard. GlobalTech will have to provide information to the certification authority to prove that it owns the GlobalTech domain. The certificate issued will contain the GlobalTech server's URL as well as the public key generated by GlobalTech and used when configuring the web server.

The final issue is that of removing invalid certificates. If a certificate is stolen, you do not want the thief to be able to masquerade as the owner of the certificates. As certificates have a fixed lifetime, eventually any stolen certificate will become invalid as it becomes out of date. However, what can we do in the interim? Certification authorities maintain Certificate Revocation Lists (CRLs) that contain stolen or otherwise invalidated certificates. If each party in a certificate exchange checks the certification authority's CRL then there is little chance of an invalid certificate being used.

The use of public keys, digital certificates and certification authorities to provide authentication and encryption is termed a Public Key Infrastructure (PKI). PKIs can be used either within an organization (you can even issue your own, self-signed certificates for this) or across the public Internet. PKI forms the basis of most efforts to create SECURE CHANNEL and KNOWN PARTNER implementations across the Internet, including IP Security Protocol (or IPSec, the standard created by the Internet Engineering Task Force).

For more information and discussion on digital certificates including their limitations, see [Schneier 2000].

Companies, such as GlobalTech, that host web servers that provide SECURE CHANNELS based on SSL will need a server certificate. The certification authority will check to see that GlobalTech is the rightful owner of the domain name and then issue a certificate on this basis. The client can then compare the server domain name in the certificate with that used to access the server. Any discrepancies between the two domain names indicate a potential security hazard. This will be flagged to the client by their software (for example a warning dialog box in a web browser) and the transaction can be aborted.

It is equally important that GlobalTech can definitively identify the client who is placing an order. The order placement functionality will not require immediate payment (such as by credit card) but will work on the usual account basis. This means that anyone with appropriate credentials can order large amounts of product that will be charged to the retailer's account. In order to reduce the risk of a fake order, GlobalTech requires that retailers who wish to use the online system obtain a certificate from one of a given set of certificate providers. To give an added level of confidence in the ownership of this client certificate, the certificate is registered by the retailer on the GlobalTech site using a pass code sent to the retailer on paper. From that point on, any interactions with the owner of that certificate are considered to be bona fide transactions performed by that retailer.

Once the client and the server have authenticated themselves to each other, the public keys contained in the digital certificates can be used to set up a SECURE CHANNEL between them. All information passing back and forth is therefore kept confidential. In this form, the three patterns – SECURE CHANNELS, DEMILITARIZED ZONE and KNOWN PARTNERS – form a reinforcing partnership, such that the DMZ protects the infrastructure that supports the SECURE CHANNELS and KNOWN PARTNERS, while KNOWN PARTNERS adds more meaning and power to the use of SECURE CHANNELS.

The risks associated with access to accounts used by public Internet customers are significantly lower than those for retailers. Additionally, most customers would not go to the trouble of obtaining and using a certificate to access the GlobalTech site. Hence, the decision was made to rely on the simpler mechanism of user name and password access for these interactions, rather than certificates.

Impact of the Pattern on Non-functional Characteristics

Availability	If the list of valid certificates is unavailable, the system cannot authenticate clients and so this would have a negative impact on availability.
Performance	There is a negative impact on performance as authentication based on digital certificates uses more encryption and so creates more overhead. There is more negative impact on performance by using encryption across the SECURE CHANNELS.
Scalability	Unaffected by this pattern.

Security

Security is improved as an attacker cannot place a false order without the retailer's digital certificate. Additionally, the associated use of SECURE CHANNELS protects information in transit.

Manageability

Manageability is negatively impacted as there are now server and client certificates to create and manage on an ongoing basis. However, if you have already set up key management for SECURE CHANNELS, part of this work may already have been done.

Maintainability

Unaffected by this pattern.

Flexibility

Unaffected by this pattern.

Portability

Unaffected by this pattern.

Cost

There is little impact on cost above and beyond that required for the underlying SECURE CHANNELS implementation.

Moving On

Our system is now as performant and secure as required. The next area for consideration is how the system can evolve to deal with more load or changed requirements.

Other Patterns

Given the nature of system control it will always be in tension with system performance. Almost all controlling measures, whether they are for administration or security, will add overhead and slow the system down.

There are clear examples of this in the way that many of the system performance patterns, such as LOAD-BALANCED ELEMENTS, DEDICATED WEB AND APPLICATION SERVERS and COMMON PERSISTENT STORE, gain much of their benefit by increasing the number of elements in the system, which means that there are more elements to configure as part of a SYSTEM OVERVIEW and more information generated from CONTINUAL STATUS REPORTING (hence more network traffic). Similarly, the addition of security measures such as SECURE CHANNELS and INFORMATION OBSCURITY will serve to slow down the overall performance of those parts of the system to which they are applied. This is why you will usually apply a mixture of control and performance patterns as the latter help to offset the negative impact on performance of the former. The only clear place where a performance pattern reinforces a control pattern is the way that DEDICATED WEB AND APPLICATION SERVERS is pretty much a prerequisite for a DEMILITARIZED ZONE.

On the other hand, the relationship between control patterns and evolution patterns is more neutral. There are some places where control patterns may help in the implementation of evolution patterns, such as a DEMILITARIZED ZONE restricting access to a SWAPPABLE STAGING ENVIRONMENT. However, the SWAPPABLE STAGING ENVIRONMENT will mean that there are more elements for a SYSTEM OVERVIEW and for some form of CONTINUAL STATUS REPORTING. There are a few more obvious tensions, such as the conflict between the DEMILITARIZED ZONE limiting the connectivity through the firewall to particular machines whereas DYNAMICALLY-DISCOVERABLE ELEMENTS should allow you to add new application servers as required.

In the next chapter we will look at patterns that help to make the system evolve more easily.

CHAPTER 9

System Evolution Patterns

Plus Ça Change

Every software project (and the system the project is developing) has to deal with changing requirements, changing personnel, advances in technology (even those that appear to be a retrograde step) and moving deadlines. Internet system projects also have to deal with the fact that, because the users are neither 'friendly' nor 'tame', the systems may be subject to changes instigated or caused by their use.

A fundamental contradiction of building Internet systems is that the rate and degree of change required is directly proportional to the success of the system. Suppose a new Internet service is launched that is capable of handling up to 1000 simultaneous users. The service launch is a success and it proves popular – the average load quickly goes from around 200 users at launch to around 1000 within a few weeks. The servers are running at near-maximum capacity much of the time.

The obvious thing to do is add more capacity, but the system architecture does not allow this to be done quickly. Plans are made for the roll-out of a new version of the system, capable of handling up to 4000 simultaneous users, in eight weeks' time. Two weeks into the upgrade plan, the service is featured on a couple of prominent news sites and user requests go through the roof (although most of these users cannot get on to the system as a cap of 1200 simultaneous users has to be set in order to avoid it slowing down to the point where it is unusable by everyone). In addition, a prominent service provider decides that they want to integrate the service with their portal. However, the technology the service provider uses doesn't fit well with the current system architecture and it needs refactoring in order for the integration to work well.

So the success of the service, something everyone on the project should be proud of, has brought a number of major headaches. Everything they considered in terms of availability, performance, scalability, manageability and security has been challenged to the point of breaking. To a certain extent the system they now need, in non-functional terms, is completely different to the one they designed, just a few months after launch.

So, what can we do? The answer lies in the creation of a system architecture that accepts the inevitability of change and allows the system to evolve. This is not to say that we introduce abstraction and generality at every point – the system could very well end up doing nothing, albeit in a very flexible way. Rather, that we adopt a number of fundamental principles and sensible approaches to architecting a system that, inevitably, will have to change.

Principles

In order to maximize availability, scalability, performance, manageability and security we have developed an architecture that consists of a relatively large number of collaborating elements. This collaboration is key: no one element or type of element particularly ensures the availability, scalability, etc. of the system – it is the combination that improves the non-functional characteristics.

This combination of element types, which works so well in improving the effectiveness and control of the system, can actively work against its evolution. In order to achieve the improvements sought we've developed an architecture that is pretty tightly coupled: the web servers must be able to communicate directly with the application servers and the application server load balancers for example. This is fine for now, but what happens if we need to change the load balancers or the application servers, perhaps upgrading them to a new version or replacing them with an entirely different product?

One way to minimize the impact of such changes is to have a much more loosely-coupled architecture, perhaps based on a Message Bus pattern [Hohpe and Woolf 2003] (examples include products from BEA and Tibco). In such an architecture, no one element would be directly aware of any other element. They would publish requests and responses as messages onto the bus and expect other elements to do something appropriate with those messages.

This is an extremely effective architecture for some types of system but not the type we are dealing with here. For a start, message bus architectures can never perform as well as those based on direct communication. Time has to be spent encoding and decoding messages and, often, bridging between the message bus and the API of the element (most web server products do not deal with messages). Perhaps more importantly though, an event- or message-based solution is not suitable for the type of system we are dealing with, which is essentially request–response based. The sheer complexity of co-ordinating all the different types of element involved in servicing even the simplest of requests makes a message-oriented solution unsuitable.

So we are settled on an architecture based on direct communication between system elements, but we want to be able to evolve these elements independently.

One-Way Dependencies

If we have two system elements that each equally depend on each other, replacing one with something different is irritatingly complex. In Figure 9.1, suppose we want to replace element B with a new element, C. We have to ensure two things: that A works with C and that C can work with A.

Sometimes the best way to ensure that B's replacement works with A is to replace A as well, perhaps upgrading to the latest version that is compatible with C. This is more expensive, time-consuming and risky (particularly if other things depend on A) than just replacing B with C.

Suppose we can ensure that we never get into this two-way dependency problem, that A only depends on B and not vice versa? This makes things a bit easier: we only need to ensure A works with C. Better still, if we want to replace A rather than B, we only need to be sure that A's replacement works with B, B should not need to be changed in any way.

So haven't we just made the problem easier to solve by saying 'let's make it easier'? Pretty much, but the type of architecture we have been looking at for our systems fits the one-way dependency model pretty well.

Figure 9.2 shows a typical three-tier architecture with a switch to load-balance the web servers and a load balancer for the application servers. In terms of dependency,

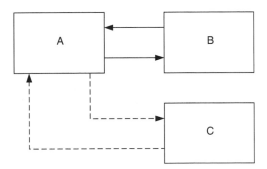

Figure 9.1 System elements with complex dependencies.

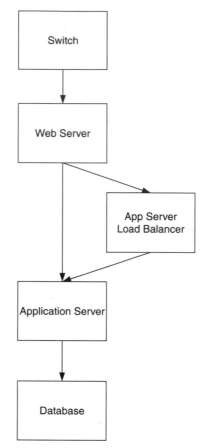

Figure 9.2 One-way dependencies in Internet technology system architecture.

the switch needs to be configured to forward requests to the correct web server, the web server needs to know about the application server load balancer and the application server (if the load balancer doesn't forward the request but merely tells the web server where to forward the request to). The application server doesn't need to know where any request it receives came from or even that a load balancer was involved in determining that it got the request.

So we could quite happily replace the web server and only affect the switch. Equally we could replace the load balancer and only affect the web server.

Standard Protocols

If we have managed to engineer our architecture so all dependencies between system elements are one-way, we can further improve our ability to evolve the system by basing the dependencies on standard protocols. The simplest example of this is the switch dependency on the web server. The switch simply needs to forward an HTTP request to a known port in order to work with the web server. If we keep the load-balancing element of the switch independent of the type of web server we are using (round-robin or based on CPU usage) then we can replace the web server with any other type of web server without needing to change the switch. Another example is using SQL in the application server when it needs to query the database.[1]

The usual argument against using such standard protocols is that they can be slower than using 'native' protocols. This may be true but using native protocols should not be the first port of call when optimizing the performance of a system. The use of native protocols introduces a hard dependency that can make the replacement of a system element very difficult or even effectively impossible. Typically, far more effective performance gains can be made by implementing some of the performance patterns described earlier.

Isolating Layers and Adapters

A third technique for improving the ability to evolve the system is to introduce a new layer or adapter where two elements have to be dependent on each other. Suppose we need to integrate our system with a supply-chain management system for placing retailer orders. The frequency of upgrades to this system is likely to be pretty low but we may need to deal with two or three over the lifetime of the Internet system. And such an upgrade can be a pretty lengthy process and have a significant impact on any system that interfaces with it.

If we're unwilling to tie the Internet system directly to the supply-chain management system, we can always introduce a mechanism that talks the Internet system's language on one side and the supply-chain management system's language on the other. Such an adapter or layer provides an interface that isolates each system from the other. This interface then becomes a point of stability in the system. The product, component or service providing the functionality can change as long as the interface stays stable. In this way, any other subsystem that uses this interface can remain stable during such a change.

DYNAMICALLY-DISCOVERABLE ELEMENTS

Estimation is a tricky business. At the start of any large Internet project, the sponsors of a project and the technical architects will attempt to estimate the number of users anticipated and to specify a system that will cope with that number of users. However, life on the Internet for most companies is anything but predictable as they

---

[1] Although, we should note, there are many inconsistencies between the way different database management systems implement and support SQL.

bring their new or updated business models to a new customer base. If business builds at an unexpected rate, the very time you need extra capacity is the very time you can least afford to take the system offline in order to add it. Some of the potential success stories of the early e-commerce days turned from heroes to villains overnight due to lack of capacity.

How can we introduce additional capacity to the system without having to take it offline?

By basing the architecture of our system on an APPLICATION SERVER ARCHITECTURE implemented as a set of LOAD-BALANCED ELEMENTS we have given ourselves a mechanism for expanding the capacity of the system relatively easily: by introducing more servers. If we split the servers according to DEDICATED WEB AND APPLICATION SERVERS, COMMON PERSISTENT STORE and PERIPHERAL SPECIALIST ELEMENTS we also have the choice of introducing servers of different types to suit our needs.

The GlobalTech system architecture has a number of points at which we can expand its capacity by adding new servers. Adding new application servers adds capacity to the dynamic functionality of the site: retailer locator, promotions, product catalogue views, etc. Adding new web servers allows us to handle more requests, particularly for the binary system assets (downloads of manuals, drivers, etc., as well as page furniture). Adding mail servers means we can increase the number of promotional emails we can send at any given time. It is also possible that we may want to reduce capacity if we have introduced extra capacity at a peak period (e.g. Christmas). After the peak we will want to recover the additional elements and redeploy them elsewhere (or send them back to the equipment rental company).

All this flexibility means that we can expand or contract the GlobalTech system's capacity in a number of different ways to cope with different types of change in demand. However, the other elements of the system need to be made aware of this additional or reduced capacity. If a web server (or the application server load balancer it talks to) does not know that there are three new application servers available, it cannot spread its load across them. It is easy to impart the initial configuration information to system elements when the system is first deployed. However, if we need to take the system out of service in order add or remove servers, we can only ever cope with changes in capacity that we can predict well ahead of time.

Use components that can discover new system elements dynamically and can start routing requests to these new elements in order to increase the capacity of the system as a whole.

We have already identified the web servers, application servers and mail servers as points in the GlobalTech system where we can extend its capacity by adding more servers. The web servers receive requests from the outermost switch so we need to use a switch that can discover new web servers as they are introduced.

Application servers receive requests from web servers but the web servers determine which application server should receive the request by communicating with the load balancer. So it is the load balancer that needs to be able to dynamically discover any new application servers. Finally, the GlobalTech application running in the application servers talks directly to the mail server when it needs to send an email. So we either need to use an application server that will transparently support dynamic discovery or else write our own discovery implementation as part of the application.

There are a couple of basic ways to implement this solution. The first is the most basic and restrictive: you can identify a set of locations (i.e. IP addresses and ports) where the discoverable system elements can be found. The element that forwards requests to the DYNAMICALLY-DISCOVERABLE ELEMENTS constantly scans these locations and updates a list of available elements based on those that it discovers. When it needs to forward a request it chooses (based on some algorithm) one in its list, checks that it is still available, and forwards the request.

The key characteristic of this implementation is that you need to be able to define all the possible locations for DYNAMICALLY-DISCOVERABLE ELEMENTS up front. As soon as you have an element at each of those locations, you need to re-configure the element that forwards requests (perhaps by taking it out of service, although you could use a DYNAMICALLY-ADJUSTABLE CONFIGURATION). This can be advantageous if you are concerned about security as, if you can secure each of the locations you have chosen, you can avoid rogue elements being introduced maliciously or by accident.

If, however, you prefer flexibility and ease of management, you can implement the solution by having any newly-introduced element add itself to the forwarding element's list of possibilities. DYNAMICALLY-DISCOVERABLE ELEMENTS, as they start up, contact the forwarding element at a known location to indicate their availability. The forwarding element can then either invalidate its cache of available elements or maintain a runtime-checked list (see DYNAMICALLY-ADJUSTABLE CONFIGURATION).

Whichever implementation you choose, the implementation and configuration is cleaner if you ensure that there are only one-way dependencies between the different layers in your application. If you do not stick to this principle, it is far more difficult to add and remove resources dynamically as it is more difficult to identify who is using them at any one time.

The dynamic discovery of system elements can be performed by hardware devices, software components or both.

Impact of the Pattern on Non-functional Characteristics

Availability   Availability is improved because newly-introduced system
                        elements can be replacements for, or supplements to, existing
                        elements. Also, the same mechanism can detect the
                        re-introduction of an existing element that has previously
                        been unavailable, perhaps due to a failure.

Performance	There is potentially a negative impact on performance because the mechanism that allows system elements to be discovered at runtime will have some processing overhead.
Scalability	Scalability is improved because new hardware and/or software can be introduced (or removed) at runtime and the system can automatically adjust to take advantage of it. This applies to both short- and long-term capacity changes.
Security	There is potentially a negative impact on security as the dynamic discovery mechanism needs to be secured to prevent rogue elements being introduced either accidentally or maliciously.
Manageability	There is potentially a negative impact on manageability as the dynamic discovery mechanism itself has to be managed in addition to the introduction of dynamically-discoverable elements.
Maintainability	Maintainability is potentially improved as elements can be introduced to replace elements that have failed or are failing.
Flexibility	The flexibility of the system is potentially improved as dynamically-introduced elements can add new functionality to the system.
Portability	Unaffected by this pattern.
Cost	Cost will increase slightly as the dynamic discovery mechanism must either be built and maintained as part of the system, or be a prerequisite for bought-in components, making those components potentially more expensive.

Moving On

The addition of more Dynamically-Discoverable Elements to a system is one way to increase the capacity of the system. However, it is not the only way. For hardware elements, we can increase the capacity of individual elements if we plan for it by deploying Expandable Hardware.

EXPANDABLE HARDWARE

Hindsight is an exact science. Looking back, we can always see what the better decision would have been now that we know how things have panned out. How many people wish that they had bought high tech stocks back in the early 1990s? And how many other people wish that they had sold those same high tech stocks before 2000? The history of an experienced system architect will be littered with such learning experiences. One of the primary things that can be learned is that there is never enough money at the start of the project to build the system you really need by the end of it. In terms of software, you often have scope to continually refactor until it meets your needs. In terms of hardware, if your first estimate was too low, you usually hit hard and painful limits as the use of the system grows.

How do we ensure the hardware doesn't impose restrictive limits on the system?

Given an Internet technology system based around an APPLICATION SERVER ARCHITECTURE you will be able to identify multiple system elements that could potentially become a bottleneck as system load grows. Some of these bottlenecks will arise due to the capacity of the hardware rather than the software, so you must decide how this will be tackled from the outset.

As noted in the introduction to this pattern, we can never be sure about the forecasts for growth in traffic for a public Internet technology application. With the help of the business people, we can estimate our anticipated number of users and their usage profile. However, users may appear more rapidly or more slowly than we anticipate. In almost all applications, there is some restriction on the amount of money initially available. It may be that the system represents a first 'toe in the water' by a company into an area such as online banking. If so, they will not pay for an initial system that can support all of their existing customers. Rather, they will want to pay for, say, a system that can support 10% of their customer base but that can expand to meet increased demand.

As part of the creation of the system architecture, you will need to estimate how much hardware you need to deliver the sort of performance required. Take the case of the database server described in the 'Costing the GlobalTech system' section of Chapter 7. Our estimate for the initial peak load of 3000 consumer and 700 retail users is a server with four processors and 6 GB memory costing $30 000. We're pretty confident that this will easily handle the initial peak load but we also know that, if the system is a success, we will need to handle nearly three times this amount.

So we have a dilemma: do we specify just the basic server we know we need; one a bit more powerful to cope with some increase in load; or a server that, at the outset is capable of coping with the maximum load it is ever going to have to face? This is not a pleasant set of options. If we spend just $30 000 for the 'base' specification, we will have to replace the server as soon as the system starts to be really successful. If we specify a server that is a bit more powerful, we have to spend more money than we strictly need and we will still have to replace it if the system is successful. In fact, only luck will make this the best choice – we will need to be a bit successful, but not as successful as we hope.

The last option is a bit scary. If we want to be sure we don't have to replace the database server (unless we far exceed all expectations) we have to spend $85 000 rather than $30 000. If we're using DATA REPLICATION, we're looking at $170 000 against $60 000. If we don't succeed to the degree we hope, we may have wasted $110 000, more than the total cost of the rest of the system. Even if we do reach the expected level of use, it may take a year or so to get to this level, so why spend the money now? We need a way to be able to gradually increase the capacity of the hardware without adding additional servers – something we can't do with a COMMON PERSISTENT STORE.

Use hardware that can be expanded to add new processors (or higher-speed processors), memory, disks and network connectivity. Ideally, size the hardware so that it can cope with the maximum predicted load when it is configured to about half its maximum capacity in these four areas.

Populating a server with half its processors, memory, disk capacity and network connectivity is not a hard and fast rule. If your initial requirements are reasonably low, but success for your system may mean you need to quadruple the capacity, you can buy a four-processor machine and populate it with just one processor and 25% of its memory and disk space. This is a very expensive way to get the capacity you initially need but gives you a lot of room for expansion. On the other hand, if you think you might just need a little 'room for manoeuvre', an initial population of 75% of capacity provides that without costing too much more than fully-loaded hardware of the same power. In our experience, however, populating a machine to half its capacity gives a good balance between initial cost and expansion potential.

Let's look at buying EXPANDABLE HARDWARE for the GlobalTech database server. A fully-laden server with four processors and 6 GB memory costs $30 000. If we bought a higher-capacity server with the same specification, but with the potential to add a further four processors and 10 GB, we would need to spend $45 000 – we're basically spending $15 000 to get the potential to upgrade later on. Populating it with the remaining four processors and 10 GB costs an additional $60 000, giving a total cost of $105 000. This is $20 000 more than buying the eight-processor, 16 GB server straight away but $10 000 less than buying the four-processor server and then replacing it with the eight-processor one (although you don't have a 'spare' four-processor server at the end).

You may do the sums shown above and consider that the extra initial cost is unwarranted at the start of the project and it is better to pay more later as the traffic grows. If it were simply down to cost then this is an easy decision to make. However, EXPANDABLE HARDWARE also gives you the ability to gradually increase the capacity of the database server in line with increase in use (you don't have to choose whether to have either the 'small' server or the 'big' one). Perhaps after a few months we add two more processors and an additional 6 GB memory, with the last two processors and remaining memory following several months after that. And we have may have the option to do this in an unplanned way. If we experience a sudden surge in demand, we will be able to obtain additional CPU and memory much faster than we would an entire server. Is this worth an additional $20 000?

So, by starting with a more expandable server, we have reduced both the cost and the risk of upgrading. This gives the optimal upgrade path based on a higher initial cost. We could also apply this pattern to other hardware resources on servers, such as hard disk capacity, and to other hardware components such as routers, switches and network-attached storage units.

So, in addition to the expandable database server outlined above, we decide to use EXPANDABLE HARDWARE for the application servers as well, despite the use of LOAD-BALANCED ELEMENTS. This increases our initial cost somewhat but gives us two separate ways in which we can increase capacity, either by introducing a new hardware server to cope with large increases in use, or by adding some memory and possibly an additional CPU to cope with smaller increases in use. We also apply the pattern to the routers and load balancers, specifying them with spare slots for additional blades to cope with the anticipated increase in load.

Impact of the Pattern on Non-functional Characteristics

Availability	There may be a negative impact on availability if there is a decision to employ a single, expandable element rather than multiple functionally-identical elements.
Performance	Unaffected by this pattern.
Scalability	Scalability is improved due to the ability to add extra capability to the existing infrastructure.
Security	Security is slightly improved as there will be fewer elements to secure than there would be with the alternative strategy of employing more functionally-identical elements.
Manageability	Manageability is improved as there will be fewer elements to administer than there would be with the alternative strategy of employing more functionally-identical elements.
Maintainability	Unaffected by this pattern.
Flexibility	Flexibility is improved as it is possible to add more functions to the system without changing the underlying hardware, by simply upgrading what you have.
Portability	Unaffected by this pattern.
Cost	The initial cost of the system is increased. However, the cost of increases in capacity are reduced. One important caveat is that the potential saving will decrease over time. The development of hardware still roughly conforms to Moore's law and in two years' time, we are likely to be able to buy a hardware server four or five times more powerful than the one we purchase today for the same price. If we have bought EXPANDABLE HARDWARE with the intention of not upgrading for a year or more we have to be aware that it might be just as cheap to buy what we need now and then completely replace it when we run out of capacity.

Moving On

The evolution patterns so far have dealt with ways to evolve a system once it is deployed. There are also ways of building the ability to evolve into an application as it and its environment is developed.

VIRTUAL PLATFORM

If the system we are building has a significant lifespan (anything over a couple of years), there is every chance that we will have to replace a number of the infrastructure elements the system is built on. This might be because we launched the system on a basic infrastructure and want to upgrade to a more 'enterprise level' set of components now the business case has been proved. Or maybe some of the elements have become obsolete and we need to replace them with more up-to-date or competitive versions. Whatever the reason, we need to reduce the impact of changes to the infrastructure as much as possible – high impact means a lengthy process of refactoring and testing the application on the new infrastructure components and a risky change to the new versions in the production system.

How do we ensure that we can change the infrastructure the system is built on without needing to make major changes to the system itself?

When you create an Internet technology system based around an APPLICATION SERVER ARCHITECTURE you will need to decide on the environment that supports your application. In older applications, you had to build almost all of the functionality you needed on top of a very low base provided by the operating system. As operating systems became more sophisticated they started to provide more of this functionality – a trend that was accelerated by the appearance of third-party libraries or components for specialized computational or business functions. More recently, higher-level platforms have appeared, such as J2EE and .NET, that provide further in-built functionality and obviate the need to access lower-level functions to achieve the desired functionality. The combination of platforms and third-party libraries or components makes up a 'technology stack' on top of which our application will run. Basically, our application functionality is now a relatively small amount of code running on top of a large 'technology stack' as shown in Figure 9.3.

If performance is your driver then you will want to dispense with any unnecessary method calls and object instantiations. The real speed comes from getting as 'close to the metal' as possible. Unfortunately, from an evolutionary point of view, the closer to the metal a particular component goes, the harder it is to evolve that component should the underlying hardware and/or software change.

In programming terms, the closest you can get to the metal is the CPU instruction. There are still bits of code around (written in C, C++ and others) which contain instructions like _asm, followed by instructions for a particular processor. Directly-coded

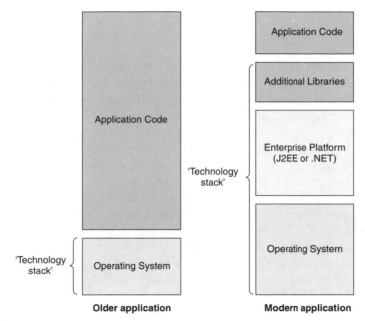

Figure 9.3 Application code running as part of technology stack.

assembly language instructions are, thankfully, no longer very common in the types of system we are interested in building. More likely though (and no less difficult to port) is the use of operating-system-specific libraries or components that can offer better performance or more powerful features than more portable versions.

Although the operating system is a fundamental part of the infrastructure for an Internet-technology system, it is by no means the only part. The web servers, application servers, peripheral servers and database servers we choose (in fact, any component) all form part of the foundations for the system we are building.

At the inception of the project to build the GlobalTech system, the architects performed an assessment of the advantages of different hardware and operating system platforms (Sparc/Solaris, Intel/Linux, Intel/Windows NT). Eventually, the architects decided to go for the Sparc/Solaris option as this gave a reasonable level of price/performance and fitted with the currently supported systems in the corporate data centre. However, the Intel/Linux option indicated a better price/performance ratio and there is a plan that the corporate data centre will soon offer support for Linux machines. The GlobalTech management is interested in seeing whether they can save money by migrating some or all of the system to Linux over time. Hence we need a technology stack that can be relatively easily ported to Linux. The management are also concerned about vendor 'lock-in'. Vendors come and go and, even if they stay, they often force upgrades onto customers that don't necessarily want them – using the argument that support for older versions is less effective (or even unavailable). So how can we be sure we are able to move platforms in the future and to swap out vendor components if it becomes necessary?

Choose a set of components and standards that insulate the system from the specifics of the infrastructure. Pick standards that are implemented by a number of different products on different platforms, and components that have versions available for different platforms.

GlobalTech opts for a J2EE application server. Although the technical team recognize that moving from one vendor's server to another is not as simple as just dropping the system code into the new server, any vendor-specific deployment or configuration information should only comprise a small proportion of the total code base. This can be further aided by intentionally isolating server-specific functionality to small areas of code. The specific server chosen also has versions proven to run on Sparc/Solaris as well as Intel/Linux so there are two axes of migration – from one vendor to another and/or one hardware and operating system platform to another.

The choice of web server is pretty simple. Functionally, different vendors' offerings are very similar and the major differences are in their non-functional characteristics. A web server is chosen for which there are proven versions available for both Linux and Solaris. The choice of database is harder. Although the J2EE application server can communicate using JDBC, there will be other code, such as stored procedures, data scripts and offload scripts, that may need to use vendor-specific features for efficiency and power. The corporate standard DBMS has proven versions for both Linux and Solaris so this is selected. There is also a concerted effort to use standard SQL constructs wherever possible and clearly identify and isolate any non-standard code so that migration to another database will be reasonably painless.

A VIRTUAL PLATFORM is a type of isolating layer as described in the principle of isolating layers and adapters, since the application is isolated from any changes to the underlying platform. However, implementing a VIRTUAL PLATFORM can be tricky because it is hard to identify the correct level of abstraction or the right way to use standardized protocols to reduce dependencies. Of course we want migration to be as painless as possible and want as much freedom of choice as we can manage. On the other hand, the chances that we decide to take the application code we've written and drop it into an entirely different infrastructure is clearly a bit far-fetched, and we don't want to compromise efficiency and effectiveness to cope with some theoretical future situation.

One area where this choice becomes very difficult is when picking an application server. Many application servers can now be bought with component frameworks that provide out-of-the-box facilities for personalization, e-commerce, product catalogues, etc. These frameworks provide an even higher level of infrastructure than the base application server – instead of building on an infrastructure that takes care of threading, transaction processing, dynamic page generation, etc., the developer is building on one that provides a shopping basket, user registration and login, hierarchical category navigation, etc. This 'application level' infrastructure helps reduce the time to implement the system in much the same way the base application server does – now the development team is customizing a bare-bones application rather than building business logic from scratch. But the use of the framework pretty much locks the system in to the framework vendor. In this case, the components that surround the application server become part of the VIRTUAL PLATFORM (see Box 9.1).

BOX 9.1 How virtual is your platform?

We should emphasize that introducing a VIRTUAL PLATFORM is not the same as deciding to use Java (which uses a Java Virtual Machine) or one of the .NET programming languages (which all use the same virtual machine). The C++ programming language does not use a virtual machine but is reasonably portable across different operating systems due to its ubiquity and use of libraries that hide any difference between those operating systems. However, defining a true VIRTUAL PLATFORM is much more than just choosing a programming language that can be ported to a different operating system or machine: we must look at the whole set of operating system(s), off-the-shelf components and products that form the environment for our application.

It is also worth making the distinction between our use of the term 'virtual platform' and the 'virtual platform' provided by an application server environment such as J2EE or .NET. In the case of the application server platform, it provides abstractions for the underlying functionality that makes it easier for developers to create powerful applications on top of it. If you refer back to Figure 9.3, an application server environment looks far more like the 'modern application' than the 'older application', and so the amount that the developer has to write is far less than it was before. The application server environments provide many benefits to the developer such as memory management and runtime code checking. Indeed, the .NET Common Language Runtime (CLR) and Intermediate Language (IL) are indistinguishable from

Java's Virtual Machine (VM) and bytecodes at a distance. Even the class libraries have many similarities (but don't tell the marketing folks at Microsoft and Sun). However, while the use of a virtual platform saves us effort (and hence time and cost) does it actually provide us with the 'virtual platform' described in the pattern?

If we first consider J2EE application servers, then in theory they provide us with a very good virtual platform. However, this only works in practice as long as you stay within the bounds of the J2EE specifications which are agreed through the Java Community Process. If you 'code to the spec' your software will run on any of the compliant application servers, given a few configuration tweaks here and there. However, most application server vendors compete not only on price/performance ratios but on added value. This means that they provide additional server-side plug-ins such as commerce server frameworks or optimized native components. As soon as you start using such functionality, the value of the virtual platform is eroded.

.NET is definitely a Microsoft-driven platform. Although there are some ports of it to other environments, at the time of writing these have not achieved any significant market share. Hence, there is a definite perception of 'lock-in' if you choose .NET. However, before dismissing .NET because of this, you should do some serious soul-searching about how portable your J2EE code really is and whether you would seriously consider changing application servers or if this is just a 'nice idea'.

Impact of the Pattern on Non-functional Characteristics

Availability	Unaffected by this pattern.
Performance	Performance is usually negatively impacted by the extra layers of processing between the application and the target hardware or operating system. However, as the different layers are written by specialists in that field (you hope), they may perform better than home-grown solutions. An example of this is that newer Java Virtual Machines can perform better than the equivalent code in C/C++, for some operations, due to the dynamic optimization they apply at runtime.
Scalability	Unaffected by this pattern.
Security	Unaffected by this pattern.
Manageability	Manageability is potentially improved if the management mechanisms are made part of the VIRTUAL PLATFORM; for example if all components report status information using SNMP.
Maintainability	Maintainability is improved as you have less of your own code in which bugs may occur. If you choose widely-used components, many of the bugs will be discovered quickly, which helps maintainability once the component is mainstream.
Flexibility	Unaffected by this pattern.
Portability	Portability is improved because the system can run on a number of different target hardware or software platforms without significant change.
Cost	The impact on cost is determined by the choice of components used to implement the VIRTUAL PLATFORM. If we adopt a standards-based approach, we may find that the elements available are cheaper than proprietary versions (they may even be freely available). However, some components may be more expensive: someone has to pay for the Linux port of our all-singing all-dancing database, for example.

Moving On

So far we have focussed on patterns for improving scalability (evolving the system to cope with more users) and portability (evolving the system to run on a different infrastructure). In both these cases, the assumption is that the functionality of the system is unchanged. However, changing the functionality to fix bugs, improve existing features and add new features is probably the most common form of system evolution we are going to have to deal with. The SWAPPABLE STAGING ENVIRONMENT and SEPARATE SYSTEM-MANAGED DATA patterns both help with migrating the system from one version to the next.

SWAPPABLE STAGING ENVIRONMENT

The functionality of the system will inevitably change over time. These changes may be to fix bugs, alter existing features or add new features. Regardless of the motivations, change to the functionality is probably the most common form of system evolution we are going to have to deal with. In an iterative or phased process, it is a fundamental characteristic of the project. Even in a 'waterfall' style of development, it is inevitably going to happen. One of the joys of developing public Internet systems is that they will be used by a set of untrained users in wholly unpredictable ways. These users will expose bugs even the most thorough testing procedures missed and they will demand features that could never have been predicted at the project's inception. So, whatever style of development process we choose, we will have to release new versions of the system. But the migration from one version of a system to another can be a lengthy and risky process at the best of times.

How do we add new functionality to the system without taking it out of service for a long period of time or taking a big risk that the new system is malfunctioning when it is brought back into service?

Our public Internet system will be built around an APPLICATION SERVER ARCHITECTURE that houses the central functionality for the system. At some point in time, this core functionality must be replaced to add new features or to deliver bug fixes. As it is a public Internet system, we cannot easily inform all our users of any potential outage required to upgrade the system. Even if we could do this, for a global application there is never a good time to take it out of service.

Time versus risk is one of the fundamental trade-offs in any migration process. The longer you take to migrate the system, the less the chance that it will be broken at the end of the process. For the migration of 'traditional' systems, the emphasis is usually on risk mitigation. A company that one of the authors worked with had reached the point where they felt they had to migrate from the version of the supply-chain management system that they were currently using to the latest version. They instigated a six-month project to populate the new version with all the data and rules of the old version and then ran a three-month pilot project with the two versions running in parallel. At the point they decided they could migrate to the new version, they shut down all access to the old version (leaving the business to run without it) for a month so they could perform the final migration before bringing the new version online. In total, the migration took ten months and the system was unavailable for one of those months.

This kind of lengthy migration process is not suitable for the GlobalTech system. We are using an iterative process to deliver the system in a number of phases. The second iteration of the GlobalTech system is nearing completion and so the new version will need to be deployed and commissioned. This new version contains major functionality improvements and requires new components in its VIRTUAL PLATFORM. Given these major changes, it is particularly important that the new version is tested in a staging environment that mimics the real environment as closely as possible. Once it has been tested in staging, it must be migrated to the live environment. The length of each iteration to some degree dictates the migration timeframe. There is little point in having an iteration that runs for three months if it takes six months to migrate the production system to the new version. Also, there are thousands of users around the world who now rely on the existing version. With the availability requirement we have, we can't afford for the system to be unavailable for a few hours, never mind weeks. We need a mechanism that allows us to migrate quickly without any significant downtime as we swap over from the old version of the system to the new version.

Introduce a staging environment into the production servers. Implement a mechanism that allows you to swap the staging environment with the production environment, effectively swapping in the new version of the system.

A 'staging environment' is a common concept in Internet technology systems. In a content-rich system it is often the environment in which new content is reviewed before it is deployed to the live site. This review usually needs to happen in an environment as close to the live site as possible so the staging environment is set up to closely mirror the live site, in terms of shape if not capacity.

One alternative is to have a duplicate set of lower-capacity hardware that is accessible only from the corporate intranet to act as the staging environment. This hardware runs the same VIRTUAL PLATFORM as the production environment and has real or 'fake' versions of external services so as to represent a realistic emulation of the production environment. The new version is then deployed into the staging environment for system testing to take place. However, there are several problems with a separate staging environment. The first is that it can be very hard and expensive to create a realistic emulation of the production environment, not only in terms of the cost of machines and software licenses but also in terms of realistic simulations of services found in the live environment. The second issue is that it is still a non-trivial task to take the application running in this separate environment and migrate it to the production servers.

Because of these issues, it is becoming increasingly common to create the staging environment on the production hardware. This ensures that the staging environment is a very close mirror of the live site and reduces the time and effort required to deploy new content as we simply have to copy the content from one environment to another on the same machine. The only real difference between the staging and production environments created on the production hardware is that there are usually fewer web, application and other server instances on the production hardware that are dedicated to the staging environment. Additionally, access to the staging server instances is restricted to known users and/or machines on the corporate intranet.

The GlobalTech system will take this concept one step further (see Figure 9.4). Rather than having fixed production and staging environments, where staging always has a smaller set of server instances than production, we will make them swappable – effectively we can dynamically choose which environment is the production and which is the staging. At the point we swap, what was the staging environment becomes the production environment and vice versa.

This arrangement requires us to make the production and staging environments identical in capacity as well as shape – at least at the point of swapping over. But this arrangement means we can cope with migrating to a new version of the system as well as content. When we want to deploy a new system version we deploy it to the staging environment, check that it functions as expected in that environment, and then swap it with the production environment when we want to migrate.

How the swapping mechanism is implemented really depends on how tolerant the business is of an unavailable system. The simplest solution is to block all access to the site at the point we want to migrate (effectively closing the outermost switch to traffic). Any ongoing sessions on the outgoing system are then killed and the outermost switch configured to forward requests to the staging environment web servers. We then allow access to the site and any new requests are forwarded to the staging environment web servers – which are now effectively the production web servers. The outgoing system is then taken out of service and what was the production environment now becomes the staging environment for the next release of the system or its content.

This is a pretty quick and dirty mechanism that is suitable for a large number of systems. As long as you give your users plenty of notice of when you're going to migrate, there shouldn't be many sessions running at the point you have to close off access. Assuming you've got all the staging servers up and running, the process of re-configuring the outmost switch should be pretty quick and the new version should be live in a matter of no more than a few minutes (an hour or two at the most). However, this solution isn't so effective if you have a number of long-running sessions (such as retailers placing orders for new stock) or if you are truly global and there is no convenient time to block access to the system.

For the GlobalTech system we decide to opt for the most 'hot-swappable' implementation we can. This requires a smart switch that can recognize the difference between a request that forms part of a running session and a request that is not part

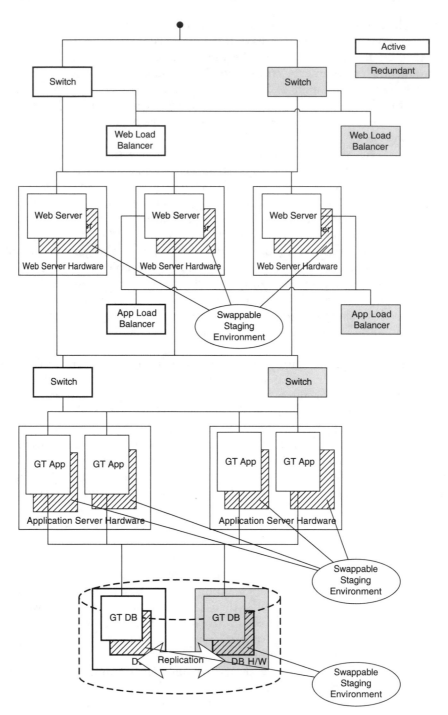

Figure 9.4 SWAPPABLE STAGING ENVIRONMENT applied to GlobalTech system.

of any session and that can be configured (at runtime) to forward requests that form part of a session to one set of web servers and requests that are not part of a session to a different set of web servers (see Figure 9.4).

We enable this behaviour at the point we wish to migrate, configuring the switch to forward requests that are not part of a session to the staging environment servers (now the production environment for new requests). Requests that are part of an existing session are routed to the outgoing production server. At this point we are effectively running two production servers – the old version continues to serve existing sessions and the new version serves new sessions. At some point all the sessions running on the old version of the system will naturally end and the outgoing system can be taken out of service. At this point the staging and production environments have swapped and we can use the new staging environment for the next release of the system or its content.

One caveat that should be mentioned relates to data migration. To have the production and staging systems running side-by-side there must either be no changes to the database schema(s) used by the system or those changes must be backwards compatible. Issues relating to data migration are discussed in the SEPARATE SYSTEM-MANAGED DATA pattern.

BOX 9.2 QA environments vs staging environments

QA environments are often confused with staging environments (and vice versa). There are usually a number of QA environments that are set up to test various different aspects of the system. There is likely to be a massively scaled-down version of the production environment that is used for basic functional testing. There will also be a number of other specialist QA environments for testing things such as scalability, performance, functionality under load, security, etc. These may well be created specifically for running a set of tests and then dismantled – particularly for large scalability and performance tests.

The key aspect of QA environments is that they are test environments; they are owned by the technical team and used to verify that the system meets technical expectations. They will often have test-specific elements such as test data feeds or stubbed back-end systems to isolate the behaviour that is being tested. They are also usually kept well isolated from the production environment to ensure there is no chance that any test elements, or elements under test, can 'leak' into the production environment.

Staging, on the other hand, is not a test environment. It is essentially a real environment and is used by the whole team to make one last check that a new version of the system both looks and performs as expected in a production situation. Early systems often had a separate staging environment that was as near as possible a copy of the production environment and the final go-live was essentially a deployment from staging to the production environment. Contemporary systems usually make no physical distinction of this kind between staging and production, preferring instead to use a SWAPPABLE STAGING ENVIRONMENT.

Impact of the Pattern on Non-functional Characteristics

Availability	Availability is improved as the system is more available throughout the evolution process.
Performance	There is potentially a negative impact on performance during the migration process as the production and staging environment servers need to run side-by-side. We could mitigate the impact by specifying hardware that is capable of running both the production and staging environments side-by-side, or even have the production and staging environments run on completely separate hardware. But these options will significantly affect cost.
Scalability	Unaffected by this pattern.
Security	Unaffected by this pattern.
Manageability	Manageability is negatively impacted during the migration process as there are twice as many elements in operation to manage and the switch-over itself has to be managed.
Maintainability	Maintainability is improved as it becomes easier to introduce fixes into the production environment.
Flexibility	Unaffected by this pattern.
Portability	Unaffected by this pattern.
Cost	The impact on cost is determined by the degree to which we mitigate the impact of the migration process on performance. If we want to avoid any performance impact we could duplicate the whole of the production environment and swap over to it when the migration process has finished. More likely we will want to spend some money expanding the capacity of the system a bit, so impact of the migration process is minimized without incurring a massive cost.

Moving On

We now have a system running on a VIRTUAL PLATFORM to make the creation, evolution and migration of functionality easier. The functionality and its content can be deployed relatively easily as the system is upgraded using a SWAPPABLE STAGING ENVIRONMENT. The SEPARATE SYSTEM-MANAGED DATA pattern considers the impact of data migration.

SEPARATE SYSTEM-MANAGED DATA

When we evolve an Internet technology system from one version to the next we are potentially changing a number of different types of application element: the page templates, the code, the configuration of the application, the data etc. With a SWAPPABLE STAGING ENVIRONMENT we can keep the system available to users as we evolve it; the degree of sophistication of the implementation governs whether the users notice any lack of availability at all. We can even evolve the schema data is stored in – we perform the data migration from the old schema as part of the process for bringing up the staging environment and, as users switch over to this environment, they start accessing the new data and schema.

However, this can only work when the data is totally under our control and most Internet technology systems have a significant proportion of data over which the system owners have absolutely no control, namely the data supplied and updated by the users.

How do we evolve the schema of the application without making it unavailable for a long period of time or risking that the new system malfunctions when it is brought into service?

Data migration is one of the fundamental problems of trying to evolve a highly-available system. As users interact with the system they change some of the data in the database. These changes can be explicitly triggered by the user, by changing their registration and profile information or submitting an order. Other changes come about indirectly such as updates to usage tracking information gathered automatically as the user navigates through the system. Users are the primary source of such externally-managed data although some systems may have other sources, such as continuous data feeds whose information is captured in a system database.

When we want to migrate the application data to a new schema we have to do this through a strictly-controlled sequence of events. The usual approach to migrating data is to perform some form of export from the old schema, manipulate the data as necessary to fit the new schema, and import. This takes a certain amount of time and is as susceptible to failure as any other intensive process. The problem with most database systems is that the data cannot be updated whilst it is being exported. So, from the point the first export starts, to the point at which the data is fully migrated to the new schema, users cannot update information – the system is effectively read-only. With the kind of data we need for the GlobalTech system, we may need to migrate hundreds of gigabytes of catalogue, support material, retailer, ordering and customer records. Such a process is going to take hours, possibly days, to carry out and validate.

There is no escaping this problem: when you need to migrate the application schema, the data being migrated cannot be updated during the migration process, and the migration process will take a finite amount of time. The key to maximising availability is to ensure that you can be selective about the parts of the schema you affect.

The GlobalTech team want to ensure that there is as little downtime as possible when migrating to new versions of the application. They will use a SWAPPABLE STAGING ENVIRONMENT to run the two versions of the code alongside each other. However both versions of the code require access to the system data. If the database schema is to change as part of the upgrade, it may be necessary to prevent all access to the system database until data has been migrated from one schema to another. Such downtime is a problem for a high-availability system so steps must be taken to minimize this downtime.

Separate the schema for system-managed data from that for externally-managed data. Migrate these schemas separately to minimize the amount of time the system is unavailable and reduce the risk of the migration failing.

In order to separate the system-managed data from that managed by an external actor, we must be able to identify the different categories of data in the system. The data manipulated by the application can be broadly split into three types: resources, system-managed data and externally-managed data.

Resources typically include static web content and images. From the point of view of this pattern, such data has already been irrevocably separated from externally-controlled data as it is completely under system control and cannot be changed by user activity.

How can we determine which parts of the system's data fall into the category of system-managed? Well, we can list some attributes of system-managed data that help us to identify it:

- Its update is controlled by the system. For example, although the contents of a product catalogue are not under the control of the system (e.g. it may be a replica of data held elsewhere in the organization), the system does retain control over when that information is updated. If the system's catalogue data is updated via a pull mechanism, that pull can be deferred to a more convenient time if the database schema is being updated. If the data is updated using a push mechanism then this could be suspended through agreement with the system pushing the data (although if this is tricky the catalogue data may be considered as externally-managed data).

- We are willing to tolerate some discrepancies between the copy of data held by the system and any copies external to the system. In many systems, the price information for products in a catalogue will change at most once a day. Once that change has been made, it is not a problem if a scheduled update later that day does not happen. Indeed, some systems in retail organizations can survive on prices that are many days old, which allows a very large update window.

- We can maintain multiple versions of the data. We could cache information from the catalogue on each application server as it is requested and only flush the cache once a day so that the information is never more than a day out of date. If we can tolerate discrepancies in the data, it should be possible to run two concurrent versions of the system, each with their own source of system-managed data.

Some people differentiate the types of data held by a system into 'operational' data (data on which the system operates, such as catalogue data or order information) and 'knowledge' data (data that governs the way that the system works, such as business rules and the contents of drop-down lists). This categorization is somewhat tangential to our categorization as system-managed data can fall into either category.

Externally-managed data has different characteristics:

- Its update is controlled by an actor external to the system. Most commonly this is a user but it may be any person or system that alters the data in the system but over which we have no control. A system that updates the system's catalogue information using a push mechanism would fall into this category if we have no control over when it attempts such updates.

- The information must remain consistent because inconsistencies will cause problems for the users of the system. In system terms, there must be one, definitive version of the data. If there is any possibility of discrepancy, this must be carefully managed.

- As we cannot handle large amounts of discrepancy in this data and it can be updated at any time by an external actor, we cannot maintain two separate versions of externally-managed data when maintaining two concurrent versions of the application.

As noted earlier, such data can be explicitly injected into the system, for example by submitting an order, or it can be generated as a consequence of using the system, for example user tracking information. The main thing is that the trigger for the update occurs in an unpredictable and uncontrollable way outside the system.

If all of the schema changes required by an application update are to system-managed data, we can create a new instance of the system-managed data on which the updated version of the application can operate. While the old and new versions of the application co-exist, they can share the same database containing externally-managed data as there are no changes to it.

Creating a new database instance for the system-managed data has some large benefits. The database instance can be created, populated and checked before the migration and then swapped over 'instantaneously'. This is particularly good if there is a lot of system data that needs to be migrated to a new schema as this can be done without having a negative impact on the performance and availability of the production system. Similarly, if you need to create a full text search index for your data then this can be done before the new database is brought online.

Alternatively, the two versions of the application can share the same instance of the system-managed data if the changes to the schema are made in a backward-compatible way. If the changes just involve adding new tables or columns to the schema without adding large quantities of new data, and there is no reliance on externally-managed data, then only a small migration is required in the form of running database update scripts. Changes to the structure of the database are a lot faster than changing the data it contains. This means that the live database can be updated at the cost of a brief outage if desired. This form of backward-compatible schema change is very useful, but it can tend to leave unused data lying around in your database. This may make the approach of creating a duplicate database for system-managed data to be used by a new version of the application more attractive.

As the externally-managed data cannot be duplicated, we have no choice but to share the database between two concurrent versions of the application. If there are any changes whatsoever to the schema of the externally-managed data then some form of outage will be required. If the changes to be made are backward-compatible, these changes can be implemented with only a short outage. However, if you want to change the schema of the externally-managed data in a way that is not backward-compatible (such as deleting a previously required column) or you need to move data around or to manipulate it in any way, a more involved migration sequence is required. The data must be exported from the old database and imported into the new one (or replicated between them). For any significant amount of data this will take some time, and don't forget that you will need to test the system once the data has been migrated before the system can be brought back online.

By separating system-managed data we are narrowing the 'surface area' affected by any change. The use of backward-compatible changes can narrow it even more. The hope for a high-availability system is that this will minimize the amount of externally-managed data whose schema needs to change. With luck you could eliminate it completely.

We can split the data in the GlobalTech system along these lines:

System-managed data	Externally-managed data
■ Product catalogue (updated by a content management system outside the Internet-based system)	■ Customer details (updated every time the customers edit their information)
■ Retail outlet information (also maintained by the content management system)	■ Shopping basket orders (created whenever the shopping basket is used to purchase goods)
■ Customer care information (also maintained by the content management system)	■ Retail orders (created whenever a retailer places an order)
■ Promotions (maintained by the content management system, an eCRM system and a campaign management system, all outside the Internet-based system)	■ Retailer details (updated whenever the retailers update their contact information)

This split allows upgrades to the catalogue, retail outlet and customer care information to be made in a relatively straightforward way when a new version is deployed.

Impact of the Pattern on Non-functional Characteristics

Availability	Availability is improved as the system is more available throughout the evolution process.
Performance	Unaffected by this pattern.
Scalability	Unaffected by this pattern.
Security	Unaffected by this pattern.
Manageability	There is a slight negative impact on manageability during the migration process as there are more elements to manage.
Maintainability	If only system-managed data is changed as part of a fix, then applying this fix causes less disruption so maintainability is improved.
Flexibility	Flexibility is improved as decoupling the system-managed data from the externally-managed data makes it easier to change and evolve the system.
Portability	Unaffected by this pattern.
Cost	The impact on cost really depends on the degree of relationship between system-managed and externally-managed data. If the two are unrelated or only loosely related (the retailer orders use the product codes, for example), the split should be easy and cheap to implement. If they are tightly related, separating the data may be very difficult and we may have to duplicate a certain amount of system-managed data in the externally-managed store.

Moving On

Our system is now as flexible as required. We have seen how the changes have accumulated in the GlobalTech system as we have examined the different patterns. In the next chapter we will take a look at the system that results from the application of the patterns.

Other Patterns

There is a natural tension between many evolution and performance patterns. The sort of overheads introduced by a VIRTUAL PLATFORM and DYNAMICALLY-DISCOVERABLE

ELEMENTS will slow down the system, so it is common to apply system performance patterns to compensate for this. Conversely, there is some degree of reinforcement as EXPANDABLE HARDWARE and DYNAMICALLY-DISCOVERABLE ELEMENTS complement performance patterns, such as LOAD-BALANCED ELEMENTS, that help to improve the scalability of the system. Similarly, the application of SEPARATE SYSTEM-MANAGED DATA can help to reduce the amount of data that has to be kept synchronized by DATA REPLICATION.

On the other hand, the relationship between control patterns and evolution patterns is more neutral. There are some places where control patterns may help in the implementation of evolution patterns, such as a DEMILITARIZED ZONE restricting access to a SWAPPABLE STAGING ENVIRONMENT. However, the SWAPPABLE STAGING ENVIRONMENT will mean that there are more elements for a SYSTEM OVERVIEW and for some form of CONTINUAL STATUS REPORTING. There are a few more obvious tensions, such as the conflict between the DEMILITARIZED ZONE wanting to limit the connectivity through the firewall to particular machines whereas DYNAMICALLY-DISCOVERABLE ELEMENTS should allow you to add new application servers as required.

In the next section, we will bring all the patterns together and examine their effect on the GlobalTech system.

PART 3

Application of the Patterns

GlobalTech Revisited

Reviewing the Architecture

In Chapter 5, we examined the requirements for the GlobalTech system. In Chapters 6 to 9, we have applied a number of patterns to evolve an architecture for the system, looking at the various non-functional characteristics and how they are affected by the introduction of each of the patterns. This chapter provides an overview of the resulting architecture and examines a number of potential variations that we may wish to explore.

Architecting for System Performance

Logical Architecture

Figure 10.1 gives an overview of the logical architecture of the GlobalTech system, evolved to improve system performance.

The system has been split into three layers contained within an APPLICATION SERVER ARCHITECTURE: the web-request handling layer that deals with incoming web requests

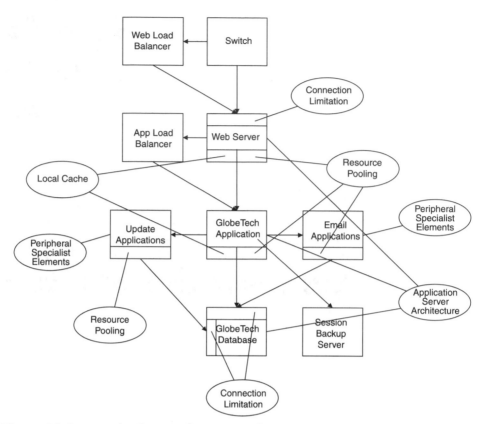

Figure 10.1 Logical architecture for system performance.

and translates them into requests for application functionality where necessary; the database layer that deals with data persistence, transactional integrity and querying; and the application layer that contains business functionality. The application layer itself consists of the GlobalTech Application and the Peripheral Specialist Elements for updates from external sources and for personalized and mass emailings.

Connection Limitation is applied in three places. The web server can limit the number of web requests it can simultaneously handle, effectively throttling the number of user requests the system as a whole has to handle at any one time. The database can also limit the number of connections it deals with to throttle the degree of data access from the GlobalTech Application and Email Applications, ensuring it has time to adequately perform queries and updates. The Update Applications bypass this limitation as they must be able to write to the database in order to function. However, they impose their own limitation on connections made to the data server, allowing the throughput of the import to be balanced against the overall performance of the database.

RESOURCE POOLING is applied in four places. The web server pools the connections it makes to the GlobalTech Application to request application functionality. The GlobalTech Application and the Email Applications each pool the connections they make to the database, as do the Update Applications. Balancing the pool sizes with limits on the number of connections should ensure that the pools are sufficiently big to give the desired improvement in performance without growing so large that they start to affect memory usage.

There are two LOCAL CACHES in the system. The GlobalTech Application caches information it writes to and reads from the database. The Update Applications invalidate this cache whenever they complete an update, thereby ensuring the cache does not contain out-of-date information. The initial implementation of the invalidation mechanism is a crude one: completion of an import totally invalidates the entire cache. If this proves to cause significant performance problems when an import is completed, the cache invalidation mechanism will be made more selective. The web server also has a LOCAL CACHE of all the binary assets used throughout the system.

We considered introducing a LOCAL CACHE for the Email Applications but the nature of these transactions (sending a confirmation email after some user-managed data has been updated and sending out both personalized and non-personalized mass mailings) means that the chance of the cache providing a sufficiently high hit ratio to justify its presence is pretty low. We may revisit this decision if the Email Applications perform badly or if they place undue stress on the database.

Deployment Architecture

Even glancing at Figure 10.2, we can see the principle of replication in full effect. Every element of the system is replicated at least once. If we were to drill further down into the detail of the system architecture we could see this principle carried through to the specification of individual elements. For example, the web, application and database hardware servers all have RAID disk arrays, and the application hardware servers have redundant network interface cards.

We can see the DEDICATED WEB AND APPLICATION SERVERS and the PERIPHERAL SPECIALIST ELEMENTS. We can also see the presence of a large number of different types of functionally-identical elements: switches and load balancers as well as different types of server. These elements are variously deployed as either ACTIVE–REDUNDANT ELEMENTS (where a single element can normally provide the required capacity and the introduction of a load balancer introduces significant cost or complexity) or LOAD-BALANCED ELEMENTS (where the use of a number of elements improves the capacity of the system and also introduces possibilities for long-term scalability through the introduction of further elements). SESSION FAILOVER provides continuous availability in the event of the failure of one of the application servers and all persistent data is in a COMMON PERSISTENT STORE that internally employs DATA REPLICATION to provide

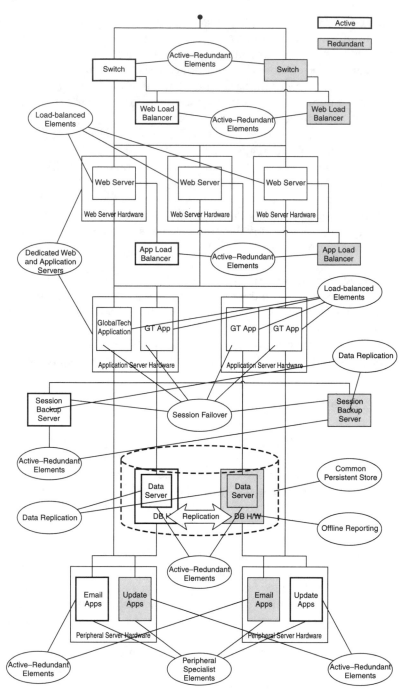

Figure 10.2 Deployment architecture for system performance.

fault-tolerant data servers. Data Replication is also used to ensure that the saved session state is available if the session backup server fails.

The redundant server in the pair that provide the Common Persistent Store provides the foundation for Offline Reporting. At regular intervals, a snapshot of the replicated data is exported into a file on the redundant hardware server. This is then transferred to a back-office environment where it is imported into a database ready for analysis.

Architecting for System Control

Logical Architecture

Continual Status Reporting is the most ubiquitous pattern – there is no element about which we do not want some management information. However, the implementation will vary significantly across the different types of elements. The switch, web server load balancers, application load balancers, and the session backup server simply need to indicate that they are up and running. The other servers need to report detailed information about their health, ranging from general memory and CPU usage to information pertinent to their specific role in the system (e.g. the number of simultaneous sessions for the GlobalTech Application).

Although not shown in Figure 10.3, Operational Monitoring and Alerting is installed in all places that have Continual Status Reporting. Monitoring agents are set up on each hardware server to monitor the status being reported by the various elements around them and to raise an alert on a channel to a back-end system should an element fail or some limit be exceeded.

In addition to reporting their status, the main server types implement 3-Category Logging to log their activities. The web servers log requests they receive, the GlobalTech Application logs error and debug information, and the database logs queries processed. The Peripheral Specialist Elements also log error and debug information.

Also not shown on the diagram are the various uses of Dynamically-Adjustable Configuration. This is mainly used to control the level of status information and logging that each of the elements performs, as well as to set any limits used by monitor agents. We also use Dynamically-Adjustable Configuration to control aspects of system performance, such as Connection Limitation levels and the sizes of pools of resources.

The major evolution in the logical architecture, from the one produced for system performance, is the introduction of a set of system elements specifically for security. The secure web server load balancer is used exclusively to handle secured requests and it balances the load between a set of web servers that are exclusive to secured requests. Using SSL and these secured servers we can establish a Secure Channel between a user and the application server that handles their requests.

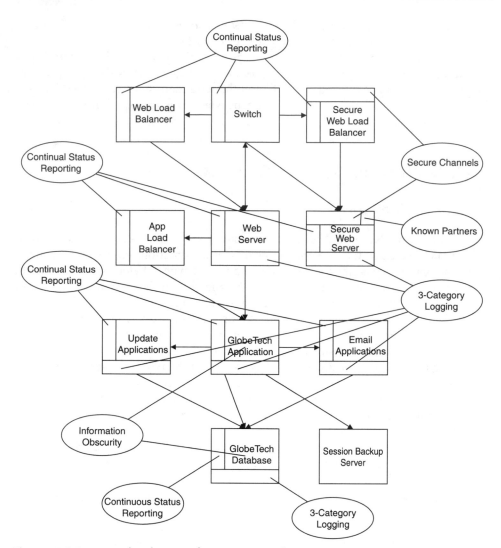

Figure 10.3   Logical architecture for system control.

In implementing SECURE CHANNELS in this way, we decided not to have a set of application servers specifically for secure requests. Arguably this would increase security even further as there is no way information from a secure request could 'leak' into a non-secure request. However, it would also massively increase the cost and the complexity of managing the system. It would also have implications for the implementation of the application: we would either have to allow sessions to be migrated from non-secure to secure servers and vice versa should the user make a secure request as part of a non-secure session, or force users to know in advance whether they are likely to carry out a secure request as part of their session. All-in-all, having separate secured application servers would be a major headache and using secure web servers in conjunction with a DEMILITARIZED ZONE (see the corresponding deployment architecture) meets our requirements.

We have also opted for a relatively simple implementation of KNOWN PARTNERS. All retailer users must have a digital certificate issued by (or on behalf of) GlobalTech to access the retailer functions of the system. These functions are only made available to a dedicated retailer domain name. Any requests to this domain must go through a secure web server which checks for the presence and authenticity of a GlobalTech certificate. Only those requests accompanied by a valid certificate are forwarded to the GlobalTech Application.

Again, the choice here is made in the face of cost and complexity implications. Keeping the GlobalTech Application unaware of the use of digital certificates means that we don't have to have special code for handling them (most web servers have certificate-authentication modules available as standard or as a chargeable option). We also don't have to have specific authentication code for the business functions – the secure web server ensures that a request for a business function is authorized and the DEMILITARIZED ZONE means we can be reasonably sure that any request for a business function comes from a secure web server. This might not be sufficient for some systems but it is good enough for GlobalTech.

The final piece of static security is the use of INFORMATION OBSCURITY to encrypt details of retailer orders and retailer details maintained in the GlobalTech system. The level of encryption is kept fairly low as this information is commonly accessed by the system but it is still sufficient to keep it obscured from casual attackers.

Deployment Architecture

With all the elements of the system continuously reporting their status in various degrees of detail we will need to implement SYSTEM OVERVIEW in various places to gain a usable overview of the system's health. Although only three are shown in Figure 10.4 – aggregating the status of the web servers, the Application Servers and the database respectively – there are actually four; the final one aggregates the status of all the other elements of the system into a single 'infrastructure' view.

The DEMILITARIZED ZONE referred to in the previous section can be seen here. An extra set of switches are introduced between the web servers and the application servers. In combination with the outermost switches, these form a DMZ into which the web servers are placed. The internal switches only allow direct requests from the web servers to the application servers using the application servers' proprietary protocol.

We can also see the physical implementation of the SECURE CHANNELS in the system, through the use of dedicated secure web load balancers and secure web servers.

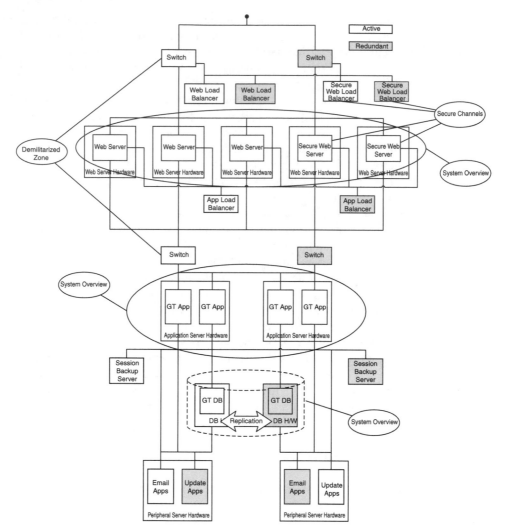

Figure 10.4 Deployment architecture for system control.

Architecting for System Evolution

Logical Architecture

There are three sets of DYNAMICALLY-DISCOVERABLE ELEMENTS (see Figure 10.5): both sets of web servers can be discovered dynamically by their respective load balancers, as can the GlobalTech Application Servers. This allows us to introduce new web servers and application servers as we need or want to.

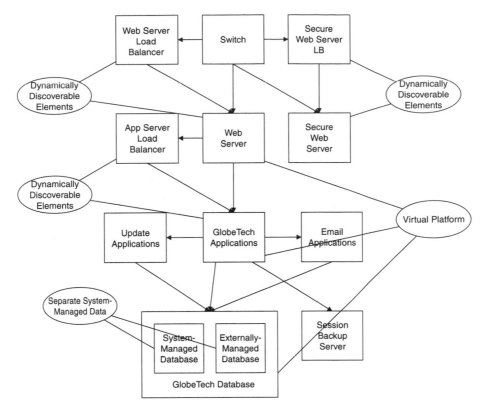

Figure 10.5 Logical architecture for system evolution.

The web servers, GlobalTech Application and database effectively sit within a VIRTUAL PLATFORM. All three products have been selected on the basis that they will run on either a Linux or a Solaris platform (either because they can be directly migrated or because there are versions of the product for both operating systems). So any code or configuration produced should be able to survive a migration from one operating system to the other. In addition, the GlobalTech Application is implemented to use strict SQL queries so that the database can be replaced if necessary.

Finally, we have introduced SEPARATE SYSTEM-MANAGED DATA to aid migration from one version of the system to another.

Deployment Architecture

EXPANDABLE HARDWARE is bought for the application and database servers and the server for the PERIPHERAL SPECIALIST ELEMENTS (see Figure 10.6). By populating all the

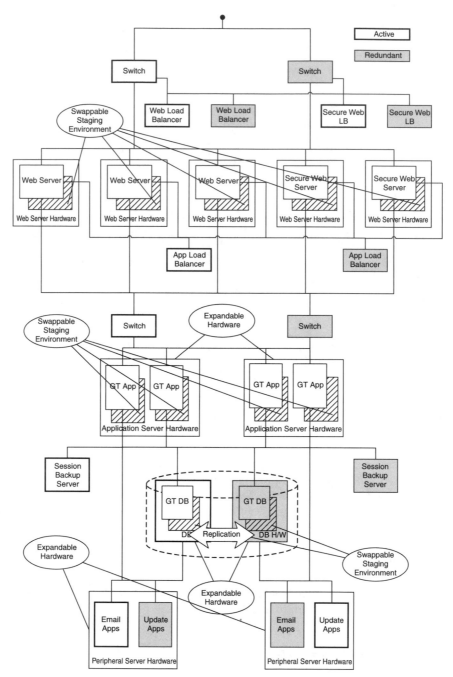

Figure 10.6 Deployment architecture for system evolution.

machines to about half their full capacity, we have the opportunity to significantly expand the system at a relatively low cost.

A SWAPPABLE STAGING ENVIRONMENT is implemented by deploying a second set of web servers, GlobalTech Applications and database schemas. We've decided against deploying a second set of peripheral applications for simplicity. The Update Applications can be closed during an upgrade without it affecting the user's perception of the system availability and both sets of servers can use the same Email Applications simultaneously. If the Email Server itself needs to be upgraded, emails can be stored during the upgrade process and then sent out when the server is brought back up.

Summary

In this chapter we have revisited the GlobalTech system and presented an overview of the architecture that has evolved through the application of all the patterns in the language. Although GlobalTech is a fictional system, we believe that it is a realistic example of the types of large-scale, high-capacity Internet technology systems that are being built in projects throughout the world today. The following chapter looks at how the patterns in the language can be applied to real projects, how they may drive architects towards a GlobalTech-style architecture or how the architectures evolved for those projects may differ from GlobalTech.

Applying the Patterns

Looking at the diagrams in the previous chapter, you may be thinking that the Glob-alTech architecture is rather more complex than the architecture of the system you work with or are planning to build. Or maybe you're thinking that the architecture looks somewhat simplistic – where is the edge caching, multiple data-centre failover and top-level security? If we're lucky, you'll be thinking that GlobalTech looks a bit like your system and you're glad to see that someone else has built something similar.

The GlobalTech architecture is clearly an exemplar – albeit one that is an amalgam of a number of real systems that the authors have been involved with (so whilst it has never actually been built, other systems that look a lot like it have been built). It is not as complex as the most complex of these systems but quite a bit more complex than the simplest. Ultimately, the GlobalTech architecture is a product of the functional and non-functional requirements placed on it. In this chapter we will look at a simpler architecture that can be evolved using the patterns in this book – an 'entry-level' high capability system if you like – and then examine how applying the patterns can produce still further architectures. This is not an academic exercise but is intended to explore how subtle changes in requirements and implementation choices can change the shape of the system and how the rest of it is implemented. An increase in the absolute level of a particular non-functional requirement may change the number and type of patterns applied. Even if the same patterns are applied in two systems, the decision to implement one of them differently can have knock-on effects for the implementation of the patterns with which it interacts. This can make the overall implementation of the two systems quite different.

The architecture of each system will be based on its functional and non-functional requirements. The number of possible combinations of varying degrees of requirement is huge. Also, there are multiple implementation choices for each pattern you apply to address these requirements. Given such a myriad of possibilities, we need a starting point from which to explore some variations, so we start with a simple system.

Not Quite the Simplest System that Could Work

High-capacity Internet technology systems have to deal with a certain level of inherent complexity, but that does not mean the system itself has to be complex. There is much to be said for simplicity in design and execution. Practitioners of extreme programming [Beck 2000] are encouraged to implement 'the simplest thing that could possibly work' while the creators of the original Java language worked on the principle of seeing how many extension features they could take away while still having a powerful language. How can we bring such simplicity to the types of Internet technology system we are examining?

Requirements

With certain caveats, we would concede that a single-box architecture (a single software element running on a single hardware server) is the simplest system that could possibly work (well, it could – possibly). However, this architecture will have problems meeting the non-functional requirements commonly set out for high-capacity Internet technology systems. Our not-quite-the-simplest architecture takes one, perhaps two, steps up the complexity ladder. It is an architecture commonly used since the late 1990s for the launch of new systems by some of the early dotcoms and a few established businesses that wished to dip their toe into the Internet waters. The main emphasis in this architecture is low cost because there was usually a fixed, and relatively small, amount of money in the funding for the initial web site. There also needed to be a story about how to grow the capacity of the system (with additional funds at certain break points) if and when the site really took off.

The non-functional characteristics for these systems were vague at best and usually expressed in relative terms. Availability was often emphasized, as everyone was paranoid that the system would be down when 'someone important' (a journalist, a highly-profitable customer, the company's owner?) went to look at it. An unavailable system equated to a failed business in many people's minds.

Scalability (long- and short-term) was also very important but much more abstract. Most businesses were committed to rapidly expanding their customer base and requirements to cope with exponentially growing numbers of users were not uncommon. However, when faced with a cost projection of what was required to support such growth, requirements were usually scaled back, with the view that coping with such a massive surge in demand is a nice problem to have compared to spending all the budget on a system to support users that might never materialize.

Performance was also typically an abstract requirement. It needed to be 'good enough' but there was not much consensus on what that really meant. In practice, performance improvements were usually retrofitted when 'someone important' decided it was too slow.

Manageability, maintainability, flexibility and portability were often second-order considerations. Although they were often part of the story about how the system would grow with its user base, they were also seen as a barrier to getting a functional system 'out of the door' – none of them provided much in the way of user-visible benefit.

Security, on the other hand, was paramount. Again, there was a fear that some security-related scandal could cause the business to fail. Depending on the nature of the business, security requirements might range from 'keep all the data secure' (to avoid the nightmare of customer details being stolen) through to a full security specification for something like an Internet bank.

So, what can we take from these broad statements in terms of more concrete non-functional requirements? Re-stating them as a set of short, sharp bullet points in the sort of language we have used throughout the rest of the book, we have:

- Cost should be reduced wherever possible.

- Failure of a single system element should not cause the system to become unavailable. However, if part of the system crashes, it is acceptable to ask users to start their current transaction again.

- Scalability should be 'allowed for' in the architecture but limited by cost:
  - Reasonable steps should be taken to provide short-term scalability (excess capacity) and medium-term scalability (easy addition of more capacity) as long as it is not too expensive.
  - If the number of users accessing the site exceeds the scalability provision, the extra requests should be bounced rather than impacting system performance for existing users.

- Performance should be increased wherever possible except where that conflicts with cost.

- Reasonable measures should be taken to ensure the confidentiality of sensitive data such as customer payment and address information. The business functionality should be protected to a reasonable degree from direct access. Both of these requirements must be balanced against cost.

■   The system should be able to evolve and adapt if the application proves to be a success. You should be able to adjust levels of requirement, such as increasing the level of security for parts of the application, as and when (or if) required. Again, this requirement is limited by cost.

Our focus for this book is the creation of systems that meet these sorts of non-functional requirements. However, the systems must do something functional as well! Fortunately, the entry-level systems all tended to have fairly similar functionality (even if the user interfaces varied dramatically). In the same way that the non-functional requirements for these entry-level systems are considerably lower than in the GlobalTech example we have used throughout the book, the functionality of these systems is also considerably simpler than that of GlobalTech. In brief, this functionality comprises:

■   A basic company web site and a web user interface for all of the functionality in the application.

■   Listing and searching of product information. Presentation of product information in summary and detail.

■   Simple shopping cart functionality to accumulate a set of products, take payment by credit card and generate shipping information to be sent to a warehouse or supplier.

■   A small amount of per user registration and customization, such as the retention of their delivery address.

This set of functional requirements helps to frame the decisions involved in architecting such an entry-level system. So, given these functional and non-functional requirements, what type of system architecture will result?

Entry-Level Architecture

With knowledge of the patterns discussed earlier in the book, we can derive a relatively simple architecture that will deliver the required level of capability. In Chapter 6, we discussed the patterns that make up the fundamental shape of the system. Let's start by considering how these patterns relate to the requirements for the entry-level system.

The functional requirements of the system indicate that we must have a web server to deliver the web user interface. We must also have at least one database containing catalogue information, order information and user details. To glue together the user interface and the database, we need to implement various functions such as online shopping, customization and catalogue searching. We could implement each of these as individual servers but, as indicated in Chapter 6, we consider the adoption of an APPLICATION SERVER ARCHITECTURE to be the starting point for a high-capability

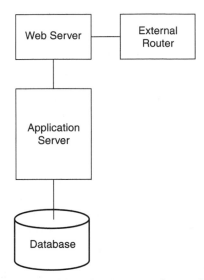

Figure 11.1   Logical architecture of entry-level system after applying APPLICATION SERVER ARCHITECTURE.

Internet technology system. As increases in availability and scalability require the raising of system capabilities, we will start from the APPLICATION SERVER ARCHITECTURE shown in Figure 11.1.

At this stage, we can start to think about applying the principle of functionally-identical elements configured as either LOAD-BALANCED ELEMENTS or ACTIVE-REDUNDANT ELEMENTS to increase the level of availability. We can apply this at a logical level by duplicating the web server and the application server and running multiple instances of each one. This means that the failure of a single software element will not cause the overall system to fail. However, if all of the web and application servers were installed on the same hardware server, the failure of this one machine would bring down the system, so the physical hardware must also be duplicated with some form of functionally-identical element. The same principle must also be applied to the external router.

Before making the choice of how each type of functionally-identical element should be implemented, we can first determine a little more about the number of elements that must be configured in this way. As it stands, the web servers, application servers and database server would be implemented on the same hardware. Although this helps the cost requirement, there are other factors to consider. The non-functional requirement for security asks that we restrict access to the business functionality from the Internet. The only way we can realistically do this is to apply DEDICATED WEB AND APPLICATION SERVERS and physically split the web servers from the application servers, otherwise the hardware servers that host the business functionality would be directly accessible from the Internet. The split allows us to route all external traffic to the hardware servers hosting the web servers and so provide a certain level of protection for the business functionality. The other factors at work here are the non-functional requirements for scalability and evolution. Each of these is far easier to achieve if this sort of split is introduced when a system is first created.

We are really making a series of trade-offs here between initial cost and capability versus cost and capability in the future. If we do not care about scalability and system evolution then we could argue the case for reducing the initial cost of the system by not splitting the web and application servers. However, this would give us far greater incremental cost when we needed to scale or evolve the system. Similarly, we could spend more initially on the security solution by creating a DEMILITARIZED ZONE around the web servers. This would make it easier to deliver increased levels of security at a later date if required. However, we do not know how likely it is that the requirement for security will increase. The financial cost of the firewall software and a machine to run it on combined with the performance cost of having business calls filtered through the firewall mean that we judge this not to be necessary as part of the initial architecture.

At this stage, we know that the web server, application server and external router in Figure 11.1 will need to be implemented as a set of functionally-identical elements that are configured to increase availability and that each of these logical elements will be deployed on its own hardware servers that are also configured as functionally-identical elements. We need to decide whether each type of element will be implemented as ACTIVE–REDUNDANT ELEMENTS or LOAD-BALANCED ELEMENTS. Part of this is a cost decision. The application servers tend to be the most expensive machines in the system as they need lots of resource to process business requests. Also, the application server software itself typically costs money (whether directly through buying a J2EE application server or indirectly by buying a Microsoft server-level operating system). To maximize the cost-effectiveness of the duplicated application servers, we decide that they should be LOAD-BALANCED ELEMENTS. As most application servers provide some form of load-balancing, this entails just a small additional cost for configuration and testing. On the other hand, the web server machines are comparatively 'cheap and cheerful' as their loading and resource usage is much lower than that of the application servers. As many web servers do not provide inherent load balancing, this would typically be implemented by a hardware content switch (a load balancer). The extra expense and complexity introduced by the content switch would outweigh the extra cost of providing two web servers that can handle the estimated user load (as compared to having two that could handle it between them). Hence, the web servers will be ACTIVE–REDUNDANT ELEMENTS. Finally, routers are typically ACTIVE–REDUNDANT ELEMENTS as they will often connect to different external 'pipes' which are themselves active–redundant. Any form of load balancing across routers tends to take place at the ISP end of the pipe. The updated logical architecture is shown in Figure 11.2.

As the application servers will be load-balanced, what approach will we take with the data? The user customization requirement needs the system to maintain some

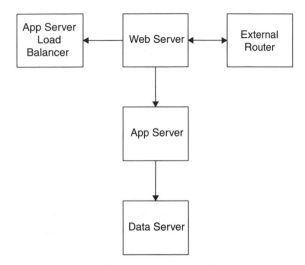

Figure 11.2 Logical architecture of entry-level system after applying LOAD-BALANCED ELEMENTS.

persistent state. Persistent state is also fairly implicit in the functional requirement for a shopping cart (for the storage of customer orders, although you could argue that this could be sent by reliable messaging to some other system). As user requests could be directed to either application server, it is not acceptable for these servers to maintain different sets of persistent data. This leads to the use of a COMMON PERSISTENT STORE since the overhead of replicating data between two load-balanced servers is too high.

We then face the question of whether the logical data server will be located on a separate physical server. If this is the case, it will add to the cost of the system since, for reasons of availability, the data server must also consist of at least two functionally-identical elements and so two machines will be required. The resource usage of the data server is somewhat orthogonal to the resource usage of the application server: the data server mainly needs disk space and reasonable memory to service requests, while the application server mainly needs high processor speed and lots of memory. If the two logical servers are physically located on the same machine, resource contention can be minimized simply by adding a bit more memory. Not only would this dramatically reduce the cost of implementing the data server, but it would also improve performance. If the two logical servers are on the same machine, the call from application server to database server becomes an inter-process call as opposed to an inter-machine call. This reduces the overhead of each database call by an order of magnitude.

The non-functional requirement for availability mandates that the data server must not itself be a single point of failure. This means that we need to apply

ACTIVE–REDUNDANT ELEMENTS or LOAD-BALANCED ELEMENTS to the data server in some form. The application servers are LOAD-BALANCED ELEMENTS. However, just because they exist on the same physical machines, the data servers do not have to use the same pattern. Indeed, most database clusters consist of ACTIVE–REDUNDANT ELEMENTS – not LOAD-BALANCED ELEMENTS. Remember, it is the software that is being balanced here, not the hardware, so software elements sharing the same physical machine can have different availability strategies. As it will contain dynamic, user-derived data, the data store must employ DATA REPLICATION between its two functionally-identical elements. The ability to cluster in an active–redundant pair and the associated replication are typical out-of-the-box features for serious database software.

The final thought around the application of functionally-identical elements and its related patterns surrounds the routing of traffic between the hardware housing the different logical elements. Network traffic must travel between the routers and the web server machines, and between the web server machines and the application/data server machines. This requires network switches between each layer of hardware. However, the non-functional requirement for availability mandates that these switches must not be single points of failure and so they themselves must be implemented as some form of redundant functionally-identical elements. As with the routers, the switches will typically be configured as pairs of ACTIVE–REDUNDANT ELEMENTS.

There is no obvious initial requirement for PERIPHERAL SPECIALIST ELEMENTS. This is not surprising as the specialist elements tend to derive from more complex functional requirements. As the functional requirements are initially quite simple, such elements do not seem to be needed.

Having applied the fundamental patterns and principles and the logically pursuant patterns, we can now use the decisions we have taken to create the deployment architecture based on the logical architecture. This deployment architecture is shown in Figure 11.3.

It should be immediately obvious that this entry-level system has a much simpler architecture than the GlobalTech system. The logical architecture has many fewer elements: the web server load balancers (for both the secure and non-secure servers), the secure web servers, the session backup server, the email server and the hardware for the data server have all been removed.

The deployment architecture is also much simpler. The web servers are now an active–redundant pair rather than load-balanced. This is because the web server can handle many more simultaneous requests than the application server (the requests are much simpler to fulfil) and the application servers will reach capacity long before the web server. The other main difference is that there are only two hardware servers to host the application servers, their load balancers, and the data servers. The active–redundant pairs for the latter two have been arranged to spread the load as evenly as possible across the two hardware servers.

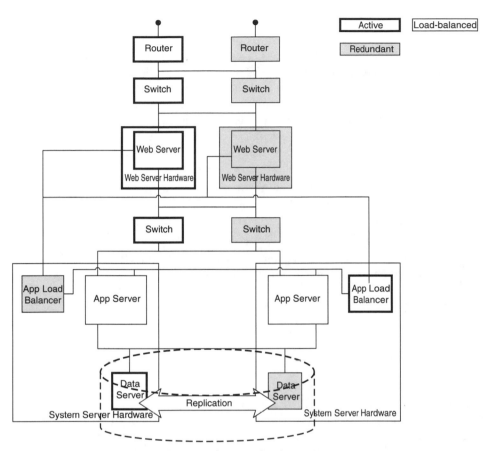

Figure 11.3 Deployment architecture for entry-level system.

Other Patterns in the Entry-Level Architecture

So far, we have defined the essential system architecture based on the functional and non-functional requirements defined for the system. Examination of those requirements together with our knowledge of the patterns defined earlier in the book lets us draw the following conclusions:

- Based on the non-functional requirement to scale in the medium term, we apply EXPANDABLE HARDWARE to the application/data server and web server hardware so that their capabilities can be upgraded more easily.

- Based on the non-functional requirement to limit the number of user sessions to the level defined in the scalability criteria, we apply CONNECTION LIMITATION at the application servers.

- Based on our own basic understanding of what is needed to support the system (i.e. our sympathy for the operations team) we put in CONTINUAL STATUS REPORTING, 3-CATEGORY LOGGING, SYSTEM OVERVIEW and OPERATIONAL MONITORING AND ALERTING. This is not simply for altruistic reasons as these are all part of the availability and the medium-term scalability strategies. To effectively deliver the non-functional requirements for availability on an ongoing basis, the operations team must be able to detect failure of elements so that they can be replaced and the correct level of availability restored. The operations team also need loading figures to predict when to add more hardware for medium-term scalability.

- Based on the functional requirement for payment for goods online and the non-functional requirement for confidentiality of payment and other customer information, the collection of credit card details and customer address information requires SECURE CHANNELS.

- The application servers we have selected can dynamically register and de-register themselves with the load balancer. This functionality comes 'out of the box' and requires only a small amount of configuration, so we will implement DYNAMICALLY-DISCOVERABLE ELEMENTS for the application servers, making it easier to add new capacity or remove failing servers. For reasons of cost, we would not implement this functionality at this stage if it were not 'out of the box'.

Another piece of 'out of the box' functionality are the pools of database connections, sockets, servlets, ASP.NET page instances and so on that are provided by the application server. This provides a very simple implementation of RESOURCE POOLING, but it may not be especially helpful without more work. Since we are not sure that this will bring any benefit in its default configuration we will not include it in the list of patterns used in the system.

So, the list of patterns and principles we have applied is as follows:

- Functionally-identical elements. Every element shown in Figure 11.3 is functionally identical to another element of the same type with which it is paired.

- APPLICATION SERVER ARCHITECTURE. The web server, application server and data server have been split out into separate components.

- ACTIVE–REDUNDANT ELEMENTS. The web servers, switches, data servers, and load balancers are all part of active–redundant pairs.

- LOAD-BALANCED ELEMENTS. The application servers are a load-balanced pair.

- DEDICATED WEB AND APPLICATION SERVERS. The application servers are deployed on different physical hardware from the web servers.

- COMMON PERSISTENT STORE. The pair of active–redundant data servers are used by both of the application servers.

- DATA REPLICATION. Updates to the data in the COMMON PERSISTENT STORE are replicated from the active data server to the redundant one.

- CONNECTION LIMITATION. The router, web server, application server and data server can all limit the number of connections they will accept.

- CONTINUAL STATUS REPORTING. Each of the web, application, and data servers continuously report their use of resources.

- 3-CATEGORY LOGGING. The web, application and data servers all log their actions and errors.

- SECURE CHANNELS. Although there is not a separate secure web server channel, we have still applied secure channels. The web server is capable of serving both secure and non-secure content and functionality through two different ports.

- DYNAMICALLY-DISCOVERABLE ELEMENTS. The application server load balancer can dynamically discover new application servers.

- SYSTEM OVERVIEW. The web servers, application servers and data servers all form a single, logical server in a SYSTEM OVERVIEW.

- EXPANDABLE HARDWARE. Both of the system hardware servers are capable of significant expansion, quadrupling their quota of processors and memory, and doubling their disk capacity.

- OPERATIONAL MONITORING AND ALERTING. The operations team will be alerted when any critical system element – such as an application server – becomes unavailable or shows signs of overloading.

The patterns we haven't applied to this system, which we did apply to the GlobalTech architecture, are:

- PERIPHERAL SPECIALIST ELEMENTS. Whereas the GlobalTech system has dedicated servers for specialist activities such as email and data import, we do not have this sort of functional requirement for this system. If email and data import capabilities are required later, then they will have to be built into the main application servers in the existing architecture. However, we can potentially evolve the system architecture to introduce separate servers for specialist activities at a later date – when a larger hardware budget is available.

- LOCAL CACHE. We generally introduce a local cache when we have to retrieve information remotely. In this architecture, only one application server has to access information remotely – the other will run on the same hardware servers as the data server. Running a cache would place extra strain on CPU and memory that already have to contend with running server processes (and possibly other processes as well). There is no proof that the benefits of running such a cache will make up for this extra load.

If we decide we need a local cache we will probably have to increase the amount of processing power and memory in the hardware servers.

- RESOURCE POOLING. Although this is relatively simple to implement, and may come 'out of the box' for some resources, knowing which resources to pool and, perhaps more crucially, the right pool sizes, is something that depends on the real use of the system. Rather than waste effort building resource pools in from the outset, the need for pools would be determined after some experience of real use.

- SESSION FAILOVER. Making the choice not to run a session back-up server of some description is difficult. However, we simply do not have the hardware budget to deploy and run additional server machines and so they cannot be included. It may be possible to preserve a small amount of session information on the client (written into the URL or in cookies) but complex session information will be lost if the application server goes down. The system will remain available (thanks to the load-balanced application servers, but the user will have to start their session again).

- KNOWN PARTNERS. Implementing a known partners scheme requires some form of secure negotiation between the client and server. Typically we want to do this with some form of token or certificate. In the GlobalTech system we used certificates with dedicated web servers for validation. Again, budget constrains our choices to the point where it is better not to provide this level of security. If we configured the active web server to validate certificates, the performance degradation would be likely to affect 'normal' users and we don't have the budget to introduce additional web servers. At a later date we can introduce known partners in a relatively low-impact way by adding secure web servers to perform the validation (as well as dedicated switches for them).

- VIRTUAL PLATFORM. With the emphasis on getting as much performance as possible from a very limited set-up, we can't really introduce a virtual platform. We need to use as many product-specific tricks and techniques as possible to achieve the best performance, availability, scalability and security that we possibly can. The next evolution of the system, which should bring greater hardware capacity, will allow us to reduce our reliance on product-specific tweaks and start to work to more abstract standards and interfaces.

- SWAPPABLE STAGING ENVIRONMENT. With our limited hardware capacity, where we don't even have enough spare processor power and memory to run a session backup server, we certainly cannot implement an entire mirror of the live environment to act as a staging environment. Without this, we're forced to take the system down if we need to upgrade it. At a later stage we hope to have enough capacity to be able to run a staging environment that can be swapped in as part of a 'hot' upgrade.

- OFFLINE REPORTING. Given the cost constraints and the limited amount of customization built into the system there is no capacity, and really no need, to implement a reporting mechanism. The only reporting in the system is a simple implementation of SYSTEM OVERVIEW for the operations team.

- DYNAMICALLY-ADJUSTABLE CONFIGURATION. Currently, we don't know how the system will be used and whether it will ever exceed its operational limits. There is only one core system (as opposed to the consumer/retailer split present in the GlobalTech system) and so there is not a huge perceived benefit in making the system overly configurable.

- DEMILITARIZED ZONE. As noted earlier, the security requirements are not stringent enough to warrant the use of a DEMILITARIZED ZONE given the level of budget for the system.

- INFORMATION OBSCURITY. The main security concern is for data in transit across the Internet. Fairly straightforward measures have been taken to secure the application functionality and data. The overhead in both development and performance are not deemed worth the security gains from encrypting data and obscuring configuration information.

- SEPARATE SYSTEM-MANAGED DATA. The future for the entry-level system is very much unknown. Although we want the system to be evolvable should it become popular, the overhead in development and performance to keep strict data demarcation of this type cannot be justified given the budget.

Which Patterns to Apply

It may be surprising that, out of the 26 patterns applied to the GlobalTech system, we have applied 14 to this new example and yet produced a much simpler architecture. Of the 12 omitted, we probably wish we could apply at least the three that would have significant benefits in terms of performance, availability, scalability and maintainability (PERIPHERAL SPECIALIST ELEMENTS, SESSION FAILOVER and SWAPPABLE STAGING ENVIRONMENT), but we're constrained by cost.

When we come to apply the patterns in this book, one of the choices we face is which of the patterns are relevant to solving our problems and which have no place in the system. If we are building a system that supports a very narrow range of users, or one that has very relaxed requirements for one or more non-functional characteristics, we may be able to discount a fair number of the patterns as being irrelevant. However, if we are producing a more general-purpose system, such as the GlobalTech system or the smaller-scale example above, the chances are that we need to apply most of the patterns to some degree or other.

Choosing the 'degree of application' is a much harder and more serious consideration when applying the patterns. It is inconceivable to us that any Internet-technology system would be taken live without some form of CONTINUAL STATUS REPORTING to let the maintenance team know what is happening. However, there is a world of difference between ensuring that the 'top' command is running on each of the hardware servers (a matter of a few hours' work at most) and implementing an SNMP reporting mechanism for every element in the system (perhaps several man-months of effort). In each of the patterns presented, we have given several examples of how that pattern can be implemented and indicated the relative scale of each of the implementation alternatives. For each pattern, however, there are many implementation alternatives – if the ones presented here don't fit, other sources will provide further alternatives or a bespoke solution can be produced.

When applying a pattern we also have to consider the consequences of applying it. For example, if we decide to implement CONTINUAL STATUS REPORTING by running the 'top' command, this decision has consequences for other patterns we may decide to apply. We may also decide we need to apply some form of OPERATIONAL MONITORING AND ALERTING but our implementation is constrained by the choice of running the 'top' command – we need to read the output and convert it into some meaningful monitoring and alerting parameters. Perhaps the implementation of the two patterns together could be simplified if we chose a slightly more sophisticated reporting mechanism (introducing the possibility of a consequently simpler monitoring and alerting mechanism).

The immediate consequences of applying particular patterns should be identifiable from the pattern relationships documented. However, there are also less-immediate consequences. If we implement CONTINUAL STATUS REPORTING and OPERATIONAL MONITORING AND ALERTING using a combination of the 'top' command and some parsing and monitoring software (probably bespoke), is it likely to be sufficient for the foreseeable future of the system? If not, how easy is it to replace with something more suitable?

A Process for Applying the Patterns?

Something we cannot do in this book is provide a one-size-fits-all process for applying the patterns – even with the standard process caveat that any organization will need to tailor it to fit their needs. How you go about applying these patterns will depend on your project process (how does 'architecture' fit into the process of producing the system from a set of requirements?), your project history (are you building a brand new system or working with some existing technology?), your technology choices (do they impose certain architectural decisions and non-functional constraints?), how you evolve your architecture (up-front on paper or as you work with the technology?) and possibly other aspects of your unique situation. A process of short-listing the patterns you want to apply, choosing a simple implementation for each of them, and then simulating on paper where that leaves you in respect to your non-functional requirements may well work for some people. Unfortunately it is likely to be unsuitable for many more people.

It is worth saying at this point that developing the architecture of a system is not some form of competitive sport. The goal of the architect is not to apply as many of the patterns as humanly possible, to produce the most complex architecture possible, or to come up with new and innovative implementations for each of the patterns. As we discussed in Chapter 2, the architect's role is to balance the many forces that are in tension in the system (and in the associated project to build and maintain the system) to produce something that is the best fit for its purpose. That best fit may well be much more simplistic than the GlobalTech example, or much more complex; the point is to find the right patterns for your system and to apply them in a way that fits your project. So the nearest to a process we can provide is a set of questions that you should ask yourself about each pattern:

- Do I really need to apply this pattern to my system? Does it help me meet the functional and non-functional requirements?

- Are there alternatives to applying this pattern (perhaps another pattern)?

- If I do apply it, do I need a simple or sophisticated implementation? What are the detailed effects of the chosen implementation on the non-functional characteristics of the system?

- If I do apply it (and choose a particular implementation) what knock-on effects does it have for other patterns I may want to apply? What about aspects of the system not covered by the patterns?

- If I do apply it (and choose a particular implementation) what consequences does it have for the foreseeable future of the system? If I am likely to replace/upgrade the solution, do I have a viable story about the replacement/upgrade? If not, do I have a viable story about the longevity of the solution?

An important aspect of answering these questions is an understanding of the relationships between the patterns. As we discussed in Chapter 4, there are two types of relationship: immediate relationships (such as 'A combines with B', 'A is required by B', or 'A is an alternative to B') and indirect relationships.

Immediate relationships help in understanding how well the patterns you are considering fit together. For example, there is an immediate relationship between DEMILITARIZED ZONE and DEDICATED WEB AND APPLICATION SERVERS; the DEMILITARIZED ZONE is easier to implement and much more effective if the web servers in it are on their own, dedicated, hardware servers. These immediate relationships are summarized in the diagram inside the back cover of this book.

Indirect relationships are found through the effect that a pattern has on the non-functional characteristics of the system. For example, it is fairly common to find a CONNECTION LIMITATION on any SECURE CHANNELS implemented. SECURE CHANNELS does not require CONNECTION LIMITATION, and neither assists in the implementation of the other, but SECURE CHANNELS does have a significant impact on the performance of the system (as perceived by the users in that channel and possibly other users on the system). Implementing CONNECTION LIMITATION helps balance out that impact by limiting the number of user requests that introduce the overhead of securing the channel. Indirect relationships help in understanding how well-balanced the system will be if you apply the patterns you are considering. The indirect relationships are governed by the interactions between the non-functional characteristics as described in Chapter 2. The effects each pattern has on the non-functional characteristics of the system is summarized in the 'Navigating the language' section in Chapter 4.

The questions above are very important to successful application of the patterns. But when these questions are asked, and when the answers are provided and to whom and by whom, needs to be determined for your unique situation.

Examples of Applying the Patterns

It is fairly self-evident that not every Internet technology system will look like GlobalTech. However, as shown by the entry-level system earlier in this chapter, if it has broadly similar non-functional requirements in most areas it will share some of the same basic structure and characteristics. As the balance of functional and non-functional requirements shifts, the shape of the system will change around this basic core to take on different forms. Many of the patterns applied will be the same as the entry-level system but the degree of application will differ and so their interaction with the patterns around them will change. Also, some of the other patterns that did not make it into the entry-level architecture will be required to meet differing non-functional requirements and these may also have an impact on the application of the core set of patterns.

Throughout the book, we have used GlobalTech as a running example of applying the patterns. This has allowed us to go into quite a lot of detail about the requirements of the system and how we can use the patterns to create a design that meets these requirements. We cannot go into such depth for many different types of system, however what we can do is to give you a flavour of how the differing requirements will affect which patterns are applied and to what degree, and hence how the 'shape' of the system will differ. To do this in a concise form, we will briefly examine some other types of large-scale system and discuss how their different requirements affect the patterns used within the system, the degree of importance of each pattern in the system and any particular implementation issues. The systems discussed are fictional – just like GlobalTech – but their requirements are typical for that type of system.

Building a Supply Chain

The Fundamental Patterns

The example system for supply chain automation is a large computer manufacturer in the UK. The system was intended to link them up to their customers throughout the European Union. These customers are essentially distributors who allow their customers (individual and corporate purchasers) to specify a PC online. The distributor sends the order on to the computer manufacturer who creates the specified computer and ships it to the customer with the distributor's 'badge' on it. This system replaced a fax-based process and the Internet was chosen over EDI as many suppliers were reluctant to invest in the purchase and ongoing upgrade of the alternative EDI software and perceived an Internet-based system as cheaper.

The system was built around an APPLICATION SERVER ARCHITECTURE, but in this case the technology used was Microsoft's .NET. Orders are submitted over HTTP in the form of XML documents. At the time the system was built, web service calls over SOAP were an option but the technology was considered too immature, although there is a strong leaning towards migration to web services over time.

The prime form of PERIPHERAL SPECIALIST ELEMENT in the system is the order-processing functionality. The web and application servers that form the APPLICATION SERVER ARCHITECTURE are principally focussed on accepting and validating messages from distributors that contain orders – order placement. A valid order is placed on a reliable message queue from which it is subsequently retrieved, processed further, recorded in the application database and then forwarded to the order fulfillment system – order processing. All of this is run from software and systems that are separate from the principal application servers; hence they are specialist elements peripheral to the main, Internet-facing application. The order-processing system has its own PERIPHERAL SPECIALIST ELEMENT in the form of an email server that is used to communicate order-processing problems to retailers.

System Performance Patterns

The availability requirements for the system were less stringent than GlobalTech. There is no need for 24×7 operation or even 24-hour operation. The availability requirement is that the system should be as close as possible to 100% availability during 'operating hours'. As the distributors are all in the European Union, this means between 6 am and 8 pm GMT (the maximum timezone difference is two hours).

As all orders are formed up by the distributor's system and then passed to the manufacturer's system, absolute performance is not critical as this can be done asynchronously once the ultimate customer has placed their order with the distributor. However, system throughput should be maintained if possible. The distributor base is fairly stable and growth forecasts are not extreme, so there are no major scalability requirements at the outset.

These availability, performance and scalability requirements led them towards the use of ACTIVE–REDUNDANT ELEMENT combinations for their web and application servers rather than LOAD-BALANCED ELEMENTS. In each case, if the active server fails, a lower specification server can take over and process orders at a reasonable rate while the active server is repaired. This saves money and reduces the complexity involved in implementing load-balancing across the web and application servers.

Simple hardware elements, such as switches and routers, are all configured as pairs of ACTIVE–REDUNDANT ELEMENTS.

In principle, orders could have been passed directly to the fulfillment system as part of the synchronous call from the distributor. However, this would require the fulfillment system to have the same high level of availability as the Internet technology system, which it does not have, and it also creates an unwanted dependency between the two systems. As they cannot be passed on immediately, the orders must be lodged in the system somewhere and the system must also keep a record of orders that have passed through it. The XML-format orders submitted via web requests are converted into messages and lodged on a reliable message queue that forms part of the system. As orders are processed, their contents are recorded in a database acting as a COMMON PERSISTENT STORE. As the database is not directly used by the application servers, there is less need for the database to be continually available (the messages can sit in the queue for a time if necessary), so a single database is used (no cluster and hence no DATA REPLICATION). This requirement would change if the system were enhanced to provide order history and status information during operating hours. If the availability requirement was the same as for the receipt of orders, the database would need to have a higher level of availability.

The use of asynchronous messaging inside the system means that order requests are processed quickly in terms of returning a receipt to the client. The actual persisting and processing of the order may take far longer but this is irrelevant to the order placement software at the client. As the interaction is system-to-system and order placement is rapid, there is no perceived need for CONNECTION LIMITATION. The rapid processing means that requests rarely fail, and if they do, a quick retry should be sufficient to deliver them.

All order submissions consist of single, independent request–response pairs. There is no attempt to keep an ongoing 'business transaction' between distributor and manufacturer as the business-level exchange of orders and associated receipts/invoices takes place over a longer period than a web session. As a result, SESSION FAILOVER is irrelevant. Similarly, LOCAL CACHE is not used as there is nothing to cache. Conversely, RESOURCE POOLING is used inherently for system resources such as threads, sockets and database connections as these capabilities are built into the .NET platform.

The system will generate reports during 'offline time'. As there are no customers for the system during this time, these reports are generated against the live database. As such, this is not an implementation of OFFLINE REPORTING, merely the generation of reports at a 'quiet time'.

System Control Patterns

As the PCs are shipped directly to customers, the system is open to abuse if someone fraudulently submits a fake order for PCs and then subsequently 'disappears'. This means that security is paramount as far as ordering goes. KNOWN PARTNERS (and hence SECURE CHANNELS) is a fundamental pattern for the system. This requires each distributor to obtain a digital certificate from a given certification authority.

There is a similar desire in terms of static security because the system is open to the Internet. The architects decided that the manufacturer's security requirements meant that they must have a DEMILITARIZED ZONE for the web servers with an associated firewall to protect the internal systems from direct attack. The use of a DEMILITARIZED ZONE confirms the need for DEDICATED WEB AND APPLICATION SERVERS. In this case, the web servers become simple forwarders of the XML orders to the application servers.

The system makes no real use of INFORMATION OBSCURITY as the manufacturer 'trusts' its partners and perceives that the use of a DEMILITARIZED ZONE, KNOWN PARTNERS and an appropriate security policy will keep their system secure enough. The main information asset maintained by the system is order history and this is not seen as important enough to warrant heavy security measures.

In terms of system management, CONTINUAL STATUS REPORTING and OPERATIONAL MONITORING AND ALERTING are essential as they support the objective of aiming for close to 100% availability during operating hours. As the system is relatively simple, a basic implementation of 3-CATEGORY LOGGING was created that delivered its information to the Windows event log on each machine. A customized SYSTEM OVERVIEW was created that mainly focussed on the status of the elements in the system – not the logging information. Again, this SYSTEM OVERVIEW was principally to support the availability requirements and so looked at loading factors and 'liveness'. Longer-term management information was generated retrospectively from log files.

A DYNAMICALLY-ADJUSTABLE CONFIGURATION is not core to the system but is used tactically to support availability if there is a perceived requirement (such as being able to alter the location of the message queue on which orders were placed). In general, the load and usage is thought to be relatively predictable and so configuration changes can be made during 'offline time'.

System Evolution Patterns

The separation of the order placement and order processing functionality means that these two parts of the system can evolve separately. The primary focus for evolution is the Internet-facing part of the system (between the Internet and the reliable message queue). For this part of the system, a SWAPPABLE STAGING ENVIRONMENT is seen as important as the system must be available during operating hours and the architects are concerned that a migration during offline time may overrun, so they want to be absolutely sure that migration is smooth. A decision was taken to apply SEPARATE SYSTEM-MANAGED DATA for the same reason.

The simplicity of the system and the use of active–redundant pairs for the web and application servers mean that there is no need for DYNAMICALLY-DISCOVERABLE ELEMENTS. Also, there is no real need for a VIRTUAL PLATFORM – they will use a Microsoft technology solution as they are a 'Microsoft shop'.

The principal route for improving system capacity, for scalability or to support more functionality is to apply Expandable Hardware to the web and application servers.

Collaborating Around the World

The Fundamental Patterns

This example involves a large-scale intranet for a global pharmaceutical company that has research, development and operations in a large number of countries around the world. The system is intended to provide collaboration and information-sharing between these widely-spread parts of the organization. Key parts of the system include the online storage of product specifications for use in preparing new production systems in plants, real-time collaboration for the design of new products and production processes, online project tracking and status reporting, and the exchange of research information between different research groups. This system had no manual predecessor, apart from hundreds of thousands of phone calls, pieces of email and physical documents. The Internet was chosen over private networks as being more cost efficient, accessible and scalable.

The system is highly oriented around content management as there are several hundred thousand product specifications, research reports and *ad hoc* documents to support. This is all supported by a third-party content management system that is fronted by an Application Server Architecture. Various other third-party applications are used for the project tracking and online collaboration features. The main objective of the Application Server Architecture is to provide a consistent integration environment and an overall structure in which to provide availability, security and management.

Some of the third-party applications are essentially Peripheral Specialist Elements. As an example, take the real-time collaboration server that allows users to share documents, parts of their screen, or other communication channels. End-user computers and the real-time collaboration system will communicate directly – their interaction will not be mediated through the core Internet technology application. Similarly, the real-time collaboration servers will be hosted on separate hardware from the Internet technology system as the requirements for this hardware will be different from that of the core application. However, the Internet technology application will control the collaboration session, such as setup and configuration.

System Performance Patterns

As the system will provide operational data for the business and will be used for real-time collaboration, high levels of responsiveness and availability are key requirements. Users will expect rapid response times and the number of timezones to be supported means that the system should provide 24×7 availability (although some short, infrequent, scheduled outages are possible over weekends). This combination leads the architects towards a highly-replicated architecture with the core functionality, such as the document serving and collaboration facilities, being implemented as many LOAD-BALANCED ELEMENTS. Only the simpler hardware-level elements, such as switches and routers, are configured as ACTIVE–REDUNDANT ELEMENTS.

Part of the availability requirement is that online collaboration should be maintained whenever possible in the face of underlying failure, which means that SESSION FAILOVER is important. The context of a collaboration session, such as the documents and communication channels currently open, must be transferred to another server should the original server fail. There may be a temporary lapse in service, but the session should 'automatically restart' to return the user to the same state as when the original server failed.

The system works with two primary sources of information – the content management system, which holds documents, project plans etc., and a database that supports custom project tracking and collaboration functionality. The importance of the information provided by the system mandates the use of COMMON PERSISTENT STORE and DATA REPLICATION for both of these data sources to maintain availability (although the mechanisms for clustering and replication will almost certainly be different in each case leading to a more complex management scenario than with a single data source).

Turning from availability towards performance, it is very important that the system does not 'grind to a halt' should it come under unexpectedly high levels of load. By applying CONNECTION LIMITATION, a consistent level of service can be maintained for current users of the system even though other users may be denied access. If this causes a problem, local administrators should be able to shut down less important user sessions (in the nicest possible way, of course) to allow access to users deemed of more immediate importance to the business. In the longer term, people can complain to their management and more funds can be found to upgrade the system.

Any patterns that can help to speed up the system have been applied. RESOURCE POOLING is one way of speeding up the system. In this case, specialist J2EE Connector implementations were used to support rapid recycling of connections to the content management and collaboration servers. The standard database connection, thread and socket RESOURCE POOLING in the J2EE platform was tuned based on beta testing. LOCAL CACHE was also applied on the web servers to speed up response times. Certain less volatile content is cached for up to 24 hours and used to satisfy requests with the same input parameters (HTTP POST or GET parameters).

Although the system is focussed largely on content delivery, not much of this content is static so that does not push towards DEDICATED WEB AND APPLICATION SERVERS. However, the cost of licensing of the J2EE application server software is deemed sufficient motivation to apply this pattern.

The context and forces of OFFLINE REPORTING are not really found in the system as one of the system's principal functions is to provide information. Hence, the generation of some reports is central to its operation and the idea that this will 'slow down core processing' does not make sense.

System Control Patterns

As the system lies at the heart of the business (and people quickly come to rely on such systems), it is vital that the system runs smoothly. CONTINUAL STATUS REPORTING and 3-CATEGORY LOGGING are both applied to a high degree when creating and configuring system elements. All system elements are required to produce SNMP status information and logs generated by the elements are retrieved to a central location on a frequent basis. The SNMP and log information feed into a sophisticated OPERATIONAL MONITORING AND ALERTING implementation that not only indicates the existence of a problem but provides a large amount of background on the symptoms of the problem and the status of the system immediately before the problem occurred. The monitoring and alerting is based on a rich, third-party management console which also provides the SYSTEM OVERVIEW used for daily operation and predictive analysis. If there is any degradation in performance that threatens the key principle of providing consistent levels of performance for existing users, the number of connections allowed to the system can be changed at various points (router, web server and application server) by implementations of DYNAMICALLY-ADJUSTABLE CONFIGURATION as appropriate to the element concerned.

Since the system will pass confidential company information across the public Internet, it will apply KNOWN PARTNERS to ensure the identity of any gateway server setting up a SECURE CHANNEL from one of the many intranets in different parts of the company. The decision to use the public Internet as the communication channel between the disparate intranets mandates the use of a firewall to defend the system from attacks originating from the Internet. This firewall forms part of a multi-layer DEMILITARIZED ZONE implementation that creates multiple security zones within the application. The reason for this is that some of the remote intranets are those of business partners rather than wholly-owned subsidiaries. Some of the information delivered by the system is confidential to the degree that it should only be made available to internal users. By creating different security zones, the architects will limit traffic that is known to originate from business partners to certain parts of the system.

The confidential nature of some of the information held by the system leads the architects to apply INFORMATION OBSCURITY to this subset. The information is stored in encrypted format and can only be accessed if the user can authenticate themselves as a member of an appropriate group. The system supports multiple groups for this purpose such as management and research. INFORMATION OBSCURITY is also used to ensure that information about how to access the database and the content management system is obfuscated.

System Evolution Patterns

EXPANDABLE HARDWARE is not applied to the main web and application servers. To increase the capacity of these elements, more servers are added to the set of LOAD-BALANCED ELEMENTS. However, EXPANDABLE HARDWARE is applied to the routers and switches to allow some expansion in capacity as uptake of the system increases. The reliance on adding new application servers as a way of expanding the capacity of the system means that a VIRTUAL PLATFORM is very important. Without a clearly-defined VIRTUAL PLATFORM, at least up to the J2EE level, the system would be at the mercy of increases in license fees by the server vendors initially chosen.

Returning finally to the original availability requirement, this has a large impact on the design for evolution. Although, in theory, upgrades can be done over weekends when the system is more lightly loaded, the management acknowledges different cultural working patterns and also the increased cost of employing multiple operations teams around the globe to coordinate updates over a weekend. This means that they want a system which is designed to allow upgrades to take place while it continues to operate (or at the cost of a very small outage). This leads to extensive use of DYNAMICALLY-DISCOVERABLE ELEMENTS – from web and application servers through to message queues and databases. The need to rapidly swap to a new version means that the production servers are configured to provide a SWAPPABLE STAGING ENVIRONMENT. However, the efforts to rapidly upgrade the system are somewhat hampered by the inability to apply SEPARATE SYSTEM-MANAGED DATA in certain areas such as the content management system. The content management system must be upgraded 'in one hit' which means that updates to this part of the system must be done as part of a scheduled outage, however costly that may prove.

Summary

In this chapter, we have shown you some principles for how you might apply the patterns in the book and some examples to show how a real system can evolve from a sequence of patterns. There is an art to applying the patterns that involves the balancing of the non-functional characteristics in the system. We hope that what we have shown you here helps you to understand more about the relationships between the patterns and so use them more successfully in the system architectures you create.

Moving on from Here

The patterns in Chapters 6 to 9 are elements in a language that captures spatial configurations in the world of Internet technology systems. These patterns have emerged as development teams have learned more about how to build performant, controllable and evolvable systems. Hopefully the pattern language will help those who read it understand more about the architectures they have developed or inherited, and arm those who face new challenges in architecting Internet technology systems.

Obviously we think architecture is important, particularly with respect to the non-functional characteristics of the system. Every system has a structure, whether or not it is captured in some form of architectural description. If this structure is not well understood, the non-functional characteristics of the system are also not understood. We believe that, in any project, there must be someone (hopefully more than one person) that cares about the structural elements, their relationships, and why the structure looks the way it does.

Having said that, we certainly don't believe architecture is a panacea for successfully producing high-capability Internet technology systems. It is simply one of a whole range of factors, albeit an important one. Some of the other factors can be far more important (sound financial and political support for the project, for example)

275

but have absolutely nothing to do with the architecture or those responsible for producing it. However, as we have worked on and learned more about Internet technology systems we have identified three factors that are often influenced by the project architects (whether they have that title or just the role) and can influence the architecture produced. These factors are the choice of technology, tool support, and the development process.

Technology

The choice of technology is probably the factor that has the most direct effect on the architect and the architecture they develop. However, the architect sometimes plays little or no role in choosing the technology their system is based on. Corporate standards and licenses, non-technical purchasing considerations, and even the business, can all determine the choice before the architect is involved, or else restrict the choice the architect can make. The architect then has to work with the technology proscribed for the system to implement the architecture required, rather than choosing the technology to fit the vision for the architecture.

We have already discussed (see Box 6.1) how application server products are becoming the 'new operating system' and we don't want to examine individual products in detail – the rate of change of these products means that this detail will date very rapidly. However, there are some interesting trends in technology that will affect the architectures of the systems we develop: Open Source Software, web services, and the development of J2EE and .NET.

Open Source Software

One of the major recent changes in the software development landscape has been the rise of open source software (OSS) or non-commercial software (NCS). Open source components come in all shapes and sizes with the largest one being probably the best known incarnation of open source, the Linux operating system. As you may already be aware (or as you may have gathered while reading this book) you can assemble a pretty convincing OSS VIRTUAL PLATFORM on which to build an Internet technology system, leaving just the purchase of hardware and the application development as up-front costs. Such an OSS VIRTUAL PLATFORM could include Linux as the operating system, Apache as the web server, JBoss and/or Tomcat as the application server and MySQL as the database engine. In terms of one of the key non-functional requirements – cost – this platform is pretty much unbeatable when looked at strictly in terms of initial procurement cost. If you consider the whole lifecycle of the project – in terms of support cost and platform maintenance, then the advantage decreases as ongoing costs will be similar to the ongoing costs of licensed software. OSS will usually require more technical support inside the organization while you will have to pay license fees for commercial software. Obviously, if you are committed to a particular set of commercial products, the cost of moving to OSS will be more as you will need to gain skills in the different parts of this new platform.

If the OSS platform gives you the functionality you need, the chances are that you can deliver the required level of performance, even if this means buying more hardware and using more of these cheap platforms instead of a single, more expensive one. High levels of availability can be achieved by taking this approach and the software is typically quite well evolved to support this – such as the DATA REPLICATION capabilities built into MySQL. In terms of security, most of the SSL-based SECURE CHANNELS you set up from your web browser are with Apache web servers. So far, so good for the OSS VIRTUAL PLATFORM, but where is the catch? For your particular project, the answer may be that there is no downside and that OSS provides you with all the features and functionality you need. However, as you build your Internet technology system and apply the patterns in this book, you may find that some holes start to appear in the characteristics and functionality of some OSS components.

Many open source projects start with a group of enthusiasts who, out of necessity, focus on the 'interesting' work (basic capabilities, performance, security) while the functionality considered 'worthy but dull' (management, documentation) is left for later. This means that for much of the early life of an OSS product, the level of some component characteristics may be low. For example, a particular component may have no form of management 'hooks' or instrumentation with which to implement CONTINUAL STATUS REPORTING.

A commercial company will pay the designers and developers to create the less interesting types of functionality. In an open source project consisting of volunteers, there is no such incentive and so these features will tend to lag. If you encounter this situation, you can address it by creating this functionality yourself (you have the source code after all). However, while this may be feasible in resource terms – the cost of development may cost less than having to buy a commercial product – it is rarely practical in terms of time.

Many vendors enhance their platforms with additional functionality that helps to speed the application development (such as commerce components or frameworks). Typically, the mainstream OSS components do not come with this type of additional functionality, but you will probably find that another OSS component or a commercial component exists to plug the gap. If you want a basic platform for OSS development, you can download and install it within a day. However, as you add more components to speed development, you start creating a more complex VIRTUAL PLATFORM. What if all the components you choose don't play nicely together? There is no guarantee that anyone has ever used the exact same set of components that you have assembled.

Don't take this section the wrong way – we like open source software and we're not saying that the large vendors are necessarily any better in particular areas. However, large software vendors, such as BEA and IBM, focus on creating an integrated product set targeted at the enterprise system market (whether they succeed in this endeavour may be open to debate). If you are looking to apply common patterns – such as Resource Pooling, Local Cache and 3-Category Logging – you will find that the vendor product suites typically have these types of capability built-in. If you are using open source solutions you may have to implement them yourself or procure a third-party solution.

Web Services

Many Internet technology systems are used for B2B or business process automation. The interface provided by these systems involves the exchange of business documents or functions with other systems. Increasingly, such systems will expose their functionality as one or more web services with interfaces that can be consumed by client systems. One of the key aspects of web services is that they use web protocols to expose their functionality. This means that they use most of the same technology and principles as the people-facing public Internet systems, and so most of the patterns still apply. Regardless of whether the system delivers HTML content to a browser or XML documents to another system, it will need to perform well, be available and scale as required. Application Server Architecture, Peripheral Specialist Elements, Load-Balanced Elements, Common Persistent Store and so on will all still be relevant when creating the system that delivers the web service. Probably the only system performance pattern that is less relevant to a system that delivers a web service is Session Failover as many web services are intended to be stateless. However, whether this attitude persists as services become more sophisticated remains to be seen. All of the system control and system evolution patterns are relevant to systems that expose web services and Known Partners is probably even more relevant than in B2C applications.

Looking at web services from a consumer's point of view, as a system architect you can use third-party web services to deliver part of your system functionality. As an example, a typical e-commerce application can (and often does) delegate credit-card payment to a third-party service. This is good as it relieves you of the necessity of processing credit card information yourself. However, your application is now dependent on this service. Before incorporating such a service in your application, you should obtain a service level agreement in terms of the availability, performance, scalability and security you need from the service. Remember that your application is only as strong as the weakest link, and the system characteristics of the web service impact those of your own application. You may decide to ensure availability of service by balancing your exposure across several third-party services in a form of Active–Redundant Elements or Load-Balanced Elements and you will certainly want to configure them as Dynamically-Discoverable Elements to replace any ailing service with another one. From the security perspective, you will need to implement Secure Channels or Known Partners with many of these services as your communication will be across the public Internet.

As systems that expose web services will be driven by automated clients, you will find that they have different patterns of application use and differing non-functional requirements. Until such a time as there is a public market for web services (the on-demand vision where you look up such services in a global registry) you will need to handle fewer unpredictable peaks. However, if your service is used by another system, peaks in their user loads may well lead to peaks in yours. You may also find it more difficult to 'retire' older versions of the service which implies the support of several concurrent versions as discussed in the SEPARATE SYSTEM-MANAGED DATA pattern. This may lead to a variation on a SWAPPABLE STAGING ENVIRONMENT with multiple swappable environments in which different versions can exist independently of each other.

J2EE

The J2EE platform originated in 1999 as an effort to standardize the set of extension APIs that a server-side Java developer should expect from a server-side Java execution environment. This standardization led to the birth of the modern Java application server as vendors of various server-side environments converged on J2EE. As the J2EE platform has evolved, it has shifted from a very network-focused platform to a more business and solution-focused environment. This reflects the typical lifecycle of many technologies:

- Develop a new and interesting toy for 'techies'. In Java terms, this was mainly the era of applets such as the 'tumbling Duke' but it also encompasses the early days of RMI. As such, it pre-dates J2EE.

- Apply this to my 'business' problem. People start to use it for pilot applications. This is the stage at which J2EE was formed from the main technologies needed for this type of application including JDBC, Web interfaces (servlets followed by JSP) and EJB components. The initial J2EE application servers appeared in response to demand for tools to support the evolving APPLICATION SERVER ARCHITECTURE.

- Create 'serious' business applications. The environment is improved to help the developers of enterprise applications. This involves technical changes such as improvements in transaction and persistence support, J2EE connectors to 'other systems' and better asynchronous support in the Java Message Service (JMS). As more parts of the functional platform come under the J2EE umbrella, it starts to resemble all or part of a serious VIRTUAL PLATFORM on which many types of application can be built. This era in the life of J2EE also involved a serious raising of the performance bar. Although this did not require any major technology changes, it involved a lot of work under the covers by the application server vendors. The J2EE application servers started to deliver higher performance with improvements in Virtual Machine speed, garbage collection, thread management and EJB lifecycle management. At this stage, RESOURCE POOLING appeared for important resources such as JDBC connections, threads and J2EE connectors.

■ Create 'robust' business applications. Once people are able to create a business application that meets the basic levels of user acceptance (a good user interface and a reasonable level of performance) focus then turns to ironing out all of the issues that made the 'version 1' applications a pain to build, maintain and administer.

It is this last point that we really want to focus on as most of the preceding changes affect what is 'inside the box' when building the application to reside inside the APPLICATION SERVER ARCHITECTURE. It was always possible to create your own implementations of SESSION FAILOVER or 3-CATEGORY LOGGING, but one of the key selling points for a platform such as J2EE is that it takes away the need to create lots of this type of 'plumbing' code and lets you focus on delivering the functional requirements of your business application. As J2EE progressed from version 1.2 through to 1.3 and 1.4, application servers became more sophisticated and started to provide clustering to support LOAD-BALANCED ELEMENTS, state management for SESSION FAILOVER and logging support even though such functionality fell outside the J2EE specification itself.

In J2EE 1.4, the main publicity was for the provision of web service support. While this is laudable and of great interest to developers, architects and even users or purchasers of the system, other functionality was added that speaks to different stakeholders. J2EE 1.4 also introduces the J2EE Management API and the Java Management Extension (JMX). The J2EE Management API defines an information model (such as the ones used by SNMP and CMIP) that includes manageable components, the servers in which they run and the deployment information for those components. The J2EE Management API builds on JMX, which specifies APIs for the creation of manageable components and for common management protocols such as SNMP and WBEM. These APIs are obviously a boon for anyone wanting to implement CONTINUAL STATUS REPORTING, SYSTEM OVERVIEW and OPERATIONAL MONITORING AND ALERTING.

The related J2EE Deployment API makes it easier to use different tools to deploy and configure J2EE applications. Another technology included at J2EE 1.4 is the Java Authentication and Authorization Service (JAAS) which builds on secure socket (JSSE) and certificate (Java Certification Path API) support delivered in J2SE 1.4 (which is a prerequisite for J2EE 1.4) to provide more support for SECURE CHANNELS and KNOWN PARTNERS. The Java Cryptography Extension in J2SE 1.4 also helps with INFORMATION OBSCURITY.

.NET

As .NET started later than J2EE, it came with a certain amount of advantage in that it was already targeted at the creation of 'serious' business applications. From version 1.0 of the .NET Framework there has been support for distribution (.NET Remoting), database connectivity (ADO.NET), web interfaces (ASP.NET) and web services together with a transactional, secure component model. A combination of Windows Server and the .NET Framework essentially provides the same sort of application server environment as found in J2EE application server products. The Windows Server operating system provides some of the same non-functional support as the J2EE application servers. For example, RESOURCE POOLING for threads and connections is provided by the Internet Information Services (IIS) which are built into the platform, and LOAD-BALANCED ELEMENTS are supported by the Windows Network Load Balancing facility which is part of the clustering capabilities.

In terms of support for the delivery of non-functional requirements, the .NET Framework provides pretty much the same level of functionality as J2EE 1.4 given that it operates in a single vendor environment (i.e. there is less focus on the ability of tools and servers to work together as they commonly come from the same source). RESOURCE POOLING is built into the platform in areas such as the management of ADO.NET Connections. The .NET Framework provides cryptography and PKI support (using the `System.Security` and `System.Security.Cryptography` namespaces) to assist in the implementation of INFORMATION OBSCURITY, SECURE CHANNELS and KNOWN PARTNERS. As with J2EE, management and the instrumentation of components is catered for through classes in the `System.Management` and `System.Management.Instrumentation` namespaces which provide access to Windows Management Instrumentation (WMI – Microsoft's WBEM implementation). This forms the basis for the inclusion of software components in CONTINUAL STATUS REPORTING and for the implementation of SYSTEM OVERVIEW and OPERATIONAL MONITORING AND ALERTING. Other relevant features include `System.Web.Caching.Cache` for implementing a LOCAL CACHE in a web-based application and the ability to configure web session state as saved in an instance of SQL Server which provides session federation (the ability to allocate individual user requests to any Web server) as well as SESSION FAILOVER.

The combination of Windows Server and the .NET Framework forms the basis for an APPLICATION SERVER ARCHITECTURE for the Windows environment. One interesting aspect of this is that since the .NET Framework is just a component added onto the system, different versions can be installed side-by-side on the same machine. This can be useful when support for multiple VIRTUAL PLATFORMS is required, such as during migration.

When Microsoft talk about .NET, they will often include their server product family, such as Commerce Server and Systems Management Server. These products are also evolving to make the non-functional side of application deployment and management easier. As an example, Microsoft have announced an intention to streamline their various management products, such as Microsoft Operations Manager and Systems Management Server, under the umbrella of Microsoft System Center which is slated to deliver a unified management infrastructure. As always, such initiatives should be judged on their delivery.

Tool Support

It's perhaps less obvious that tool support can influence the architecture of a system, or be influenced by the architect, in the same way that the choice of technology can. But we have found that there are particular types of tools that can assist architects in making some of the decisions they have to make or can support the architecture developed.

Testing Tools

Availability, scalability and performance can all be tested objectively using automated testing tools (manageability, maintainability, flexibility and portability are much more subjective characteristics and security is often best tested using a manual process). We can write a set of tests and run them against the system to determine how well it performs with an average user load. We can then ramp up the load to see how well the system copes and whether the simulated users still experience acceptable performance. We can also introduce various failures into the tests to see how the system deals with the loss of certain system elements under certain loads or conditions.

This type of testing can be invaluable to an architect. Although the patterns for system performance that we have presented describe ways to structure your system for greater availability, scalability and performance, we can't tell you how big your servers need to be, or how many you need to have (although we have provided some ideas in the 'How many servers do you need?' section in Chapter 7). Sizing can be one of the most unpleasant jobs that an architect has to do. Unless you are building a system exactly like one you have built before, there is a lot of reliance on vendor metrics (and we all know exactly how reliable and objective they are), comparison with systems of dubious similarity, and plain guesswork. If you under-size, everyone will be upset when the system struggles to cope with its 'normal' load, and if you over-size, the financial controller will be upset at how much money you've 'wasted'. Performance and scalability testing can give you hard data to input into sizing. Of course, you need some sort of system in place in order to get useful sizing data but, in a long-term and evolutionary process (see below) getting data in the first one or two phases can assist in evolving the system over a much longer period of time.

Like sizing, designing the detail of the system architecture for flexibility and portability can require a lot of guesswork. As the requirements for the system change, new and unexpected uses for it will be uncovered. As the technology the system is built on changes, there will be opportunities to utilize new functionality and the necessity to move away from obsolete technologies. A VIRTUAL PLATFORM gives you the right shape for portability; applying principles such as isolating layers and adapters and one-way dependencies improves the system's flexibility. But no-one can know exactly what the future holds and, unless your VIRTUAL PLATFORM abstracts out exactly the right details of the underlying technology, and all the adapters and one-way dependencies are in exactly the right places, there will be times when the architecture simply can't absorb a required change. Unfortunately, as with sizing, it is often deemed to be the architect's job to ensure the system is 'as flexible and portable as possible', although the fact that there can't be a negative impact on the other non-functional characteristics, particularly performance, is left unsaid.

War Story

One of the authors once worked on a project to produce the next generation of a computationally-intensive system. The reason for this new version was that, whilst the system did its job very well, it required a lot of programming effort to make it do anything new. The vision for the new version was that it was to be 'pluggable' – any new functionality would be developed in isolation and simply slotted in when it was ready. Unfortunately, there wasn't really a lot of detail on the types of things that should be pluggable. New computations, certainly, but also new ways of looking at data, new ways of transforming the data, new interface components; in fact just about anything currently in the system and a number of things not yet thought of.

Needless to say, all this flexibility could not come at the expense of performance, the system still had to do what it currently did at least as fast (and a small increase in speed would be nice). After some months of requirements capture, design, re-capture of new requirements and re-design, the project stalled completely, much to the relief of the author who had come to believe that the task was impossible.

Functional testing tools can support the architect in making the system portable and flexible. Functional tests simply check that, given a certain stimulus, the system reacts as expected. Good functional test coverage allows an architect to apply the 80/20 rule to the need for portability and flexibility: we can do the 20% of the work that will give us 80% of the portability and flexibility we need. When we come up against the remaining 20% that isn't as flexible or portable as we would desire, we have a suite of tests that will help us to ensure any rapid port or change in functionality works as we expect. As an example, consider porting an application from one J2EE environment to another. The choice of J2EE (or a subset of J2EE technologies) is the 20% of the work that gives us 80% or more of the portability required. Once the components of the application have been ported and installed, a set of functional tests will allow us to identify any parts of the application that do not work due to inconsistencies between the two J2EE environments – we do not have to spend a lot of time sitting around and scratching our head to figure out what problems the differences might cause. The set of functional tests lets us defer extensive consideration of the precise porting (or flexibility) issues until the time at which they are relevant. In a sense, ensuring that the system has good functional test coverage is a way of architecting for portability, flexibility and even maintainability without actually changing the structure of the system itself.

Configuration Management Tools

Internet technology systems are, by their nature, extremely complex beasts. Where a software application used to consist of the source code, some statically-bound libraries, and, perhaps, a database schema with some system data, a contemporary Internet technology software application may consist of:

- Source code, both application code and dynamic server page templates
- Statically-bound libraries
- A database schema and system data
- An object–relational database mapping definition
- Application server configuration information
- Binary assets such as images, drivers and documents
- Executable business rules
- Search indexes
- Web service definitions
- Component configuration information
- Resource bundles containing text for internationalization
- Error code message mappings and configuration information to integrate with the SYSTEM OVERVIEW

And all this just for the software application. To this list we need to add configuration information for many of the elements in the system, further data and schema definitions for peripheral elements, and so on.

Such a list of artefacts indicates the increase of complexity in developing Internet technology systems. However, the real increase in complexity comes not from having more types of artefacts to manage, but from the dependencies between those artefacts. The application will only be able to store and retrieve persistent data if it is using the right version of the object–relational mapping definition and the database has been set up with the corresponding version of the database schema and system data. The application will only work correctly if the application server configuration information is correct, and the system will only work correctly if the configuration information for all the system elements is consistent.

This increase in complexity is a direct result of the use of the patterns and the technologies that we have discussed in this book, a necessary increase in complexity to achieve the type of high-capability system we're interested in. The architect, or someone else on the project, needs to ensure that this level of complexity is manageable for the architecture to be usable. If the development team cannot cope with the number of types of artefacts, and the dependencies between individual artefacts, the architecture – and the non-functional characteristics it embodies – cannot be realized.

Good version control and configuration management is absolutely essential for the realization of any non-trivial architecture. Being able to ensure that the correct versions of artefacts are being used, all the required artefacts are present, and that they are all consistent with each other, is vital. Having the right configuration management tool can make the difference between a necessarily complex architecture being fit for purpose or being completely unmanageable (see [Berczuk 2002] for a discussion of configuration management patterns and available tools).

War Story

One of the authors worked as the system architect on an Internet technology project that consisted of multiple components distributed across multiple physical tiers. The original intention was that each of these components could be deployed individually, thus easing the administrative overhead of upgrading parts of the system and reducing the risk associated with a whole system upgrade (if it ain't broke – don't fix it). However, a combination of uncertainty about dependencies, an unstable target platform and a high level of FUD (fear, uncertainty and doubt) surrounding deployment and application configuration finally defeated the configuration management efforts and every component of the application ended up being deployed each time an upgrade to any of them was needed.

Build and Deployment Tools

There is some overlap between configuration management and build and deployment. Although the tools are very different, the impact on the architecture is the same. There is no point having a configuration management system that ensures all the right artefacts are present and will work together, if there is no way of getting all those artefacts out onto the production hardware (or the development and QA hardware for that matter). However, such deployment is also a non-trivial task and is complicated by the fact that it is frequently viewed as one of the more 'dull' aspects of a project and is potentially neglected or handed over to more junior members of the team.

The build and deployment process must be executed with skill and diligence and should really be overseen by a fairly senior member of the team even if they do not do all of the work themselves. The build must include any and all relevant components of the system and these must be included as part of the deployable package. The system deployment must be ready to go – it must 'hit the ground running'.

When the project starts, builds are small and deployment is done into an internal development environment. As the project progresses, the size of the build and the 'distance' across which it needs to be deployed increases. An increasing skew between the developer environment and that into which the application must be deployed makes the build and deploy process more difficult but also more important. A classic example of this is security, since developer workstations usually have security configured at a low level to enable easy sharing and debugging but the live environment will have security configured to a high level to restrict access. Part of the deployment process must ensure that the expected security settings are applied to each component and this propagation of configuration information must be achieved in a repeatable manner.

A number of the patterns introduced in this book are likely to require some support from the build and deployment process for successful implementation. If we have DEDICATED WEB AND APPLICATION SERVERS and have implemented a LOCAL CACHE on the web servers for binary assets, we need to ensure that all binary assets are deployed to all web servers. If we rely on LOCAL CACHES for the application servers, we may want to 'warm up' these caches as part of the deployment process so that there isn't a period after deployment when the performance is poor because the caches are empty. If we have a DYNAMICALLY-ADJUSTABLE CONFIGURATION, we need to ensure that the configuration is correct for each of the elements on each of the servers. And so it goes on. It is important that the build and deployment tools and process support the architecture, otherwise they can break it in some quite unexpected ways.

War Story

One of the authors worked on a project where there were a significant number of pages that needed to be accessed using SECURE CHANNELS, implemented with SSL and a dedicated secure web server. The use of the SECURE CHANNEL was made configurable because SSL wasn't used in the development and QA versions of the system to avoid the need to administer a number of certificates (there was a single QA version of the system that had its own CA-certified certificate). Almost inevitably, the first deployment of the system of the production system went live with the SECURE CHANNEL still disabled. This was picked up on pretty quickly and, due to the use of DYNAMICALLY-ADJUSTABLE CONFIGURATION, was rectified without any interruption to the service. Just as inevitable, though, was the fact that the second and third times the system was deployed (each with some minor bug fixes), no one thought to ensure the SECURE CHANNEL was set up correctly. Eventually, the build and deployment process was updated to ensure the SSL configuration was automatically updated whenever the configuration file was deployed to the production servers.

Development Process

The degree to which the development process affects the architect and architecture really depends on the type of process. If the project chooses a waterfall-type process, the architecture is likely to be defined well ahead of any development work and the role of the architect is to define the complete architecture, possibly with no direct communication with the people who are to build it. However, we have never seen a traditional waterfall process used successfully on an Internet technology project, although we've seen it tried on a number of occasions.

Internet technology projects, perhaps more than other types of system development project, must deal with rapidly changing requirements and technology (the technology used in Internet systems is still developing rapidly). In the early days of the 'dotcom era' the constant 'requirements churn' was due to the mad scramble for the hearts and minds of users (closely followed by the hearts and minds of investors) – plus the fact that a lot of people didn't really know what they wanted their systems to do because no-one knew what Internet systems were really capable of.[1] Obviously we've moved on from that era but businesses are still learning how to use the Internet, and the ways the Internet allows businesses to operate frequently throws up new opportunities for partnership and cooperation that inevitably affect the Internet and extranet systems of the partner organizations. Just because the dotcoms no longer command the headlines or the investment community's interest doesn't mean that Internet technology projects are any less volatile than they used to be.

Many projects have responded to the volatility in requirements and technology by adopting some form of agile development process. The use of such a process brings a wealth of benefits for the creation of software components to be used in a system, not least the ability to rapidly re-purpose or re-engineer bits of the application as requirements or technology change. This ability to change the application rapidly is usually substituted for a formal software architecture phase, and the role of the software architect is down-played or completely absent.

So where does this leave the system architecture and the system architect? Hardware is, by its nature, much less easy to refactor. If you spend your hardware budget on one big server and then realize you really need two medium-sized machines, you can't just split it in half. Some fore-thought and architectural consideration is required. This architectural consideration also needs to be extended to how the software is spread across the system hardware, if not to the internals of the application itself.

Agile processes do not obviate the need for architectural thinking; the architecture and the architect role needs to fit in with the agile process. In an agile team, the

---

[1] Perhaps the one exception to this was Amazon.com who really blazed the trail of Internet technology systems. Certainly in Europe they were seen as a yardstick by which to compare any Internet technology system, not just B2C e-commerce systems. Developers would know to expect a deluge of new and changed requirements for the system they were building soon after Amazon released a new version of their system or announced a major new feature.

architectural decisions will tend to be shared out between the more senior developers and those decisions will evolve over time (see [Fowler 2003a]). This is the approach to architecture that we have taken over the past few years – evolving the system architecture over several development phases of the system.

An Evolutionary Approach to Architecture

No successful and enduring architecture can be produced in one shot. A system's architecture does not appear in a flash of inspiration and then remain constant throughout the lifetime of the system. Even in traditional waterfall-style processes the architecture will take time to develop and then will be required to change over time (although the aim is to reduce the need for change as much as possible).

When implementing software components using an iterative and incremental process, we tend to produce many versions of the system, usually each one a small but significant improvement on the previous version. In order to deliver value to the customer, rather than simply deliver software, we tend to pick the functions that deliver the most value or represent the greatest risk first. As the system evolves from iteration to iteration the body of functions supported grows and grows. Usually new functions are added but, sometimes, old functions are altered in the light of feedback from the users. Perhaps what they thought was going to be useful proves less so, perhaps using the system has revealed a better approach to the problem, perhaps something has proved so useful that enhancing it is more important than adding functionality not currently supported.

The benefits, and liabilities, of evolutionary development have been well documented (you can examine [Brooks 1995], [Beck 2000] and [Beck 2003]). An evolutionary approach to architecture brings the same benefits to the non-functional characteristics of the system that evolutionary implementation brings to its functionality. In order to achieve the 'goodness of fit' that is unique to the system being built, the evolutionary approach tackles the primary requirements first – producing the architecture that best supports those requirements – and then evolves it to support the secondary requirements over time.

The primary requirements are those that deliver the most value or represent the greatest risk. Which particular requirement or requirements are primary will depend on the system being built. A banking extranet system will probably have security as its primary requirement. Availability and performance are also very important but security cannot be compromised. In order to improve these characteristics, other non-functional characteristics of the system will have to suffer. If the extranet is the online banking system for a high-street bank, security, availability, performance and scalability are probably the primary requirements.

A small-scale extranet, with specialist functions for high-value individuals, may well have security and manageability as primary requirements with availability, performance and scalability relegated to secondary considerations. Of course, this doesn't mean that we ignore availability, performance and scalability altogether, just that we focus on security and manageability and make decisions about the others only in the light of the security and manageability we need to achieve.

Using the patterns in this book, the person or people playing the role of the system architect can guide the functional development to ensure that the characteristics required for that iteration of the system are considered. In order to kick off the evolutionary process, an initial architecture is required. This may be directly derived from the fundamental patterns presented or may be a bit more elaborate, incorporating a basic implementation of a number of patterns for system performance, control and evolution. As more is learned about the system and the non-functional characteristics required, further patterns can be applied.

This type of architectural refactoring does not come for free (or even cheaply). At times it can be a daunting process, particularly if you are facing a major change to the system such as retro-fitting a set of security mechanisms or introducing a completely new level of scalability and performance. But it is possible – particularly with good technology and tool support.

Conclusion

Change has been one of the constant factors in the computer industry over the past five decades. Changes to a system are largely driven by external factors, whether that is a change to the functional or non-functional requirements imposed on the system or whether the change is broader – such as a new technology or approach to system development. The amount of change a system must cope with will depend on the lifespan of the system and the volatility of the environment in which it is deployed. The functional and non-functional requirements of almost all systems change as they are developed. The longer the system is in operation, the broader the scope of changes that will be demanded of it. Also, the longer a system is in operation, the more the environment around it will change.

It is unlikely that you will be able to insulate your system from changes to requirements, and it is certain that you cannot stop the environment around it changing. You have probably concluded that we think of systems as organisms that must adapt as they grow and as the world around them changes. In architectural terms, if the system is to live and evolve, it must take on different shapes over time and the system architect must guide the evolution from shape to shape, refactoring as required. We believe that the patterns in this book, and the relationships between them, form the foundation upon which you can base this system-level, pattern-driven refactoring and evolution. Change can be unsettling due to fear of the unknown or the uncertainty associated with new situations. Internet technology is no longer new or unknown as evidenced by the patterns in this book. Armed with this map of the landscape, we hope you can become a better guide for the stakeholders in your systems.

They always say time changes things, but you actually have to change them yourself.
(Andy Warhol)

Reference Patterns

This appendix contains cut-down forms of the patterns in the book – what we call 'reference patterns'. The detail of each pattern and an in-depth discussion of the implementation options are contained in the main pattern chapters. However, we realize that it is not particularly convenient to have to read through the whole narrative to find the essential points of the pattern. There are times when you will be reading a different part of the book and you come across a reference to a pattern with which you are unfamiliar. In this case, you can refer to the reference form of it in this appendix. This cut-down form of the pattern will allow you to quickly grasp its intent and then get back to the part of the book you were reading.

This appendix can also be used as a quick reference. Each reference pattern contains the problem statement, context information and resulting context – the impact on non-functional characteristics of the system. We would hope that you can look up a particular pattern in this appendix to assess whether it is appropriate to your problem/context combination and delivers the desired non-functional characteristics. If so, you can then look at the main pattern for the implementation detail and discussion. If the pattern is not quite what you are looking for, each reference pattern lists related patterns and principles that may help to achieve the desired level of particular non-functional characteristics.

The reference patterns are listed in the order that they appear in the book. Table A.1 is in alphabetical order to enable you to quickly cross-reference the patterns to the pages on which their details or reference entries appear.

Table A.1   Patterns and their Discussions in this Book

PATTERN NAME	DETAILS	REFERENCE
3-Category Logging	161	324
Active–Redundant Elements	93	298
Application Server Architecture	71	292
Common Persistent Store	113	307
Connection Limitation	132	311
Continual Status Reporting	146	319
Data Replication	122	309
Dedicated Web and Application Servers	108	305
Demilitarized Zone	178	331
Dynamically-Adjustable Configuration	171	328
Dynamically-Discoverable Elements	213	339
Expandable Hardware	216	341
Information Obscurity	185	333
Known Partners	203	337
Load-Balanced Elements	97	300
Local Cache	137	315
Offline Reporting	140	317
Operational Monitoring and Alerting	155	322
Peripheral Specialist Elements	79	295
Resource Pooling	135	313
Secure Channels	194	335
Separate System-Managed Data	230	347
Session Failover	103	303
Swappable Staging Environment	225	345
System Overview	166	326
Virtual Platform	220	343

Fundamental Patterns

APPLICATION SERVER ARCHITECTURE

Problem

What is a good starting point for the architecture of an Internet technology system?

Context

You are creating an Internet technology system that requires many different types of functionality and high levels of non-functional characteristics such as availability, manageability and performance.

Example

The GlobalTech system requires a product catalogue, registration and personalization, online ordering for retailers and various information-based applications such as the retail outlet finder, and online troubleshooting. Each of these has its own concerns and must be logically separated to some degree. As part of the separation, each could be implemented on its own hardware as a set of 'collaborating semi-autonomous applications'. However, they must all combine at different times and in various ways to deliver a 'seamless' experience for the user.

Forces

- Different functionality could be delivered by different applications but each one then is a single point of failure.
- Repeated interactions between separate applications can be costly.
- Different applications scale at different rates.
- Each application will need to be managed separately which adds greatly to the management overhead of the system.
- The interactions between many different applications can create a system that is complex and difficult to maintain.

Solution

Adopt an APPLICATION SERVER ARCHITECTURE: group all core system functionality in a single application. Internally partition the application according to the preferred logical architecture.

Example Resolution

If we had decided to adopt the 'collaborating semi-autonomous applications' architecture outlined above for the GlobalTech system, we would have ended up with a complex architecture consisting of seven or so separate applications. Adopting an APPLICATION SERVER ARCHITECTURE means that we lump all this complexity into a single application as shown in Figure 6.2.

Resulting Context

- Availability isn't improved over the 'collaborating semi-autonomous applications'. As discussed previously, the fact that some applications could continue to function when others have failed or been taken down is of dubious benefit. However, the availability of the APPLICATION SERVER ARCHITECTURE is really no worse.

- Performance is likely to be significantly improved. Whereas we had all the semi-autonomous applications collaborating (using some form of inter-process or inter-server communication, possibly via the database) to render pages or perform complex functions, now we have a single application, although parts of this may still require inter-process communication depending on implementation choices.

- The application of this pattern does not in itself improve the scalability of the system. However an APPLICATION SERVER ARCHITECTURE lays the foundation for a highly-scalable system.

- Security is marginally improved due to having only one application and one database to worry about securing.

- Manageability is significantly improved: whereas we had many applications to manage, now we only have one. Even when we add more complexity to the architecture to achieve scalability, etc., we shall see that an APPLICATION SERVER ARCHITECTURE lays the foundation for a more manageable system.

- Because all the logically separate software 'modules' are part of the same application, we don't have to worry about complex communication mechanisms. However, we have not lost the benefits of having well-defined sets of functionality which can, potentially, help to isolate bugs. On the whole, maintainability is improved.

- This type of system architecture is not as flexible as the 'collaborating semi-autonomous applications architecture'. Whilst we have a similar partitioning, which gives us some degree of flexibility, we are have abandoned the semi-autonomous nature that caused us performance, management and maintenance headaches. This means that we can't just add new functionality without impacting the existing system.

- An APPLICATION SERVER ARCHITECTURE provides a foundation where manageability, performance, availability and scalability can be addressed more easily (and, hence, more cheaply). Whether it is actually cheaper to adopt an APPLICATION SERVER ARCHITECTURE than the 'collaborating semi-autonomous applications' approach is debateable. Certainly, running the application in the .NET framework or a J2EE application server can potentially reduce costs; the cost of purchasing the infrastructure can easily be offset against the cost of building all the functionality provided from scratch. Even if we were to build the 'collaborating semi-autonomous applications' using J2EE servers, we would need many more server instances which can potentially affect license costs.

Implementation

This pattern applies only to software.

Related Patterns and Principles

Functionality that does not fit within the core of the APPLICATION SERVER ARCHITECTURE can be implemented as a PERIPHERAL SPECIALIST ELEMENT.

PERIPHERAL SPECIALIST ELEMENTS

Problem

Should we integrate all software elements into the application server, leaving us with a single, internally-partitioned application that implements all system functionality?

Context

You have created an Internet-technology system using an APPLICATION SERVER ARCHITECTURE. You now need to introduce some functionality that falls outside the 'mainstream' system functionality as it is only used by a sub-set of users, only runs for a limited time, or interfaces in an unusual way to the outside world. This addition must not degrade the characteristics of the overall system.

Example

There are several areas of GlobalTech functionality that, whilst being specific to GlobalTech and unlikely to be implemented using off-the-shelf software, can be considered 'specialist' or 'extraordinary':

- The daily creation of 'personalized' emails to a group of users. The target group is dynamically determined each time the process is run. One day it might be every user registered, another it might be every user that has logged in during the past month, and on yet another it might be every user that has purchased a particular type of product.
- Update of the retailer catalogue. Certain elements of the product catalogue information (relating to lead times and pricing bands) are retailer-specific. This information is updated in the supply-chain management system and then sent out to other systems as one or more messages.

- Update of the non-retailer product catalogue information, retailer database and retail outlet finder. The raw data for these changes is deposited as a set of files on the servers housing the database. Every so often, daemon processes on the application servers will wake up and look for update files. If an update file is found, its contents will be processed and changes will be made to the database.

Forces

- The functional and non-functional characteristics of the 'extraordinary' functionality often differ from those of the mainstream application functionality.
- We do not want the development and maintenance of the 'extraordinary' functionality to impact the development and maintenance of the mainstream application functionality.
- The use of an APPLICATION SERVER ARCHITECTURE makes the system easier to manage, but having all relevant application functionality on every type of element can make those elements highly complex and so difficult to create and maintain.
- The overall performance and scalability of the system is improved through the use of an APPLICATION SERVER ARCHITECTURE, but we don't want the application behaviour delivered to an individual user interacting with a particular element to be negatively impacted by the execution of 'extraordinary', CPU- or bandwidth-intensive behaviour on behalf of other users or as a system support function.

Solution

Separate 'extraordinary' functionality from the core application and implement it in specialist or dedicated elements. Place these elements at the periphery of the application – integrated with it but executed, maintained, secured and managed independently from it.

Example Resolution

Evolving the GlobalTech APPLICATION SERVER ARCHITECTURE to split out PERIPHERAL SPECIALIST ELEMENTS from the main application gives us the structure shown in Figure 6.4.

Resulting Context

- On the whole, the availability of the core application is improved due to splitting out specialist functionality. If the Retailer Update Application fails, the core application can continue to function (assuming the failure of the update doesn't render the retailer data completely invalid).

■ Overall system performance is potentially improved as PERIPHERAL SPECIALIST ELEMENTS are often introduced to carry out a task that is particularly expensive or complex and so would lead to (probably unpredictable) performance degradation if they were run as part of the core application. The performance of the specialist elements will also be improved if they are hosted on their own dedicated hardware rather than sharing with the core application.

■ The scalability of the overall system is largely unaltered, but the separation of extraordinary functionality allows it to be scaled independently from the core system elements.

■ As it introduces more and different elements into the system, the use of PERIPHERAL SPECIALIST ELEMENTS can make security more of a challenge. However, by separating these elements from the mainstream their security can be individually tailored.

■ Manageability of the extraordinary functionality is improved because each specialist application can be managed appropriately. However, manageability of the system as a whole is negatively impacted because different management procedures and techniques have to be introduced for each application.

■ The use of PERIPHERAL SPECIALIST ELEMENTS can improve the maintainability of the system as any problem with the specialist functionality is isolated in its own application.

■ PERIPHERAL SPECIALIST ELEMENTS frequently deliver additional, non-core, functionality in a flexible manner.

■ Portability is largely unaffected when we consider the main application and the bespoke specialist servers we have built. Unless we choose to implement them in different technologies, porting the core application and specialist servers is likely to be as easy or as difficult as porting one application with both core and specialist functionality. Choosing to implement specialist functionality using off-the-shelf products (commercial or non-commercial) can affect portability. An SMTP server is likely to be available for many operating systems and there are a number of different SMTP server products to choose from so portability is improved. On the other hand, if we choose a proprietary search engine technology we may become tied to that vendor and the operating systems they support.

■ On the face of it, choosing to split out specialist behaviour like this will increase our costs: we will probably increase the number of hardware servers and we have increased our maintainability problem (a major source of ongoing cost). However, we have to trade this off against potential savings: use of off-the-shelf products (commercial or non-commercial) can save money compared to developing the functionality ourselves. Also, adding separate hardware servers isn't necessarily more expensive. If we were to host all applications on a single server, it would have to be very powerful. By placing the specialist applications on optimized hardware (and reducing the capacity of the Core Hardware accordingly) we may not spend much more money than buying a single big server – maybe we can even reduce the hardware budget.

Implementation

This pattern applies equally to hardware and software. Hardware elements might be introduced for a data link or specialist switching function. Software elements might take care of administrative or data trawling functions.

Related Patterns and Principles

- This pattern works with APPLICATION SERVER ARCHITECTURE to make the core system architecture simpler.
- If you have multiple PERIPHERAL SPECIALIST ELEMENTS performing one task, you can configure them as functionally-identical elements.

System Performance Patterns

ACTIVE–REDUNDANT ELEMENTS

Problem

There is always a possibility that part of your system may be taken out of action. How do we ensure that the system as a whole continues to function?

Context

We are implementing an enterprise-level Internet technology system based around an APPLICATION SERVER ARCHITECTURE where high availability is one of the prime non-functional requirements.

Example

The GlobalTech system has some fairly stringent availability requirements. It should be down for no more than one hour per month for minor upgrades to system software or hardware, and for no more than four hours per quarter for major upgrades. There is no server (hardware or software) under consideration that can guarantee this level of availability.

Forces

- The system will have a required level of availability which must be delivered even in the face of hardware or software failure.
- The system needs to be maintained and upgraded over time. Even with planned downtime there may be a need to upgrade or fix a system element whilst ensuring the system remains available.

Solution

Provide alternative capacity for your critical system elements by duplicating those elements. Redirect users to the duplicate should the active element become unavailable.

Example Resolution

The GlobalTech system introduces redundant switches and servers that will automatically swap in should the active one fail, as shown in Figure 7.1.

Resulting Context

- Availability of the system is improved due to the presence of a redundant element that can take over in the event the active element fails or has to be taken out of service for maintenance.
- There will be a very small (possibly insignificant) impact on performance due to the introduction of the 'failover' mechanism that switches in the redundant element should the active one fail.
- There may be a negative impact on security due to the additional element and failover mechanism, both of which have to be secured.
- There is a negative impact on manageability as one element has been replaced by two and the failover mechanism also has to be managed.
- The impact on cost can be significant: where we once had a single element, we now have two (plus the cost of implementing the failover mechanism). If the elements are identical, we have basically doubled the cost of introducing that element. We can mitigate this by introducing a cheaper version of the element as the redundant one (see the functionally-identical elements principle) but this restricts our implementation choices: we would definitely want to switch back to the active element as soon as it is introduced back into service.

Implementation

This pattern must be applied equally to hardware and software. Software elements are, perhaps, more prone to failure than hardware because they are inherently more complex. They are also likely to be the elements that need to be taken out of service for maintenance (usually to have their functionality upgraded). However, this isn't to say that hardware is immune to failure or requires no maintenance. And there is no point having a single hardware element running an active–redundant pair of software elements. If the hardware fails, the system is down.

Related Patterns and Principles

- LOAD-BALANCED ELEMENTS is an alternative solution to a similar problem.
- SESSION FAILOVER is required if the element maintains rich state.
- If the element being replicated is a database, you will probably need to apply COMMON PERSISTENT STORE and DATA REPLICATION.

LOAD-BALANCED ELEMENTS

Problem

How can the system continue to function when elements become unavailable and when system load increases beyond the capacity of a single element?

Context

We are implementing an enterprise-level Internet technology system based around an APPLICATION SERVER ARCHITECTURE where high availability is one of the prime non-functional requirements. We have rejected the use of ACTIVE–REDUNDANT ELEMENTS because the reduction in performance and scalability when a lower-capacity redundant element is in service is too severe, and the cost of having full-capacity redundant elements is too high.

Example

The requirement for the GlobalTech system is to support a peak of 3000 consumer and 700 retailer users at the outset. Given the complexity of the GlobalTech Application, this translates to one *very* big server which will cost a lot of money to buy. Doubling this cost to introduce a redundant element is probably not feasible so we might opt for a lower-capacity redundant version. We want one that is only a fifth to a quarter of the cost. This doesn't translate directly to 20–25% of the capacity so perhaps it can only handle 600 consumer and 100 retail users. In the event of failure or maintenance, the system performance is going to be very poor, possibly rendering the system totally unusable even under moderate load.

Forces

- The system will have a required level of availability which must be delivered even in the face of hardware or software failure.
- The system needs to be maintained and upgraded over time. Even with planned downtime there may be a need to upgrade or fix a system element whilst ensuring the system remains available.
- When implementing ACTIVE–REDUNDANT ELEMENTS, the number of users accessing a reduced capacity redundant server could be restricted to a level matching its capabilities. However, this will effectively make the server unavailable to the remaining users which is not satisfactory.
- Specifying a redundant server to the same level as that of the active server means that there will be no degradation in performance, but is economically unacceptable for most organizations.
- The system has a required level of performance in the face of a particular user load which it needs to maintain even though hardware and software elements will be taken out of service due to failure or the need for maintenance.
- The system will need to deliver a consistent level of performance in the face of increased user load. There must be some way of increasing the system capacity should this load exceed original estimates.

Solution

Use multiple elements of similar capability and balance the load continuously across them to achieve the required throughput and response. To increase capacity, add further elements to the load-balanced set.

Example Resolution

Figure 7.2 shows how the GlobalTech system mixes active–redundant and load-balanced elements.

Resulting Context

- Availability is improved. As with ACTIVE–REDUNDANT ELEMENTS, loss of an element due to failure or maintenance does not mean the system ceases to function. However, the reduction in capacity of the system is determined by the proportion of load the element takes, not the capacity of the redundant element. In cases where we would have to have a much lower capacity redundant element for reasons of cost, LOAD-BALANCED ELEMENTS are likely to provide better capacity. Unlike ACTIVE–REDUNDANT ELEMENTS, LOAD-BALANCED ELEMENTS can also cope with multiple failures or failure during maintenance.

- There is a negative impact on performance as the load balancer needs to determine the element to which it should forward a request.

- Scalability is greatly improved. With ACTIVE–REDUNDANT ELEMENTS we can only scale the system by increasing the capacity of the active element (possibly only by replacing it). Using LOAD-BALANCED ELEMENTS, we can increase the capacity of the system by adding new elements to the load-balanced set. The load balancer will ensure they receive their 'fair share' of requests and the system is scaled.

- There is a negative impact on security due to the introduction of additional elements that need to be protected.

- There is a large negative impact on manageability. We now have a number of additional elements to manage and that number can grow according to our scalability needs.

- Cost may not be too severely impacted. Depending on the type of hardware, the cost of buying a large number of medium-capacity servers may actually be lower than the cost of buying one high-capacity and one low capacity (redundant) server. It may be a bit more expensive, but it is rare that it is a lot more expensive. The cost of the load balancer needs to be added to the cost of the system.

Implementation

Both software and hardware load balancers are available. The actual load balancing tends to be across software elements, with the load balancing across hardware achieved as a consequence of the software elements running on that hardware.

Related Patterns and Principles

- The ACTIVE–REDUNDANT ELEMENTS pattern is an alternative solution that addresses one of the problems.

- The SESSION FAILOVER pattern is required if the element maintains rich state.

Session Failover

Problem

If users interact with a server and build up state on that server, they will be unhappy if the state is lost when the server becomes unavailable. How do we ensure state is preserved in the event of server failure?

Context

We are implementing an enterprise-level Internet-technology system based around an APPLICATION SERVER ARCHITECTURE where high availability is one of the prime non-functional requirements. We are ensuring that availability using ACTIVE–REDUNDANT ELEMENTS or LOAD-BALANCED ELEMENTS (or a mixture of the two). The system maintains interaction state in the form of a user session held on the server.

Example

The GlobalTech system maintains extensive in-memory state for the retailer ordering functionality: the retailer assembles their order over a number of individual requests using a variety of tools (e.g. previously ordered items, various searches, promotional codes, etc.). The order state is kept in memory until the retailer places the order with GlobalTech. The process of assembling an order may take any length of time from a couple of minutes up to several hours.

Forces

- Failures in software or hardware may well occur while the user is in the middle of interacting with the system but we cannot allow that failure to interrupt the user's interaction or the server to lose important data.

- Having either a redundant or load-balanced, functionally-identical element that can take over from a failed element means that the user can continue interacting with the system, but that element needs to be able to get at the state of the user's interaction for the user to be able to continue that interaction uninterrupted.

- Storing the state information either as part of the request URL or one or more cookies means that any element involved in fulfilling the request can get at the information, but the nature of the interaction means the amount and sensitivity of the information makes this choice inappropriate.

Solution

Implement a mechanism that holds session information whilst the user is interacting with the system and makes this information available to the duplicate servers in the system.

Example Resolution

We introduce a session persistence mechanism into the GlobalTech system in the form of a session backup server. We save session state whenever it is changed in response to a request. We introduce request-based failover so that the system software tries to load session state from the session backup server whenever it receives a request that forms part of a session it doesn't recognize (see Figure 7.3).

Resulting Context

- Availability is improved as the user's session state is maintained even if the requests need to be directed to a new server due to the loss of the one that had been maintaining that state.

- There is likely to be a negative impact on performance due to the need to save the user's session state periodically.

- We have introduced some new system elements – the session backup server and its redundant pair – that need to be secured. We also have a mechanism that saves the state information in some way. We have to ensure that sensitive information is not stored as part of the state or is obscured in some way (see INFORMATION OBSCURITY).

- There is a negative impact on manageability due to the introduction of a new mechanism and associated elements that all have to be managed.

- Maintainability can be marginally improved as it is possible to retrieve information about the state of user sessions in the event of system failure.

- The cost is most likely to be affected by whether dedicated session backup servers (both software and hardware elements) are purchased. This maximizes availability but has significant expense. Alternatively we could run the session backup servers on other hardware servers (such as the Core Hardware in the GlobalTech example) and save some expense, but with a slight decrease in availability.

Implementation

This pattern applies essentially to software. The state is maintained as part of a software component and the session backup server is usually implemented in software. Hardware is only required to host the backup server – sometimes this hosting is provided by a dedicated hardware server, sometimes the backup servers live on the same hardware server as the system software.

Related Patterns and Principles

- ACTIVE–REDUNDANT ELEMENTS and LOAD-BALANCED ELEMENTS both require SESSION FAILOVER if those elements maintain rich state.

- If dedicated session backup servers are used, they can be deployed either as ACTIVE–REDUNDANT ELEMENTS or LOAD-BALANCED ELEMENTS.

- SESSION FAILOVER can employ DATA REPLICATION techniques if several backup servers are deployed as LOAD-BALANCED ELEMENTS.

DEDICATED WEB AND APPLICATION SERVERS

Problem

How can we independently scale, tune and improve the availability of the 'web' and 'application' elements of the system?

Context

We are implementing an enterprise-level Internet technology system based around an APPLICATION SERVER ARCHITECTURE for which good performance is a fundamental requirement in order to make the system usable.

Example

In the GlobalTech Application we have software web and application servers that perform different tasks. However, if these servers are deployed on the same hardware, the hardware cannot be tuned or scaled for the individual types of server – they are lumped together leading to sub-optimal performance and increased licensing and configuration cost.

Forces

- Only a small amount of the response returned to the user may involve application server functionality.

- It is difficult to optimize a hardware server for both memory-intensive computation and disk or network I/O.

- The web and application servers will usually scale at different rates, with the web server being able to handle more concurrent users than the application server.

- Application server software licenses tend to cost more money than web server software and these licenses are usually on a per processor basis, so more hardware servers running the application server will cost more money regardless of whether that capacity is used or not.

- If the web and application servers are bound together, failure of a web server will result in no requests being delivered to the associated application server.

Solution

Deploy the web server and application server software onto dedicated hardware servers that are optimized to support these different types of functionality.

Example Resolution

As Figure 7.5 shows, the GlobalTech system introduces separate tiers of web and application servers. Both are deployed as LOAD-BALANCED ELEMENTS.

Resulting Context

- Availability is improved due to the separation of the web servers from the rest of the system software – a web server can fail without impacting any particular system software instance as it did in previous versions of the architecture.
- Performance can be improved depending on the degree to which the web and application hardware servers can be optimized. This will depend on the type of application and its interface – sites with lots of graphics or large binary assets to be downloaded, or particularly complex functionality, are likely to benefit most from the split.
- Scalability is improved due to the ability to independently scale the web server and system software load-balanced pools.
- There is a negative impact on security in the sense that there are now a number of new elements that need to be secured. However, DEDICATED WEB AND APPLICATION SERVERS does provide the foundation for the DEMILITARIZED ZONE security pattern.
- There is a negative impact on manageability due to the need to separately manage the web servers and system software, plus the additional load balancers.
- Maintainability is potentially improved as problems specific to the web servers will be isolated on those machines. Equally, the web servers and the system software stack can be fixed independently if necessary.
- The introduction of a number of new hardware servers has an initial negative impact on cost (plus the purchase of the additional load balancers). However, the use of optimized or specialist hardware should prove cheaper in the long run – scaling the system doesn't necessarily require new hardware of all types to be purchased.

Implementation

The split between web and application servers is generally carried out on both the hardware and software elements. This means that both hardware and software can be tuned for the web and application server functions.

Related Patterns and Principles

■ COMMON PERSISTENT STORE is usually employed in addition to DEDICATED WEB AND APPLICATION SERVERS to give the 'classic' three-tier Internet system architecture.

■ The web and application servers are deployed as either ACTIVE–REDUNDANT ELEMENTS or LOAD-BALANCED ELEMENTS.

■ We can further improve manageability and maintainability by introducing appropriate isolation layers or one-way dependencies.

■ The use of DEDICATED WEB AND APPLICATION SERVERS paves the way for implementing a DEMILITARIZED ZONE to improve the security of the application data and functionality housed in the application servers.

COMMON PERSISTENT STORE

Problem

If the system employs multiple elements to deliver a particular part of the system functionality, how do we ensure that those elements present a consistent view of the data in the system?

Context

We are implementing an enterprise-level Internet technology system that has to store persistent information between user sessions. We have DEDICATED WEB AND APPLICATION SERVERS deployed as either ACTIVE–REDUNDANT ELEMENTS or LOAD-BALANCED ELEMENTS. We are using SESSION FAILOVER so that any application server can take over from any other in the event of failure or the need for maintenance.

Example

In the GlobalTech system we have a lot of types of data that may change through users interacting with the system. Customer profiles, customer orders, retailer profiles and retailer orders are all going to be created and maintained by the users of the system and so this data needs to be consistent across all the servers that the user may interact with. We could look at propagating changes from the server on which the user creates or changes data to the other servers in the load-balanced pool (in a form of DATA REPLICATION) but this is a complex and difficult process. It requires every system software instance to be able to access the database of every other system software instance to ensure they are all up-to-date. Instead we need a single consistent data set that all servers access and update.

Forces

- Storing persistent data locally to the application server is simple and fast but means that each application server has a different view of the system's state.

- Failures in software or hardware may well occur while the user is in the middle of interacting with the system and has caused data to be written to a persistent store. We cannot allow that failure and subsequent SESSION FAILOVER to leave the user with an inconsistent view of the system.

- Load-balancing between application servers, or having an active–redundant pair, means that there is a chance (possibly very high) that the user will access the system using different application servers each time they start a new session. We cannot allow the 'behind the scenes' use of different servers to give the user an inconsistent view of the system.

Solution

Store all application data in a COMMON PERSISTENT STORE and have all the servers access it.

Example Resolution

In the GlobalTech system, the COMMON PERSISTENT STORE is implemented as a database management system running on its own hardware server, as shown in Figure 7.6.

Resulting Context

- Availability is severely impacted by the introduction of the COMMON PERSISTENT STORE as a single point of failure.

- There is potentially a negative impact on performance by the introduction of a network gap. This can be somewhat mitigated by optimizing the database hardware server but the degree of traffic between the application and the database is likely to outweigh the benefits of this optimization.

- Because the COMMON PERSISTENT STORE is the only element of its type in the system, and one that is likely to be involved in most, if not all, user requests, it becomes a bottleneck for scalability. If it reaches the limits of its capacity, we can only replace it with a higher-capacity element.

- Although we have introduced another element to the system, security is potentially improved as we can take security measures to protect the persistent data – something we particularly care about.

- There is a negative impact on manageability by the addition of yet another hardware server and its corresponding software element.

- Maintainability is potentially improved as problems specific to the COMMON PERSISTENT STORE are isolated to its server. However, we have an issue of availability if the database hardware server or the database cannot be maintained while they are in service.

- Cost is potentially greatly impacted. When we had one database per application, it only required a relatively small amount of resource to function – the memory and CPU utilization will have been dominated by the application. Now we have a single hardware server that has to support a software element processing all queries from all applications, it will need to be a substantial server. Any saving made by being able to further optimize the application server hardware is likely to be small in comparison.

Implementation

The COMMON PERSISTENT STORE is usually deployed to its own hardware. However, a variation could be employed where the system hardware is used to house persistent storage software. This reduces hardware requirements (and, hence, cost) but means that the system has more work to do to remain available in the event of hardware failure.

Related Patterns and Principles

- Implementation using ACTIVE–REDUNDANT ELEMENTS and DATA REPLICATION will be required to avoid the COMMON PERSISTENT STORE becoming a single point of failure.

- Lack of performance due to the introduction of the separate data store can be addressed by LOCAL CACHE and SEPARATE SYSTEM-MANAGED DATA.

- Lack of scalability in the data store can be addressed by EXPANDABLE HARDWARE.

DATA REPLICATION

Problem

To deliver high availability we must introduce some level of duplication of system elements. However, if those elements store data, no inconsistency can be tolerated between them. How can this inconsistency be prevented?

Context

We are implementing an enterprise-level Internet technology system where high availability is one of the prime non-functional requirements. The system needs to store data persistently and does so using a COMMON PERSISTENT STORE.

Example

The GlobalTech system uses a COMMON PERSISTENT STORE to hold catalogue data, retailer information, user registration data, and order data.

Forces

- We need a COMMON PERSISTENT STORE to ensure a consistent view of the system across all application servers (whether active–redundant or load-balanced) but failure of the persistent store means that any service requiring access to persistent data, for retrieval or update, cannot be delivered.
- Introducing a number of persistent stores to ensure availability defeats the object of a common store – there needs to be one and only one copy of the data.

Solution

Deploy the COMMON PERSISTENT STORE as a pair of ACTIVE–REDUNDANT ELEMENTS. Implement a mechanism that replicates the data between them and ensures the transaction is not completed until the data is available on both the active and redundant elements.

Example Resolution

For the GlobalTech system we have opted for a DBMS that supports clustering and data replication, as shown in Figure 7.10.

Resulting Context

- Availability is improved by replacing the single point of failure with a pair of ACTIVE–REDUNDANT ELEMENTS.
- There is a significant negative impact on performance for any operation that involves writing data to the database.
- As long as the security mechanisms work in the same way for a pair of ACTIVE–REDUNDANT ELEMENTS as they do for a single server, security is unaffected.
- There will be a negative impact on manageability due to the need to manage the active–redundant pair of elements and the DATA REPLICATION mechanism.
- Maintainability should be unaffected unless there are problems with the DATA REPLICATION mechanism itself, in which case there may be some uncertainty as to the state of the data set the application is using.

- DATA REPLICATION is usually implemented using proprietary mechanisms that have their own non-functional characteristics. If the database is accessed using SQL, potentially it can be swapped with another SQL-compliant database, but the new database may not have a DATA REPLICATION mechanism or it might work in a very different way.

- The simplest way to implement such a complex mechanism as DATA REPLICATION is to buy a persistent storage product that supports it. This can be very expensive, particularly when compared with other products that don't support DATA REPLICATION but otherwise meet all the functional and non-functional requirements for the sore. Bespoke solutions can be developed but these are usually reasonably complex and so take time and money to develop and maintain.

Implementation

This pattern is usually implemented in software, often as part of the database management system. Additional hardware is introduced to give tolerance to both hardware and software failure and maintenance.

Related Patterns and Principles

- DATA REPLICATION can be used to provide a COMMON PERSISTENT STORE with high availability.

- One way to improve the performance and reduce the complexity of this pattern is to apply SEPARATE SYSTEM-MANAGED DATA.

- Implement a LOCAL CACHE for the application instances to reduce the load on the persistent store and free more resource for it to replicate its data.

- Use of CONNECTION LIMITATION can also reduce the strain on the persistent store.

CONNECTION LIMITATION

Problem

Sometimes you have more users than you can comfortably service, which degrades the service for all users. How do we ensure that all the users we service receive a minimum level of service?

Context

We are implementing an enterprise-level Internet technology system where high performance is one of the prime non-functional requirements. The system consists of an APPLICATION SERVER ARCHITECTURE with DEDICATED WEB AND APPLICATION SERVERS and a COMMON PERSISTENT STORE.

Example

In the GlobalTech system we have a set of web servers that we believe can comfortably handle around 7500 simultaneous users. However, we only have enough application instances to serve around 4000 simultaneous users. We have the option of adding more servers to scale the application but this takes time and we don't see it as being necessary at the moment (or worth the cost). However, suppose something unexpected happens (like a range of GlobalTech products win a major design award, for example) and 6000 users do all turn up at the same time: the web servers will cope but the application servers will struggle and everyone will experience poor performance.

Forces

- We want to serve as many users as possible but we also want to make sure that each individual user has a good experience. Having many users accessing a constrained resource at the same time will give a proportionately slower experience the more users we allow.
- It is usually not financially justifiable to specify each element of the system to meet the anticipated peak load. Even if you do, sudden spikes could possibly exceed this peak and degrade performance.

Solution

Limit the number of users that can connect to the system, or requests that can connect to a system element, at any one time to avoid resource contention and the associated poor performance.

Example Resolution

We introduce a limitation on the number of requests the system will accept. Additional users will be redirected to a static holding page. We also introduce a limit to the number of requests each individual application server will process in order to maintain overall responsiveness and balance in the system.

Resulting Context

- There is a negative impact on availability as we reject any requests over a set limit. However, this is availability from the user's point of view rather than system availability – some users are still able to access the system even though others can't.

- We can guarantee a level of performance regardless of the demand for the system.

- Perhaps strangely, scalability is improved by limiting the number of connections to the system or a particular system element. Our view of scalability is that it defines the system's ability to cope with increased load without degrading performance significantly. By imposing the CONNECTION LIMITATION pattern we can ensure good scalability up to that limit and then prevent degradation due to overloading.

- There is a slight negative impact on manageability due to the need to manage the connection limit.

- The cost of implementing a connection limit is pretty low. A number of products support this concept as standard but even a bespoke implementation is not that big a job.

Implementation

This pattern applies to both software and hardware.

Related Patterns and Principles

- RESOURCE POOLING can further improve performance.

- A LOCAL CACHE of persistent stores can reduce the need to limit connections as a request may be able to work with the data in the cache rather than going to the database.

RESOURCE POOLING

Problem

How do we maximize the utilization of limited or expensive resources?

Context

We are implementing an Internet technology application based around an APPLICATION SERVER ARCHITECTURE. We need to provide resources to processes or threads that are expensive to initialize and we have implemented CONNECTION LIMITATION to optimize the use of these resources.

Example

In the GlobalTech system, we could potentially have 3700 concurrent users at peak load even from the outset. If every process that services one of these users requires a database connection to do its work, then this means we need a 3700-user license. Although this gives us the required performance, it also gives us a mighty budget headache.

Forces

- We want to maximize overall system performance (throughput) by limiting connections but we also want to maximize individual user performance (end-to-end).
- It is not usually financially justifiable to specify enough capacity in expensive resources for each projected user of the system.
- Resource usage tends to vary over the course of a request. Not all resources are required for the whole lifetime of the request.
- Obtaining and initializing resources is typically expensive in terms of time and processing power. This initialization should be avoided where possible.

Solution

Implement a pool of resources from which it is relatively inexpensive to acquire such resources and to which they can quickly be released when no longer required.

Example Resolution

Each of the application servers in the GlobalTech system has a pool of connections that it uses to connect to the database server cluster. The pool is limited in size by licensing constraints. The business components will obtain a database connection just before they need it and release it as soon as they have finished with it.

Resulting Context

- Performance is improved due to the reuse of limited resources that can be expensive to create or initialize.
- Sharing of valuable resources allows more users to connect to the system than we otherwise could.
- There is a slight negative impact on manageability due to the need to manage the resource pool.
- Many products support resource pooling as standard and bespoke implementation is not a significant investment.

Implementation

This pattern applies to both hardware and software.

Related Patterns and Principles

- The CONNECTION LIMITATION pattern prevents the pool of resources from needing to grow too large or too often.

- Using a LOCAL CACHE can reduce the number of times we need to connect to the database.

LOCAL CACHE

Problem

How can we speed up access to information distributed across multiple servers?

Context

We are implementing an enterprise-level, Internet technology system that uses DEDICATED WEB AND APPLICATION SERVERS together with a COMMON PERSISTENT STORE.

Example

The GlobalTech database is housed on its own hardware server. This introduces a performance problem as all queries and resultant data have to travel over the network connection between each application instance and the database.

Forces

- A COMMON PERSISTENT STORE ensures information integrity but this means that all system elements have to compete for the resource, potentially introducing a bottleneck.

- A distributed architecture with a COMMON PERSISTENT STORE gives advantages in reliability and robustness but means that data access has to be inter- rather than intra-process.

- Data integrity is of prime importance but much data is slow-changing and a system element may read the same piece of data many times before it changes.

Solution

Identify information that changes infrequently compared to the frequency with which it is accessed and cache it locally to where it is used.

Example Resolution

Each of the application servers in the GlobalTech system caches data that it reads from the DBMS. When this information is next required by an application component, it can be retrieved from the local cache without reference to the database.

Resulting Context

- Potentially there is a minor improvement in availability. If the COMMON PERSISTENT STORE fails, some data is still available in the LOCAL CACHE. However, only a subset of functionality is likely to remain available; functions such as ordering require access to the store, not merely to a cache.
- Performance is improved by the local availability of data or assets that would otherwise have to be retrieved from a remote store.
- We need to consider the type of information being held in the LOCAL CACHE. If the information is sensitive, introduction of the cache has a negative impact on security as we have to protect the cache as well as the persistent store.
- There is a slight negative impact on manageability as we have to manage the cache and any caching parameters that can be 'tuned'.
- The cost of implementing a LOCAL CACHE depends on its sophistication. It is relatively easy to build and maintain a very simple cache and the cost is minimal. However an adaptive cache that holds frequently updated information is hard to build and products that perform this function can be expensive to buy.

Implementation

This pattern applies to both hardware and software.

Related Patterns and Principles

- LOCAL CACHE can be implemented to overcome overheads introduced by COMMON PERSISTENT STORE and DEDICATED WEB AND APPLICATION SERVERS.
- The identification of cacheable data and the implementation of the cache is eased by the application of SEPARATE SYSTEM-MANAGED DATA.
- If the cache is to hold sensitive data, we may need to apply some form of INFORMATION OBSCURITY to it.
- OFFLINE REPORTING employs a similar principle to achieve a very different effect: by caching data locally to a reporting and analysis tool, we can avoid adversely affecting the performance of the running application.

OFFLINE REPORTING

Problem

How can we extract important information from a system without significantly impacting the ability of that system to do its job?

Context

We have implemented a high-capability Internet technology system that gathers data as it processes user transactions. This data contains useful business information about those transactions including who performed the transaction, when it took place, how it related to other transactions and how the system behaved during the transaction. By performing suitable analysis on this data, the business can detect trends in product sales and customer demographics. The system operations team can also use such data to predict system load and detect potential overload.

Example

The GlobalTech system gathers information such as orders placed, duration of transactions and page views. This information can be analysed to determine which products were commonly bought together. This can be further refined when it is split on a demographic basis (e.g. retailers who are identified as operating in a higher-income area). There may be many such analyses that are required – some standard and some *ad hoc* – as the business tries to determine the best combination of offers and marketing to suit the needs of its customers. Using live system data as the basis for such analyses puts an additional, intensive load on the system database and degrades the performance of the system.

Forces

- Lots of intensive data processing is required to create useful reports, but such processing slows down the live system.
- Reporting tends to be historical and/or predictive. In either case, the data does not need to be completely up-to-the-minute.
- Users of the reporting mechanisms are internal to the organization, while the main application is focused at delivering information to external users.
- Users of the reporting mechanisms are inside the internal firewall. Providing access to specific parts of the external system will require a more complex firewall configuration.
- If a report is generated from live system data, all of the updates from a (long running) business transaction may not have been applied when the report is generated, potentially giving misleading results.

- *Ad hoc* reports generated in real-time may be required against the data.
- For a simple system, it would be possible to minimize such contention by running reports 'overnight', i.e. at a time of low system load. For systems that are used 24×7, there may be no ideal timeslot at which user load is sufficiently low that running a heavy report would not impact system responsiveness.

Solution

Periodically snapshot data that needs to be analysed. Export this snapshot from the live system environment so that any reporting can be carried out 'offline'.

Example Resolutions

For the GlobalTech system we will implement a bespoke snapshot mechanism for each of the three main areas of interest. Implementing three separate mechanisms means we can run the snapshots at different times. The queries required to generate the snapshots will have an impact on the database, but nowhere near as big an impact as running the reporting against it. We can also parameterize the snapshot mechanisms as much as we like, for example specifying that we're only interested in how users view certain areas of the site, or the profiles of new customers.

Resulting Context

- Performance is improved as we have isolated an essential but 'expensive' process from the live system.
- There is potentially a negative impact on security as we create snapshots of potentially sensitive data. These snapshots need to be protected from anyone who should not have access to them. We also have to be careful that our export mechanism does not leave security holes that could be used to gain access to the corporate environment.
- There is a negative impact on manageability due to the introduction of new mechanisms and system access points that have to be managed.
- The implementation cost really depends on the sophistication of the snapshot and export mechanisms. If we don't mind exporting the whole database in a single, unparameterized snapshot and the database product supports snapshots being taken whilst it is still running, this should be a simple and cheap mechanism to implement. If we want to be more selective about what we snapshot and how we export it, we will need to build a bespoke solution, which could be reasonably expensive to build and maintain.

Implementation

This pattern applies only to software.

Related Patterns and Principles

- Information about the system could be fed into the SYSTEM OVERVIEW to give us a picture of trends in using the system and how they relate to its 'health'.

- SEPARATE SYSTEM-MANAGED DATA may make it easier to create the snapshots as we are only interested in data created and modified by users or as a consequence of their actions. If we store all data in the same database, we may take snapshots of the data that we own and modify, which is pointless.

- If the export mechanism needs to make use of the public Internet, we may wish to set up SECURE CHANNELS and even KNOWN PARTNERS to make sure the data cannot be intercepted when it is exported. We might also want to use INFORMATION OBSCURITY to hide sensitive information held in the snapshot in case an unauthorized person gains access.

System Control Patterns

CONTINUAL STATUS REPORTING

Problem

To control your system effectively you need to be armed with information at regular intervals about what each system element is doing. How do you obtain this information?

Context

We have an Internet-technology system in operation that uses a number of different hardware and software servers. The system has stringent requirements for performance, scalability and availability. The failure of any system element could potentially impact the level of capability in these areas. In order to prevent system crashes or predict when new capacity is needed, you must have some current and historical data on system usage.

Example

Figure 8.1 presents a simplified view of the GlobalTech architecture (the switches and load balancers have been omitted) that shows that there are a number of elements that we need to manage.

The web servers, application servers and database servers (both hardware and software) all play vital roles in the system. If one of the web servers fails, the load on the other two web servers increases by 50%. This could lead to poor performance for the users or even to the failure of one of the remaining web servers. This sequence of events may well go unnoticed unless you can determine the health and capacity of the web servers.

Forces

- When the system is deployed into the live, staging or test environments, operational, security and practical considerations mitigate against the use of standard development techniques (such as debugging) to examine the internal state of the system.

- Internet technology systems are subject to huge and unpredictable variations in their use. This makes it difficult to decide which system elements we need status information from and what degree of information is needed.

- Monitoring every system element involves more effort (cost) to set up and degrades performance and reduces manageability due to the increased data generated. However, in the type of architecture we are evolving, every element has a vital role to play and, consequently, can significantly affect the overall health of the system if it fails or is subject to excessive load.

- Generating lots of information from a system element involves more effort (cost) to set up, degrades performance and reduces manageability due to the increased data generated. The amount and type of information required depends on the purpose for which the information is used. Restricting the information generated may prevent the correct diagnosis of problems.

- It may be cheaper and more manageable to have system elements store status information about themselves and analyse that information off-line or at set intervals. But this does not give us the ability to react immediately to changes in use that might threaten the health of the system.

Solution

Define a reporting interface or protocol for every type of system element that can seriously affect the operational health of the overall system (usually all or nearly all of them). Have each individual system element continuously report its status according to its type. Log some or all of the data generated so that it is available for subsequent offline analysis.

Example Resolution

In the GlobalTech system, we add status reporting capability to the web servers, application servers and data access servers. Using a variety of reporting techniques, including the SNMP protocol, each of the components reports its use of limited resources such as memory, CPU and disk space (all); sockets (web servers); database connections (application servers); and cursors (data access servers). The type and amount of information generated, the frequency of generation and the protocol used to export it depends on the requirements of any monitoring, alerting or prediction systems that use it.

Resulting Context

- Availability is potentially improved as the generated information can be used to identify and predict element failure or overload.
- There is a negative impact on performance because of the overhead of the continuous reporting.
- Security is potentially reduced as extended system information is available to any intruder who has the capability of monitoring network traffic.
- Manageability is improved because up-to-date information about each element's condition is continuously available.
- Maintainability is potentially improved because management information can sometimes be useful in diagnosing a fault or problem. For example, requests for dynamic pages failing when the data access servers take more than 30 seconds to pass back the result set may indicate a pre-defined time-out in the database drivers used by the application servers).
- The cost of introducing continuous reporting for every type of system element is always going to be significant whether the element supports reporting out of the box or not. This cost is justified because continuous status reporting is at the heart of a controllable system.

Implementation

Reporting must be performed by virtually every system element regardless of whether it is hardware or software. For simple elements such as a hardware switch, the status information may be as simple as an indicator that it is still functioning. For more complex elements such as the hardware database server, there may be a large amount of highly-detailed information.

Related Patterns and Principles

- Combining all the detailed information reported into a single SYSTEM OVERVIEW makes the monitoring of management information easier.
- CONTINUAL STATUS REPORTING is a prerequisite for OPERATIONAL MONITORING AND ALERTING.
- CONTINUAL STATUS REPORTING forms the basis of 3-CATEGORY LOGGING. The use of DYNAMICALLY-ADJUSTABLE CONFIGURATION allows the level of logging to be changed.

OPERATIONAL MONITORING AND ALERTING

Problem

How do we make it possible for human operators to spot potential problems in the large volume of information generated by status reporting from a complex or high-volume Internet-technology system?

Context

We have an Internet-technology system in operation that uses a number of different hardware and software servers. The system has stringent requirements for performance, scalability and availability. The failure of any system element could potentially impact the level of capability in these areas. The system has been configured according to CONTINUAL STATUS REPORTING so that it generates status and management information.

Example

The system is configured with LOAD-BALANCED ELEMENTS for its major components. However, failure of such an element will still need to be addressed. If one of the load balancers for the web servers fails, then the second load balancer will continue to process the entire user load. However, the system will now have a much reduced level of availability (it now has a single point of failure – namely this second load balancer) and it may also have reduced performance if higher levels of user load are intended to be shared between the two load balancers.

Forces

- To reduce cost and simplify procedures, we will need to restrict the number of people on the system operations team. However, there are many parameters that can indicate immediate or potential problems in a system, and a large amount of generated data becomes increasingly difficult for a limited system operations team to process manually in a timely fashion (i.e. soon enough to avert system failure).

■ Monitoring all of the system elements is costly (in terms of time at least) and will impact performance and manageability due to the amount of data generated. However, in the type of architecture we are evolving, every element has a vital role to play and, consequently, can significantly affect the overall health of the system if it fails or is subject to excessive load.

■ It may be cheaper and more manageable to have system elements store status information about themselves and analyse that information off-line or at set intervals. But this does not give us the ability to react immediately to changes in use that might threaten the health of the system.

Solution

Use CONTINUAL STATUS REPORTING to report the status of all system elements at an appropriate frequency. Implement an automated, OPERATIONAL MONITORING AND ALERTING process that watches for indicators of a failing system and warns the system operations team – allowing them to take preventative action if possible.

Example Resolution

We introduce an automated monitoring component that 'watches' a defined set of resources for each of the system elements. We set predefined thresholds for the different types of resource – if any system element reaches one of these thresholds an alert is sent to the operations team warning them of the possibility of failure.

Resulting Context

■ Availability is improved as the alerts can help the operations team prevent the system from becoming partially or wholly unavailable.

■ There is a negative impact on performance because a reasonably high level of continuous reporting is required on some system elements to support the required level of monitoring.

■ Manageability is improved as there is no need to manually monitor the system.

■ Cost is increased, regardless of whether a specific management application is purchased or custom solutions are built. This cost is justified as it makes the system manageable for less money than employing many operations people.

Implementation

This pattern applies to all system elements that generate status information, regardless of whether they are hardware or software.

Related Patterns and Principles

- OPERATIONAL MONITORING AND ALERTING needs CONTINUAL STATUS REPORTING to be implemented to provide the system information on which monitoring is performed.

- OPERATIONAL MONITORING AND ALERTING is similar to SYSTEM OVERVIEW as it will require fairly high-level information (usage and 'dead or alive') from each system element. However, the timescales in OPERATIONAL MONITORING AND ALERTING are far more immediate.

- OPERATIONAL MONITORING AND ALERTING should be combined with 3-CATEGORY LOGGING to provide background on the logical actions the system was performing at the point of any element failure.

- Implementing DYNAMICALLY-ADJUSTABLE CONFIGURATION for major system elements and their parameters means that runtime information can be acted upon without the need for major maintenance.

3-CATEGORY LOGGING

Problem

If the system fails, or performance degrades, how do we know what the various elements in the system were actually doing at the time?

Context

We are building an Internet-technology system that will be subject to failure. We will need to determine the cause of failure so we can take actions to prevent it.

Example

The GlobalTech system uses CONTINUAL STATUS REPORTING to give an up-to-date picture of its health. OPERATIONAL MONITORING AND ALERTING will highlight the failure of system elements and any excessive load. However, if an application server goes down when it isn't under excessive load or resource-constrained we will have no idea what else might have caused the failure.

Forces

- The system element information generated for OPERATIONAL MONITORING AND ALERTING provides us with a picture of the system's health during normal execution, but we also need to see what the system was doing to re-trace the sequence of events or activities that may have contributed to a system failure.

- To successfully debug a hardware or software element you need a lot of diagnostic information, but the generation of diagnostic information decreases the performance of the system element and you do not know beforehand precisely what information may be needed.

- You cannot know beforehand which elements of the system will fail, but recording diagnostic information for all elements in the system will take up a prohibitively large amount of storage space.

- We need to be able to re-trace the sequence of events or activities that may have contributed to a system failure. CONTINUAL STATUS REPORTING provides us with an up-to-date snapshot of the system but doesn't necessarily provide the historical information we require.

Solution

Implement a mechanism to log information about system events and system execution. This mechanism should log three categories of data: debug data (usually execution-trace information such as which component methods have been called and with what parameters), information (simple warnings about the system condition such as timeouts or missing data), and error data (things that go very wrong such as failure to connect to a database or loss of connection between web server and load balancer).

Example Resolution

We introduce two areas of logging into the GlobalTech system. The web server logging functionality is turned on to give a list of http requests received and responses passed back. We also introduce a convention for logging information from software components in the application server. Every exception unexpectedly thrown is logged as an error and every method has a debug logging statement at the beginning that indicates the method called and the parameter values it was called with. We treat the database like a black box (the internal workings of the database are not our concern) and simply turn on its default error logging.

Resulting Context

- There is a negative impact on performance because the logging mechanism introduces a processing overhead.

- Manageability is improved because the logged information can also be used by system managers to monitor system execution.

- Maintainability is improved as the logging gives support and development engineers the information they need to track errors in the system or trace its execution.

- Cost is increased as it will take time and effort to add and configure the logging for different system elements. However this cost can be very quickly recouped as less time is spent on troubleshooting during the time the system is in production.

Implementation

Usually it is the software components that log information, debug messages and errors. However, some hardware devices will come with in-built logging capabilities.

Related Patterns and Principles

- 3-CATEGORY LOGGING is a form of CONTINUAL STATUS REPORTING that is specific to software components, where the status of a component consists of the current point in its lifecycle.
- 3-CATEGORY LOGGING provides a way of discovering what the system is doing and OPERATIONAL MONITORING AND ALERTING provides a way of seeing how well it is doing it.
- Consider using the DYNAMICALLY-ADJUSTABLE CONFIGURATION pattern to allow the level of 3-CATEGORY LOGGING to be altered while the system is running.

SYSTEM OVERVIEW

Problem

With a large number of system elements, each generating information, how do we assess the whole system's current health or identify long-term trends?

Context

Our Internet-technology system consists of many system elements that provide high-performance and high-availability services to users. We have implemented CONTINUAL STATUS REPORTING and OPERATIONAL MONITORING AND ALERTING for the system to generate status information from the critical system elements and monitor their health. We have implemented 3-CATEGORY LOGGING to generate information about the execution of the system.

Example

The GlobalTech system has implemented CONTINUAL STATUS REPORTING and OPERATIONAL MONITORING AND ALERTING for its web servers, application servers, data access servers, load balancers, network switches and routers. With all system elements in operation we have 26 streams of status data:

- three web servers, both software and hardware (six elements in total)
- four application server software instances running on two hardware servers (six elements in total)
- two data access servers, both software and hardware (four elements in total)
- two load balancers for each tier of servers, web and application (four elements in total)
- two network switches for each segment (four elements in total)
- two routers where the external pipe comes into GlobalTech (two elements in total)

Each of these elements is reporting data on between four and 20 measurable characteristics.

Forces

- We need to monitor individual system elements for failure or excess load, but we also need a picture of the system's overall health.
- We want to standardize the monitoring of the system as much as possible, but we also want to ensure that appropriate tools are used to gather the different types of information required.
- We want to be able to examine long-term trends in the system's health, but the sheer volume of data produced makes this a difficult data-mining job.

Solution

Provide a mechanism to aggregate the monitoring and logging information generated by CONTINUAL STATUS REPORTING and 3-CATEGORY LOGGING. Merge the information and abstract from it to give an overview of the system.

Example Resolution

All of the elements in the GlobalTech system are allocated to management groups (web servers, database server cluster, etc.). The status of each of these groups is represented by a single set of indicators including a current status flag and the level of load. This SYSTEM OVERVIEW is emailed to the operations team every 30 minutes.

Resulting Context

- Although performance of the management function is negatively impacted because of the introduction of an extra layer of communication, the performance of the system itself is unchanged.

- Scalability is improved indirectly as the need for extra capacity will be determined in good time and additional capacity can be added (finances permitting).

- Manageability is improved because all system elements are considered as a single entity for monitoring.

- Flexibility is improved as a new reporting agent or monitoring agent can be implemented under the abstracting layer without impacting existing agents.

- Cost is increased as the creation (or purchase) of an additional layer is required.

Implementation

We need to aggregate our picture of the health of both the software and hardware system elements in order to gain our system overview.

Related Patterns and Principles

- SYSTEM OVERVIEW complements the APPLICATION SERVER ARCHITECTURE, PERIPHERAL SPECIALIST ELEMENTS, SEPARATE WEB AND APPLICATION SERVERS and COMMON PERSISTENT STORE patterns to provide a system that is well-distributed but still easy to monitor.

- CONTINUAL STATUS REPORTING provides the management information on which the overview is based.

- SYSTEM OVERVIEW is easier to implement when we have implemented functionally-identical elements.

DYNAMICALLY-ADJUSTABLE CONFIGURATION

Problem

If the system is reaching the limit of a non-functional characteristic, how can you react to this change in usage without interrupting system operation?

Context

The deployed Internet-technology application has met its original non-functional requirements using various mechanisms. The load on the system will change in unpredictable ways and will probably fail to meet the original non-functional requirements.

The behaviour of system elements is governed in part by their configuration settings. These settings must be changed to alter the contribution of a system element to the overall non-functional characteristics of the system.

Example

We have applied CONTINUAL STATUS REPORTING in combination with the OPERATIONAL MONITORING AND ALERTING and SYSTEM OVERVIEW patterns to give both immediate detailed information and longer-term summary information about the health of our system. This alone does not give us the ability to cope with potential fluctuations in demand.

Forces

- Ideally our system would be self-repairing: if there is a large increase in user demand it should somehow re-configure itself to cope with that demand. But such self-repairing systems are extremely difficult to build and require the builder to predict most of the situations that are likely occur and to implement suitable remedies for all of those situations.

- We can deduce a lot from the raw data produced by CONTINUAL STATUS REPORTING and 3-CATEGORY LOGGING and can identify potential remedies from these diagnoses. But we need to be able to implement those remedies in a timely manner such that they can prevent problems occurring (or mitigate the after-effects of a problem that has occurred).

- We could implement remedies fairly quickly by taking part of the system out of service, introducing the remedy to that part then bringing it back into service (this works well with a system that is architected for high availability). But such an approach often exacerbates the problem it is trying to resolve.

- If the non-functional characteristics of a system are based wholly or in part on a set of built-in limits or settings then it cannot respond to unexpected changes in usage without being redeployed. But elements that read their configuration from external sources are more complex and slower to initialize.

- Elements that can adapt their configuration while still operating are very complex to implement (or expensive to buy) and so may be less reliable.

Solution

Identify key parameters that fundamentally affect the non-functional characteristics of the system. For each of these parameters, introduce a mechanism to allow elements to reload their configuration information at runtime.

Example Resolution

To keep response times acceptable under heavy load, the GlobalTech team introduce two points at which to throttle the number of requests using the CONNECTION LIMITATION pattern. The two points are at the web servers and at the application servers (limiting the number of HTTP requests and simultaneous sessions respectively). These limitations are split between business and consumer users – there is a limit for each different type of user that can be altered independently. These limits for requests and sessions are made configurable at runtime so that they can be altered on the fly.

Resulting Context

- There is a negative impact on performance because the constant reading of configuration information introduces processing overhead.
- Manageability is improved as the system's characteristics can be more easily altered to cope with unexpected conditions.
- Cost is increased due to the effort required to implement the dynamic re-configuration mechanism.

Implementation

This pattern typically applies to software elements, however certain types of hardware (e.g. switches) usually have a set of configurable parameters that can be altered at runtime.

Related Patterns and Principles

- CONTINUAL STATUS REPORTING provides the information about the system's health that is required to inform the values set for configurable parameters.
- DYNAMICALLY-ADJUSTABLE CONFIGURATION is usually split into different types of configuration along the lines used to create a SYSTEM OVERVIEW.
- Many other patterns can be implemented with configurable parameters. For example, 3-CATEGORY LOGGING can have its performance improved by making the logging points configurable. It is standard practice to run error logging permanently but it can significantly reduce logging overhead for the

majority of the time if you only run information and debug logging when they are required.

■ This pattern shares many ideas with the Configurable System pattern [Sommerlad 1999].

DEMILITARIZED ZONE

Problem

Internet technology systems, particularly those facing the public Internet, are regularly subject to attacks on their functionality, resources and information. How do we protect our systems from direct attacks?

Context

An APPLICATION SERVER ARCHITECTURE has been adopted to deliver an Internet technology application. The application holds information on users and provides important functionality for users. The application is exposed to an environment which contains potential attackers.

Example

The GlobalTech system holds customer profiling information, dealer order information and commercially sensitive sales information, any of which could be stolen or corrupted by an attacker. This information will be shared with GlobalTech's corporate systems making them liable to attack as well.

Forces

■ The risk of attack will be higher if the potential rewards from the attack are high in terms of financial gain or publicity. Any countermeasure must be commensurate with the perceived threat.

■ We must make intrusion into both the hosting company's systems and the web application itself as difficult as possible.

■ We want to make the system open and easy to use for legitimate users, but as the level of security is increased it becomes more difficult to use the system.

Solution

Provide a region of the system that is separate from both the external users and the internal data and functionality – commonly known as a DEMILITARIZED ZONE

(DMZ). Restrict access to this region from the outside by means of limiting network traffic flow to certain physical servers. Use the same techniques to restrict access from servers in the DMZ to the internal systems.

Example Resolution

The GlobalTech system implements a DEMILITARIZED ZONE by deploying its DEDICATED WEB AND APPLICATION SERVERS on opposite sides of a firewall. The internal firewall will only allow through traffic from the web servers to dedicated locations and ports on the application servers. All other access to internal resources is denied. The web servers and the internal firewall are also defended by a filtering router connected to the outside world.

Resulting Context

- There may be a negative impact on availability as the firewall becomes a single point of failure (standard procedure is for a firewall to 'fail closed', i.e. in the event of failure it will deny all connections to the protected systems).

- There is a negative impact on performance due to the overhead of network traffic filtering and the necessity of physical separation between the web servers and the application servers as defined in DEDICATED WEB AND APPLICATION SERVERS. If this has not already been done to improve another non-functional characteristic, it must be done to implement a DMZ and so will add multiple extra network hops for each user transaction.

- The scalability of the underlying application is unaffected. However, the additional elements (such as filtering routers and firewall software) must be able to scale to the desired number of users and concurrent connections.

- Security is improved because fewer systems are exposed to attack and multiple firewall artefacts must be breached to compromise security.

- There is a negative impact on manageability since the very restrictions that limit access to internal data may make it difficult to access the application from an internal monitor.

- Cost is increased as extra elements must be procured to build the DMZ. These include not only the filtering routers, firewall software and firewall host, but also the extra network equipment, such as switches and cabling, used in the DMZ itself

Implementation

This pattern usually requires a combination of hardware and software.

Related Patterns and Principles

- A DEMILITARIZED ZONE is usually combined with DEDICATED WEB AND APPLICATION SERVERS so that the web servers can be deployed in the zone and the application servers behind the internal firewall.

- For improved application security, SECURE CHANNELS need to be employed in addition to a DEMILITARIZED ZONE.

- To help make it more difficult for an attacker to compromise the individual elements in a DEMILITARIZED ZONE, you may use INFORMATION OBSCURITY to hide the roles of particular elements.

INFORMATION OBSCURITY

Problem

How do we ensure that sensitive data gathered and stored by our system is protected from unauthorized access?

Context

An APPLICATION SERVER ARCHITECTURE has been adopted to deliver an Internet technology application. The application gathers customer data as part of its normal operation. The system holds a variety of configuration information that could be of use to a potential attacker. The application is exposed to an environment which contains potential attackers. This has probably led to the use of a DEMILITARIZED ZONE to provide a level of protection for the system.

Example

E-commerce applications and other online systems manipulate a lot of information – some of which is sensitive, such as credit card details. A cracker breaching the system should not find it easy to discover this information and make use of it for commercial gain or fraudulent purposes.

Forces

- Data needs to be accessible by different parts of the system but should not be easily viewable by potential intruders.

- Encryption and decryption are comparatively slow and expensive (in resource terms) and so should be avoided unless necessary.

- Much data is non-sensitive in nature and does not need protecting.

- The level of encryption used should be weighed against the likelihood of unauthorized access to the data.

Solution

Grade the information held by the system for sensitivity. Obscure the more sensitive items of data using encryption and obfuscation techniques

Example Resolution

All 'public' data, such as catalogue information held in caches and in memory on the web servers is held in plain text. However, credit card details are held in encrypted form. The only place in the system that such details appear in plain text is in memory on the application server as it is delivering this information to the credit card processing agency.

Resulting Context

- Availability should not be negatively impacted, but care should be taken not to introduce single points of failure in the form of encryption key distribution and management services.
- There is a negative impact on performance if an obscurity mechanism is introduced because of the processing overhead associated with the mechanism. This is particularly true of complex encryption algorithms with long key lengths.
- Scalability should not be negatively impacted, but any mechanisms used by the obscurity policy, such as encryption key distribution and management services, should themselves be scalable.
- Security is improved by data obscurity because, even in the event of an attack during which the attacker gains access to the file system, system memory and application database, any sensitive data is not usable by the attacker. Security is also improved by configuration obscurity as any attacker will find it more difficult to obtain the information they need to crack the system.
- There is a negative impact on manageability as additional configuration will be needed for any encryption mechanism (such as key management).
- Obfuscation techniques, in particular, can affect the maintainability of the system as the developers have to remember obscure names for configuration files, etc.
- Flexibility may be negatively impacted as you may need to maintain back-compatibility with existing encrypted data or obscured configuration.

■ There is a negative impact on portability as you must ensure that any new platform supports the encryption mechanisms you wish to use.

■ Cost is probably increased as the extra requirements of encryption may require either additional general capability to support software encryption or dedicated encryption hardware. You may also need to buy additional encryption software depending on what comes with your existing platforms and tools.

Implementation

This pattern mainly applies to software, although hardware acceleration may be used.

Related Patterns and Principles

■ INFORMATION OBSCURITY is often employed in conjunction with SECURE CHANNELS.

■ The use of a DEMILITARIZED ZONE can reduce the level of encryption required in parts of the system as the risk of access is diminished.

SECURE CHANNELS

Problem

How do we ensure that data being passed across public or semi-public space is secure in transit?

Context

The system is implemented using an APPLICATION SERVER ARCHITECTURE and DEDICATED WEB AND APPLICATION SERVERS. The system architecture probably also includes a DEMILITARIZED ZONE in which the web servers reside. Both web browser clients and business-to-business clients access application functionality and data via the web servers. This interaction takes place across the public Internet or across a shared corporate network space. The web servers must access the application servers for application functionality and pass data back and forth across the same public or semi-public space. Information passing across the public Internet and across shared corporate networks could be subject to eavesdropping.

Example

Customers must pass sensitive information between their systems (browser or B2B system) and the GlobalTech system. This information is open to attack (interception or tampering) as it passes across the public Internet between the two systems. Even in the DEMILITARIZED ZONE, traffic between the web servers and application servers is somewhat insecure as parts of the DEMILITARIZED ZONE may be attacked from the outside, captured by an attacker and used as a base for monitoring traffic in the DEMILITARIZED ZONE.

Forces

- The basic protocols used by Internet technology systems were not designed to be secure.
- Some data needs to be made available outside the system's defence mechanisms but it still needs protecting.
- Much data made available outside the system's defence mechanisms is non-sensitive in nature and does not need protecting.
- Encrypting data is a significant overhead on system performance.
- It is easier to provide encryption solutions with known partners, but many customers of the system cannot or will not install specific software or hardware for this purpose.

Solution

Create secure channels that obscure sensitive data in transit using encryption and client–server authentication.

Example Resolution

In the GlobalTech system, all catalogue data is transferred between client and server in plain text. When a dealer wants to place an order, or a retail customer wants to log in, they are redirected to the HTTPS port. The SSL-based HTTP server listening on this port will authenticate the server to the client and will encrypt the sensitive order or password information flowing between client and server.

Resulting Context

- There is potentially a negative impact on availability if the obscurity mechanism causes server-affinity, which undermines effective failover.
- There is a negative impact on performance from the processing overhead if you introduce an obscurity mechanism for data in transit.
- There is potentially a negative impact on scalability if the obscurity mechanism causes server-affinity, which undermines effective load-balancing.

- Security is improved because data that is captured in transit is not usable by the attacker.
- There is a slight negative impact on manageability as there are now arte-facts of the SECURE CHANNEL to be managed, such as SSL server certificates.
- The choice of obscurity mechanism and its level of support on multiple platforms may have a negative impact on portability.
- Cost is increased as you must obtain and maintain one or more server cer-tificates for your SECURE CHANNEL. Also, you may need to increase the hard-ware specification of your web servers or buy dedicated encryption hard-ware to mitigate the associated performance overhead.

Implementation

This pattern mainly applies to software, although hardware acceleration may be applied in some cases.

Related Patterns and Principles

- This pattern is commonly employed in conjunction with a DEMILITARIZED ZONE.
- This pattern underpins the KNOWN PARTNERS pattern.

KNOWN PARTNERS

Problem

How can we validate the identity of business partners so we can be sure they are who we think they are when we want to collaborate with them?

Context

The system is implemented using an APPLICATION SERVER ARCHITECTURE and DEDICATED WEB AND APPLICATION SERVERS. The system architecture probably also includes a DEMILITARIZED ZONE in which the web servers reside. We have implemented an extranet system to expose internal functionality and data to chosen business partners across the Internet or a semi-public space.

Example

The GlobalTech system allows retailers to place orders and review order status across the public Internet. GlobalTech must ensure that only legitimate retailers can place orders and that orders can be definitively associated with particular retailers.

Forces

- Steps need to be taken to validate external users, but if these are too complex the system will not be used.
- Customers should be able to easily perform business transactions online but the organization needs to validate that they are really who they claim they are.
- We want to make the system as open and as easy to manage as possible behind its external defences. However, exposure of sensitive business functionality needs tighter security than public-facing parts of the system.
- Validation should work both ways so that a customer is sure that they are communicating with the correct system.

Solution

Ensure that access to system functionality and data is restricted to known partners who must authenticate themselves in a secure manner.

Example Resolution

When providing extranet access to functionality, all access to the web servers is restricted based on digital certificates. The client must provide a digital certificate to gain access to the extranet functionality and the server must provide a digital certificate to the client to prove their identity. Once this authentication has taken place, data is exchanged in a secure manner using HTTPS.

Resulting Context

- If the list of valid certificates is unavailable, the system cannot authenticate clients and so this would impact availability.
- There is a slight negative impact on performance as authentication based on digital certificates uses more encryption and so creates more overhead. There is more impact on performance by using encryption across the SECURE CHANNELS.
- Security is improved as an attacker cannot place a false order without the retailer's digital certificate. Additionally, the associated use of SECURE CHANNELS protects information in transit.
- There is a negative impact on manageability as there are now server and client certificates to create and manage on an ongoing basis. However, if you have already set up key management for SECURE CHANNELS, part of this work may already have been done.

■ There is little impact on cost above and beyond that required for the underlying SECURE CHANNELS implementation.

Implementation

This pattern mainly applies to software.

Related Patterns and Principles

■ KNOWN PARTNERS is often employed in conjunction with the DEMILITARIZED ZONE pattern.

■ The KNOWN PARTNERS pattern uses SECURE CHANNELS both internally and externally.

System Evolution Patterns

DYNAMICALLY-DISCOVERABLE ELEMENTS

Problem

How can we introduce additional capacity to the system without having to take it offline?

Context

We have an Internet technology system based around an APPLICATION SERVER ARCHITECTURE implemented as a set of functionally-identical servers. The same principle is applied to web servers as part of DEDICATED WEB AND APPLICATION SERVERS, the COMMON PERSISTENT STORE and PERIPHERAL SPECIALIST ELEMENTS. We want to evolve our system by adding new elements to it. An example would be the addition of more web servers or application servers to achieve better scalability and availability.

Example

The GlobalTech system's three-tier architecture and functionally-identical web servers and application servers allow availability and scalability to be improved through the addition of more of these servers. At the system's launch, a number of web and application servers are chosen to give the system a particular capacity. As the system's user population grows, we will need to increase this capacity by adding more of each of these types of server.

Forces

- If demand exceeds system capacity we will want to introduce new elements to meet it. The converse is true if demand is consistently below capacity.

- Additional capacity is of no benefit if existing elements are not aware of it or cannot make use of it. Other system elements must also be aware of any reduction in capacity and alter their behaviour accordingly.

- If the system must be taken out of service to adjust its capacity or configuration then this limits the speed with which more capacity can be added. For a 24×7 operation it may even rule out any change in capacity.

Solution

Use components that can discover new system elements dynamically and can start routing requests to these new elements in order to increase the capacity of the system as a whole.

Example Resolution

The two element types in the GlobalTech architecture of which we are likely to introduce new elements are the web servers and the application servers. The web servers receive requests from the outermost switch so we need to set the switch up to discover new web servers as they are introduced. Application servers receive requests from web servers but the web servers determine which application server to send the request by communicating with the load balancer. So it is the load balancer that needs to be able to dynamically discover any new application servers.

Resulting Context

- Availability is improved because newly-introduced system elements can be replacements for, or supplements to, existing elements. Also, the same mechanism can detect the re-introduction of an existing element that has previously been unavailable, perhaps due to a failure.

- There is potentially a negative impact on performance because the mechanism that allows system elements to be discovered at runtime will have some processing overhead.

- Scalability is improved because new hardware and/or software can be introduced at runtime and the system can automatically adjust to take advantage of it.

- There is potentially a negative impact on security as the dynamic discovery mechanism needs to be secured to prevent rogue elements being introduced either accidentally or maliciously.

- There is potentially a negative impact on manageability as the dynamic discovery mechanism itself has to be managed in addition to the introduction of dynamically-discoverable elements

- Flexibility is improved because dynamically introduced elements can add new functionality to the system.

- Maintainability is potentially improved as elements can be introduced to replace elements that have failed or are failing.

- Cost will increase slightly as the dynamic discovery mechanism must either be built and maintained as part of the system, or be a prerequisite for bought-in components, making those components potentially more expensive.

Implementation

This pattern applies to both hardware and software.

Related Patterns and Principles

- DYNAMICALLY-DISCOVERABLE ELEMENTS requires a form of system-level DYNAMICALLY-ADJUSTABLE CONFIGURATION in order to work.

- The introduction of one-way dependencies to reduce the dependence of system elements on each other makes DYNAMICALLY-DISCOVERABLE ELEMENTS easier to introduce.

EXPANDABLE HARDWARE

Problem

How do we ensure the hardware doesn't impose restrictive limits on the system?

Context

We have an Internet technology system based around an APPLICATION SERVER ARCHITECTURE with a variety of hardware system elements, any of which could become a roadblock to scalability as the system grows.

Example

The GlobalTech architects must decide on their initial hardware specification. They know that initially the system must support peaks of 3000 public Internet customers and 700 retailers. The agreed level of expansion is to peaks of 7000 public Internet users and 2000 retailers.

Forces

- You can never be totally sure of your system usage forecasts.
- Budgets are frequently restricted when a system is first specified. Additional funds to expand the system may only become available once the system is deployed.
- Different system elements scale at different rates. Adding a certain amount of memory to an application server may allow it to serve additional users but the same amount of memory added to a web server may allow it to serve far more additional users.
- The addition of new servers or network channels provides us with a powerful mechanism for scalability but the addition of a complete new server is an expensive and complex activity that brings a step, rather than incremental, improvement in scalability.
- New servers or chassis elements are usually costlier than additional capacity to plug into an existing unit.
- In some cases, such as clustered databases, you cannot scale by adding more functionally-identical elements.

Solution

Use hardware that can be expanded to add new processors (or higher-speed processors), memory, disks and network connectivity. Ideally, size the hardware so that it can cope with the maximum predicted load when it is configured to about half its maximum capacity in these four areas.

Example Resolution

The GlobalTech architects decide to implement LOAD-BALANCED ELEMENTS across both the web server tier and application serve tier from the outset. This reduces the need for EXPANDABLE HARDWARE on these elements. However, they still decide to specify systems that are not fully loaded with key resource such as memory and disk as the system requirements anticipate an increase in load of more than 100% over time. The key area for EXPANDABLE HARDWARE is in the routers and load balancers. These are specified with spare slots for additional blades to cope with the anticipated increase in load.

Resulting Context

- There may be a negative impact on availability if there is a decision to employ a single, expandable element rather than multiple functionally-identical elements.

- Scalability is improved due to the ability to add extra capability to the existing infrastructure.

- Security is slightly improved as there will be fewer elements to secure than there would be with the alternative strategy of employing more functionally-identical elements.

- Manageability is improved as there will be fewer elements to administer than there would be with the alternative strategy of employing more functionally-identical elements.

- Flexibility is improved as it is possible to add more functions to the system without changing the underlying hardware, by simply upgrading what you have.

- The initial cost of the system is increased. However, the cost of increases in capacity is reduced.

Implementation

This pattern applies only to hardware.

Related Patterns and Principles

Multiple functionally-identical elements may be used as an alternative to EXPANDABLE HARDWARE or as a complementary strategy.

VIRTUAL PLATFORM

Problem

How do we ensure that we can change the infrastructure the system is built on without needing to make major changes to the system itself?

Context

We are implementing an Internet technology system based around an APPLICATION SERVER ARCHITECTURE. When we evolve the system we may want to change the infrastructure that it runs on. In the context of our multi-server approach, this infrastructure is more than just the operating system it runs on and the programming language we have implemented it in. It consists of every product we have bought as part of the system 'technology stack'.

Example

The GlobalTech system is to be deployed to a set of Solaris servers in the corporate data centre. However, the corporate data centre is soon to offer support for Linux machines and the GlobalTech management is interested in seeing whether they can save money by migrating some or all of the system to Linux over time. We need a technology stack that can be relatively easily ported to Linux.

The management is also concerned about the dependency on product vendors. It is a volatile time in the technology markets and they are concerned about vendor lock-in for political and economic reasons. Where we choose a product as part of the system we want to make sure the chances of being locked into it are minimized.

Forces

- We want to be able to cope with differences between target platforms but to have as much commonality as possible in the development across those platforms.

- We can use technologies and components from particular vendors or groups of vendors to abstract the underlying platform, but this locks us into those vendors to some degree.

- We want the system to run as quickly and efficiently as possible, but we cannot write every software component as a custom component.

Solution

Choose a set of components and standards that insulate the system from the specifics of the infrastructure. Pick standards that are implemented by a number of different products on different platforms, and components that have versions available for different platforms.

Example Resolution

A J2EE application server is chosen for the application. Selecting a version proven on both Linux and Solaris should make it possible to migrate from one operating system to the other without requiring the application code to be re-written. The choice of a J2EE component model does not really mean we can 'drag and drop' our application code from one vendor's J2EE server to another, but the significant differences should be relatively small and, if we are careful, isolated to chosen sections of the code.

The web server and database chosen both have implementations for both Solaris and Linux at the version we are using. Again, there may be minor differences in the non-functional characteristics on each operating system but the changes required to the system code and configuration should be minimal.

Resulting Context

- There is usually a negative impact on performance by the extra layers of processing between the application and the target hardware or operating system. However, as the different layers are written by specialists in that field (you hope), they may perform better than home-grown solutions.

- Manageability is potentially improved if the management mechanisms are made part of the VIRTUAL PLATFORM; for example if all components report status information using SNMP.

- Maintainability is improved as you have less of your own code in which bugs may occur. If you choose widely-used components, many of the bugs will be discovered quickly, which helps maintainability once the component is mainstream.

- Portability is improved because the system can run on a number of different target hardware or software platforms without significant change.

- The impact on cost is determined by the choice of components used to implement the VIRTUAL PLATFORM.

Implementation

The pattern will be implemented in software but could be used equally to make the system portable between different hardware or software platforms.

Related Patterns and Principles

VIRTUAL PLATFORM is a very specific type of isolation layer.

SWAPPABLE STAGING ENVIRONMENT

Problem

How do we add new functionality to the system without taking it out of service for a long period of time or taking a big risk that the new system is malfunctioning when it is brought back into service?

Context

We are implementing an Internet technology system based around an APPLICATION SERVER ARCHITECTURE. The system is used by a large user base that is outside our control and cannot necessarily be easily informed of any potential outage. The users expect the system to be continuously available.

Example

The second version of the GlobalTech system needs to be deployed and commissioned. The new version contains major functionality improvements and takes advantage of new components in its VIRTUAL PLATFORM. However, there are thousands of users around the world who now rely on the existing version. We cannot take the application out of service for more than a few minutes without causing them serious inconvenience. How do we mitigate the risk involved in swapping the users rapidly onto a new and unproven system?

Forces

- There is never a good time to have a long service outage on a publicly accessible, 24×7 global application.
- The application must be tested in a staging environment before it is introduced into the production environment.
- The staging environment must be as close to the production environment as possible.
- The time taken to migrate to the new version of the system must be shorter than the time taken to create a new version.

Solution

Introduce a staging environment into the production servers. Implement a mechanism that allows you to swap the staging environment with the production environment, effectively swapping in the new version of the system.

Example Resolution

For the GlobalTech system we decide to opt for the most 'hot-swappable' implementation we can. This requires a smart switch that can recognize the difference between a request that forms part of a running session and a request that is not part of any session and that can be configured (at runtime) to forward requests that form part of a session to one set of web servers and requests that are not part of a session to a different set of web servers.

Resulting Context

- Availability is improved as the system is more available throughout the evolution process.

- There is potentially a negative impact on performance during the migration process as the production and staging environment servers need to run side-by-side.

- There is a negative impact on manageability during the migration process as there are twice as many elements in operation to manage and the switch-over itself has to be managed.

- Maintainability is improved as it becomes easier to introduce fixes into the production environment.

- Cost impact is determined by the degree to which we mitigate the impact of the migration process on performance.

Implementation

In our terms, this is very much a software pattern as the two environments share the same hardware.

Related Patterns and Principles

- If you have staging and production environments running in parallel using the same data, it is a good idea to SEPARATE SYSTEM-MANAGED DATA as much as possible.

- The use of a VIRTUAL PLATFORM tends to make it easier to maintain two distinct environments on the same hardware.

SEPARATE SYSTEM-MANAGED DATA

Problem

How do we evolve the schema of the application without making it unavailable for a long period of time or risking that the new system malfunctions when it is brought into service?

Context

We are implementing an Internet technology system based around an APPLICATION SERVER ARCHITECTURE. The production hardware is configured with a SWAPPABLE STAGING ENVIRONMENT to keep the system highly available as it is evolved.

Example

The GlobalTech team want to ensure that there is as little downtime as possible when migrating to new versions of the application. They will use a SWAPPABLE STAGING ENVIRONMENT to run the two versions of the code alongside each other. However both versions of the code require access to the system data. If the database schema is to change as part of the upgrade, it may be necessary to prevent all access to the system database until data has been migrated from one schema to another. Such downtime is a problem for a high-availability system so steps must be taken to minimize this downtime.

Forces

- The system holds data that is updated due to some external actor, such as the users of the system.
- Any form of data migration will take a finite amount of time but while the data is being migrated it cannot be updated as there is a risk of inconsistency and corruption.
- We want the system to have a high degree of availability, so hours of downtime are not acceptable.
- The system may have very large amounts of data that need migrating. The more data to be migrated, the more time it will take.

Solution

Separate the schema for system-managed data from that for externally-managed data. Migrate these schemas separately to minimize the amount of time the system is unavailable and reduce the risk of the migration failing.

Example Resolution

We can split the data in the GlobalTech system along these lines:

System-managed data	Externally-managed data
- Product catalogue	- Customer details
- Retailer outlet information	- Shopping basket orders
- Customer care information	- Retailer orders
- Promotions	- Retailer details

This split allows upgrades to the catalogue, retail outlet and customer care information to be made in a relatively straightforward way when a new version is deployed.

Resulting Context

- Availability is improved as the system is more available throughout the evolution process.
- There is a slight negative impact on manageability during the migration process as there are more elements to manage.
- If only system-managed data is changed as part of a fix, then applying this fix causes less disruption so maintainability is improved.
- Flexibility is improved as decoupling the system-managed data from the externally-managed data makes it easier to change and evolve the system.
- The impact on cost really depends on the degree of relationship between system-managed and externally-managed data.

Implementation

This pattern applies to software.

Related Patterns and Principles

- This pattern is usually combined with a SWAPPABLE STAGING ENVIRONMENT to smooth the evolution of the system.
- The data under discussion is usually managed in a COMMON PERSISTENT STORE that consists of two clustered databases that use DATA REPLICATION to remain synchronized.

Bibliography

Alexander, C. (1964) *Notes on the Synthesis of Form*. Harvard University Press.
  A formal treatise containing descriptions of the way that forces interact in building architecture, and mathematical formulae.
Alexander, C. (1979) *The Timeless Way of Building*. Oxford University Press.
  A classic work that serves as an introduction to a pattern-based theory of architecture.
Alur, D., Crupi, J., and Malks, D. (2000) *Core J2EE Patterns*. Prentice Hall.
  A catalogue of common patterns used when designing software systems to run on the J2EE platform.
Anderson, B., and Dyson, P. (1998) *State Object Pattern in Pattern Languages of Program Design 3*. Addison Wesley.
Anderson, R. (2001) *Security Engineering: A guide to building dependable distributed systems*. Wiley.
Bass, L., Clements, P., and Kazman, R. (1998) *Software Architecture in Practice*. Addison Wesley.
  Oft-quoted and fairly definitive work on software architecture.
Beck, K. (2000) *Extreme Programming Explained*. Addison Wesley.
  An explanation of the principles of extreme programming which is big on iterative development and testing.
Beck, K. (2003) *Test-Driven Development*. Addison Wesley.
  A deeper exploration of the way you can develop software better by writing tests first.
Berczuk, S. (2002) *Software Configuration Management Patterns*. Addison Wesley.
  A good discussion of many of the issues around using software configuration management techniques to provide stability in the face of rapid change, and a set of patterns to help achieve stability.
Brooks, F. (1995) *The Mythical Man Month*. Addison Wesley.
  The classic work on the management of system development and why it has changed so little in general terms over the past 40 years.
Buschmann, F., Meunier, R., Rohnert, H., Sommerlad, P., and Stal, M. (1996) *Pattern-Oriented Software Architecture*. Wiley.
  One of the key early patterns books, which encapsulates a lot of useful design patterns in real-world contexts.

Clarke, R., Dempsey, G., Ooi, C. N., and O'Connor, R. F. (1998) *A Primer on Internet Technology*. Available at http://www.anu.edu.au/people/Roger.Clarke/II/IPrimer.html
    A discussion of basic Internet technology.

Cockburn, A. (2001) *Writing Effective Use Cases*. Addison Wesley.

Fowler, M. (1997) *Analysis Patterns*. Addison Wesley.

Fowler, M. (2003a) 'Who Needs an Architect?', *IEEE Software Magazine July/August*. IEEE. Available at http://www.martinfowler.com/ieeeSoftware/whoNeedsArchitect.pdf.
    A discussion of architects and architecture particularly notable for the differentiation between hands-off and hands-on architects.

Fowler, M. (2003b) *Patterns for Enterprise Application Architecture*. Addison Wesley.
    A very comprehensive catalogue of the patterns and principles used in modern software architecture and a guide to their combination and use.

Gamma, E., Helm, R., Johnson, R. and Vlissides, J. (1995) *Design Patterns*. Addison-Wesley.
    The Gang of Four book that started it all in terms of applying the principle of patterns to software and hardware systems.

Henney, K. (2000) 'A Tale of Two Patterns'. Available at www.curbralan.com (select 'Papers' and go to the Java report section).
    The site contains various distributed design patterns spread over a series of articles.

Hohpe, G., and Woolf, R. (2003) *Enterprise Integration Patterns*. Pearson Education.
    A description of common patterns for EAI systems. Parts of it are available at http://www.enterpriseintegrationpatterns.com.

IEEE (2000) *Recommended Practice for Architectural Description of Software-Intensive Systems*. IEEE.
    A discussion on the use of architectural views, but no actual definitions of views you may want to use.

Marcus, E., and Stern, H. (2000) *Blueprints for High Availability*. Wiley.
    A very good book on the details of creating high-availability systems, what can go wrong and how to avoid it. The second edition was published in 2003.

Netscape (1996) *Secure Sockets Layer Protocol*. Available at http://developer.netscape.com/docs/manuals/security.html#SSL.

Pye, D. (1963) *The Nature of Design*. Studio Vista. Page 301.

Schneier, B. (1996) *Applied Cryptography*. Wiley.

Schneier, B. (2000) *Secrets and Lies*. Wiley.

ServerWatch Available at http://www.serverwatch.com.
    Good information on various software Internet servers.

Sommerlad, P. (1999) *Configurable System Pattern*. Submitted to EuroPlop.

Glossary

Alerting Bringing a problem to the attention of an automated or manual mechanism that can (potentially) resolve the underlying problem. An example is sending a pager message to the duty system administrator. Other channels for alerts include emails and GUI-based indicators (e.g. the image of a router goes red on screen when it fails).

Alerting agent A software entity that makes it easier to generate alerts based in specific system events. The alerting agent may be a custom piece of software or it may be bought in. The alerting agent may be built into the same software entity as the monitoring agent, so that different messages can be sent through various alerting channels based on rules configured in the monitoring agent.

ASP.NET Part of Microsoft's .NET Framework that allows developers to easily write dynamic web content that is run on the server-side and generates HTML to be sent to a browser.

Authentication The act of proving your identity to a third party.

Common Management Information Protocol (CMIP) A text-based status reporting protocol that provides for system elements to send information about their status to a monitoring tool. It is intended to address problems with SNMP and eventually to supersede it. It runs over TCP/IP.

Confidentiality   Ensuring that information passed in messages or permanently stored is only accessed by those authorized to do so.

Cracker   Someone intent on breaking into a system, usually for a malevolent purpose (see Hacker).

Digital certificate   A digital document containing the public key of a person or organization and information about their identity. The digital certificate is digitally signed by a certification authority to give a qualified guarantee of its authenticity.

Digital signature   A guarantee that the contents of the associated digital document have not been altered since the signature was created. The signature is an encrypted version of a hash value generated from the contents of the associated document. The encryption is based on the private key of the signer and so you can use their public key (contained in their digital certificate) to decrypt the hash value and compare it to one freshly generated from the associated document. If the two values match, the document has not been altered since it was signed.

Encryption   The obscuring of data by passing it through an encryption algorithm.

Encryption algorithm   A mathematical process that obscures information. The original information (plaintext) is converted into obscured ciphertext. Encryption algorithms rely on a piece of data called a key to make the generated ciphertext unique. Encryption algorithms can be symmetrical (the same key encrypts and decrypts), asymmetrical (there are two keys – one for encryption and one for decryption) or one-way (you can never retrieve the original plaintext even if you have the key).

File Transfer Protocol   See FTP.

Filtering router   A filtering router examines network packets as it transfers them from one network to another. If the source, destination or protocol of a particular packet (or a combination thereof) conflicts with a set of rules configured on the router, the packet is discarded. Filtering routers are commonly used as part of a firewall.

Firewall   A hardware or software element that performs a security task related to the restriction of access to the system from the outside. Examples of firewalls range from a router that uses packet filtering to block unwanted traffic through to a dedicated, multi-homed host system running a sophisticated piece of firewall software, such as Firewall-1. Multiple firewalls may be used in a particular security architecture, such as a DEMILITARIZED ZONE.

FTP   A text-based way of requesting and retrieving the contents of files on remote systems. FTP runs over TCP/IP.

Hacker   An expert in computer systems who is interested in continually pushing the boundaries of what is possible and exploring the options and limitations of utilities and services. 'Hacking' is an attitude that can be used for good or bad purposes (see Cracker).

Hashing   A way of generating a unique value from a set of digital data. Hashing is commonly used as part of integrity mechanisms as a hash can be generated from some digital data and then encrypted to create a digital signature.

HTML   A way of marking up text with tags to indicate how that text should be displayed in a web browser. You can also create forms from a selection of simple GUI elements.

HTTP   A text-based way of requesting and retrieving pages from a web server. HTTP runs over TCP/IP.

HTTPS   A secure form of the HTTP protocol that uses SSL to create a SECURE CHANNEL between the client and the server for the duration of a web session.

HyperText Markup Language   See HTML.

HyperText Transfer Protocol   See HTTP.

Integrity   Ensuring that the contents of a message are not tampered with or being able to detect such tampering.

Internet Inter-ORB Protocol (IIOP)   Part of the CORBA specification, used as the underlying protocol for J2EE's RMI distribution mechanism.

IPSec   A standardized way of creating Secure Channels at the IP layer of the TCP/IP protocol. IPSec is based on the use of public and private keys.

Logging   The recording of system-level information to a given, persistent location. An example is HTTP request information being written to a file by a web server.

Management console   A piece of software that helps the operations team amalgamate information gathered from monitoring agents to create one form of System Overview.

Monitoring   The act of receiving and interpreting information generated by system elements. An example would be listening for particular SNMP messages sent from a specific subset of the system elements, such as network card failures on the routers.

Monitoring agent   A software entity that makes it easier to monitor a system. There may be different monitoring agents for different parts of the system or a single, overarching monitoring agent for the whole system. Such software could be written specifically for the project or it could be bought in (e.g. HP OpenView). An example is a management console that receives SNMP alerts and processes them based on a set of rules.

Post Office Protocol (POP)   A text-based protocol for retrieving email messages from an email server. The main variant of POP is POP3 which runs over TCP/IP.

Public key and private key   A pair of encryption keys that work together. Information encrypted by one of the keys can only be decrypted by the other. Public keys are made widely available and private keys are kept secure. Such keys form the basis of integrity and authentication mechanisms.

Redundant Array of Inexpensive Disks (RAID)   A set of variations for configuring an array of disks so that one disk can fail without losing data or disk access capability.

Reporting agent   A software entity that logs information. This may be part of a functional element (such as the HTTP logging functionality built into a web server or SNMP reporting functionality embedded in a switch or router), or it may be a separately-installed piece of software (for example, a daemon or service that takes snapshots of system resource usage and writes them to a database). Typically, each element in the system will house or be co-located with a monitoring agent.

Secure Sockets Layer (SSL)   Encryption mechanisms used on top of standard TCP/IP sockets technology to provide privacy and authentication services for Internet technology systems.

Simple Mail Transfer Protocol (SMTP)   A text-based way of sending email messages from email client to email server and from one email server to another. SMTP runs over TCP/IP.

Simple Network Management Protocol (SNMP)   A text-based status reporting protocol that provides for system elements to send information about their status to a monitoring tool. SNMP runs over TCP/IP. The system information reported as part of SNMP is referred to as a Management Information Base (MIB) and the asynchronous reporting of information is referred to as an 'SNMP trap'.

Simple Object Access Protocol (SOAP)   A way of encoding messages in XML to make them interoperable between systems. Most SOAP traffic is passed over HTTP.

SSL   See Secure Sockets Layer.

TCP/IP   The Internet Protocol (IP) provides the basic addressing and packet exchange protocol used on the Internet. The Transmission Control Protocol (TCP) creates end-to-end connections on top of IP.

TOP (or top)   A Unix command that monitors system load, CPU usage, memory usage etc.

Transmission Control Protocol/Internet Protocol   See TCP/IP.

Virtual Private Network (VPN)   An encrypted channel between a host and a network or between two networks. It gives the appearance that all of the hosts are on the same network so that they can interoperate normally. However, as the channel is encrypted, it can be used to link networks and hosts across the Internet or other semi-public space.

WS-Security   An initiative under the auspices of the World Wide Web Consortium for adding a security infrastructure to the exchange of SOAP messages and other Web Service interactions.

XML   eXtensible Markup Language (XML) is a way of marking up text with tags to define the structure of the data. There is a whole family of standards around XML that define data typing, data conversion and data searching.

Index

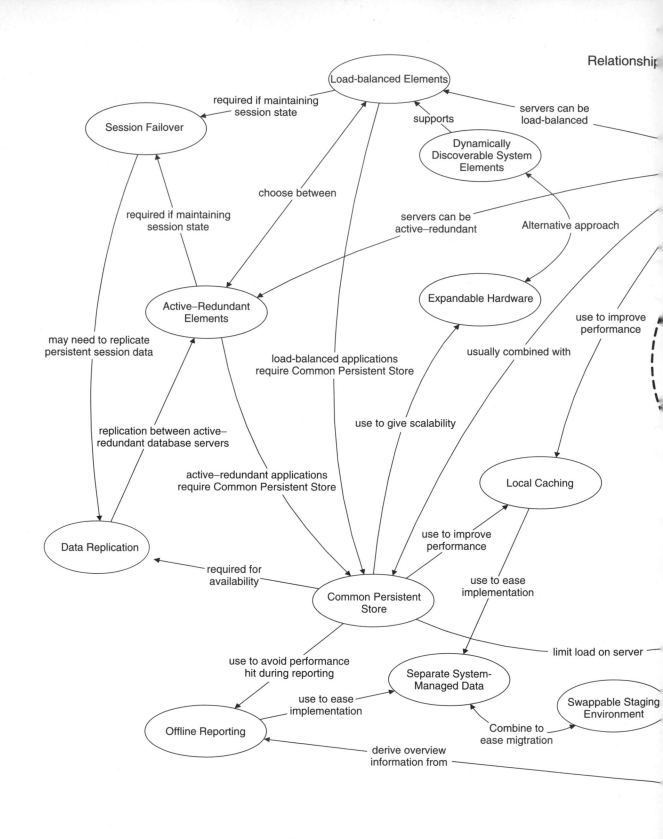